D0209276

The Economic Impact of Knowledge

Dale Neef
G. Anthony Siesfeld
Jacquelyn Cefola
Editors

BUTTERWORTH
HEINEMANN

Boston Oxford Johannesburg Melbourne New Delhi Singapore

338.064
E19

Copyright © 1998 by Butterworth–Heinemann

 A member of the Reed Elsevier group

All rights reserved.

No part of this publication may be reproduced, stored in a retrieval system, or transmitted in any form or by any means, electronic, mechanical, photocopying, record-
ing, or otherwise, without the prior written permission of the publisher.

 Recognizing the importance of preserving what has been written,
Butterworth–Heinemann prints its books on acid-free paper whenever possible.

 Butterworth–Heinemann supports the efforts of American Forests and the Global
ReLeaf program in its campaign for the betterment of trees, forests, and our environment.

Library of Congress Cataloging-in-Publication Data
The economic impact of knowledge / Dale Neef, G. Anthony Siesfeld
  Jacquelyn Cefola, editors.
      p. cm.—(Resources for the knowledge-based economy)
    Includes bibliographical references and index.
    ISBN 0-7506-7009-6 (alk. paper)
    1. Technological innovations—Economic aspects. 2. Research,
  Industrial. 3. High technology industries. 4. International trade.
  5. Intellectual property. 6. Competition, International. I. Neef,
  Dale, 1959– . II. Siesfeld, Gerald Anthony. III. Cefola,
  Jacquelyn. IV. Series.
  HC79.T4E2527 1998
  338′.064—dc21   98-14676
                                                               CIP

British Library Cataloguing-in-Publication Data
A catalogue record for this book is available from the British Library.

The publisher offers special discounts on bulk orders of this book.
For information, please contact:
Manager of Special Sales
Butterworth–Heinemann
225 Wildwood Avenue
Woburn, MA 01801-2041
Tel: 617-928-2500
Fax: 617-928-2620

For information on all Butterworth–Heinemann publications available,
contact our World Wide Web home page at: http://www.bh.com

10 9 8 7 6 5 4 3 2 1

Printed in the United States of America

Contents

University Libraries
Carnegie Mellon University
Pittsburgh PA 15213-3890

Introduction to Series—
Why Knowledge, Why Now?

Why is there such an upsurge of interest in knowledge? In 1996 there were at least six major conferences on the subject; three new journals focusing on knowledge (sometimes loosely called intellectual capital or organizational learning) were published; and many major firms in the United States and Europe added positions such as chief knowledge officer, organizational learning officer, and even a few vice presidents for intellectual capital!

Why the focus on a subject that, at some levels, has been around since the pre-Socratic philosophers? Is it yet another one of the multitudinous management enthusiasms that seem to come and go with the frequency of some random natural phenomena? We don't think so! Many of us doing research on this subject have seen the rise and fall of many of these varied nostrums—all of which attempted to offer firms a new road to achieving a sustainable competitive advantage. However, when much of the shouting dies down, we conclude that, excluding monopolistic policies and other market irregularities, there is no sustainable advantage other than what a firm knows, how it can utilize what it knows, and how fast it can learn something new!

However, this still does not answer the questions why knowledge, why now? Let us list some very broad trends that seem to be playing a significant role in the current development of knowledge:

A) The globalization of the economy, which is putting terrific pressure on firms for increased adaptability, innovation, and process speed.

B) The awareness of the value of specialized knowledge, as embedded in organizational processes and routines, in coping with the pressures of globalization.

C) The awareness of knowledge as a distinct factor of production and its role in the growing book value to market value ratios within knowledge-based industries.

D) Cheap networked computing, which is at last giving us a tool for working with and learning from each other.

While many can argue for and against the significance of these trends, we feel that the preponderance of evidence points to the increasing substitution of brain for brawn within our organizations and our social lives. Yet we have developed few conceptional tools to better work with "wetware."

It is with these forces in mind that we offer the following volume to you. While there are, as yet, few agreed-upon standards and analytic frames and definitions, there are enough serious articles and books to help managers get some real traction in dealing with the crucial yet elusive subject of knowledge.

After all, we have had about five hundred years of thought concerning the other major factors of production, for example, land, labor, and capital. Let these volumes start the process of codifying knowledge about knowledge in order for us to better manage in the twenty-first century.

Laurence Prusak,
Series Editor

Part One

The Effect of Knowledge on National Economies

Introduction—
Rethinking Economics in the Knowledge-Based Economy

Dale Neef

What happens to our understanding of economics when the vast majority of people within our economy are employed to create ideas, solve problems, or market and sell services rather than to produce any tangible goods? How do we monitor and influence an economy in an "unbounded" global environment where land in the form of office space or manufacturing infrastructure is no longer important, where labor can be employed wherever it is most cost-effective worldwide, and where capital is equally available to finance a project in Bangkok or in Detroit? How must we rethink our standard economic models in a knowledge-based economy where the only "natural" resources of real value—those which give our nation "comparative advantage"—are intangible, that is, dependent upon what our people "know"? These are the types of issues with which economists are now beginning to wrestle as the transition to a knowledge-based economy continues to create changes as fundamental to our economic infrastructure as those witnessed during the Industrial Revolution.

In the first section of this three-part anthology I have selected six articles through which we will be examining the changing global environment and exploring some of the most contentious economic issues of our time, including:

- The effects of knowledge-based, "weightless" growth on advanced economies;
- How nations and organizations need to prepare for the accelerated pace of technological change;
- The effect of the newly emerging global market framework on organizations and nations;

- How governments need to create Research and Development strategies in order to best support their nation's own "comparative advantage" in knowledge in an era of "non-national" organizations;
- The need for a global "knowledge police" to protect the rights of individuals and organizations in a global economic environment where intellectual property and newly invented technologies are easily "pirated" or reverse-engineered.

As we explored in volume four of this series, *The Knowledge Economy*, a fundamental change in the behavior of all major developed economies is now taking place, characterized by a marked shift away from traditional manufactured goods production and toward a service-based economy dependent upon high-skill professional service and technology companies. Today nearly 85 percent of Americans are employed in the service economy and some 65 percent of these in the "high-skill" areas. Indeed, this high-skill, high-technology arena in the United States is now the fastest growing area for investment, and accounts—directly or indirectly—for nearly 8 out of 10 new jobs being created.[1] It is also where the money is being accumulated: by the millennium, the top 20 percent of the labor force considered to be knowledge workers—design engineers, research scientists, software analysts, lawyers, biotechnology researchers, financial, business and tax consultants, marketing specialists, etc.—will earn more than the other four-fifths of the workforce combined.[2]

The effects of this shift toward a knowledge-based, "weightless" economy are also reflected in the more traditional realm of manufacturing, where high-skill industries have doubled their share of manufacturing output to 25 percent since 1975.[3] Even the manufacturing process itself is becoming knowledge based, as raw material or physical assembly costs have plummeted to a national average of only 15–30 percent of total product value. As Alan Greenspan pointed out in 1996, America's total output, measured in tons, is little more than it was 100 years ago—despite a twenty-fold increase in real GDP value.[4]

In the past, the cost of producing manufactured goods came predominantly from raw materials, plant and labor costs. Very little value was added through the highly standardized labor processes of the production line. Today, that formula has been reversed. Intangible inputs that are dependent upon employee knowledge and skills—creativity and design proficiency, customer relationships and goodwill, innovative marketing and sales techniques—account for an average of 70 percent of the value of automobiles, and an incredible 85 percent of the value of high-technology goods such as microchips or CDs.[5] Today, and in the future, it is "brain" and not "brawn" that is the key to economic growth.

1. Wyckoff, Andrew, "The Growing Strength of Services," *OECD Observer*, No. 200, June 1996.
2. Tapscott, Don, *The Digital Economy*, p. 7.
3. "The Knowledge-based Economy," *OECD*, 1996
4. "The World Economy Survey," *The Economist*, September 28, 1996, p. 43.
5. "The World Economy Survey," *The Economist*, September 28, 1996, p. 43.

All of this means that unlike our typical goods-production economies of the past, an ever-increasing proportion of the output of the economy today is in the form of "intangibles"—services whose effect are not easily measured by traditional accounting methods of quantity or volume. Equally important, it means that companies and therefore the nation as a whole are growing increasingly dependent for their financial success upon high-skill knowledge workers—a group who are making up an ever-increasing proportion of every organization, in both the service and manufacturing sectors alike. In short, the knowledge-based economy is already upon us.

CHAPTER 1: KNOWLEDGE-BASED GROWTH AND THE ACCELERATED PACE OF CHANGE

Most contemporary economists agree that the knowledge-based economy has characteristics that may be very different from those found in traditional economic models, and although it is by no means certain yet that we need to scrap the fundamental tenets of economic theory that we have worked with for the past 200 years, changes in the global economy challenge many of our traditional economic notions.

In the past, it was usually a unique combination of land, labor, and capital that gave a nation its "comparative advantage." Today, things are different. As an ever-increasing percentage of economic growth arises from the burgeoning knowledge sector, a nation's comparative advantage comes instead from its collective ability to leverage what its citizens know. Traditional factors of economic growth—that is land, labor, capital, and indeed, to a large extent current fiscal policies—seem less relevant (if not obsolete) when seen in the context of a global, knowledge-based economy.

Until recently, for example, land—location, availability of natural resources, transportation advantages such as rivers or natural harbors—was part of the basis for economic development and success. "Where" something was done often dictated "what" was done. But traditional factors such as natural resources and raw materials are far less important now than they were just ten years ago. Not only are raw materials now an ever-decreasing proportion of the value of goods within the advanced economies, but modern extraction, production, and transportation methods have meant that natural resource prices themselves have fallen some 60 percent since 1975 (and will probably fall 60 percent more in the next twenty years). This all makes traditional natural resource–based production much less profitable, and the natural advantages of land much less important.[6]

Physical assets, too, are less important. As the manufacturing base continues to shrink from the effects of automation, the "workerless factory," outsourcing, and relocation of plants to nations with lower labor costs, less and less physical plant of any sort is required in advanced economies. A similar trend can be seen in

6. Thurow, Lester, *The End of Capitalism,* p. 67.

the service sector, where modern computing and communications tools tied together in an electronic environment have revolutionized the way in which companies view the need for physical assets. Many organizations now consist of little
more than a sales force, coordinating management offices, and a series of distribution hubs. Office space has been rationalized with new "hotelling" techniques
greatly reducing traditional office requirements. Many workers today are mobile
and essentially nomadic, spending their time in airports or in hotels, working on
laptops connected to "virtual" networks. Although innumerable social and personal difficulties arise from this new scenario, the fact remains that organizations
in the knowledge-based economy are maintaining only a fraction of the physical
assets that they had in 1980, and land as a key factor for providing comparative
advantage has been rendered virtually meaningless.

Similarly, the traditional notion of labor itself providing the means for retaining a national comparative advantage requires rethinking in the global,
knowledge-based economy. Since the onset of industrialization, the vast majority
of employment (and thus national economic prosperity) in advanced economies
has traditionally been found in low- to medium-skill, "make or move" type jobs,
where virtually anyone could be trained to complete the work. In the past, labor
was seen as a commodity much like any other—as interchangeable as the assem-
bly-line parts with which the employees worked—and over the past fifty years advanced economies have come to expect a continued high standard of living to be
gained from those low- and medium-skill jobs. However, all of that is changing.
Most employment in advanced economies is now within the service sector, and as
labor-based manufacturing continues to be shed or outsourced globally, low- and
medium-skill work in advanced economies will become increasingly less well paid
and more difficult to find. To make matters more difficult, unlike the low- and
medium-skill labor markets of the pre-1990s, inclusion in the highly skilled labor
force of the knowledge-based economy is unlikely to be automatic or universal.
The transition from blue-collar to knowledge work is not an easy one.

The economic principles concerning capital, too, have changed dramatically.
With the development of electronic currency trading and financial markets in major cities worldwide, capital is no longer restricted to local investment boundaries.
With global capital markets exchanging some 1.3 trillion dollars every day, investment funds can be obtained quickly for development anywhere in the world.[7] The
very nature of the concept of capital intensity—where investment was once restricted only to those nations which had the indigenous wealth and infrastructure—is no longer applicable. In 1995 an amazing $170 billion in private capital
was invested in developing economies, and between 1991 and 1995 total flows of
foreign direct investment doubled to $315 billion as American and European
companies invested in low-wage nations such as Mexico, Brazil, or China. Indeed,
some 10 percent of U.S. pension funds are invested in Asia alone.[8] In the global,

7. Mathews, Jessica, "Power Shift," *Foreign Affairs,* January/February 1997, p. 57.
8. "All of a Sudden Every Banker is a World Banker," *The Economist,* July 27, 1996, p. 61; "Bal-
ancing Act," *The Economist,* January 4th, 1996, p. 71.

knowledge-based economy, capital investment is no longer restricted to wealthy nations. Global capital markets and their complex, interactive exchange networks make investment impersonal, unencumbered by national sentiment or long-term planning. Today, finance seeks out profits, wherever they may be around the globe.

Finally, we also know that one effect of concentrating an ever greater number of our most knowledgeable people on high-skill problem solving and the development of high-technology products (and paying them more to do it) is that the pace of change will continue to accelerate. Because knowledge-based business seems to grow under its own effect—creating markets that never before existed, attracting and producing more innovation, unconstrained by land, labor, or capital—it is in large part unpredictable. The computer industry provides a typical example, where some 70 percent of revenue today comes from products which didn't even exist two years ago. Even at the national level a sharp comparison can be drawn between the four decades which it took for Japan to become a leading car and computer manufacturer and the little more than five years it has taken for Taiwan to gain a large share of the world's PC markets, or other new Asian "Tiger" economies, such as Thailand and South Korea, to develop highly competitive automotive industries.

An entirely new level of volatility permeates the world economy today. In fact, of the Fortune 500 companies in 1955 (most of which were natural resource–based), 70 percent are now out of business. One of the most curious economic characteristics of knowledge is that it often makes previous goods, services, and knowledge obsolete. Entire industries may spring up, thrive, and be eliminated in a decade, as knowledge-based growth continues to shorten product life cycles, compress development cycles, drive new product prices downward, and increase the competition for technical standards.[9] Just a few examples illustrate the enormity of technological improvement resulting from this focused commercialization of knowledge-based work over the past several years.

In agricultural, manufacturing, and low-skill service sectors, machines are quickly replacing the need for low- and medium-skill human labor. So extensive have the technological advances been in agriculture that the percentage of farm-based workers has dropped from 75 percent in 1900 to some 25 percent of the U.S. working population after World War II. Farm labor accounts for less than 3 percent of employment in America today.[10] Similarly, in the realm of manufacturing, the scale of productivity improvement from automation is astounding. During the last thirty-five years the world's largest 500 multinational corporations grew by some 700 percent in real terms (from $721 billion in sales in 1971 to $5.2 trillion in 1991) even while decreasing the total number of employees.[11] One good

9. "The World Economy Survey," *The Economist,* September 28, 1996, p. 10.; James M. Utterback, "Mastering the Dynamics of Innovation," Harvard Business School Press, Boston, 1994, as cited by Tapscott, *Digital Economy,* p. 10.; Howitt, Peter, "On Some Problems in Measuring Knowledge-based Growth," *Implications of Knowledge-based Growth for Micro-Economic Policies,* p. 15.
10. "The World Economy Survey," *The Economist,* September 28, 1996, p. 7.
11. Greider, William, *One World, Ready or Not,* p. 21.

example of near-automated production is US Steel, which in 1980 employed 120,000. Today the company employs fewer than 20,000.[12] In fact, the percentage of the workforce involved directly in manufacturing in the United States has dropped from 33 percent post-war to less than 17 percent—and may drop as low as 12 percent by the end of the decade. Some estimate that within thirty years as little as two percent of the world's current labor force may be needed to produce all the goods necessary for total demand, worldwide.[13]

In high-technology areas such as computing and telecommunications, the pace of change is even more incredible. Communications and computing capabilities—capturing, codifying, and disseminating information and knowledge—has improved exponentially in terms of speed and cost. Since 1975 the combination of global telecommunications and computing has increased its information-carrying capacity by over a million fold. In telecommunications, new optic fiber networks—each wire smaller than the size of human hair—are each able to transmit the data equivalent of the entire *Encyclopedia Britannica* in five seconds. In 1960 a transatlantic cable from the United States to Britain could carry only 138 conversations at one time. Today new fiber-optic design allows for 1.5 million conversations simultaneously. The same accelerated pace of improvement can be seen in the computing industry, where today's $2,000 laptop computer is much more powerful than a $10 million mainframe computer was in 1975, and a typical CD-ROM can now hold 360,000 pages of text.[14]

So how do businesses find their way ahead in such a rapidly changing global marketplace? In Chapter 1, "Uncertainty and Technological Change," Nathan Rosenberg, Professor of Public Policy and Economics at Stanford University, explores the difficulties associated with anticipating the future impact of successful innovation—those discoveries, which have the effect of producing further innovations and investments broadly throughout business and society—when we can only think of new technologies in terms of old frameworks. No one, for example, could have predicted that the invention of the laser would be the basis for fundamental and diverse new CD, surgery, printing, and telecommunications technologies. Similarly, no one anticipated that the computer—developed for the purpose of rapid calculation, but now used for everything from complex design to aircraft cockpits, satellite technology, and worldwide reservation systems—would so fundamentally change technology, economics, and society.

Part of the problem, he explains, is that new technology begins in a primitive state and with properties whose usefulness cannot be immediately appreciated. This is why some 80 percent of R&D funding is devoted to improving products that already exist. Moreover, many inventions have origins in an attempt to solve very specific, narrowly defined problems, whereas major innovation often requires a combination of "complementary technologies" in order for any single

12. Drucker, Peter, *Post-Capitalist Society*, p. 64.
13. Rifkin, Jeremy, *The End of Work*, p. 8.
14. "The World Economy Survey," *The Economist*, September 28, 1996, pp. 3–4.

technology to be effective. Optic fiber technology, after all, is of no value unless placed within the context of computer-driven, digital telecommunications. In today's climate of "relevance" funding by government, Professor Rosenberg examines what incentives, institutions, and policies are likely to lead to a lessening of uncertainties and provide the greatest "foresight" in promoting future innovation.

CHAPTER 2: CONVERGENCE—GLOBAL COMPETITION IN THE KNOWLEDGE-BASED ECONOMY

In the knowledge-based economy it is the production of ideas, not goods, that is the source for economic growth, and the reason that new computing and telecommunications technologies are so economically revolutionary in their nature is that they allow ideas—in the form of techniques, research results, diagrams, drawings, protocols, project plans, chemical formulae, marketing patterns, etc.—to be distributed instantaneously and in a coherent way to anyone, anywhere around the world. As a result of these advances in computing and telecommunications the emergence of an interconnected global environment is becoming more apparent. This "unbounded" economic framework, in turn, provides organizations not only with vast new market opportunities, but also with an enormous potential pool of labor worldwide as improved communications and low-cost transport allow direct access to low-wage, low-skilled workers globally.

But this trend has gone well beyond simply allowing advanced economies to take advantage of low labor costs in foreign countries. Developing economies (those that we used to think of as "third world") themselves have rapidly adapted to the advances in operational techniques, automation, computing, and telecommunications technologies and are quickly building a highly competitive production infrastructure capable of manufacturing high-quality products at a fraction of the labor costs of the traditional "advanced" economies.

Their success can be illustrated, in part, by looking at the tremendous growth rates they have witnessed in the last several years. Since 1969, East Asia's proportion of the world's economic output has leapt from 4 percent to over 25 percent, with the average Asian national growth rate rising to 7.5 percent in the first quarter of 1997. In 1978 China's exports totaled only $9.8 billion, but by 1994 their exports had shot to $121 billion—making China the eighth largest exporter of manufactured goods in the world. South Korea's GDP has grown 177 percent since 1980, and Thailand's GDP has risen 235 percent in the past twenty years.[15]

Moreover, this growth is not exclusively low-skill, low-wage labor. In many cases Asian education levels meet or exceed those of the traditional developed economies (United States student scores were 28th and 27th, respectively, among

15. Tapscott, Don, *The Digital Economy*, p. 6; "China," *The Economist*, August 17, 1996, p. 18.

nations in high school mathematics and science achievement tests), and the R&D and productivity investment rates rival OECD levels.[16]

Accordingly, not only are new markets being opened up for consumer-based goods, but for the first time these developing economies are able to contribute directly to the development of those goods at every stage of production, often in cooperation with other developing economies. Samsung, for instance, invested $1 billion on TV set and white goods production in Brazil and Mexico in 1996, and Hyundai just set up a $500 million regional reciprocal manufacturing center in Brazil, Colombia, and Venezuela. As a result, much of the work that was once the exclusive domain of the OECD nations is now quite competently done in India, Singapore, Thailand, Latin America, or Eastern Europe at much lower labor costs.[17]

All of this means that for the first time in history products can be made and sold almost anywhere on the globe. Design and test elements of manufacturing can be accomplished in parallel, and the results conveyed electronically. Market trends can be sensed and responded to with much greater accuracy and speed. The entire supply chain, when organized effectively, can be accomplished globally, without boundaries, at a fraction of the cost it would require to complete in a single domestic economy subject to traditional high- and low-skill labor supply and demand. Transportation-based technologies have revolutionized the speed and cost structures of shipping goods around the world. New sea-going carriers, electronic scheduling, advanced port management, and revolutionary new designs for the container-carrying fleet have combined with an ever-growing air cargo fleet to crisscross the globe twenty-four hours each day.

Since the 1950s, the United States has prospered, at least in part, because it boasted a uniquely low-leveraged economic infrastructure where raw materials, low- to medium-skill labor, and the availability of capital were more abundant and less expensive than in other economies. Many economists now warn that within the next decade, those same characteristics, and therefore the traditional economic mainstays of the post-war Western economic miracle (automobiles, white goods, textiles, and even high-value electronics) may be permanently transferred to low-wage, developing economies. In advanced economies like the United States, Sweden, or Britain, low- and medium-skill production will increasingly be either moved away to low-cost labor markets globally, or abandoned altogether, forcing a further shift toward the "knowledge-based" industries or services where advanced economies still retain a "comparative advantage."

One particularly worrying aspect of these changes is the issue of convergence, where the United States, in particular, seems to be falling behind other advanced economies in crucial measurements of productivity. The United States now maintains less than 25–30 percent of world GDP—a figure which has dropped

16. "World Education League: Who's Top?," *The Economist*, March 29, 1997, pp. 21–23.
17. "Crossing the Pacific: Asian Investment in Latin America," *The Economist*, August 24, 1996, p. 51.

from 70 percent post-war, and halved since 1960 when the United States boasted over 50 percent.[18] In 1971, 280 of the largest 500 multinationals were American owned and based. Today the United States can claim ownership of only 157, while Europe has surpassed the United States with 168 and Japan has jumped from 53 to 199.[19] Part of the problem is that knowledge- and service-based work—which now makes up some 70–80 percent of an advanced economy's output—is notoriously difficult to measure accurately (as Tony Siesfeld discusses in Part 3 of this anthology). But some economists believe that there are more sinister implications behind this trend.

Is there danger in convergence, or is it a natural evolution toward post-war equilibrium to be expected and encouraged? There is much debate about how quickly the gap is closing and what it will mean to the United States. In Chapter Two, two of the most distinguished political economists of our time, Robert Heilbroner from the New York School for Social Research and Lester Thurow, former Dean of MIT's Sloan School of Management, explore the key issues around these contentious issues in "Falling Behind: The Productivity Problem."

Heilbroner and Thurow contend that despite strong growth and the appearance of a healthy economy, there are many indications that productivity levels in the United States, particularly, are falling behind European and Asian nations. Part of the problem is no doubt related to the severe shift toward services that is becoming apparent in the U.S. economy. After all, security guards, doctors, and lawyers, by the nature of their work and pay structure, are peculiarly resistant to measures that reduce cycle time or create broad productivity increases. Indications are that even as the blue-collar sector is shrinking its productivity levels are rising; while as the white-collar service sector grows (now over two thirds of the workforce) productivity rates continue to fall.

But the shift toward a "weightless" economy can only explain part of the productivity issue. Although the service sector is larger in the United States than in Europe as a whole, many European and Asian nations are only marginally behind in the growth of services. More importantly, say Heilbroner and Thurow, key areas of the American economy such as mining, petrochemical, and construction have witnessed a steady decline, comparatively, in output per worker. Why?

One reason is that the American public—and therefore industry—has failed to invest, both in terms of capital equipment and in terms of medium- to long-range R&D. German families, for example, save about 15 percent of their annual income, the Japanese save some 20 percent, while Americans, by comparison, save less than 5 percent. Because of notoriously high levels of consumer spending, over the past fifteen years there has been very little available capital in America for making the key investments necessary in order to take full advantage of new operational technologies.

---

18. Spence, Michael, "Science and Technology Investment Policy in the Global Economy," *The Mosaic of Economic Growth*, edited by Ralph Landau, p. 176.
19. Greider, William, *One World*, p. 22.

A second reason, according to Heilbroner and Thurow, is that unlike most European and Asian countries, the trend in the United States is for less, not more, cooperation with government in terms of public/private, long-term economic planning. This, combined with unprecedentedly high levels of consumption, a focus on short-term over long-term investment, an emphasis on military-based R&D, and the tendency of U.S. businesses to focus locally rather than globally, has resulted in an alarming trend which finds the United States "falling behind."

CHAPTER 3: TECHNOLOGY, R&D, AND ECONOMIC GROWTH

So how do highly developed economies like the United States, the EU 15, and Japan continue to compete in the knowledge-based economy? It is becoming apparent that it certainly won't be effective in the long term to attempt to subsidize low-wage, low-skill manufacturing industries which can ultimately never hope again to compete with developing economies with their low-wage infrastructure and expectations. Most economists agree that the answer is to use our "comparative advantage" in the knowledge-based work that we do best, and many contend that government sponsored investment in research and development will remain the key to retaining and exploiting that knowledge-based comparative advantage.

Richard Nelson, Professor of Economics at Columbia University, and Paul Romer, Professor of Economics at Stanford University and the key intellectual force behind new knowledge-based growth theories, contend in their article "Science, Economic Growth and Public Policy," that the United States, with its increasing focus on individual and direct R&D grants, is ignoring and thus underestimating the enormous indirect value that "open" public-funded research has on society and the economy as a whole. Focusing on "mission-oriented" research within individual and knowledge-retentive companies rather than broader "core research" at universities and government institutions may mean that valuable fundamental knowledge from which might spring thousands of new ideas is not shared throughout the economy. In the knowledge-based economy, those nations which promote a broader "sharing" of knowledge gained through R&D, they contend, will see greater benefits to society as a whole. Ultimately, in its drive for efficiency, the United States may well be restricting, rather than encouraging, the free flow of knowledge and innovation.

Yet, at a time of general reduction of government spending and influence, calls for lower taxes, and the shift of traditional government responsibilities to a local level, the debate surrounding the most effective focus and method for supporting research and development is heating up. The debate is further fueled by the growing realization that as organizations become more "non-national" in nature, governments in the United States, Germany, or Britain may find themselves essentially subsidizing R&D which is then "absorbed" by companies in foreign markets, adding to the prosperity of other national economies. In his essay "Science and Technology Investment Policy in the Global Economy," A. Michael Spence, Dean of the Stanford Graduate School of Business, suggests that the mechanisms that the United States uses for developing and deploying technology have changed little since they were put in place after World War II, when America was in a unique position, by virtue of its enormous economic dominance, of being both the largest producer and greatest user of technology. In the global, knowledge-based economy, the current flow of knowledge is almost exclusively one-way, however, and the United States risks becoming a large net supplier of technology and human capital to the rest of the world. What is the solution?

One alternative is to attempt to "close" the system through protectionist measures which would guard our return on investments in R&D and innovation. Such a course in a global, knowledge-based economy, suggests Spence, is rife with difficulties. A second approach is to begin to agree with industrialized nations around the globe to all invest similarly proportionate amounts in science and technology R&D with the goal of developing an open, "free trade" in ideas to governments, universities, and companies worldwide.

CHAPTER 4: WHO WILL BE THE GLOBAL KNOWLEDGE POLICE?

As the previous articles make clear, one of the most compelling problems arising from the unbounded, knowledge-based economy is that historically there has been little agreed international law governing such critical issues as antitrust, copyright, or patents. This international "free-for-all" market has resulted in a general hesitancy to distribute new products and services in emerging markets, and has meant tremendous losses for those who create new products only to see them reverse-engineered or copied outright in foreign markets. The scale of the problem is enormous. As Bruce Lehman points out, up to 8 percent of all products and services worldwide are pirated with costs to the United States alone estimated to be as high as $200 billion annually. China, for example, is thought to have a market for "pirated" music (primarily CDs) worth $168 million—almost the same size as its entire "legitimate" music market in total.[20] Similarly, software piracy accounted for lost sales estimated to be as high as $15 billion in 1996, with piracy rates emerging as high as 43 percent for Britain, 67 percent for Japan, and an amazing 94 percent for Russia.[21]

So how do we protect the knowledge that helps us as a nation to leverage our comparative advantage? In Chapter 4, Bruce Lehman, Under Secretary of State for Labor, explores some of the key issues to be resolved in a global, knowledge-based economy where new ideas, products, or services can be copied in-

20. Lehman, Bruce, "Intellectual Property," *Columbia Journal of World Business,* Spring 1996, p. 15; "Chinese Piracy: A Case for Copying," *The Economist,* November 23, 1996, p. 73.
21. "Intellectual Property," *The Economist,* July 27, 1996, p. 58.

stantly, and presents an upbeat assessment of recent developments in this key area in his article "Intellectual Property: America's Competitive Advantage in the 21st Century."

CHAPTER 5: THE RISE OF THE NON-NATIONAL ORGANIZATION

The last chapter of Part One examines one final aspect of the global, knowledge-based economy: the growing influence of "non-aligned" multinational companies. As the world moves toward an "unbounded" global economy, organizations of all types are becoming more geographically decentralized, and thus less aligned with any particular nation than in the past. New regional agreements on tariff reductions, combined with growing market saturation for consumer goods domestically, have driven many companies toward global extension and the development of a more "non-national" character, where cross-border operations extend into complex loose alliance networks of vendors, outsourcing agents, and distribution channels worldwide.

A new breed of international conglomerates is beginning to emerge as large firms scramble to gain influence in this new global marketplace. The global economy can create strange bedfellows: IBM and Siemens, for example, are working together to produce a 16-megabyte chip in France. Daimler-Benz executives are in talks with Mitsubishi on joint ventures, and Ford completes joint production with Nissan while owning one quarter of Mazda. It all can be alarmingly complex, as William Greider notes, when "NEC and IBM both own equity stakes in Bull, the French computer company, which own a majority of Honeywell, and Honeywell is in alliance with NEC, which, of course, competes with IBM.[22]"

Similarly, in the telecommunications field national giants are scrambling to align, creating new and alarmingly powerful "non-national" communications giants such as World Partners (AT&T and sixteen other companies in thirty-one countries), and Global One (Deutsche Telecom, France Telecom, and Sprint). As these and other telecommunications giants continue to emerge, it will mean that any activity that can be conducted through a screen and a telephone wire—writing software, secretarial services, airline revenue accounting, processing insurance claims—will be able to be done without regard to geography or nation.[23] This trend is already well advanced, with some 100 American firms outsourcing their software "code cutting" overnight via electronic networks to India where programmers are typically paid less than 25 percent of the American rate. In fact, it is estimated that some four million "virtual aliens" are already employed directly in the American workforce, existing outside of the nation's borders, undercutting domestic labor rates, working in an ill-defined tax framework, connected only through a growing electronic communications network. Indeed, this global tele-

22. Greider, William, *One World, Ready or Not,* pp. 174, 180–183.
23. "A Marriage of Convenience," *The Economist,* November 9, 1996, pp. 71–72.

communications infrastructure already essentially exists beyond the controlling powers of any single nation.[24]

If burgeoning markets and low-cost labor regimes are the "pull" that draws organizations into new global markets, the high tax rates and high labor costs that are now integral to the economic framework of advanced economies are increasingly being seen as the "push" for companies to relocate. Nestlé, a Swiss company, now has some 98 percent of its production capacity outside of their host nation. Similarly, Toyota is now over 70 percent non-Japanese, and Motorola's American employee level has declined to 56 percent.[25] This continued evolution toward truly global markets may mean that, for large-scale enterprises, it will no longer be possible to remain wholly domestic either in production or sales. In the next few years, as companies continue to become more and more global in nature, the traditional commitment to national prosperity and patriotism will give way to organizational loyalty.

As a result, the very nature of the role of national governments in the global, knowledge-based economy is changing. In the past, a nation's comparative advantage was based upon a combination of natural resources, labor, capital, and a balance of governmental, social and economic stability within its borders. National governments could monitor and to some extent control what goods were produced within their borders, what products and services were sold by their people, and how much money their citizens were eventually allowed to keep in the local currency. Indeed, internally, their ability to tax and control interest rates have been their two main tools for wielding influence and power over capitalist organizations and the economy as a whole.

However, our traditional understanding of economic activity which arose from the theories of Adam Smith, Alfred Marshall, or even John Maynard Keynes, was based on the idea that even accounting for import and export trade, every nation's economy was essentially "bounded." Borders could be sealed, taxes could be raised or lowered, tariffs imposed, duties focused on specific goods in order to provide incentives and punishments. Governments could assist indigenous industry through subsidies, grants for Research & Development or through advantageous trade legislation. Is this all still the case in the global, knowledge-based economy?

CHAPTER 6: POWER SHIFT: THE AGE OF NON-STATE ACTORS

Jessica Mathews, Senior Fellow at the Council on Foreign Relations, suggests in her article "Power Shift: The Age of Non-State Actors," that it is not probable that government assistance will continue in the global, knowledge-based

---

24. "The Software Industry Survey," *The Economist,* May 25, 1996, p. 15.
25. Rosecrance, Richard, "The Rise of the Virtual State," *Foreign Affairs,* July/August 1996, p. 52; Greider, William, *One World,* p. 91.

economy. She maintains that with the development of electronic communications, capital markets, advanced transportation, and easily transferable technologies, the very nature of multinational industrial ownership may change. In the future, governments will have less and less control over business as organizations become members of "non-national" conglomerates, deftly moving their assets and skills around the world in order to avoid any legislated pressures (such as labor laws or taxation) that governments attempt to place on them.

After all, of the world's largest economies in 1997, fifty were corporations. Sales revenues for General Motors alone were roughly equal to the combined GNP of any ten African nations, and today around 400 of the world's largest companies account for over one half of the world's total output.[26] Within the next decade we may well find that the knowledge-based economy has undermined the very nature of the nation-state.

The key characteristics, then, of the new economic framework are knowledge-based business, new technologies, and unbounded globalization. Depending upon one's perspective, this transition can mean opportunity or Armageddon, but most economists agree that however difficult it may be to adjust to these new realities, it will be much more difficult to resist them. As comparative advantage (for nations, or, in the near future, non-national organizations) becomes increasingly dependent upon access to ideas, human capital, and the ability to create innovative new products and services, understanding and adjusting to the impact of knowledge becomes paramount.

26. Stopford, John M. "The Impact of the Global Political Economy on Corporate Strategy," Carnegie Bosch Institute, Working Paper No. 94-7, p. 3.

1

Uncertainty and Technological Change

Nathan Rosenberg

I would like to begin with two generally accepted propositions about technological change: it is a major ingredient of long-term economic growth, and it is characterized by a high degree of uncertainty. Understanding the nature of these uncertainties and the obstacles to surmounting them is not a trivial matter. Rather, it goes to the heart of how new technologies are devised, how rapidly they diffuse, the ultimate extent of that diffusion, and their eventual impact on economic performance and welfare.

In view of the great uncertainties attached to the innovation process, it is hardly surprising that innovating firms have, historically, experienced high failure rates. Quite simply, the vast majority of attempts at innovation fail. But to describe the high failure rate associated with past innovation is to tell only a part of the story, and perhaps not the most interesting part. Indeed, I want to suggest that the more intriguing part of the story, with which I will be mainly concerned, has been the inability to anticipate the future impact of successful innovations, even after their technical feasibility has been established. This statement remains valid whether we focus upon the steam engine 200 years ago or the laser within our own lifetimes.

I will suggest that uncertainty is the product of several sources and that it has a number of peculiar characteristics that shape the innovation process and therefore the manner in which technological change exercises its effects on the economy. Since I will be primarily concerned with what has shaped the trajectory and the economic impact of new technologies, my focus will be confined to technologies that have had significant impacts. A study that included unsuccessful as well as successful innovations might yield insights of a very different nature.

I should also say at the outset that while I am not primarily concerned with the recent formal literature on growth theory (specifically the "new growth the-

Reprinted from THE MOSAIC OF ECONOMIC GROWTH, edited by Ralph Landau, Timothy Taylor, and Gavin Wright, with the permission of the publishers, Stanford University Press. © 1996 by the Board of Trustees of the Leland Stanford Junior University.

ory"), I am surprised that that literature has, so far at least, omitted any mention of uncertainty. While the rate of innovation is surely a function of the degree to which investors can appropriate the gains from their innovation, a number of central features of the innovation process revolve around uncertainty. At the very least, there is a risk/return tradeoff to be considered when evaluating projects that reflects the uncertainty attaching to appropriability. But the kinds of uncertainties that will be identified here go far beyond the issue of appropriability.

One further caveat seems appropriate. The discussion that follows is "anecdotal" in nature. However, the anecdotes have been deliberately selected to include many of the most important innovations of the twentieth century. Thus, if the characterizations offered below stand the test of further scrutiny, the analysis of this chapter will have captured distinct features of the innovation process for technologies whose cumulative economic importance has been immense.

It is easy to assume that uncertainties are drastically reduced after the first commercial introduction of a new technology, and Schumpeter offered strong encouragement for that assumption. His views have proven to be highly influential. In Schumpeter's world, entrepreneurs are compelled to make decisions under circumstances of very limited and poor quality of information. But in that world the successful completion of an innovation resolves all the uncertainties that previously existed. Once this occurs, the stage is set for imitators, whose actions are responsible for the diffusion of a technology. Perhaps it should be said that the stage is now set for "mere imitators." Schumpeter was fond of preceding the noun "imitators" with the adjective "mere." The point is one of real substance, and not just linguistic usage. In Schumpeter's view, life is easy for the imitators, because all they need to do is to follow in the footsteps of the entrepreneurs who have led the way, and whose earlier activities have resolved all the big uncertainties.

It is, of course, true that some uncertainties have been reduced at that point. However, after a new technological capability has been established, the questions change and, as we will see, new uncertainties, especially uncertainties of a specifically economic nature, begin to assert themselves.

The purpose of this chapter is to identify and to delineate a number of important aspects of uncertainty as they relate to technological change. These aspects go far beyond those connected with the inventive process alone. In addition, as we will see, they reflect a set of interrelated forces that are at the heart of the relationship between changes in technology and improvements in economic performance.

SOME HISTORICAL PERSPECTIVES

Consider the laser, an innovation that is certainly one of the most powerful and versatile advances in technology in the twentieth century, and one that is still surely in the early stages of its trajectory of development. Its range of uses in the thirty years since it was invented is truly breathtaking. A list of uses would include precision measurement, navigational instruments, and a prime instrument of chemical research. It is essential for the high-quality reproduction of music in compact discs (CDs). It has become the instrument of choice in a range of surgical procedures, including extraordinarily delicate surgery upon the eye, where it is used to repair detached retinas, and gynecological surgery, where it now provides a simpler and less painful method for removal of certain tumors. It is extensively employed in gall bladder surgery. When this chapter was being revised in manuscript, its pages were printed by a laser jet printer. Lasers are widely used throughout industry, including textiles, where it is employed to cut cloth to desired shapes, and metallurgy and composite materials, where it performs similar functions.

But perhaps no single application of the laser has been more profound than its impact on telecommunications, where, together with fiber optics, it is revolutionizing transmission. The best trans-Atlantic telephone cable in 1966 could carry simultaneously only 138 conversations between Europe and North America. The first fiber optic cable, installed in 1988, could carry 40,000. The fiber optic cables being installed in the early 1990s can carry nearly 1.5 million conversations (Wriston, 1992, pp. 43–44). And yet it is reported that the patent lawyers at Bell Labs were initially unwilling even to apply for a patent on the laser, on the grounds that such an invention had no possible relevance to the telephone industry. In the words of Charles Townes (1968, p. 701), who subsequently won a Nobel Prize for his research on the laser, "Bell's patent department at first refused to patent our amplifier or oscillator for optical frequencies because, it was explained, optical waves had never been of any importance to communications and hence the invention had little bearing on Bell System interests."

Let me cite some further major historical instances where the common theme is the remarkable inability, at least from a later perspective, to foresee the uses to which new technologies would soon be put. Western Union, the telegraph company, was offered the opportunity to purchase Bell's 1876 telephone patent for a mere $100,000, but turned it down. In fact, "Western Union was willing to withdraw from the telephone field in 1879 in exchange for Bell's promise to keep out of the telegraph business." But if the proprietors of the old communications technology were myopic, so was the patent holder of the new technology. Alexander Graham Bell's 1876 patent did not mention a new technology at all. Rather, it bore the glaringly misleading title "Improvements in Telegraphy" (Brock, 1982, p. 90).

Marconi, who invented the radio, anticipated that it would be used primarily to communicate between two points where communication by wire was impossible, as in ship-to-ship or ship-to-shore communication. To this day the British call the instrument the "wireless," precisely reflecting Marconi's early conceptualization. Moreover, the radio in its early days was thought to be of potential use only for private communication: that is, point-to-point communication, rather like the telephone, and not at all for communicating to a large audience of listeners. Surprising as it may seem to us today, the inventor of the radio did not think of it as an instrument for broadcasting. Marconi in fact had a conception of the market for radio that was the precise opposite of the one that actually developed. He visualized the users of his invention as steamship companies, newspapers, and navies. They required directional, point-to-point communication, that is, "narrowcasting" rather than broadcasting. The radio should therefore be capable of transmitting over great distances, but the messages should be private, not public (Douglas, 1987, p. 34).

The failure of social imagination was widespread. According to one authority, "When broadcasting was first proposed . . . a man who was later to become one of the most distinguished leaders of the industry announced that it was very difficult to see uses for public broadcasting. About the only regular use he could think of was the broadcasting of Sunday sermons, because that is the only occasion when one man regularly addresses a mass public" (Martin, 1977, p. 11).

The wireless telephone, when it became feasible in the second decade of the twentieth century, was thought of in precisely the same terms as the wireless radio. J. J. Carty, who was chief engineer of the New York Telephone Company, stated in 1915 "The results of long-distance tests show clearly that the function of the wireless telephone is primarily to reach inaccessible places where wires cannot be strung. It will act mainly as an extension of the wire system and a feeder to it" (Maclaurin, 1949, pp. 92–93).

The computer, in 1949, was thought to be of potential use only for rapid calculation in a few scientific research or data processing contexts. The notion that there was a large potential market was rejected by no less a person than Thomas Watson, Sr., at the time the president of IBM. The prevailing view before 1950 was that world demand could probably be satisfied by just a few computers (Ceruzzi, 1987).

The invention of the transistor, certainly one of the greatest inventions of the twentieth century, was not announced on the front page of the *New York Times*, as might have been expected, when it was made public in December 1947. On the contrary, it was a small item buried deep in the newspaper's inside pages, in a regular weekly column titled "News of Radio." It was suggested there that the device might be used to develop better hearing aids for the deaf, but nothing more.

This listing of failures to anticipate future uses and larger markets for new technologies could be expanded almost without limit. We could, if we liked, amuse ourselves indefinitely at the failure of earlier generations to see the obvious, as we see it today. But that would be a mistaken conceit. For reasons that I propose to examine, I am not particularly optimistic that our ability to overcome the ex ante uncertainties connected with the uses of new technologies is likely to improve drastically. If I am right, a more useful issue to explore is what incentives, institutions, and policies are more likely to lead to a swifter resolution of these uncertainties.

Much of the difficulty, I suggest, is connected to the fact that new technologies typically come into the world in a very primitive condition. Their eventual uses turn upon an extended improvement process that vastly expands their practical applications. Thomas Watson, Sr., was not necessarily far off the mark when he concluded that the future market for the computer was extremely limited, if one thinks of the computer in the form in which it existed immediately after the Second World War. The first electronic digital computer, the ENIAC, contained no less than 18,000 vacuum tubes and filled a huge room (it was more than 100 feet long). Any device that has to rely on the simultaneous working of 18,000 vacuum tubes is bound to be notoriously unreliable. The failure in prediction was a failure to anticipate the demand for computers after they had been made very much smaller, cheaper, and more reliable, and when their performance characteristics, especially their calculating speed, had been improved by many orders of magnitude; that is to say, the failure was the inability to anticipate the trajectory of future improvements and the economic consequences of those improvements.

If space permitted, the history of commercial aviation could be told in similar terms, as could the history of many other innovations. With respect to the introduction of the jet engine, in particular, the failure to anticipate the importance of future improvements occurred even at the most eminent scientific levels. In 1940 a committee of the National Academy of Sciences was formed to evaluate the prospects for developing a gas turbine for aircraft. The committee concluded that such a turbine was quite impractical because it would have to weigh fifteen pounds for each horsepower delivered, whereas existing internal combustion engines weighed only slightly over one pound for each horsepower delivered. In fact, within a year the British were operating a gas turbine that weighed a mere 0.4 pounds per horsepower (U.S. Navy, 1941, p. 10).

This is an appropriate place at which to make a very simple, but nonetheless fundamental, observation: most R&D expenditures are devoted to product improvement. According to McGraw-Hill annual surveys over a number of years, the great bulk of R&D (around 80 percent) is devoted to improving products that already exist, rather than to the invention of new products. Thus, it is incorrect to think of R&D expenditures as committed to the search for breakthrough innovations of the Schumpeterian type. On the contrary, the great bulk of these expenditures need to be thought of as exhibiting strongly path-dependent characteristics. Their main goal is to improve upon the performance of technologies that have been inherited from the past. A moment's reflection suggests that this should not be surprising. The telephone has been around for more than 100 years, but only recently has its performance been significantly enhanced by facsimile transmission, electronic mail (e-mail), voice mail, data transfer, on-line services, conference calls, and "800" numbers. The automobile and the airplane are each more than 90 years old, the camera is 150 years old, and the Fourdrinier machine, which is the mainstay of the papermaking industry today, was patented during the Napoleonic Wars. Clearly the improvement process deserves far more attention than is suggested by Schumpeter's frequent recourse to the derisory term "mere imitators." Equally clearly, a world in which most R&D expenditures are devoted to improving upon technologies that are already in existence is also a world in which technological change can hardly be characterized as exogenous.

So far it has been suggested, by citing important historical cases, that uncertainty plays a role in technological change that goes far beyond the uncertainty associated with technological feasibility alone. Indeed, the uncertainty associated with the eventual uses of the laser or the computer might, more appropriately, be characterized as "ignorance" rather than as "uncertainty." That is to say, along any particular dimension of uncertainty, decision makers do not have access to an even marginally informative probability distribution with respect to the potential outcomes. It is not difficult to demonstrate that ignorance plays a large part in the process of technological change! However, rather than arguing over the differences between Arrovian and Knightian uncertainty (which is how economists phrase this distinction between measurable and unmeasurable uncertainty), the next section of this chapter will outline a number of important dimensions along which uncertainty plays a role in the rate and direction of inventive activity and diffusion. Taken together, we have very little information, even retrospectively, about the relationships among these different dimensions. If uncertainty exists along more than one dimension, and the decision maker does not have information about the joint distribution of all the relevant random variables, then there is little reason to believe that a "rational" decision is possible, or that there will be a well-defined "optimal" investment or adoption strategy.

DIMENSIONS OF UNCERTAINTY

Why is it so difficult to foresee the impact of even technologically practicable inventions? Much of the relevant literature emphasizes the huge uncertainty that has attached to the question "Will it work?" This is clearly a major source of uncertainty, but the fixation upon workability has served to distract attention from several other, more subtle and overlapping sources. We turn now to a consideration of these sources.

First, it is not only that new technologies come into the world in a very primitive condition; they also often come into the world with properties and characteristics whose usefulness cannot be immediately appreciated. It is inherently difficult to identify uses for new technologies. The laser (Light Amplification by Stimulated Emission and Radiation) represents, at one level, simply a light beam formed by the excitation of atoms at high energy levels. It has turned out that laser action can occur with a wide range of materials, including gases, liquids, and solids. The uses to which this capability has been put have been growing for thirty years, and will doubtless continue to grow for a long time, just as it took many decades to explore the uses to which electricity could be put after Faraday discovered the principles of electromagnetic induction in 1831.[1]

An essential aspect of both electricity and the laser is that neither represented an obvious substitute for anything that already existed. Neither had a clearly defined antecedent. Rather, each was a newly discovered phenomenon that was the outcome of pure scientific research.[2]

---

1. It is recorded that a skeptical MP turned up at Faraday's laboratory shortly after his discovery of electromagnetic induction and asked him in a rather supercilious tone what it was good for. Faraday is supposed to have replied, "Sir, I do not know what it is good for. But of one thing I am quite certain: some day you will tax it."
2. In fact, Einstein had already worked out the pure science underlying laser action in 1916, in a paper on stimulated emission. From the point of view of the history of science, it might be said that

In the field of medical diagnostics, it has frequently happened that after some new visualization technology has been developed, it has taken a long time to learn how to translate the new observational capability into clinically useful terms. This has been the case with respect to CAT scanners, magnetic resonance imaging (MRI), and most recently echocardiography. Often a great deal of time-consuming additional research has been required before it was possible to make a reliable, clinically helpful interpretation of what was already being visualized in terms of the diagnosis of a disease condition in the heart, lungs, or brain.

This is presently the case with respect to PET—positron emission tomography. PET scanners are powerful tools for providing a quantitative analysis of certain physiological functions, unlike CAT and MRI, which are valuable for anatomical observation. Thus, it has a great potential for providing useful information on the effectiveness, for example, of drug therapy for the treatment of various diseases, such as brain tumors. But quite aside from the huge cost of this technology, its clinical application in such fields as neurology, cardiology, and oncology has so far been limited by the continuing difficulties of translating observations and measurements of physiological functions into specific, meaningful clinical interpretations.

There is a related point in the currently burgeoning field of medical innovation. The inherent complexity of the human body and, perhaps equally important, the heterogeneity of human bodies have rendered it extremely difficult to tease out cause-effect relationships, even in the case of medications that have been widely used for long periods of time. Aspirin (acetylsalicylic acid), probably the world's most widely used drug, has been in use for over a century, but only in the last few years has its efficacy been established for reducing the incidence of heart attacks as a consequence of its blood-thinning properties.

Although the discovery of negative side effects has received far more public attention, the discovery of unexpected beneficial new uses for old pharmaceutical products is a common, and often serendipitous, experience. Another significant case in point has been the applications of adrenergic beta-blocking drugs, one of the more significant medical innovations of our time. These compounds were originally introduced for the treatment of two cardiovascular indications, arrhythmias and angina pectoris. Today they are used in the treatment of more than twenty diverse conditions, largely as a result of new uses that were uncovered after they had been introduced into cardiology. These include such non-cardiac indications as gastrointestinal bleeding, hypertension, and alcoholism (Gelijns, 1991, pp. 121, 269). Similar experiences could be related with respect to AZT (currently employed in the treatment of AIDS patients), oral contraceptives, RU-486, streptokinase, alpha interferon, and Prozac. More generally, the widespread "off-label" use of many drugs is a good indication of the pervasiveness of ex ante uncertainty in medical innovation.

there was "nothing new" when laser technology was developed some 45 years later, although in fact a Nobel Prize was awarded for the achievement. From the point of view of technological change and its economic and social impact, the development of the laser was, of course, a major event.

Second, the impact of an innovation depends not only on improvements of the invention, but also on improvements that take place in complementary inventions. For the lawyers at Bell Labs to have had some appreciation of the importance of the laser for telephone communication, they would have required some sense of the technology of fiber optics, and the ways in which lasers and fiber optics might be combined. The laser was in fact of no particular use in telephone transmission without the availability of fiber optics. Telephone transmission is being transformed today by the combined potential of these two technologies. Optical fibers did in fact exist in a rather primitive form in the early 1960s, when the first lasers were developed, but not in a form that could accommodate the requirements of telephone transmission. In fact, it is interesting to note that an excellent book on the telecommunications industry, published as recently as 1981, provides no discussion whatever of this new fiber optic technology (Brock, 1982). As is often the case, it took a number of years for some of the attractive properties of fiber optic technology to become apparent: the lack of electromagnetic interference, the conservation of heat and electricity, and the enormous expansion in bandwidth that fiber optics can provide—the last feature a consequence of the fact that the light spectrum is approximately 1000 times wider than the radio spectrum.

The general point is that the impact of invention A will often depend upon invention B, and invention B may not yet exist. But perhaps a more useful formulation is to say that inventions will often give rise to a search for complementary inventions. An important impact of invention A is to increase the demand for invention B. The declining price of electricity, after the introduction of the dynamo in the early 1880s, stimulated the search for technologies that could exploit this unique form of energy. But the time frame over which such complementary innovations could be developed turned out to vary considerably. The search gave rise almost instantly to a burgeoning electrochemical industry, employing electrolytic techniques (aluminum), but a much longer period of time was required before the development of the complementary electric motor that was to become ubiquitous in the twentieth century. Similarly, a main reason for the modest future prospects that were being predicted for the computer in the late 1940s was that transistors had not yet been incorporated into the computers of the day. Introducing the transistor, and later integrated circuits, into computers were, of course, momentous events that transformed the computer industry. Indeed, in one of the most remarkable technological achievements of the twentieth century, the integrated circuit eventually became a computer, with the advent of the microprocessor in 1970. The world would be a far different place today if computers were still being made with vacuum tubes.

The need to develop complementary technologies may have a great deal to do with the apparent failure of computer technology in the last couple of decades to raise the level of U.S. productivity growth above its rather dismal recent levels. Robert Solow has made the observation that we see computers everywhere today except in the productivity statistics. But it appears to be typical of truly major innovations that they take a long time to absorb. The historical experience with respect to the introduction of electricity offers many earlier parallels. If we date the beginning of the electric age in the early 1880s, with the invention of dynamos, it was fully forty years—into the 1920s—before the electrification of factories began to show up in terms of significant measured productivity growth (Du Boff, 1967; Devine, 1983; Schurr, 1990).

Major new technological regimes take many years before they replace an established technology. The delay is due partly to having to develop numerous components of a larger technological system—an issue that will be addressed shortly. Restructuring a factory around an electric power source, in place of the earlier steam engine or water power, commonly required a complete redesign and restructuring of a factory facility. It represented, among other things, a revolution in the principles of factory organization. The layout of the machinery in the factory now had far more flexibility than it did with the old power sources. Learning how best to exploit a new, highly versatile power source with entirely different methods of power transmission inside the plant involved decades of experimentation and learning. Indeed, such technological innovations commonly require significant organizational changes as well.

Moreover, firms that had huge investments in manufacturing plants that still had long productive lives ahead of them were naturally reluctant to discard a facility that was still perfectly usable. As a result, if we ask who were the early adopters of electricity in the first twenty years of the twentieth century, it turns out that they were mainly new industries that were setting up production facilities for the first time, like producers of "tobacco, fabricated metals, transportation equipment and electrical machinery itself." In the older, established industries the introduction of electric power had to await the "physical depreciation of durable factory structures," and the "obsolescence of older-vintage industrial plants sited in urban core areas" (David, 1990, p. 357).

The general point is that a radical new technology such as a computer must necessarily have a very long gestation period before its characteristics and opportunities are well understood and can be thoroughly exploited. In 1910 only twenty-five percent of U.S. factories used electric power. But twenty years later, in 1930, it had risen to seventy-five percent. History suggests that we should not be terribly surprised. For comparison, if we date the beginning of the modern computer (a much more complex general-purpose technology than electricity) from the invention of the microprocessor in 1970, we are still only a quarter-century into the computer age. It took some forty years or so before electric power came to play a dominating role in manufacturing. History strongly suggests that technological revolutions are not completed overnight. If this is correct, it should be a source of optimism. The great economic benefits of the computer may still lie before us!

Third, as a closely connected point, major technological innovations often constitute entirely new technological systems. But it is difficult in the extreme to conceptualize an entirely new system. Thus, thinking about new technologies is likely to be severely handicapped by the tendency to think of them in terms of the old technologies that they eventually replace. Time and again, contemporaries of a new technology are found to have thought about it as a mere supplement that would offset certain inherent limitations of an existing technology. In the 1830s and 1840s, railroads were thought of merely as feeders into the existing canal system, to be constructed in places where the terrain had rendered canals inherently impractical (Fogel, 1964). This is precisely the same difficulty that was later encountered by the radio. Similarly, the telephone was originally conceptualized as primarily a business instrument, like the telegraph, to be used to exchange very specific messages, such as the terms of a prospective contractual agreement. This may, of course, explain why Bell's telephone patent was, as mentioned earlier, titled "Improvements in Telegraphy."

It is characteristic of a system that improvements in performance in one part are of only limited significance without simultaneous improvements in other parts. In this sense, technological systems may be thought of as comprising clusters of complementary inventions. Improvements in power generation can only have a limited impact on the delivered cost of electricity until improvements are made in the transmission network and the cost of transporting electricity over long distances. This need for further innovation in complementary activities is an important reason why even apparently spectacular breakthroughs usually have only a slowly rising productivity curve flowing from them. Within technological systems, therefore, major improvements in productivity seldom flow from single technological innovations, however significant they may appear to be. At the same time, the cumulative effects of large numbers of improvements within a technological system may eventually be immense.

Fourth, an additional and historically very important reason why it has been so difficult to foresee the uses of a new technology is that many major inventions had their origins in the attempt to solve very specific, and often very narrowly defined, problems. However, it is common that once a solution has been found, it turns out to have significant applications in totally unanticipated contexts. That is to say, much of the impact of new technologies is realized through intersectoral flows. Inventions have very serendipitous life histories (Rosenberg, 1976, Chap. 1).

The steam engine, for example, was invented in the eighteenth century specifically as a device for pumping water out of flooded mines. In fact, it was for a long time regarded exclusively as a pump. A succession of improvements later rendered it a feasible source of power for textile factories, iron mills, and an expanding array of industrial establishments. In the course of the early nineteenth century, the steam engine became a generalizable source of power and had major applications in transportation: railroads, steamships, and steamboats. In fact, before the Civil War, the main use of the steam engine in the United States was not in manufacturing at all but in transportation. Later in the nineteenth century, the steam engine was, for a time, used to produce a new and even more generalizable source of power—electricity—which, in turn, satisfied innumerable final uses to which steam power itself was not directly applicable. Finally, the steam turbine displaced the steam engine in the generation of electric power, and the special features of electricity—its ease of transmission over long distances, its capacity for making power available in "fractionalized" units, and the far greater flexibility of electricity-powered equipment—sounded the eventual death knell of the steam engine itself.

Major innovations, such as the steam engine, once they have been established, have the effect of inducing further innovations and investments over a wide frontier. Indeed, the ability to induce such further innovations and investments is a reasonably good definition of what constitutes a major innovation. It is a useful way of distinguishing between technological advances that are merely invested with great novelty from advances that have the potential for a major economic impact. But this also highlights the difficulties in foreseeing the eventual impact, since that will depend on the size and the direction of these future complementary innovations and associated investments.

The life history of the steam engine was shaped by forces that could hardly have been foreseen by British inventors who were working on ways of removing water from increasingly flooded coal mines in the eighteenth century. Nevertheless, the very existence of the steam engine, once its operating principles had been thoroughly understood, served as a powerful stimulus to other inventions.

I have been stressing here the observations that innovations often arise as solutions to highly specific problems in a particular industry, and that their subsequent inter-industry flow is bound to be highly uncertain. This is because the uses of a new technology in a quite different industrial context are especially difficult to anticipate. Yet in some cases a new technological capability may have multiple points of impact on another industry.

Consider the impact of the computer upon the air transportation industry. I would suggest that the changing performance of commercial air transportation has been influenced at least as much by the application of the computer to new uses in this industry as by the R&D spending that has taken place within the industry itself. Consider seven substantial impacts of computers on the airline industry:

1. Supercomputers now perform a good deal of fundamental aerodynamic research, including much of the research that was formerly performed in wind tunnels.
2. Computers have been a major source of cost reduction in the design of specific components of aircraft, such as wings. They played an important role in the wing designs of the Boeing 747, 757, and 767, as well as the Airbus 310.
3. Computers are now responsible for much of the activity that takes place in the cockpit, including, of course, the automatic pilot.
4. Computers, together with weather satellites, which routinely determine the shifting locations of high-altitude jet streams, are now widely used in determining optimal flight paths. The fuel savings for the world commercial airline industry is probably well in excess of $1 billion per year. (Note that this is yet another important case of the economic impact of a technology, the computer, depending upon a complementary technology that was developed many years later, weather satellites.)
5. Computers and computer networks are at the heart of the present worldwide ticketing and seating reservation system.

6. Computer simulation is now the preferred method of instruction in teaching neophytes how to fly.
7. The computer, together with radar, has become absolutely central to the operation of the air traffic control system, which would be difficult to imagine without it.

One important implication of this discussion is that R&D spending tends to be highly concentrated in a small number of industries. However, each of these few industries needs to be regarded as the locus of research activity that generates new technologies that may be widely diffused throughout the entire economy. Historically, a small number of industries have played this role in especially crucial ways: steam engines, electricity, machine tools, computers, transistors, and so on. This reinforces the earlier suggestion that we may even define a major or breakthrough innovation as one that establishes a new "framework for the working out of incremental innovations. In this sense, incremental innovations are the natural complements of breakthrough innovations. Breakthrough innovations, in turn, have often provided the basis for the emergence of entirely new industries."

The fifth and final constraint is rather less precise than the rest but, I believe, no less important. It is that the ultimate impact of some new technological capability is not just a matter of technical feasibility or improved technical performance; rather, it is a matter of identifying certain specific categories of human needs and catering to them in novel or cost-effective ways. New technologies need to pass an economic test, not just a technological one. Thus, the Concorde is a spectacular success in terms of flight performance, but it has proven to be a financial disaster, costing British and French taxpayers several billions of dollars.

Ultimately, what is often called for is not just technical expertise but also an exercise of the imagination. Understanding the technical basis for wireless communication, which Marconi did, was a very different matter from anticipating how the device might be used to enlarge the human experience. Marconi had no sense of this. On the other hand, an uneducated Russian immigrant to the United States, David Sarnoff had a lively vision of how the new technology might be used to transmit news, music, and other forms of entertainment and information into every household (and eventually automobile) in the country. Sarnoff in brief, appreciated the commercial possibilities of the new technology. Sarnoff's vision, of course, eventually prevailed under his leadership of RCA after the First World War (Bilby, 1985).

Similarly, Howard Aiken, a Harvard physics instructor who was a great pioneer in the early development of the computer, continued to think of it in the narrow context in which its early development took place—that is, purely as a device for solving esoteric scientific problems. As late as 1956 he stated, "If it should ever turn out that the basic logics of a machine designed for the numerical solution of differential equations coincide with the logics of a machine intended to make bills for a department store, I would regard this as the most amazing coincidence that I have ever encountered" (Ceruzzi, 1987, p. 197). That is, of course, precisely how it turned out, but it was hardly a coincidence. A technology originally invented for one specific purpose—the numerical solution of large sets of differential equations—could readily be redesigned to solve problems in entirely different contexts, such as the making out of bills for department stores. But it obviously was not obvious!

The essential point, of course, is that social change or economic impact is not something that can be extrapolated out of a piece of hardware. Rather, new technologies need to be conceived of as building blocks. Their eventual impact will depend on what is subsequently designed and constructed with them. New technologies are unrealized potentials that may take a very large number of eventual shapes. What shapes they actually take will depend on the ability to visualize how they might be employed in new contexts. Sony's development of Walkman is a brilliant example of how existing technologies—batteries, magnetic tapes, and earphones—could be recombined to create an entirely new product that could provide entertainment in contexts where it could not previously be delivered— where, indeed, no one had previously even thought of delivering it, like to joggers and walkers. To be sure, the product required a great deal of engineering redesign of existing components, but the real breakthrough was the identification, by Akio Morita, of a market opportunity that had not been previously identified.

Although many Americans continue to believe that the VCR was an American invention, that is simply an unsupportable perception. The American pioneers in this field, RCA and Ampex, gave up long before a truly usable product had been developed. Matsushita and Sony, on the other hand, made thousands of small improvements in design and manufacturing after the American firms had essentially left the field. These developments were closely connected to another point. A crucial step forward in the development of the VCR was the realization that there was a potential mass market in households if certain performance characteristics of the product, especially the size of its storage capacity, could be sufficiently expanded. Although the initial American conception of the VCR had been of a capital good to be used by television stations, some American as well as Japanese participants were aware of the much larger home market possibilities. The crucial difference seems to have been the Japanese confidence, based upon their own manufacturing experience, that they could achieve the necessary cost reductions and performance improvements. The rapid transformation of the VCR into one of Japan's largest export products was therefore an achievement of both imagination and justified confidence in their engineering capabilities (Rosenbloom and Cusumano, 1987).

The limited view once held by Americans of the potential for the VCR bears some parallels with the disdain of the mainframe computer makers toward the personal computer as it began to emerge about fifteen years ago. It was then fashionable to dismiss the PC as a mere "hacker's toy," with no real prospects in the business world, and therefore no serious threat to the economic future of mainframes (*New York Times,* Apr. 20, 1994, p. ci).

REVIVING OLD TECHNOLOGIES—
OR KILLING THEM OFF

My analysis has focused on barriers to the exploitation of new technologies. But of course, in highly competitive societies where there are strong incentives to innovation, those incentives apply to improving old technologies as well as to inventing new ones. In fact, innovations often appear to induce vigorous and imaginative responses on the part of firms that find themselves confronted with close substitutes for their traditional products. It is not at all uncommon to find that the competitive pressure resulting from a new technology leads to an accelerated improvement in the old technology. Some of the greatest improvements in wooden sailing ships took place between 1850 and 1880, just after the introduction of the iron-hull steamship and the compound steam engine, which were to displace sailing ships by the beginning of the twentieth century. Included were drastic improvements in hull design that allowed greater speed, more cargo in proportion to the tonnage of the ship, and, above all, the introduction of labor-saving machinery that reduced crew requirements by no less than two-thirds. Similarly, the greatest improvements in gas lamps, used for interior lighting, occurred shortly after the introduction of the incandescent electric light bulb (Rosenberg, 1976, Chap. II).

A major feature of the postwar telecommunications industry is that research has increased the capabilities of the already-installed transmission system, in addition to leading to the development of new and more productive transmission technologies. Every major transmission system—a pair of wires, coaxial cables, microwaves, satellites, fiber optics—has been subject to extensive later improvements in message-carrying capabilities, often with only relatively minor modification of the existing transmission technology. In some cases, there have been order-of-magnitude increases in the message-carrying capability of an existing channel, such as a 3/8-inch coaxial cable, and such productivity improvements have "frequently led to the postponement of the introduction of new generations of transmission technologies." For example, time-division multiplexing allowed an existing pair of wires to carry twenty-four voice channels or more rather than the single channel that it originally carried. The same pattern is observed in fiber optic technology. When AT&T began field trials with fiber optics in the mid 1970s, information was transmitted at 45 megabytes per second. By the early 1990s, the standard for new fiber optic cables had reached 565 megabytes per second, with reliable sources predicting capacities of nearly 1,000 megabytes per second in the near future.

But it is not only the case that the introduction of new technologies often has to await the availability of complementary technologies and that, in the meantime, established technologies may achieve renewed competitive vigor through continual improvements. New technologies may also turn out to be substitutes rather than complements for existing ones, thus drastically shortening the life expectancy of technologies that once seemed to warrant distinctly bullish expectations. The future prospects for communication satellites declined quite unexpectedly during the 1980s with the introduction of fiber optics and the huge and reliable expansion of channel capacity that they brought with them. In turn, fiber optics, whose first significant application was in medical diagnostics in the early 1960s, may now be approaching the beginning of the end of its useful life in that field. Fiber optic endoscopes had made possible a huge improvement in minimally invasive techniques for visualizing the gastrointestinal tract. Recently, new sensors from the realm of electronics, charged couple devices (CCDs), have begun to provide images with a quality of resolution and degree of detail that could not possibly be provided by fiber optic devices. The CAT scanner, certainly one of the great diagnostic breakthroughs of the twentieth century, is giving way to MRI, which possesses an even more powerful diagnostic capability. Uncertainties of this sort impart a large element of risk to long-term investments in expensive new technologies. The competitive process that eventually resolves these uncertainties is not the traditional textbook competition among producers of a homogeneous product, each seeking to deliver the same product to the market at a lower cost. Rather, it is a competition among different technologies, a process that Schumpeter appropriately described as "creative destruction." Thus, it is no paradox to say that one of the greatest uncertainties confronting new technologies is the invention of yet newer ones.

The simultaneous advances in new technology, along with the substantial upgrading of old technology, underlines the pervasive uncertainty confronting industrial decision makers in a world of rapid technological change. One would have to be very optimistic, as well as naive, to think that some intellectual paradigm can be developed to handle all the relevant variables in some neat and systematic way. But it may be plausible to believe that a more rigorous analysis of the issues that have been raised here may lead to a considerable improvement in the way we think about the innovation process.

We can now return to the point made earlier: the lack of knowledge about the relationships between these different dimensions of uncertainty prevents us "from understanding the total effect of uncertainty upon technological change." For example, two dimensions of uncertainty, discussed above, concern the refinement of complementary technologies and the potential for any technology to form the core of a new technological system. Even at the simplest level, it is difficult to be precise about the interaction between these different effects. The existence and refinement of complementary technologies may exercise a coercive and conservative effect, forcing the novel technology to be placed inside the current "system." Alternatively, however, complementary technologies may be exactly what is necessary for the practical realization of an entirely new system. My point is not to decide one way or the other on these issues; instead, it is to argue that a research program that neglects these interactions may be missing a very large part of how uncertainty has shaped the rate and direction of technological change and, by extension, the historical growth experience.

CONCLUSION

It is not part of my warrant to offer policy recommendations. However, a few closing observations may be in order. The research community is currently being exhorted with increasing force to unfurl the flag of "relevance" to social and economic needs. The burden of much that has been said here is that we "frequently simply do not know what new findings may turn out to be relevant, or to what particular realm of human activity that relevance may eventually apply." Indeed, I have been staking the broad claim that a pervasive uncertainty characterizes not only basic research, where it is generally acknowledged, but also the realm of product design and new-product development—that is, the D of R&D. Consequently, early precommitment to any specific, large-scale technology project, as opposed to a more limited, sequential decision-making approach, is likely to be wasteful. Evidence for this assertion abounds in such government-sponsored projects as weapons procurement, the space program, research on the development of an artificial heart, and research on synthetic fuels.

The pervasiveness of uncertainty suggests that the government should ordinarily resist the temptation to play the role of a champion of any one technological alternative, such as nuclear power, or any narrowly concentrated focus of research support, such as the War on Cancer. "Rather, it would seem to make a great deal of sense to manage a deliberately diversified research portfolio, a portfolio that is likely to illuminate a range of alternatives in the event of a reordering of social or economic priorities or the unexpected failure of any single, major research thrust. Government policy ought to be to open many windows and to provide the private sector with financial incentives to explore the technological landscape that can only be faintly discerned" from those windows. Thus, my criticism of the federal government's postwar energy policy is not that it made a major commitment to nuclear power that subsequently turned out to be problem-ridden. A more appropriate criticism is aimed at the single-mindedness of the focus on nuclear power that led to a comparative neglect of many other alternatives, including not only alternative energy sources but also improvements in the efficiency of energy utilization.

The situation with respect to the private sector is obviously different. Private firms may normally be expected to allocate their R&D funds in ways that they hope will turn out to be relevant. Private firms are very much aware that they confront huge uncertainties in the marketplace, and they are capable of making their own assessments and placing their "bets" accordingly. Bad bets are, of course, common, indeed so common that it is tempting to conclude that the manner in which competing firms pursue innovation is a very wasteful process. Such a characterization would be appropriate were it not for a single point: uncertainty. In fact, a considerable virtue of the marketplace is that in the face of huge uncertainties concerning the uses of new technological capabilities, it encourages exploration along a wide variety of alternative paths. This is especially desirable in the early stages, when uncertainties are particularly high and when individuals with differences of opinion (often based upon differences in access to information) need to be encouraged to pursue their own hunches or intuitions. Indeed, it is important that this point should be stated more affirmatively: the achievement of technological progress, in the face of numerous uncertainties, requires such differences of opinion.

Finally, a further considerable virtue of the marketplace is that it also provides strong incentives to terminate, quickly and unsentimentally, directions of research whose once-rosy prospects have been unexpectedly dimmed by the availability of new data, by some change in the economic environment, or by a restructuring of social or political priorities. For a country that currently supports more than 700 federal laboratories with a total annual budget of over $23 billion, more than half of which is devoted to weapons development or other defense-related purposes, that is no small virtue.

REFERENCES

Bilby, Kenneth, *The General: David Sarnoff and the Rise of the Communications Industry.* New York: Harper and Row, 1985.

Brock, Gerald W., *The Telecommunications Industry.* Cambridge: Harvard University Press, 1982.

Ceruzzi, Paul, "An Unforeseen Revolution: Computers and Expectations, 1935–1985." In Joseph J. Corn, ed., *Imagining Tomorrow,* Boston: MIT Press, 1987, pp. 188–201.

David, Paul, "The Dynamo and the Computer: An Historical Perspective on the Modern Productivity Paradox." *American Economic Review Papers and Proceedings,* May 1990, 355–61.

Devine, Warren, Jr., "From Shafts to Wires: Historical Perspectives on Electrification." *Journal of Economic History,* June 1983, 43(2), 347–72.

Douglas, Susan, *Inventing American Broadcasting, 1899–1922.* Baltimore: Johns Hopkins University Press, 1987.

Du Boff, Richard, "The Introduction of Electric Power in American Manufacturing." *Economic History Review,* Dec. 1967, 509–18.

Fogel, Robert, *Railroads and American Economic Growth.* Baltimore: Johns Hopkins University Press, 1964.

Gelijns, Annetine, *Innovation in Clinical Practice.* Washington, D.C.: National Academy Press, 1991.

Maclaurin, W. Rupert, *Invention and Innovation in the Radio Industry.* New York: Macmillan, 1949.

Martin, James, *Future Developments in Telecommunications.* Englewood Cliffs, N.J.: Prentice-Hall, 1977.

Rosenberg, Nathan, *Perspectives on Technology.* New York: Cambridge University Press, 1976.

Rosenbloom, Richard, and Michael Cusumano, "Technological Pioneering and Competitive Advantage: The Birth of the VCR Industry." *California Management Review,* Summer 1987.

Schurr, Sam, et al., *Electricity in the American Economy.* New York: Greenwood Press, 1990.

Townes, Charles, "Quantum Mechanics and Surprise in the Development of Technology." *Science,* Feb. 16, 1968.

U.S. Navy, "Bureau of Ships, Technical Bulletin No. 2. Jan. 1941." As cited in James Martin, *Future Developments in Telecommunications,* Englewood Cliffs, N.J.: Prentice-Hall, 1977, p. 11.

Wriston, Walter B., *The Twilight of Sovereignty.* New York: Charles Scribner's Sons, 1992.

2

Falling Behind: The Productivity Problem

Robert L. Heilbroner and Lester C. Thurow

One of the greatest shocks to our national ego has been the dawning realization that when it comes to standards of living, America is no longer number one. Indeed, in the world ranking of average standards of material well-being, we are probably something like number ten, and if Japan continues to catch up with us, we will soon become number eleven. In some cases, such as Saudi Arabia or Abu Dhabi, this ranking is a statistical artifact, produced by averaging together the astronomical incomes of a small ruling clique with the still abysmal living standards of the masses of the population. But that is not the case with industrialized nations such as Sweden or Switzerland or Denmark, nor will it apply if and when Japan overtakes us. The basic reason, of which we are uncomfortably aware, is that American productivity is today lower than that of a number of other advanced nations. We simply produce less per person than they do.

How could it happen that the United States, so long the envy and admiration of the world, could have fallen on such parlous times? There are two approaches to this question, one positive, one negative. The positive approach emphasizes that the loss of American leadership can better be seen as the long-overdue assertion of European and Japanese economic strength and ability. When all is said and done, a nation's productivity reflects its reservoir of skills and talents and morale, as well as its stocks of machinery and its access to resources. The nations that are now at the head of the world's parade of incomes are all there because their resources, equipment, and human capital have put them there. Swedish or German engineering, for instance, has always been as good as any in the world. The Japanese educational system is a marvel of discipline and application. Even the Saudis, benefiting from their oil, are only enjoying a claim to wealth that we too once enjoyed when the Mesabi Range or the Great Plains gave us (or still give us) a God-given advantage over everyone else.

Reprinted with the permission of Simon & Schuster from ECONOMICS EXPLAINED, Revised and Updated Edition by Robert L. Heilbroner and Lester C. Thurow. Copyright © 1982, 1987, 1994 by Robert L. Heilbroner and Lester C. Thurow.

So the positive side of the productivity story is that Europe has finally over-come the setbacks of two devastating world wars and that Japan has finally come into her own. To the extent that the world is a safer and better place as a commu-nity of equals, we can only applaud their rise to riches, even if it means that the era of cheap tourism and unchallenged American superiority is gone forever.

But there is also a negative side to the productivity issue. The newly rich have not merely claimed their rightful place in the sun. Americans have lost their own place because we have suffered a decline in productivity compared with our Western allies. In the 1980s, industrial productivity rose by about two percent per year in West Germany and by about 3 percent per year in Japan. But it rose less than 1 percent annually in the United States. During 1989–90, we not only lost out comparatively to our main competitors, but we actually ran backward! Pro-ductivity fell by 1 percent over those two years, until it finally rebounded to 2.7 percent in 1992—good, but not spectacular.

WHAT HAS HAPPENED TO PRODUCTIVITY?

What lies behind the phenomenon of "falling behind"? The ups and downs of the last few years suggest that there is a short-term process at work as well as a longer-term one. The short-term process is not particularly dangerous. It arises be-cause measured productivity—the number of cars, or tons of steel, or ton-miles of freight produced by an average employee—rises or falls depending on whether we are in a boom or a recession. During recessions, although employers may be forced to lay off some of their working force, they try to hang on to skilled over-head personnel even if they aren't fully occupied, because employers know that when the turn comes it isn't easy to hire a knowledgeable bookkeeper, or a sales-man who knows the line, or a versatile draftsman. Thus sagging output is appor-tioned among a working force that is somewhat larger than it could be, and the inevitable result is a fall in average output per employee. That is also why produc-tivity bounces back quickly as soon as production picks up steam, for output can be increased without having to hire another bookkeeper, salesman, or draftsper-son. Hence, in upswings, productivity data look good.

These short-term reasons caution against overreacting to newspaper head-lines warning of precipitous drops in productivity. But they do not account for the continuing, year-by-year deterioration of American performance. For instance, the 1985 fall in productivity took place in a year of economic growth. Something more fundamental must have been going on.

The first place where we should direct our attention is the shift that has been going on in the allocation of America's productive effort. If we compare the 1980s with the 1950s—or with a century before that—we can see that there has been a steady streaming of labor and capital out of agriculture, first into industry and later into the service sector. To put it anecdotally, a typical worker in 1900 was a farmhand, in 1940 a factory hand, in 1990 an office worker. Put in economic terms, this has resulted in a rise in American productivity in the earlier years when the industrial sector was gaining, and a fall in recent years when the service sector has been swelling. Today about 75 percent of all employees work in some kind of service industry, whether it be a law firm, H & R Block, or the local hospital. This is a higher percentage, by far, than is found in any other industrial nation.

To be sure, the term "services" covers a very wide spread of businesses and occupations. The technical definition includes some businesses in which productivity is very high. It also embraces the field in which productivity is typically only fifty percent of the level in manufacturing. What is significant for our purpose is that certain areas within the vast service sector, marked by abnormally low productivity, are also areas in which employment has mushroomed in the last decade. Outstanding among these are personal business services, such as lawyers and accountants, health and hospital care, and education. In the last two fields, output per worker is worth far less per hour and has been growing far more slowly than elsewhere in the economy. Indeed, the 600,000 persons we now employ in our private security forces have a purely negative effect on productivity, because they add to cost but do not contribute anything to output.

This is not to say that security guards—or police—may not be necessary, or that nursing homes are a waste. On the contrary, it is likely that we have too few policemen or guards, and everyone knows that our nursing facilities are inadequate. Alas, that only demonstrates that we may have to pay the price of a somewhat lower average productivity to achieve a society that provides amenities and safety and good government. Just the same, it is one reason why our productivity has fallen.

A second reason is that a number of important industries have encountered specific productivity problems. One of these is mining, where the decline has been especially marked. Here the blame can be attributed to two very different factors. In the case of oil production (which is included in mining), it is nature that is the problem. We have simply entered a state of geological depletion in America: less oil is produced in old wells, and new wells have to be drilled deeper and yield fewer bonanzas. This is a problem that is likely to intensify, even if we learn to extract oil from shale or to recover the oil left in old rock formations.

A second part of the mining problem lies in the coal industry. Here the difficulty is not geological but social. Stricter safety and environmental measures impose higher costs on coal mining, particularly to repair the damage done by strip-mining operations. These measures add to the amount of labor needed to produce each ton of coal, and pull down our productivity as a consequence. The same is true of copper mining. As with the need for security personnel or nursing homes, we may set very high store by environmental protection, but we must also recognize that there is a price to be paid in terms of measured output per working person.

Mining is not the only industry that has slipped. So has productivity in the utility industry, partly because of very high energy costs. More interesting—because we do not really know why productivity has fallen—is the case of the construction industry. The data unmistakably point to a steady fall in the output per worker in this large area of activity. Why? Perhaps because we aren't building as many Levittowns, with their cookie-cutter designs. Perhaps because many important construction projects in nuclear energy have ground to a halt. Perhaps because construction is just more complicated than it used to be. Perhaps because the old work ethic is gone. The fact is that we do not know the answer. All we know is that productivity is off in construction, and that too pulls down the national average.

THE PRODUCTIVITY CHALLENGE

Taken together, the shift to services, the fall in mining output, and the sag in construction account for about one third of our total drop in productivity over the past few decades. Thus there are obviously other industries and other reasons behind the productivity problem. Here we are going to zero in on one and only one of these additional explanations. It is the failure of American industry to invest in enough modern capital equipment to stay abreast of its Western partners. Capital equipment alone is certainly not the secret of productivity, but it is a very important part of the problem, as we shall see.

This brings us to cars and steel. Why did these industries fare so badly, vis-à-vis their international competitors? One reason seems to concern internal management, another "external" management. Internal first. Americans are used to thinking of themselves as non-bureaucratic. But that is a self-image that simply will not stand up against an analysis of the way we organize a great deal of production. To put it bluntly, we are white-collar top-heavy. It takes many more office workers for us to produce a car than is the case with our main competitor, Japan.

It isn't just cars. During the 1980s, American firms laid off about 6 percent of their blue-collar work force. Over that same period, output rose by thirty percent, despite the decline in production-floor employees. This means that factory-floor productivity per employed worker must have risen significantly—and it did, at just under three percent a year. Meanwhile, however, those same firms were hiring fifteen million new white-collar workers. White-collar employment rose by thirty-three percent—faster than the gain in output. The conclusion follows irrefutably—while blue-collar productivity was rising, white-collar productivity was falling. And since there are now almost two white-collar workers for every blue-collar worker on American payrolls, their decline in efficiency far outweighed the gain in factory-floor output per person.

Why are American firms more bureaucratic than foreign ones—including the foreign ones that have plants here, where they must abide by the same rules and regulations as American companies? No one knows. But there is a growing awareness that traditional American managerial ways must be changed if we are to hold our own in the free-for-all of world competition.

Then there is the "external" problem of management. We can illustrate it through the instances of both the steel and auto industries. Both industries made catastrophically wrong decisions that affected their ability to compete. Steel decided not to go into oxygenation and continuous casting, and the auto industry decided not to abandon the big car. Both decisions were terribly wrong, particularly because our international competition decided otherwise.

That is not quite the end of the analysis, however. Why did American managers make such wrong decisions? One reason seems to be a difference in the time horizon over which Americans and foreign managers have been trained to think. Americans concentrate on the "bottom line" today. Junking steel plants and auto-assembly lines that were still making money during the early 1970s would have required the decision to accept very poor or negative bottom lines then, in exchange for prospects of high growth and very satisfactory bottom lines five years ahead. European and Japanese managers have been trained to think in terms of long-range growth; Americans, in terms of short-period profits. The result has been extremely costly for us.

But even that is not quite the full explanation of the failure of the auto and steel industries to modernize. The changeover from existing equipment to new plant and equipment required not only an escape from the short-run bottom line mentality, but also relatively easy availability of capital. The decision to modernize steel, like the decision to "down-size" cars, required literally billions of dollars of investment. GM alone had to spend twenty billion dollars between 1974 and 1980. In Europe and Japan that capital was much more readily available than in the United States.

In part this was the case because the propensity of these nations to save is much higher than in America. We have noted that, before West Germany swallowed up East Germany, West German families saved about fifteen percent of their annual incomes, and Japanese families save about twenty percent of theirs, whereas Americans typically save only 5 percent of their incomes. Even if we add corporate savings to the pot, in the United States only about one seventh of all our income is available for the replacement of old capital and the formation of new capital. In the former West Germany and Japan, the availability of total savings is about one and a half to two times as great as ours. Hence it is not surprising—although it is certainly disquieting—to learn that on a per capita basis Japan invested $2.50 in new plant and equipment in 1992 for every $1 invested in the United States.

Capital was also more readily available abroad because many foreign industrialized nations use the power of government to support—even to finance—their big, internationally oriented businesses. This is particularly the case in Japan, where the closely coordinated activities of the Japanese government, its big banks, and its largest corporations have given rise to the business-government cooperative effort we call "Japan Incorporated." The Japanese government, working closely with its banks and industrial leaders, typically chooses one or two firms to serve as the leaders in a given industry, secures large bank credits for these firms, and thus paves the way for the leaders' massive entry into the international arena, equipped with the latest technology. To some extent, this kind of government-private coordination has been used by Western nations as well. Even in Germany, where there is much less leadership by government, there has been a unified effort to make capital available when needed.

The best example is Airbus Industrie, a collective effort of the British, French, Spanish, and German governments to break into the aircraft manufacturing business. Almost twenty years and $26 billion were required, but in the end European governments created a manufacturer who has essentially driven McDonell Douglas to the Orient and who now threatens Boeing's dominant world position.

Thus another reason why American steel and auto manufacturers failed to meet the challenge from abroad was that they did not compete on even terms. Admittedly, the Americans made very costly mistakes in judging the market and in paying too much heed to immediate profits. But these mistakes also reflect the absence of a public-private structure that might have lifted sights higher and provided the wherewithal to attempt ambitious programs. In a word, American enterprise has not learned how to organize its effort in a new setting that is global in scope, and where the traditional division between government and business is blurring. We may not like this emerging way of economic life, but it exists and must be taken into account when we inquire why we have fallen behind.

This is by no means a full analysis of the productivity puzzle. For example, we have paid no heed to the warnings of those who blame the military for our lagging productivity, claiming that too much engineering and scientific talent and too much skilled manpower go into totally unproductive armaments. Nor have we considered what the Japanese call "hard productivity"—the productivity that results from high technology and massive capital—as against "soft productivity"— the increase in output that reflects stronger morale and a genuine feeling of teamwork. How far this belated appreciation of the dignity of labor can go in the face of the imperatives of profit and the conventional wisdom of efficiency is a matter that may prove of decisive importance for the future.

But rather than continue with a long list of contributory elements, we prefer to end with two key points. The first is already apparent from our survey and would only become more evident if we continued the analysis. It is that there is no quick fix for the problem. There is no way of rapidly reversing the drift into the service sector. There is no way of making nature more bountiful. We may temper our environmental concerns, but it is no longer possible to ignore them. The mentality of American management will not change overnight. The savings propensities of American families will not double tomorrow. And the long-standing mutual suspicions between government and business make it very difficult to find ways of meeting the new public-private challenge from abroad. An infrastructure program will not bring productivity results for four to six years. In a word, the productivity problem will not go away quickly.

Second, improving productivity will be painful, not agreeable. It may mean, for instance, phasing out industries or firms that cannot hold their own in the international battle for markets. With how much enthusiasm will the American apparel trade agree to that? Under the banner of Helping American Productivity, how willingly will Chrysler's inefficient work force migrate to the sun belt, where new jobs may or may not await them in some other line of work? Raising savings requires that we cut back on our propensity to consume: "Buy now, pay later" is not compatible with "Invest now, grow later." If we are serious about raising investment, we must be serious about discouraging the national love affair with "living it up."

Thus it is not going to be easy or pleasant to reverse the trend of American productivity. There is no single great ailment to which a single great restorative effort can be applied. Everyone wants productivity to be restored—starting with the other guy's problem. Yet, if we are to compete in international markets with the Japanese and Germans, productivity must be raised, and raised dramatically. If we cannot find the political will to impose the necessary costs on ourselves in some fair manner, we will simply not solve the problem. Having fallen behind, we will stay behind.

3

Science, Economic Growth, and Public Policy

Richard R. Nelson and Paul M. Romer

Major long-term policy changes often flow from decisions made in times of stress. Thus, choices about how to fight World War II ultimately led to the large-scale sustained support of university research by the federal government that has lasted over the half-century since World War II. The economic threat we face today is less acute than the security threat we faced then. Nevertheless, this threat may lead to a fundamental realignment of science and technology policy and a major change in the economic role of the university.

In the midst of the debate about how government support for science should be structured after World War II, Vannevar Bush prepared his famous report, "Science—The Endless Frontier." Although the specific institutional recommendations from the report were not adopted, it set the terms for the subsequent intellectual debate about science policy. In an analysis of Bush's report, Donald E. Stokes (1995) notes that Bush advocated government support for the kind of abstract science done by scientists such as Niels Bohr, the physicist who played a pivotal role in the development of quantum mechanics. Bush argued that public support for that kind of science would lead to advances in the work done by someone like Thomas Edison, who takes existing knowledge and puts it to commercial use. (The argument comes from Bush but the examples of Bohr and Edison come from Stokes.)

We are beginning to see a decisive shift on the part of the government toward direct rather than indirect support for the "Edisons." If Edison were alive today, setting up General Electric, he could apply for direct grants from such government programs as SBIR (Small Business Innovative Research), ATP (Advanced Technology Program), and TRP (Technology Reinvestment Program). He could pursue CRADAs (Cooperative Research and Development Agreements) with the National Laboratories. He could form a consortium of for-profit firms and get

From *Challenge*, March/April 1996, pp. 9–21. Reprinted by permission from M. E. Sharpe, Inc., Armonk, NY 10504.

government matching money to develop a specific technology such as flat panel display screens. The government would also be much more willing to help him establish commercially valuable intellectual property rights over any fundamental discoveries that he might make. Some policy makers would encourage him to patent the sequence data on gene fragments, the scientific and practical importance of which no one had yet understood.

As many students of science and technology have pointed out, there are good reasons to be dissatisfied with the "linear model" of the relationship between science and practical technology that is implicit in Bush's report. According to this now discredited model, the government merely puts resources into the Bohr-end of a production line and valuable products come out at the Edison-end. There are, however, equally good reasons to be worried about a strategy that sharply shifts government policy toward direct support of R&D in industry, giving government money to Edison-like activities and strengthening property rights across the board. And the reasons for concern are amplified if such a policy shift involves a drying up of public support for basic research at universities.

One important limitation of the linear model—the one we will focus upon here—is that it is blind to basic research undertaken with practical problems in mind—work in which the Bohrs are directly motivated to lay the scientific basis for the work of the Edisons. In the map laid out by Stokes, such work is epitomized by the research of Louis Pasteur, a scientist whose research was primarily guided by practical problems, which led him to explore fundamental scientific questions. Basic economic analysis suggests that different institutional arrangements be used to support the work of a Bohr and an Edison, but the example of Pasteur indicates that one wants to have strong linkages between the two. Both of these kinds of work are more productive when they rub up against each other.

Universities in the United States have enjoyed unique success in promoting this kind of interaction. Before World War II, they did this by catering to the needs of the private business sector. They provided the home for new scientific fields such as metallurgy, which was developed expressly to advance steel-making technology. After the war, universities in the United States became world-class centers of Bohr-style science, but they also gained new strength in the Pasteur-like activities. In large part, this took place because such government agencies as the National Institutes of Health and the Department of Defense provided massive support for what came to be called "mission-oriented" basic research.

We now have the opportunity to adjust the set of practical problems that animate Pasteur-style science within the university. We could reduce our emphasis on problems in the areas of defense and health. We could pay more attention to the broad range of scientific and technical challenges that arise in the private sector. This change can be implemented without endangering our national strength in Bohr-style science. It can be accomplished without trying to privatize Pasteur-style science and without creating strong property rights that could impede the free flow of knowledge that is generated by this work. Indeed, our argument is that the preservation, with reorientation, of Pasteur-style science within the university will both strengthen Bohr-style science and help us meet the changing practical demands we are putting on science.

We are concerned that this is not adequately understood. Instead of offering new and different opportunities for the Pasteurs of the university, policy makers may try to convert both the Bohrs and the Pasteurs into Edisons. Fearful of this prospect, the Bohrs and Pasteurs may fight any proposal for readjustment. Government leaders may therefore bypass the university in frustration and fund the Edisons of the private sector directly. Over time, the work that was previously done by Pasteurs in the university will be shifted to the private sector through a combination of direct grants, matching money, and stronger property rights, where it will become Edison work, not Pasteur work. The Bohrs may acquiesce in this privatization and eventual destruction of Pasteur-style science because it buys them protection from political demands for changes in their part of university research. We could end up with the kind of separation that we have avoided until now, with the Bohrs working in isolation from the Edisons, and with little work in the Pasteurs' quadrant. We will then have lost the unique features that made our universities so successful in generating good science and strong economic growth.

In this paper, we try to outline the economic principles that should guide the choice of which path to take. We start by outlining the forces that brought us to this junction.

THE CURRENT POLICY CONTEXT

Before describing what economists know about the connections between science, technology, and economic growth, it is important to lay out the economic context of the current debate about science policy. This context has been shaped by the erosion of the very large and widespread technological and economic lead that the United States had over other countries during the 1960s and the worldwide slowdown in income and productivity growth since the early 1970s. The erosion of the U.S. lead is easy to explain and probably was inevitable. The slowdown in growth is not well understood.

It is important to recognize that the post-World War II economic and technological dominance of the United States was the consequence of two distinct waves of economic growth. The first wave, which dates from the late nineteenth century, began at a time when U.S. universities were not strong centers of scientific research. The act that created the land-grant college system in the 1870s described the mission of these institutions as the development of the "agricultural and mechanic arts." Such research as did take place tended to reflect this strong practical orientation. European intellectuals were disdainful of the vocational orientation of American universities. And as late as the 1930s, young American scientists who wanted advanced scientific training generally went to Europe to get it.

The early U.S. successes in such industries as automobiles and steel were not the result of any particular American strength in science. Instead, firms here achieved dominance in the techniques of mass production in large part because they operated in the world's largest common market. They had access to many consumers and to ample supplies of inexpensive raw materials. But universities also played an important role. Because of the unusual practical orientation of the U.S. system of higher education, U.S. industry had access to a large pool of well-trained engineers and was able to develop professional managers to a far greater degree than was the case in Europe.

The second major wave of American economic success was in "high-technology" industries. These developed after World War II and were made possible by rapidly developing American capabilities in science. Indeed, World War II was a watershed in American science and technology in several respects. After the war, the federal government became the principal patron of university research. By the middle 1960s, the American university research system had clearly become the world's best across a spectrum that included almost all fields of science. This improvement in the quality of American science was accompanied by major procurement and industrial R&D programs of the department of defense and, for a period of time, NASA. These programs created the initial market for some of the high-technology goods that made the first use of the rapidly developing body of scientific knowledge. On the other hand, in many cases the market for high-technology goods drew forth the science that made these goods possible.

Increased government support for science was accompanied by two other developments. One was the large increase in the number of young Americans earning a university education. While only a small fraction of college majors were in the natural sciences or engineering, the sheer numbers of Americans receiving undergraduate and postgraduate training meant that by the late 1960s the fraction of scientists and engineers in the U.S. work force stood well above the fraction in Europe and Japan. Second, both private and public monies flowing into industrial R&D increased greatly. By the late 1960s, the U.S. ratio of industrial R&D to GNP was far higher than in any other country. All these factors combined to give firms in the United States a commanding position in such high-technology fields as computers, semiconductors, aircraft, and pharmaceuticals.

The late 1960s marked another watershed. By that time American economic dominance was clearly beginning to erode, as Japan and the advanced industrial nations of Western Europe began to catch up. There were two basic factors behind this process of catching up. One was the rapid integration of the economies of the industrialized nations. Reductions in transportation costs and the removal of trade restrictions meant that manufactured products and raw materials could move more readily between countries. In addition, increased flows of direct foreign investment let firms from the United States put their knowledge and technology to work in many other countries. The other factor in the process of catching up was the investment that other countries were making in science and engineering education and in research and development. Together these developments made it possible for several countries to achieve rough parity with—and in some cases go beyond—the United States in traditional areas of mass production. The U.S. high-technology industries, however, have generally continued to do well in the face of strengthening foreign competition.

Most economists believe that convergence among the advanced industrial nations was inevitable. In a world where transportation and communication costs are falling and where governments remove artificial barriers, the same forces that operate within the borders of the United States will operate between countries. At the time of the Civil War, economic activity in the southern states of the United States was very different from that in the industrialized Northeast. Because of the greatly increased mobility of goods and firms that has been the result of advances in transportation and communications technology since that time, economic activity in the two regions now looks much the same.

At the same time that the convergence between the industrialized nations was taking place, productivity and income growth slowed significantly from the pace it had achieved during the quarter-century after World War II. This slowdown occurred first in the United States, but is also apparent in the other industrialized economies. Economists are still uncertain as to exactly what lay behind the global slowdown beginning in 1970, or to put the question in another way, why growth that proceeded at unprecedented rates during the 1950s and 1960s has returned to levels that are closer to historical norms. In any case, economists are nearly unanimous in holding that the rapid growth of other nations was not a cause of the slowdown in growth in the United States.

Nevertheless, the combination of convergence and slow growth blended together to create a public perception that the United States is suffering from a serious relative decline in its economic performance. This perception has changed the nature of the policy discussion in the United States regarding the appropriate role of the government in supporting technology and science. The loss of the dominant position held by American firms has caused the policy discussion to focus on measures that could enhance their competitive position. The productivity slowdown, which manifests itself most dramatically in stagnation of the wages paid to low-skilled workers, has generated additional support for government measures that would directly spur economic growth.

The slowdown has also meant that government revenues have not grown as rapidly in the last thirty years as they did during the 1950s and 1960s. The slowdown in the rate of growth of private income has increased political resistance to increased tax rates. As a result, political support for the strategy of dealing with national problems by spending public money has fallen. Also, as seems always to be the case when times get harder, there has been growing disenchantment with government policies and programs that were widely regarded as appropriate and efficacious during earlier, better economic times.

One important manifestation has been growing dissension about whether the large-scale U.S. government support for basic research, primarily at universities, is worth what it costs. Increasingly, there are suggestions that university research support ought to be more closely targeted on areas and activities that are deemed likely to feed directly into technological innovation.

This dissatisfaction certainly has influenced the design of the new technology programs. Except in the area of defense procurement, the government traditionally has used the university as an intermediary when it wanted to encourage economic and technological development in the private business sector. The new technology programs cited in the introduction largely bypass the university. Many directly influence research activity within firms and, for the first time, attempt to do so in areas where the federal government will not be the primary user of the goods being developed.

Several other factors further complicate the situation for universities. The end of the cold war already poses a serious threat to existing defense-related support for university research in such fields as electrical engineering, computer science, and materials science. Growing concern about health care costs may soon threaten research support for the biomedical sciences. An increasing number of young scientists who had expected to follow an academic career are finding that path blocked by a lack of jobs. Universities are responding to the feared cutbacks in government research funding by soliciting more support from industry.

At the same time that public support of university basic research has come under attack, some of the private organizations that did path-breaking basic research—Bell Labs, IBM Yorktown, Xerox PARC—have been cutting back on expenditures or reallocating their energies to projects that have quicker payoffs or where the results more easily can be kept proprietary. Some of these same companies also are pulling away from their previous support of academic research.

The current debate about government support for science and technology reflects all this. Decisions made now will determine how scientific research in universities and technological development in industry will evolve, perhaps for decades to come. Behind every position in this debate there lies a set of assumptions about the relationships between science, technological innovation, and economic growth. It is to these relationships that we now turn.

TECHNOLOGY AND ECONOMIC GROWTH

From the very beginning, economists have appreciated the importance of technical advance. One of the most striking parts of Adam Smith's pioneering analysis of economic principles, The Wealth of Nations, was his famous description of productivity improvement in the making of pins. A good part of that description involved technical advances.

From the beginning, technological advance was seen as the force that could offset diminishing returns. Diminishing returns—the notion that the marginal benefits decrease as the effort in any activity increases—is fundamental to any explanation of how a market economy allocates resources. Classical economists reasoned as follows: the amount of food produced by each agricultural worker is very high when there are few workers on a given area of land. Output per worker diminishes as more people work the given amount of land. This kind of reasoning leads to a very pessimistic view of the prospect for sustained economic growth. As Thomas Malthus and others pointed out, in the absence of some offsetting influence, diminishing returns in agriculture implies that the output of food per person will fall as the population increases. The inevitable outcome would be famine and starvation.

By the end of the nineteenth century, it was clear that this dismal forecast was completely wrong. Population and food output had each increased dramatically. Economists observed that discovery and invention kept Malthus's bleak prediction from coming true. With a fixed set of technological opportunities, the return in any activity did indeed diminish. But over time, new techniques of production have been introduced. Initially, these new activities offered high returns. As resources were shifted into them, the returns fell, but new discoveries and new techniques kept the process going.

Economists were preoccupied with other questions during the first half of this century, especially with macroeconomic stabilization because of the worldwide disruptions experienced during the interwar period. When they returned to the study of long-run trends in the 1950s, both the empirical studies and the theoretical writings affirmed the importance of technical advance to economic growth. Technological change was understood to have a direct effect on growth by increasing the amount of output that can be produced with fixed quantities of capital and labor. The direct effect is what economists try to measure with estimates of "total factor productivity growth" or the "growth accounting residual." Early estimates attributed most of the growth in per capita income to this effect alone. More recent estimates have attributed a larger fraction of growth to the accumulation of physical and human capital and have reduced the fraction directly attributable to technology.

In any case, estimates of this direct effect of technological change tell only part of the story. Technical advance also has an indirect effect because it raises the return on investments in physical and human capital. If there were no technological advance, returns on both of these types of capital would be reduced to zero.

Capital accumulation would stop. In a fundamental sense, all economic growth, even the growth that is directly caused by capital accumulation, can ultimately be attributed to technological change.

A second line of work tried to measure the rate of return on investments in technology. In one famous and revealing calculation, Zvi Griliches showed that the investment in agricultural research that produced hybrid corn generated benefits that were about seven times larger than the costs and yielded an internal rate of return of about forty percent. Other calculations found similar rates of return on research investments in other parts of agriculture and in manufacturing. These estimates measure the social rate of return because the entity that does the research—either the government or the private firm—often fails to capture all of the benefits. In the jargon of the field, much of the benefit comes in the form of "spillovers" that are captured by others.

The existence of a differential between private and social returns is essential if we are to understand why high rates of return on research and development could persist. If all firms could capture all of the benefits and earn 40 percent return on investments in R&D—a return that is much higher than returns on other forms of investment—many firms would increase their R&D investments. As they did, the return to research would be driven down to a more normal level. Because large returns to investment in research apparently still are available, we can infer that private investors have difficulty capturing all of the benefits from their investments.

The divergence between the private and social return to R&D investment provides an important justification for policies that would encourage R&D. From the point of view of society, the income-maximizing strategy is to invest first in those activities that offer the highest rate of return. From the point of view of society as a whole, this criterion suggests that we are not investing enough in the activities that generate technological advance. To address the question of how this deficiency could be resolved, we need a precise understanding of what these activities are and what the government can do to influence them.

THE ECONOMICS OF SOFTWARE

Although economists have long appreciated the centrality of technical advance in the process of economic growth, a complete understanding of the key processes, investments, and actors that combine to produce it has not come easily. Indeed, these processes are very complex and variegated. Economists broadly understand that the advance of technology is closely associated with advances in knowledge. It also is clear that new knowledge must be embodied in practices, techniques, and designs before it can affect an economic activity. Beyond this, different economic analyses focus on or stress different things.

Some discussions stress the "public good" aspects of technology, seeing new technology as ultimately available to all users. Others treat technology as largely a "private good," possessed by the company or person that creates it. Many economists have studied research and development as the key source of new technology. Those that have focused on R&D done by private, for-profit business firms naturally assumed that the technology created through corporate R&D is, to some extent at least, a private good. By contrast, economists who have stressed the "public good" aspects of technology have focused on government investments in R&D, "spillovers" from private R&D, or both. (These spillovers are another manifestation of the divergence between the public and private returns noted above.) Still others argue that a single-minded emphasis on organized R&D as the source of technical advance sees the sources too narrowly. They point to evidence that learning-by-doing and learning-by-using are important parts of the processes whereby new technologies are developed and refined.

Another matter on which economists have been of different minds is whether technical advance and economic growth fueled by technical advance can adequately be captured in the mathematical models of economic equilibrium that economists developed to describe a static world. Joseph Schumpeter and economists proposing "evolutionary" theories of growth have stressed that disequilibrium is an essential aspect of the process. By contrast, recent theories that descend from neoclassical models presume that the essential aspects of technical advance and economic growth can be captured by extending the static equilibrium models.

While we do not want to underplay the important open questions about how economists ought to understand technical advance, a workable consensus for policy analysis seems to be emerging from these divergent perspectives. Technology needs to be understood as a collection of many different kinds of goods. These goods can have the attributes of public goods and private goods in varying proportions. Some are financed primarily by public support for R&D, others by private R&D. Both business firms and universities are involved in various aspects of the process. Other parts of technology are produced primarily through learning-by-doing and learning-by-using, both of which can interact powerfully with research and development. There are aspects of the process that are quite well treated by equilibrium theories, with their emphasis on foresight, stationariness, and restoring forces. Still other aspects are better suited to the evolutionary models, with their emphasis on unpredictability and the limits of rational calculation.

One way to summarize this emerging view is to focus on three types of durable inputs in production. We will take our imagery and language from the ongoing digital revolution and refer to these three different types of inputs as hardware, software, and wetware. Hardware includes all the nonhuman objects used in production—both capital goods such as equipment and structures and natural resources such as land and raw materials. Wetware, the things that are stored in the "wet" computer of the human brain, includes both the human capital that mainstream economists have studied and the tacit knowledge that evolutionary theorists, cognitive scientists, and philosophers have emphasized. By contrast, software represents knowledge or information that can be stored in a form that exists outside of the brain. Whether it is text on paper, data on a computer disk, images on film, drawings on a blueprint, music on tape—even thoughts expressed in human speech—software has the unique feature that it can be copied, communicated, and reused.

The role of software, hardware, and wetware can be discerned in a wide variety of economic activities. Together they can produce new software, as when a writer uses her skills, word processing software, and a personal computer to write a book. They can produce new hardware, for example, when an engineer uses special software and hardware to produce the photographic mask that is used to lay down the lines in a semiconductor chip. When an aircraft simulator and training software are used to teach pilots new skills, they produce new wetware.

These three types of inputs can be discerned in activities that are far removed from digital computing. In the construction of the new city of Suzhou in mainland China, the government of Singapore says that its primary responsibility is to supply the software needed to run the city. The hardware is the physical infrastructure—roads, sewers, buildings, etc.—that will be designed according to the software. The wetware initially will be the minds of experts from Singapore, but eventually will be supplied by Chinese officials who will be trained in Singapore to staff the legal, administrative, and regulatory bureaucracies. The software comprises all the routines and operating procedures that have been developed in Singapore, examples of which range from the procedures for designing a road, to those for ensuring that police officers do not accept bribes, to instructions on how to run an efficient taxi service.

Traditional models of growth describe output as a function of physical capital, human capital, and the catch-all category, "technology." The alternative proposed here has the advantage of explicitly distinguishing wetware (i.e., human capital) from software. This is an essential first step in a careful analysis of the intangibles used in economic activity. The next step is to identify the reasons why software differs from both hardware and wetware.

Economists identify two key attributes that distinguish different types of economic goods: rivalry and excludability. A good is rival if it can be used by only one user at a time. This awkward terminology stems from the observation that two people will be rivals for such a good. They cannot both use it at the same time. A piece of computer hardware is a rival good. So, arguably, are the skills of an experienced computer user. However, the bit string that encodes the operating-system software for the computer is a nonrival good. Everyone can use it at the same time because it can be copied indefinitely at essentially zero cost. Nonrivalry is what makes software unique.

Although it is physically possible for a nonrival good to be used by many people, this does not mean that others are permitted to use it without the consent of the owner. This is where excludability, the second property, comes in. A good is said to be excludable if the owner has the power to exclude others from using it. Hardware is excludable. To keep others from using a piece of hardware, the owner need only maintain physical possession of it. Our legal system supports each of us in our efforts to do this.

It is more difficult to make software excludable because possession of a piece of software is not sufficient to keep others from using it. Someone may have surreptitiously copied it. The feasible alternatives for establishing some degree of control are to rely on intellectual property rights established by the legal system or to keep the software, or at least some crucial part of it, secret.

Our legal system assigns intellectual property rights to some kinds of software but not others. For example, basic mathematical formulas cannot be patented or copyrighted. At least at the present time, there is no way for the scientists who develop algorithms for solving linear programming problems to get intellectual property rights on the mathematical insight behind their creation. On the other hand, the code for a computer program, the text of a novel, or the tune and lyrics of a song are examples of software that is excludable, at least to some degree.

The two-way classification of goods according to excludability and rivalry creates four idealized types of goods. Private goods and public goods are the names given to two of these four types. Private goods are both excludable and rival. Public goods are both nonexcludable and nonrival. The mathematical principles used to solve linear programming problems are public goods. Because they are software, they are nonrival; it is physically possible to copy the algorithms out of a book. Because the law lets anyone copy and use them, they are nonexcludable.

In addition to private goods and public goods, there are two other types of goods that have no generally accepted labels but are important for policy analysis. The first are goods that are rival but not excludable. The proverbial example is a common pasture. Only one person's livestock can eat the grass in any square foot of pasture, so pasture land is a rival good for purposes of grazing. If the legal and institutional arrangements in force give everyone unlimited access to the pasture, it is also a nonexcludable good. Frequent allusions to "the tragedy of the commons" illustrate one of the basic results of economic theory: Free choice in the presence of rival, nonexcludable goods leads to waste and inefficiency.

The fourth category, and one of central importance to the study of technical advance, is of nonrival goods that are excludable, at least potentially. We stress the term "potentially" here because society often has a choice about the matter. It can establish and enforce strong property rights, in which case market incentives induce the production of such goods. Alternatively, it can deny such property rights. Then if the goods are to be provided, support through government funding, private collaborative effort, or philanthropy is needed. Many of the most important issues of public policy regarding technical advances are associated with this latter choice. For rivalrous goods, establishing and enforcing strong property rights is generally a good policy (although there are exceptional cases). But for nonrivalrous goods, the matter is much less clear.

By and large, society has chosen to give property rights to the kind of software commonly called "technology" and to deny property rights but provide public support for the development of the software commonly referred to as "science." Establishing property rights on software enables the holder of those rights to restrict access to a nonrival good. When such restriction is applied—for example, by charging a license fee—some potential users for whom access would be valuable but not worth the fee will choose to forego use, even though the real cost of their using it is zero. So putting a "price" on software imposes a social cost—positive-value uses that are locked out—and in general the more valuable the software is to large numbers of users, the higher will be the cost. To cite just one example that influences the choices of working scientists, there are experiments that could be carried out using PCR (polymerase chain reaction) technology that would be done if the scientists involved could use this technology at the cost of materials involved. Some of these are not being done because the high price charged by the current patent holder makes this research prohibitively expensive.

Note that this is very different from what is entailed in establishing property rights on rival goods. Only one user can make use of a rival good at any one time. So property rights, or options to sell them, encourage the rival good to be used by those to whom it is most valuable.

Our legal system tries to take account of the ambiguous character of property rights on software. We give patents for some discoveries, but they are limited in scope and expire after a specific period of time. For rival goods this would be a terrible policy. Imagine the consequences if the titles to all pieces of land lapsed after seventeen years. For some nonrival goods, such as works of literature or music, we grant copyright protection that lasts much longer than patent protection. This can be rationalized by the argument that costs from monopoly control of these goods creates relatively little economic inefficiency. For other goods, such as scientific discoveries and mathematical formulas, the law gives no protection at all. This presumably reflects a judgment that the cost of monopoly power over these goods is too high and that we are better off relying on such nonmarket mechanisms as philanthropic giving and government support to finance and motivate the production of these types of software.

One important distinction between different types of software is the difference in the amount and variety of additional work that needs to be done before that software makes an actual contribution that consumers would be willing to pay for. Property rights on software that is directly employed by final consumers can lead to high prices—consider the high prices on some pharmaceuticals—and cut out use by some parties who would value use, but will not or cannot pay the price. For software such as this, however, that is close to final use, it is possible for users to make reasonably well founded benefit-price calculations.

It is quite otherwise with software whose major use is to facilitate the development of subsequent software. Any market for software, such as mathematical algorithms and scientific discoveries far removed from the final consumer, would risk being grossly inefficient. Over time, many producers have to intervene, making improvements and refining the basic idea, before such software can be finally embodied in a technique, practice, or design that produces value and is sold to a final consumer. Economic theory tells us that the presence of monopoly power at many stages in this long and unpredictable chain of production can be very bad for efficiency.

In the worst case, property rights that are too strong could preempt the development of entire areas of new software. In the computer software industry, people capture this dilemma by asking the rhetorical question, "What if someone had been able to patent the blinking cursor?" The point applies equally well to many other important discoveries in the history of the industry—the notion of a high-level language and a compiler, the iterative loop, the conditional branch point, or a spreadsheet-like display of columns and rows. Extremely strong property rights on these kinds of software could have significantly slowed innovation in computer software and kept many types of existing applications from being developed.

In the production of computer software, basic software concepts are not granted strong property rights. Software applications, the kind of software sold in shrink-wrapped boxes in computer stores, is protected. This suggests a simple dichotomy between concepts and final applications that mirrors the distinction noted in the beginning between the search for basic concepts by a Niels Bohr and the search for practical applications by a Thomas Edison. As the work of Pasteur would lead us to expect, this dichotomy hides important ambiguities that arise in practice. At the extremes, the distinction between concepts and applications is clear, but in the middle ground there is no sharp dividing line. Courts are forced to decide either that software for overlapping windows or specific key sequences should be treated as essential parts of an application that are entitled to patent or copyright protections, or that they are basic concepts that are not given legal protection. In the realm of software, there are many shades of gray. The simple dichotomy nevertheless serves as a useful framework for guiding the economic and policy analysis of science and technology, for science is concerned with basic concepts, and technology is ultimately all about applications.

SCIENCE AND TECHNOLOGY

One of the dangers in drawing sharp policy distinctions between basic concepts and applications arises because progress in the development of both types of software is most rapid when they interact closely. The ideal policy treatment of these two types is different, but if badly designed policies interfere with this interaction, they can do great harm.

Most important, new technologies come into existence in an embryonic and imperfect form. In many cases, people have only a limited understanding of both the underlying basic concepts and of the range of possible applications. It took some time and effort after the "discovery" of the transistor at Bell Labs before transistors were developed that could be used in practical applications. It took many years for the transistor to evolve from its early free-standing state into collections of transistors in integrated circuits and many more for the development of higher-density and faster circuits. Many researchers working in many different firms contributed to these developments. In the beginning, no one anticipated the many uses to which it would be put. If Bell Labs had had extremely strong property rights over the use of the transistor, many of the most important improvements in design and new uses for it might never have been discovered.

The story of the laser follows along similar lines. When it was first invented, AT&T, which had rights to the invention, could not see a way in which it would ever be used in the communications business. Successive generations of the laser have turned out to have a wide range of applications, the vast majority of them outside the telephone system. One important application, however, has been in fiber optics, which currently is revolutionizing that system.

In the cases of both the transistor and the laser, the history of technological development is marked by great uncertainty and considerable differences of opinion regarding how to make the technology better. It took wide participation in the process of refinement and exploration to produce the many applications that consumers now buy.

In most of the technologies whose development has been studied in detail, technical progress proceeded through a lengthy, complex evolutionary process. At any time, there were a number of different actors who were attempting to develop variants or improvements on prevailing technology. They competed with each other and with prevailing practice. Some turned out to be winners, and others were losers. The winners often enjoyed wide market success. At the same time they provided a new base from which subsequent technological advance, often made by others, could progress.

Most innovations that arise in the private sector are a mixture of new concepts and applications that are ready for sale. Successful inventors can make a profit, at least for a time, on the sale of applications, because they generally are protected. Even if the legal system does not provide effective protection, first-mover advantages and secrecy are often enough to let someone earn a profit by selling a new application. In almost all cases, the basic concepts became public software, available for the rest of the technological community, both in the private sector and in the university, to build on.

As the discussion from the last section suggests, strong property rights that interfered with widespread participation would reduce the diversity in the evolutionary process and slow progress. But weak property rights create spillovers. They reduce the private incentives for doing research and induce a divergence between the social and private rates of return to research. An effective social system for inducing technological progress will therefore tolerate weak property rights on basic concepts but will subsidize some types of research to offset the tendency for a research effort to be too low. Because both the search for concepts and the search for applications can lead to important new discoveries, both are candidates for subsidies. Since World War II, a significant portion of the subsidies in the United States have taken the form of unrestricted support for university research into basic concepts (as provided, for example, by the National Science Foundation), but an even larger fraction was devoted to support for research in basic concepts that were relevant to practical applications in the areas of defense and health.

Before the war, there was research support from the government in the field of agriculture and private philanthropic support for some areas of basic science. The bulk of the subsidies, however, were directed at training scientists and engineers, most of whom went to work in the private sector. Some of this support came from the federal government, through its grants of land to the states. Some came from the operating budgets of the states themselves. Important support also came from the philanthropic activity of such people as George Eastman and Arthur D. Little (who helped create chemical engineering at MIT) or such organizations as the Carnegie Foundation and the Rockefeller Foundation (which fostered the development of physics, the social sciences, and molecular biology).

In the cases of both the laser and the transistor, fields of scientific study grew up around the new technologies. The advent of the transistor provided a whole new agenda for research for electrical engineering and materials science. The laser has had a major effect on such fields as physical chemistry and has revitalized the field of optics. These scientific fields worked backwards from applications and tried to uncover the basic concepts that helped explain how and why they worked.

In both of these cases, the original inventions drew extensively on scientific knowledge. After their achievement, the technologies themselves became the subject matter of scientific research. In turn, the growing body of scientific understanding about the technologies provided important inputs into their refinement and further development.

Technological progress was quite rapid both before and after World War II, in environments that provided very different kinds of support for science and technology. The history of specific technological areas shows that the development of basic concepts and applications are intimately intertwined. Both of these observations suggest that it is pointless to ask whether applications or basic concepts are the prime movers in generating scientific and technological progress. Since each can encourage the other, neither can be singled out. This has not, however, stopped people from trying.

In the 1950s and 1960s, scholars studying technical advance debated the relative importance of "perceptions of demand" or "opportunities opened by science." Implicit in this debate were two different views about policy options for stimulating technical advance and economic growth. The interpretation based on scientific opportunity was associated with a science-push policy: Support scientific research, and the economic and technical benefits will follow. The perceptions of the demand view seemed to suggest that measures designed to increase economic activity in the private sector should be given the highest priority.

A number of studies indicated that if one looked into the perceptions that motivated the initiation of particular projects, the key factor was almost invariably "perception of a demand." Studies have documented that scientific understanding and techniques often played a critical role in successful inventive efforts, but that the understandings and techniques drawn upon often tended to be relatively "old." A study funded by the Department of Defense, "Project Hindsight," explored the key scientific and technical breakthroughs that enabled the development of a number of important weapons for the military. The study found that almost invariably these breakthroughs came about as the result of research addressed to particular needs, rather than "basic research" done with little awareness of or concern about those problems.

The NSF responded by funding "Project Traces," which looked farther back in the history of various technological advances and found that many of them were in fact made possible only because of earlier "basic research." David Mowery and Nathan Rosenberg, in an article summarizing and criticizing this debate (1979), argued that it was pointless to focus on either "perception of demand" or "perception of a technological opportunity" as the only factor stimulating a particular technological effort. They pointed out that it made sense to invest only in cases where both a scientific opportunity and a practical demand were present.

In many technologies, the early findings continue to hold up—much of the science being drawn upon in the private sector is not new science. There are, however, some areas in which the connections between university research and commercial application are relatively close: pharmaceuticals, certain other chemical technologies, various fields of electronics, and more recently, biotechnology. In these fields, inventors seem to draw on science that is quite recent.

The nature of the interaction between application and the development of basic concepts was illuminated by a survey research project conducted about ten years ago. Industry executives in charge of R&D were asked about the importance of various bodies of basic and applied science for technical advance in their industry. They were also asked about the relevance of current research in these scientific areas. Most respondents rated the relevance of a "science" much higher than the relevance of "university research in that science." But evidence supports the interpretation that effective industry R&D in a specific field almost always requires that the scientists and engineers working in industry had to be trained in universities so that they are familiar with the basic scientific understandings and techniques. In many cases, however, new advances in science were not exploited in industrial R&D. If we separate the wetware (educational) and software (research) outputs of the university, for most businesses it was the output of wetware that mattered.

The responses regarding what fields of university research were most relevant to technical advance in industry were interesting. For the most part the industrial respondents tended to score most highly the relevance of university research in the engineering fields and in such scientific fields as materials science and computer science—fields in Pasteur's quadrant. Most of the respondents stated that university research in basic disciplines such as mathematics and physics was not particularly relevant to technical advance in their lines of business. But this does not mean that basic research in the fundamental disciplines is not relevant to technical advance. It suggests that the results of basic research in such fields as mathematics and physics influence technical change indirectly, by improving and stimulating research in the more applied scientific and engineering disciplines.

POLICY IMPLICATIONS

There is no inherent danger in moving toward an environment where economic and commercial opportunities are given more explicit weight in determining broad areas of "national need" and where national security and health carry less weight. This change poses little risk, provided it does not reduce the fraction of research that is focused on fundamental concepts and does not shorten the time horizon over which payoffs are measured. The best way to avoid such a shift would be to preserve the institutional arrangements for supporting research that have worked so well. Universities have offered an extremely effective environment for exploring basic concepts and pursuing distant payoffs. A shift toward commercial and economic objectives should be accomplished by changing the emphasis in university research, not by pushing that research into the private sector. There must continue to be a place in the university for modern-day Pasteurs.

The returns from this attempt to adjust priorities will be larger if it is accompanied by two complementary developments. One is a change in orientation of advanced training programs in the sciences and engineering. They should move toward training people for work in the private sector and away from the presumption that PhDs, or at least good ones, get recycled into academia. It may be possible to go a long way toward this goal merely by changing the attitudes and expectations that permeate the graduate faculty. Changing attitudes and expectations will not be easy, but the alternative is to stand by while the number and quality of people getting advanced training in the sciences declines. In an era of rapidly unfolding technological opportunities, it would be perverse to cut back on advanced training in science.

If university research and graduate training are to be oriented more toward the needs of industry, it is also important that mechanisms for interaction between university and industry scientists and engineers be widened and strengthened. Universities and companies might strive for a significant increase in the extent to which industry scientists spend periods of time in academia and academic scientists in industry. These exchanges might even be supported by government funds. Rather than giving money directly to firms to do research on specific topics, the government might also explicitly subsidize the training of students who will go to work in the private sector. By taking these steps, the government could subsidize the inputs that go into private-sector research instead of contracting with firms for specific research outputs. This would let market demands and market perceptions of opportunity continue to be the primary forces that allocate resources between specific research projects in the private sector. It would avoid the pork-barrel politics that can arise when the government writes checks to business firms.

As the arguments from the previous section make clear, it is generally not good practice to establish "property rights" on the output from scientific research. This is true whether that research is directed at practical problems facing the military, health professionals, or business firms. There are important efficiency advantages in a system where the government subsidizes the production of fundamental concepts and insights and gives them away for free. The Bayh-Dole Act of 1980 marked a major retreat from the principle that knowledge subsidized by the government should circulate freely, and the continuing argument about issues such as whether "gene fragments" ought to be patentable clearly reflects strong pressures to move even further in this direction. Even as we strengthen property rights on the applications end of the software spectrum, we should not establish private property rights on bodies of knowledge and techniques that have wide and nonrivalrous applications, particularly when many of these applications are in further research and development. A renewed attention to the needs of industry need not be associated with a major change in our intellectual property rights regime. There is no reason to treat science as being "private" rather than "public" knowledge.

World War II produced a new set of principles about the role of the federal government in support of science. The arguments presented in Vannevar Bush's report captured some of these principles. The major support that the defense department and the National Institutes of Health provided for mission-oriented basic research reflected others. This new understanding encompassed the traditional principle that private funds should be the main support for commercial applications of science. To this was added a new set of principles about science: Government funds should be used to finance the search for new fundamental concepts and insights.

These principles are as relevant today as they were then. We should adjust the details of science and technology policy in response to changing circumstances. But we should not change our principles.

4

Science and Technology Investment and Policy in the Global Economy

A. Michael Spence

In this short chapter, I want to try to set out some of the characteristics of the American system for developing and deploying technology and some of the evolving features of the economic environment, principally in its international dimensions, that should influence how the current system performs and how it should be adapted in the future.

Part of the system of developing and deploying technology is in the public and non-profit sectors. But a very important part resides firmly in the private sector, both in the United States and increasingly around the world. In Figure 4.1, I have tried to put the elements of the U.S. science and technology system on a single piece of paper. I will be speaking about the relative size of these elements, their internal characteristics, and the ways in which they relate to each other. This sounds more formal than it will turn out to be. But I have found it useful in discussions about these general subjects to try to avoid situations in which conversations (sometimes quite heated) apparently about the same subject turn out to be about two or more different aspects of the system.

Now let me state in the most general terms where I am going, and then turn to the details. I will assume that most of the readers are familiar with the U.S. system for developing and deploying technology. I want to argue that the U.S. system currently in place was built immediately after World War II, at a time when the United States was the only substantial economy intact and capable of both developing and deploying technology.

I want to thank my colleagues at the Graduate School of Business at Stanford University and those who served with me on the National Research Council's

Reprinted from THE MOSAIC OF ECONOMIC GROWTH, edited by Ralph Landau, Timothy Taylor, and Gavin Wright, with the permission of the publishers, Stanford University Press. © 1996 by the Board of Trustees of the Leland Stanford Junior University.

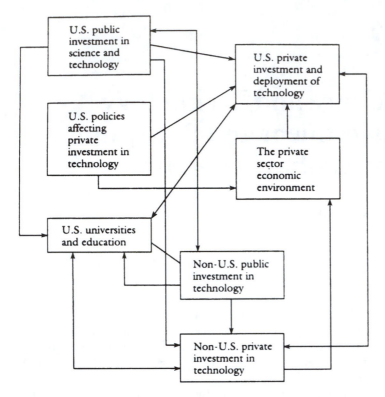

FIGURE 4.1 Elements of a global science and technology system.

Board on Science, Technology, and Economic Policy for their useful critical comments. Also, thanks to Ralph Landau for his numerous comments and insights.

I will then argue that this is no longer true, in fact that it has been getting steadily less true for thirty years. I will try to identify two or three broad options for adapting to the new circumstances. On the way by, so to speak, I want to rely on a recent report from the Board on Science, Technology and Economic Policy of the National Research Council (1994), to suggest that there are some problems in the U.S. private sector and in policies that surround it, principally in the areas of saving, investment, and the cost of capital, that bear on these issues and that affect the U.S. economy's ability to take advantage of technology to improve productivity, competitiveness, growth, and per capita income.[1]

1. The two main papers from the conference on which the report was based are Hatsopoulos and Poterba (1994) and Porter (1994). Note that the report of the NRC and the conference volume have the same name. The conference volume will eventually include the NRC report as well as the supporting papers. However, as of this writing, the NRC summary is available on its own from National Academy Press in Washington, DC.

Finally, let me give away the answer, or the option I think we should prefer. It is that we should try to maintain most of the features of our current system for developing civilian technology, augment it a little to compensate for the vacuum that the withdrawal from defense will leave, and attempt to persuade our principal industrialized partners to do approximately the same thing. In a nutshell, this system would involve all developed nations investing proportionate amounts in science and technology, in a system which is open, so that the results are available to research personnel in governments, universities, and companies on a global basis.

The alternatives are to continue on the present course and hence continue to be a very large net supplier of technology and human capital to the rest of the industrialized world, or to undertake an elaborate sequence of steps, the intent of which would be to partially close the U.S. system in the global sense so that the benefits of U.S. investment become more proprietary from a national point of view. The problem with the first of these is that it will continue to come under increasing adverse political pressure. The underlying issue will be: "Why should a large asymmetry continue to exist at taxpayer expense when there is a much more even distribution of wealth than there was thirty or forty years ago?"[2] This kind of pressure will lead to a tendency to adopt the second alternative: closing the system. The problem with it, I will argue, is that to close the U.S. system even partially, one will have to take measures that affect all the players (government labs, universities, companies, and investors) and that reduce dramatically the efficiency of the national investment in technology.[3]

SOME OBSERVATIONS ABOUT THE GLOBAL ECONOMY AND RELATED MATTERS

The U.S. approach to science and technology was put in place after the Second World War, using the model of the war effort to generate science and technology and to respond to the technological demands of the cold war. Whatever the U.S. fraction of industrial country GDP was at the time (a conservative estimate would be sixty-five to seventy percent), it has now declined to thirty to thirty-five

2. It might be objected here that the data show that Germany and Japan have national investment rates in R&D that are as high or higher than the United States. This is true if you add together public and private R&D investment and particularly if you remove the defense R&D in the United States. However, though the data are less good, I would argue that there remains an imbalance in the upstream, non-proprietary, open segment of the R&D portfolio, where the free-rider problem is potentially greatest and our system most vulnerable to the criticism implied by this question.
3. Cohen and Noll (in this volume) argue that we are well on the way down the competitive path with respect to technology. This is the path I am referring to as "closing the system." Cohen and Noll are certainly right about the directional shift and the consequences in terms of efficiency. I guess my view would be that there is still the opportunity to adopt the other option, what I call the multilateral approach at the end of this chapter.

percent. The amount of technology generated by public sect investment and private investment outside the United States has therefore increased tremendously, as has the ability of economic actors in other nations to absorb the technology generated here.

These trends will continue. It is almost certainly true—indeed, it is becoming commonplace to predict that a large fraction of world growth will be in Asia and Latin America in the next two decades.[4] Eastern Europe may also be a center of growth. (The reader will find in the chapter by Rowen in this volume a very interesting forecast of global economic growth in the next few decades.)

In addition, these regions—especially parts of Asia and eastern Europe—have quite highly developed human resources but do not yet have the incomes and prices of the most advanced industrial countries of Europe, North America, and Japan. These emerging economies thus have large advantages as places to locate high-quality, low-cost manufacturing facilities; one large global company that has moved aggressively into eastern Europe estimates that it has at least a thirty percent cost advantage in manufacturing there relative to comparable facilities in western Europe. As long as the world economy remains relatively open, these cost differentials will cause, in fact force, a fairly rapid evolution in the advanced industrial countries. One can see some of the effects both in countries like Korea and in the United States and Japan.

The direction of this evolution is not easy to predict or characterize accurately. The notion that all U.S. workers will end up in non-tradable, low value-added per worker services is surely wrong, because of exchange rates adjustments and the infeasibility of running permanent large trade deficits. A trend in the advanced industrial countries, however, toward exportable services industries based on expertise and human capital is entirely feasible and even likely. It is also likely that these activities will include using information technology to direct global manufacturing and distribution systems. I sometimes ask the Stanford business school students what the Gap, Nike, and (almost) Sun Microsystems have in common. The answer is that in a certain sense they are quite completely vertically integrated from product development through to the final consumer. The only step they do not undertake in-house is manufacturing.[5]

The pattern is far from clear, however. In the 1980s, the computer industry changed its basic structure from vertically integrated (like IBM) to a series of horizontal market bands in each of which there is intense competition. I think it is fair to say that economists do not yet have a comprehensive framework for under-

4. I recently had the opportunity to look at the figures on per capita consumption of electricity in China, the same figures the principal suppliers of power generation capacity are looking at. To move China to even low-to-moderate per capita consumption levels by industrial country standards will require the opening of power plants in the 1000 to 2000 megawatt range every month for the better part of twenty years. Similar statements could be made about roads, information systems, and a host of other parts of what we normally think of as infrastructure.

5. Benetton is often cited as the extreme example of the corporation as architect of the system as it contracts out virtually every step of the value-added chain.

standing the forces that cause the shifting pattern of vertical integration, disintegration, alliances, and changes in economic relationships among companies in the value-added chain in various industries and sectors.

But whatever emerges from this process, it is a reasonably good guess that technology, particularly information and communication technology, will play a central enabling role. And the transitions will be accompanied by substantial investments in technology and in capital that is complementary to the new technology.

THE U.S. ECONOMIC ENVIRONMENT

I would like to step back now for a short period and look at the U.S. economy in terms of adaptability, investment, and savings.

The good news first: U.S. companies were confronted in the late 1970s and early 1980s with the effects of substantial innovation in manufacturing in Japan, including an orientation to quality, effective supply-chain management, and continuous incremental process improvement. After a lag, U.S. companies (and I might add schools of management) have responded. There is clearly an improved situation with respect to relative productivity as a result of taking the international challenge seriously. U.S. firms have made major efforts to increase efficiency, speed, and quality; the automobile and semiconductor industries serve as vivid examples. Further, in the deployment of information technology to improve on best practice in both internal processes and supply-chain management, it appears to this observer that U.S. companies and U.S. technology are (on average) in the lead.

The less good news comes from the more macroeconomic long-term view of the economy. I will not dwell on this, but I need to mention it because it bears directly on the development and use of technology in the private sector, which we have already seen is potentially important to the future.[6]

Savings and Investment

The U.S. savings rate has been well below industrial country norms for all of the 1980s and thus far in the 1990s. The savings rate net of the federal deficit is under three percent of GDP and at times recently has fallen close to zero. Even leaving aside the federal deficit, the national savings rate is low, on the order of seven to eight percent of GDP. It is also below the national levels of net investment, so for several years the United States has been a net importer of capital.[7]

---

6. The discussion that follows relies heavily on National Research Council (1994).
7. As economists recognize, but much public discussion does not, this excess of domestic investment over domestic savings, plus some accounting identities, explains the trade deficit.

There are two consequences of having low savings rates relative to other countries and relative to domestic investment. To the extent that capital markets are integrated on a global basis, the shortfall of capital in the United States raises global interest rates and the cost of capital. In itself, this is not a disaster. But at a time when the demand for capital in Asia, Latin America, and eastern Europe is huge, it is certainly not helpful that the world's richest country is a net absorber of capital. A second consequence involves the partial integration of global capital markets. It is generally agreed that integration in fixed income securities is quite far along and more advanced than integration with respect to equity.[8] To the extent that equity markets are not fully integrated globally, a savings shortfall in the United States has the effect of differentially raising the cost of equity capital in the United States.

There are other causes of an elevated cost of capital in the United States, such as the tax system, so I do not wish to appear to be basing the entire case on savings behavior and the amount of integration in global financial markets. Below, I will discuss some of the direct evidence that the U.S. cost of capital is higher than in other industrial countries.

United States investment rates as a percentage of GDP have been below the average for other industrial countries for at least fifteen years. The rates of productivity growth have been similarly below average for longer than that. Meanwhile, the measured return on corporate investment in the United States has been above that of Japan and Germany. This suggests that the costs of capital faced by U.S. companies have been and continue to be above those used by companies in other countries. In addition, there is quite a bit of qualitative evidence that U.S. publicly traded corporations interact with many financial investors who have relatively short time horizons, which is what one expects of investors who face a higher cost of capital.[9]

In terms of the focus of this chapter, the key connection is that long-term investments in private sector technology are most appropriately financed by equity. With technology investments, there is often little in the way of measurable collateral or tangible assets that normally accompany the use of debt financing. A higher cost of equity is therefore a problem for private technology investment, and in turn, a problem for an economy like ours, which will evolve in the shifting patterns of global competition in part based on its capacity to invest in and deploy new technology.

It would take me too far afield here to document the evidence, the arguments, and the counterarguments for these propositions. The point I want to make is just that if we are entering a period of relatively rapid evolution in most

---

8. There are reasons for this. The information flows required to support full integration of equity markets are very substantial. There is, of course, partial integration of equity markets through the dependence of asset prices, including equity on interest rates, which increasingly are set in global markets.

9. These comments are summaries of the work of Hatsopoulos and Poterba (1994), Porter (1994), and Landau (1994).

advanced industrial countries, as I and many others expect, then impediments to long-term investments in critical intangible assets like technology, human capital, and training and the development of new products and markets are a worrying handicap. And having a high relative cost of equity capital is precisely such an impediment.

IMPROVING THE MACROECONOMIC ENVIRONMENT

A report of the Board on Science, Technology and Economic Policy (STEP) of the National Research Council (NRC) (1994) recommended a number of changes in policy that are intended to improve the U.S. macroeconomic environment for saving and investment: I recap the substance of those recommendations here. I believe that without changes of this type, more microeconomic technology policies will not translate into the desired effect on overall economic productivity.

Any democratic political system creates substantial pressures to deal with immediate short-term problems. These need to be counterbalanced with a longer-term view. It would be desirable for the administration and Congress to set specific longer-term goals with respect to private investment, net saving, and productivity growth. I believe that the American public would and should support such efforts, if they were publicly explained and justified.

The STEP board of the NRC argued that having net saving and investment rates of eight to ten percent of GDP over a five- to ten-year period would contribute measurably to enhancing productivity and wage growth in the United States. Such rates would also not hurt and would probably help the global economy. It would make the U.S. neither a net importer nor a net exporter of capital, and it would put U.S. domestic investment in the range of other advanced industrial countries. To advance these objectives, the tax system would have to be changed over the next decade in accordance with several key principles:

1. Steady movement toward a progressive consumption-based tax system, in which saving and investment income are taxed less or not at all and consumption is taxed more.[10]
2. Eliminating the double taxation of that part of corporate income paid as dividends to holders of equity, to close the gap between the return on the corporate investment and the return to the financial investor.
3. Reducing the investment subsidy for residential real estate, and using these revenues to reduce taxes on corporate investments.
4. As an interim measure, extending the favorable tax treatment of long-term gains on corporate stock to equity investments in companies regardless of size. This would have the dual effects of partially reducing the

---

10. The Nunn-Domenici proposal is a recent example of such an approach.

double taxation of corporate income and encouraging longer-term investments and time horizons among financial investors.

5. Over time, government dissaving (that is, the budget deficit) needs to be eliminated to restore the rate of saving to an appropriate level and to stem the growth of interest payments as a fraction of the federal budget. Interest payments now represent about fourteen percent of the federal budget. Even after taking into account the planned effects of the 1993 deficit reduction measures, interest costs are expected to consume the same share of federal spending by the end of the century.

6. Private saving needs to be increased. The tax measures mentioned above should help. But since economists do not now have a systematic understanding of the large differences in savings rates across countries, it is therefore difficult to know what other measures might be effective in encouraging private savings.

7. Expand the cadre of long-term investors, by giving management and directors restricted stock and options, and by removing various impediments to institutional investors holding large equity positions of particular companies.

Over an extended period of time, these steps will improve the environment for corporate investment, and particularly for longer-term investments in technology. Without such measures, the availability of funds and the high required after-tax returns on investment threaten to diminish U.S. economic performance in the critical areas of productivity growth and new market development.

THE U.S. SCIENCE AND TECHNOLOGY SYSTEM

The U.S. system for generating science and technology and deploying it has been in place for forty years. It has had and retains many attractive features. Among them are the following.

1. There has been a broad portfolio of basic science and civilian technology invested in by the federal government.

2. As a result of the peer review system, that investment has been quite efficient as measured by results per dollar invested.

3. Overhead, being tied to direct funding, has in effect also been subject to the peer review system, and hence based upon a measure of merit.

4. By conducting a substantial fraction of the research in universities, the country has obtained as a joint product a highly educated scientific and engineering workforce.

5. The system has been open, so results once produced are relatively freely available. This by itself dramatically increases the efficiency of the whole system. The system is open not just domestically but internationally.

6. Defense, a substantial fraction of the total national R&D investment, has been mission-oriented, more proprietary from a national point of view

than either basic science or civilian technology investment, and characterized by variable (over time) spillovers into the civilian R&D sector. The majority view appears to be that defense R&D spillovers into the civilian sector have declined substantially and steadily over time.

7. The National Academies have assembled the ablest scientific and engineering talent in the country and made it available at marginal cost to the government in the form of advice on matters of science and technology.

8. In the private sector, the availability of knowledgeable venture capital and substantial research capacity in large corporations helped ensure that technology was rapidly developed and used commercially.

9. The private sector's culture and legal environment have been tolerant of spin-offs, which have been the source of much innovation and growth in many high-technology sectors. Schools of engineering and medicine have also been sources of spin-offs with similar effects.

10. Intellectual property, while a complex area of the law, has been reasonably effective in ensuring adequate returns to the investor in technology, without stifling new product development or the creation of new enterprises.

11. There has been some evolution in policy surrounding the system in the area of joint technology ventures, whether among private firms or with government as a partner. Initially, antitrust was hostile to this kind of collaboration, since it looked as if it might be a concealed form of price collusion. More recently, the prevailing view is that in many contexts, international competition is a sufficient regulatory device to protect consumers. The Advanced Technology Program of the National Institute of Standards and Technology (part of the Department of Commerce) is now conceived of as a collaboration between government and groups of companies. It is projected to grow substantially in the federal budget. There remain issues in this area to be resolved, such as who has access to the technology funded in part with public funds. In general there remains a wide range of opinion about whether there is some middle ground between public investment in technology (mostly upstream) and individual corporate private investment in which there is underinvestment. I suspect that the prevailing view in Washington is that the public sector science and technology investment is somewhat overbalanced toward upstream, basic research, and thus that the government science and technology portfolio should shift somewhat (though not dramatically) toward the downstream, applied, commercial applications.

What, Then, Is New?

The international environment for the creation and dissemination of science and technology is changing, which raises questions of what modifications, if any, would be appropriate technology practices and policies. Let me list some of these changes, in no particular order.

As the industrial and industrializing countries grew over the last forty years, their capacity to produce and to absorb technology increased, too. Although the U.S. science and technology system was formally open in the 1950s, it was *de facto* mostly of benefit domestically. But now, the openness of the U.S. system produces major benefits on a worldwide basis.

There is now substantial production and absorption of technology outside the United States. It is undertaken by both government investment and private corporations. As a result, the complexity of the international flows of technology, and the activities required by companies to ensure that they have access to the most advanced technology, have increased substantially. One gets an impression of this complexity from Figure 4.1, presented earlier.

The investment in defense-related technology will likely decline in the United States as a result of the end of the cold war. From a national perspective, this component of the R&D portfolio tended to be more proprietary, in the sense that the fruits of this spending rebounded to U.S. companies. To the extent that the defense R&D is replaced by civilian R&D under the current system, the effect will be even more openness from a global perspective. Of course, if the federal government reduces R&D without a corresponding increase in the civilian sector, the total commitment of resources to science and technology will decline.[11]

In the past, there have been major basic science research programs in corporations. IBM and AT&T are perhaps the leading examples. Under global competitive pressure, this corporate support for basic research has declined and is unlikely to return.

The United States (and to some extent the United Kingdom) have become the global training centers for high-level scientific and engineering personnel. There is an asymmetry here. It is not that other advanced countries are incapable of providing advanced scientific education, or completely avoid doing so. Rather, the flows tend to be one-way because of the relative universality of the English language in scientific communication. There are tens of thousands of foreign citizens of great ability in U.S. postgraduate degree programs. Upon graduation, many of these stay in the United States and expand the scientific base here. Others return to their countries. There is then an implicit transfer of technology in the process.[12]

Before considering possible ways of thinking about the consequences of these changes in the international environment, it is important to dispose of one notion. It is commonly thought that the substantial U.S. public sector investment in science and technology is a source of competitive advantage. There are undoubtedly what might be called local or neighborhood effects in the transfer of

11. Even if one thinks that the spillovers from defense R&D have been low, the reduction in defense R&D will still reduce the resources devoted to training scientific and engineering manpower. The latter do move between the defense and civilian sectors.

12. This asymmetry created in part by language need not be permanent. It is quite possible that in two or three decades, the volume of science and technology investment and training in Asia will be such that Chinese will become an important second international language for scientific education.

technology from the public domain to the private sector. It would be hard to live for long in Silicon Valley and argue that these do not exist. On the other hand, except for defense, public investment in technology occurs in a largely open global system. In such an environment, public investment in technology could not be a long-run source of advantage, because the technology generated by public investment has been, by choice, very accessible. It is more like an international public good.

DIRECTION FOR TECHNOLOGY POLICY AND INVESTMENT

If one accepts the general direction of the preceding analysis, there are some issues to be considered and some conclusions to be drawn. In general terms, it is important that government policies (including those not normally thought of as strictly technology policies) be conducive to vigorous private sector investment in technology and in complementary assets.

To maintain a healthy level of private sector investment in technology, it is necessary to ensure that the availability and cost of capital is competitive. That probably means moving over time toward a system in which investment and saving is taxed less and consumption is taxed more. This is not a new idea. But it may be gaining ground. The most recent proposal is the Nunn-Domenici proposal for a progressive consumption-based tax system using the apparatus of the current income tax system. There have been several proposals for tax integration, the elimination of double taxation of income flows from equity investment (for example, see U.S. Department of the Treasury, 1992). There are other ways of lowering the taxation of income from investment, and hence the cost of capital, for investment in productive intangible assets like technology. For example, the STEP board has proposed that the non-taxation of mortgage interest on residential real estate for principal amounts in the higher ranges be phased out and replaced with reduced taxes on capital gains from longer-term holdings of equity (National Research Council, 1994).

In the longer term, increasing the savings rate will be necessary. That means reducing the federal deficit and finding a way to increase the private savings rate. To the extent possible in our political system, it is also desirable to avoid policies that create rather than reduce risk in the private sector investment process. Unpredictable variations in policy will tend to create risk and deter investment. This is important in regulated areas like the environment and health and safety.[13]

13. Many believe that our tax system creates perverse incentives for U.S. multinationals to put their R&D activity abroad, and that the tax system does not put the United States on a level playing field with international competitors. Since much of the tax system evolved during the period when U.S. technology was the dominant force, it is probably a good time to undertake a thorough reexamination of its provisions and their consequences with respect to R&D.

On the issue of direct government investment in science and technology, the central issue is whether there are adaptations of the current system that are wise in view of the changed international environment. Let me start by clarifying what the objectives are. For this purpose, I will take the objective of public investment in science and technology to be to contribute materially to the steady improvement in the standard of living and quality of life of U.S. citizens. Notice that this objective is different from "winning" in some global competitive battle. Also, the adoption of this objective does not preclude that those in other countries also benefit from U.S. science and technology investment—my proposed objective is neutral on that point. I emphasize these points simply because I have found in discussions of these issues that proponents of alternative approaches often have quite different underlying objectives.

Given the characteristics of the current science and technology system, its continuation with little modification is one option. Other countries will then continue adapting to the U.S. system. They will take the upstream part of the U.S. research system as an international public good and then invest in ways that are complementary and that further their goals. In most countries, there is not much point in trying to match or duplicate the massive U.S. investment in biomedical science. The smart thing to do, and what is in fact being done, is for other countries to rely on the United States for much of the basic science and advanced scientific research and training, and then to devote relatively more of their own resources to supporting the downstream, private sector, and relatively more proprietary parts of the science and technology value-added chain. Historically, in most countries, this has meant that the relative size of the private R&D sector (relative, that is, to the public investment) is larger than it is in the United States, not because the U.S. private sector investment in technology is small, but rather because the public investment is large.

Over time, if this scenario were to be played out, it would lead to increasing skepticism from U.S. policy makers and legislators. We have seen this pattern before.

For example, prior to the end of the cold war, there began to be concern in the area of defense that the United States was providing a disproportionate share of what amounted to a public good for the democratic part of the world. What seemed quite natural 25 years ago—given the large differences in size and wealth—will increasingly seem less natural and equitable. We also see a similar pattern in international trade negotiations in the postwar period. For a couple of decades, the United States was prepared to play a leading role in promoting free trade, provided that the general evolution proceeded under the auspices of the multilateral GATT, implicit in which was the notion that while there might need to be a period of asymmetrical behavior as the industrializing countries grew and recovered, the goal was a symmetric multilateral system supported by all the industrialized countries. By and large, the direction of movement has been consistent with the intent. But when other countries do not evolve quickly enough toward the prescribed multinational behavior as they become richer, friction results.

In the area of science and technology, these concerns could take two broad directions. One direction would be a series of actions which attempted to confine the benefits of U.S. science and technology investment as much as possible to the domestic economy; in a phrase, to close the system at least partially. The second direction is to maintain the openness, but seek through international negotiation to reach an agreement that all advanced countries will adopt a broadly similar approach and contribute proportionately (in very gross terms) to a global public good of a science and technology base. This seems to me similar in broad terms to the pattern in trade and the still-evolving pattern in defense. Let me refer to the latter as the multilateral approach and to the former (that is, partially closing the domestic system) as the competitive approach.

My view is that the multilateral course is vastly preferable, for a number of reasons.

The first point I want to make is that the incentive structure of this situation is not zero-sum. Certainly, the multilateral approach is designed to cause mutual benefits to accrue to all the parties. There is a free-rider problem with which the multilateral approach is designed to deal. If all nations adopted the competitive approach and tried to close off their science and technology to the extent possible, the world would be a poorer place.

The second point is that the multilateral approach is consistent with specialization by country. Specialization will require some sophistication in the system of accounting. But there is no reason in principle why one or a few nations could not become the leading suppliers of advanced environmental technology while others do biomedical science and still others invest more heavily in materials.[14] Because of its size, the United States is likely to have the broadest portfolio for the foreseeable future. The multilateral approach is also consistent with having certain countries specialize in science and technology. That is to say, the country-level investments need not coincide exactly with the location of the activity. If the United States has a comparative advantage in science and technology investment, then the public and private sectors in other countries can put investment resources into these activities in the United States. The multilateral approach refers mainly to the origins of the resources to be invested in the international public good, and not to the balance of the locations in which the investments are carried out.[15]

But the main point I want to make is that the competitive approach, despite its likely political appeal, has problems. To close the U.S. system even partially,

14. Timothy Taylor pointed out that in the interests of promoting goodwill in the multilateral approach, it would be useful if each of the advanced countries did not invest in one or two technologies, so that the mutual dependence and reciprocity would be more visible.
15. I am indebted to Robert Hall for making this useful distinction and a related point, that requiring balance in the location of the activity could lead to large inefficiencies. There are potential problems. Foreign investment in U.S. institutions that develop technology can be (and has been) seen as buying American technology cheaply, rather than as sharing in the investment in international public goods. It will therefore be important to underscore in policy discussions that such investments are reciprocal and part of an overall system that is fair.

one would need to take a series of policy actions the effect of which would be not only to reduce the outflow of technology internationally, but also to substantially reduce the internal openness of the system.[16] Consider Silicon Valley, or any one of many advanced centers of biomedical science in the United States. Upon close inspection you will find companies and university sciences interacting daily. You will find investors, venture capitalists, and entrepreneurs in constant contact. New companies are started and then taken public or purchased by larger companies. In biotechnology, many companies make marketing contracts with multinational pharmaceutical companies. Large companies increasingly enter into alliances with multinationals based outside the United States to develop new and expensive technologies: the IBM-Siemans-Toshiba joint venture for the 25 6-megabyte memory chip would be an example.

Even trying to close this system is difficult to imagine. If a serious attempt were made to do so, the required steps would substantially interdict the flow of scientific and technical information in the U.S. economy, within the scientific community, and between that group and the private sector. The openness of that complex system has been one of the most important contributors to the efficiency of the science and technology investment process.

Let me put this point differently and slightly more technically. The wisdom of the U.S. science and technology system has been the combination of substantial public investment combined with low-to-negligible appropriability of technology, at least until one gets well down in the value-added chain toward product development. The low appropriability increases efficiency by reducing redundancy. But it also reduces private sector incentives for investment in basic research by lowering the returns for such investment. The substantial public investment restores those returns sufficiently to induce private investment at the appropriate downstream points.

I do not detect a strong inclination to move in the direction of the competitive approach. Hence I do not want to leave the impression that there is an imminent threat of such a move. Rather, I suspect that the problem will be one of continuing and escalating tension and public criticism surrounding the commitment of public funds to science and technology in an environment in which it is relatively easy to demonstrate that the benefits are dispersed globally at a rapid rate. Ultimately, that could lead directly to reduced investment in technology. The best defense against this line of argument seems to me the multilateral approach, which would make it possible to argue that the direction of movement is one in which advanced countries contribute to the base of knowledge in science and technology in such a way as to benefit everyone. Although I have not made the

---

16. The efficiency cost of doing this can be enormous. The chapter by Nathan Rosenberg in this volume points out that there is a large unpredictable element in the process of advancing technology. An advance in one area can unlock an impasse in another seemingly unrelated area. The openness promotes the finding of these linkages promptly and also reduces redundant and wasted effort.

point here, it is perhaps obvious that if our science and technology system is open to advanced countries, it will necessarily be open to developing ones, as well.

This general stance is responsible and consistent with America's general approach in international economic relations. I would hope that the administration, Congress, and the influential National Academies would take up the issue of U.S. science and technology policy in a global economy and that after due consideration and debate they would push us in the multilateral direction.

REFERENCES

Hatsopoulos, George N., and James M. Poterba, "America's Investment Shortfall: Probable Causes and Possible Fixes." In the conference volume of *Investing for Productivity and Prosperity.* Washington, D.C.: National Academy Press, 1994.

Landau, Ralph, "From Analysis to Action." In the conference volume of *Investing for Productivity and Prosperity.* Washington, D.C.: National Academy Press, 1994.

National Research Council, *Investing for Productivity and Prosperity.* Washington, D.C.: National Academy Press, 1994.

Porter, Michael, "National Investment Systems." In the conference volume of *Investing for Productivity and Prosperity.* Washington, D.C.: National Academy Press, 1994.

U.S. Department of the Treasury, *Integration of the Individual and Corporate Tax Systems: Taxing Business Income Once.* Washington, D.C.: U.S. Government Printing Office, Jan. 1992.

5

Intellectual Property: America's Competitive Advantage in the Twenty-first Century

Bruce A. Lehman

Three forces reshaped the U.S. economy during the 1980s—globalization, the creation and application of new technologies, and the shift to a knowledge-based economy. By looking at the historic role of intellectual property rights in U.S. economic growth, one can see not only that an ability to create and adapt has always been the driving force in the U.S. economy, but that it will continue to be its strength in the future. This historical perspective leads to a fundamental conclusion: In the next century, U.S. economic growth and competitiveness will largely be determined by the extent to which the United States creates, owns, preserves, and protects its intellectual property, and the extent to which the federal government can foster economic growth by creating incentives for private sector investment in research and development, promoting stronger intellectual property protection abroad, reducing barriers to trade and serving U.S. business interests throughout the world.

THE COMPETITIVENESS QUESTION

During the late 1980s, numerous articles and books bemoaned the impending decline of U.S. industrial competitiveness. Why, then, a decade later, has the U.S. economy once again proven to be the leading source of industrial and technological innovation in the world, and why has the United States seen quarter after quarter of economic growth with low inflation, low unemployment and high cor-

From THE COLUMBIA JOURNAL OF WORLD BUSINESS, Vol. 31, #1 (Spring 1996), pp. 6–16. Reprinted by permission of Jai Press, Inc.

porate earnings? U.S. economic growth has always been based on an ability to adapt to economic change that resulted from the creation and application of new technologies and new business practices, from the continued expansion of markets for the country's goods and services, from competition in a climate favorable to new business creation, and from the pro-growth, pro-investment, pro-technology practices and policies of a strong federal government.

Three forces reshaped the U.S. economy during the 1980s—globalization, the creation and application of new technologies, and the shift to a knowledge-based economy. By looking at the historic role of intellectual property rights in U.S. economic growth, one can see not only that an ability to create and adapt has always been the driving force in the U.S. economy, but that it will continue to be its strength in the future. Furthermore, although the role of the government in encouraging economic growth is an under-appreciated, yet critical, component of U.S. economic history, this historical perspective leads to a fundamental conclusion: In the next century, U.S. economic growth and competitiveness will largely be determined by the extent to which the United States creates, owns, preserves and protects its intellectual property, and the extent to which the federal government can foster economic growth by creating incentives for private sector investment in research and development, promoting stronger intellectual property protection abroad, reducing barriers to trade and serving U.S. business interests throughout the world.

THE HISTORIC ROLE OF INTELLECTUAL PROPERTY IN ECONOMIC GROWTH

After freeing the colonies from the British empire, the founders of the United States faced an equally daunting challenge—economic independence. The colonial economy was extractive in nature, tapping its vast resources for agriculture, fishing and hunting. With very little domestic technological innovation, the colonies were net importers of technology, purchasing new tools and technologies from abroad and importing technical knowledge through immigration. Until the U.S. Constitution was adopted, many colonies and states granted individual patents using special acts of legislature. In some cases, such as the steam-powered riverboat, competing patents from various states made protection of inventions difficult and litigious.[1]

Recognizing the important role that the invention of new technologies plays in creating new products and expanding the economy, the founders of the new nation wisely included a provision in the constitution to "promote the progress of

1. For a thorough examination of early American Industrialization, see Thomas C. Cochran, *Frontiers of Change: Early Industrialism in America* (New York: Oxford Press, 1981), which covers our history through approximately 1855; also Carroll Pursell, *The Machine in America: A Social History of Technology* (Baltimore: Johns Hopkins University Press, 1995).

science and the useful arts by securing for a limited time to authors and inventors the rights to their respective works."[2] That provision, the basis for copyright and patent law in the United States, provides incentives to create and innovate. That provision also began the second American revolution, the creation of an industrial economic base. From the War of Independence to the Civil War growth in the U.S. economy came from what can be loosely called proto-industrialization, the invention and improvement of steam-power engines, metal refining, machine tool production, etc., and from the more traditional method of increasing sources of land, labor, capital, etc.

Thomas Jefferson said of this new system that "the issue of patents for new discoveries has given a spring to invention beyond my conception." Jefferson, as secretary of state and one of three officials responsible for granting patents (the others being the secretary of war and the attorney general), is considered the first commissioner of patents. It is said he examined every application filed between 1790 and 1793, when the provision for examination of inventions was eliminated. For the next 43 years, patents were granted to anyone who submitted an application and the fee, a system that severely diminished the value of patents.[3] In 1836, the examination provision was reestablished, improving the quality and value of patents. Every applicant was required to file a specification, a drawing and a model for examination. The patent term was set at 14 years with a 7-year extension allowed at the discretion of the commissioner.[4]

The founding fathers also understood that government plays a vital role in fostering economic growth and independence by promoting the research and development of these new technologies and by investing in transportation infrastructure. In one of the earliest examples of military spending leading to commercial applications, the newly formed federal government paid Eli Whitney (popularly known as the inventor of the cotton gin) to create a system of interchangeable parts for guns. Previously, each gun was manufactured individually. Whitney created a method for manufacturing interchangeable parts so that when a part broke, only the part (rather than the entire gun) needed to be replaced.[5] Whitney's work on interchangeable parts is but one of hundreds of examples of early American industrialization. All of these inventors came for protection to the U.S. Patent and Trademark Office (hereafter, the PTO) which has, since 1790, granted almost 5.5 million patents.

2. U.S. Constitution, art. 1, sec. 8, clause 8.
3. See Judith A. McGaw, *Early American Technology: Making and Doing Things from the Colonial Era to 1850* (Chapel Hill, NC: University of North Carolina Press, 1994).
4. For an example of how this new system worked see McGaw, "A Patent Transformation: Woodworking Mechanization in Philadelphia, 1830–56."
5. Two books on the role of inventors and economic growth highlight the role of individual inventors in shaping the new industrial paradigm: Jonathan Hughes, *The Vital Few: The Entrepreneur and American Economic Progress* (New York: Oxford University Press, 1986); and Harold C. Livesay, *American Made: Men Who Shaped the American Economy* (New York: Harper Collins, 1979).

The patent system retained a central role in promoting the growth and development of early American technology. The records of the PTO were recognized as a vital national treasure. When Dr. William Thornton, the first superintendent of the PTO (1802–1828), learned on August 25, 1814, that the PTO was about to be burned by the British, he quickly mounted his horse and rode to confront the soldiers. He pleaded with Colonel Jones to spare Blodgert's Hotel (then the home of the PTO) saying that "to burn what would be useful to mankind would be as barbarous as formerly to burn the Alexandria Library for which the Turks have been ever since condemned by all enlightened nations." The hotel was the only government building that escaped destruction.

Many historians recognize that by the middle of the 1850s, proto-industrialization was complete. In 1853, U.S. economic independence had become firmly established as demonstrated by the visit to the United States by members of the English Parliament to view a New York exhibition of what had become known as the "American system of manufacturers." A few years later, in 1861, the patent term was increased to seventeen years from the date of issue with no extensions. President Lincoln, the only president to hold a patent, recognized the important role of patent protection in the economy saying, "the patents system added the fuel of interest to the fire of genius."[6]

In the late nineteenth century, America was transformed into a national industrial economy powered by oil, gasoline and machines. This era saw the continuation of trends established during the era of proto-industrialization. As in the early part of the century, economic growth in the late 1800s was based on the creation of new technologies, the development of new forms of energy—such as oil and gas—and the development of new business practices, particularly the growth of national corporations and mass production.[7] Furthermore, the strides made in the late 1800s owed much to earlier innovations by individual inventors and to earlier investments by the federal government, building transportation and communication infrastructure and promoting science and technology.

What was different about the late nineteenth century was the synergy between new technologies, new infrastructures and new business practices. This new synergy, the industrial paradigm, transformed the U.S. economy into a modern, high-tech, mass-production economy. One need only recall the stories of Henry Ford and the automobile, Thomas Edison and the phonograph, Andrew Carnegie

6. During his travels as a young man, his boat ran aground on the Mississippi River. Later, he had a similar experience on the Great Lakes. When he was a congressman from Illinois, he invented "A Device for Buoying Vessels over Shoals," and received patent number 6,469 on May 22, 1849. His patent model is part of the Smithsonian collection.

7. For a general overview of this subject, see Jonathan Hughes, *American Economic History* (Glenview, IL: Scott, Foresman and Company, 1990). Several business history books by Alfred D. Chandler give detailed descriptions on this subject: *Strategy and Structure: Chapters in the History of the American Enterprise* (Cambridge, MA: MIT Press, 1962); *The Visible Hand: The Managerial Revolution in American Business* (Cambridge, MA: Belknap Press, 1977); and *Scale and Scope: The Dynamics of Industrial Capitalism* (Cambridge, MA: Harvard Press, 1990).

and steel, John D. Rockefeller and oil, or the Wright brothers and airplanes, to understand the dramatic impact this had on the U.S. economy, American life and the nature of American society.[8] The transformation also led to the need for government to become involved in the economy in order, among other things, to protect public health and safety.[9] As in the era of proto-industrialization, the PTO continued to provide incentives to create and invest through patent protection.

In this new economy, giant corporations and new industries used new methods for manufacturing to mass produce industrial and consumer goods. Some of these industrial goods, such as railroads, automobiles, trucks and airplanes, sped the massive quantities of consumer goods to a newly integrated national marketplace. Advertising, marketing and public relations functions were created by corporations looking to stimulate demand for this huge quantity of goods by creating a mass market, and to manage and influence public opinion about the role these new industrial giants would play in American society.[10]

One outgrowth of this new mass market was the need to identify the myriad of new products for consumers. The nation's first federal trademark law was passed in the 1870s. Trademarks are the fingerprints of commerce. They identify goods and services available in the marketplace and, as indicia of origin, provide valuable information to consumers about the qualities of these goods and services. Today, corporations routinely spend millions of dollars on marketing and advertising to promote brandname recognition of their products and services and to differentiate themselves from their competitors. American trademarks are symbols of quality and value that are recognized and desired throughout the world.

Another result of this massive burst of technological invention was the creation and growth of a uniquely American entertainment industry that today dominates the world. New inventions—from radio and television to movies, to sound recordings—have provided new venues through which the creative expression of musicians, actors and other artists could be commercialized.[11] These artistic expressions are protected by copyright law.

8. See Robert H. Weibe, *The Search for Order 1877–1920* (New York: Hill and Wang, 1967).

9. Several books on the history of governmental involvement in our economy provide broad overviews of this issue: Jonathan R.T. Hughes, *The Governmental Habit: Economic Controls From Colonial Times to the Present* (New York: Basic Books, 1977); Thomas K. McCraw, *Prophets of Regulation* (Cambridge, MA: Belknap Press, 1984); and Morton Keller, *Public Policy and Economic Change in America 1900–1933* (Cambridge, MA: Harvard Press, 1990).

10. For a discussion of the role and influence of these new corporations in our society during the twentieth century, see Louis Galambos and Joseph Pratt, *The Rise of the Corporate Commonwealth: United States Business and Public Policy in the 20th Century* (New York: Basic Books, 1988).

11. For a general history of broadcasting see Christopher H. Sterling and John M. Kittross, *Stay Tuned: A Concise History of American Broadcasting* (Belmont, CA: Wadsworth, 1978). For a more detailed examination of the invention and development of radio and its role in our society, see Tom Lewis, *Empire of the Air: The Men Who Made Radio* (New York: Harper Collins, 1991).

INTELLECTUAL PROPERTY AND THE
COMPETITIVENESS ANSWER

The Short-Term View: Going Global

Corporate takeovers and downsizing were watershed events during the 1980s. This decade of tremendous upheaval and change appeared to have many troubling effects on established patterns of work and employment with the benefits of these transactions to our economic performance not yet evident. Instead, one only saw the immediate and wrenching impact these changes had on workers throughout the country and a growing disparity in the allocation of income and assets. Unfortunately, many of those same American workers have not yet felt the benefits of these changes.

Today, we see that these changes were part of a larger trend—the restructuring of corporate America to create leaner, more efficient and more competitive industries. This type of restructuring is not a new phenomenon. As the U.S. economy grew from a local to a regional to a national to a global economy, economic change and social upheaval marched hand in hand with increases in economic might. During each of these transitions, however, leaders have been called upon to transform the role of the federal government in society as a means of mitigating the consequences of these changes.

A Broader Perspective: Technology-Driven Change

New technologies and materials that grew out of decades of Cold War military spending on research and development were applied to already existing industries during the 1980s, elevating these industries to a new level of competitiveness. Technology has helped corporations lower the cost of production, raise return on investment and equity, improve inventory control and turnover, shorten production cycles, and improve productivity through the use of computer-aided design and manufacturing. Beyond transforming mature industries, these new technologies and materials have also grown into major industries, adding new sources of growth to the economy. Materials such as graphite are now commonly used in a variety of products, and fiber optic cable, the basic product used to construct the information superhighway, is now produced in massive quantities. Computer chips, hardware, software, pagers and cellular phones, are all recently developed technologies that have created new industries and are protected by intellectual property laws.

The Big Picture: The New Paradigm

The economy of the 1980s changed dramatically due to globalization and the invention and application of new technologies. But a far broader trend, the shift from an economy based on the industrial paradigm of the nineteenth century to a twenty-first century knowledge-based economy, has been driving these changes in our economy, Further, in the new knowledge-based economy, it is ideas, innovation and intellectual property that are the driving forces. Both new corporations and restructured corporations and industries are finding that one of their most valuable assets is their intellectual property, and that their competitive strategies worldwide depend heavily on protecting that intellectual property. This new reality plays to the country's economic strength: the use of advanced technologies and materials, the globalization of business, and the creation and ownership of intellectual property.

Some of the fastest growing U.S. industries—software publishing, biotechnology and pharmaceuticals, and entertainment—reflect this new paradigm for trade, technology and economic growth. They are globally competitive, investment-intensive, intellectual property-based industries. Furthermore, tapping larger, global markets using new technologies and materials to become more efficient producers and creating new intellectual property products has made all U.S. industries more competitive. One would expect that their profits and value would increase. In 1980, the Dow Jones Industrial Average was about 1,000. Fifteen years later, the Dow broke 5,000.

TODAY'S NEW PARADIGM: INTELLECTUAL PROPERTY IN A WORLD OF IDEAS

Henry Ford understood the industrial paradigm and came to symbolize his era by creating a mass-produced automobile. His inventions, protected by patent law, formed the basis for a new corporation and a new industry that created thousands upon thousands of jobs. These new industrial corporate giants soon realized, however, that they needed to rationalize and make predictable the process of invention and innovation. As a result, they formed huge corporate laboratories, places that during this century have been responsible for a large portion of the technological advances Americans use every day. Thomas Edison's Menlo Park in New Jersey serves as an early example of the newly created business of invention. Both individual inventors and corporate laboratories then turned to the PTO to gain patent protection for their inventions.[12]

A similar process of synergistic creativity is taking place in the digital electronics marketplace. Many of today's cutting-edge technology companies, such as Microsoft, Motorola and Hewlett-Packard, started by individual creators and innovators, are, like their industrial counterparts, in the business of invention and innovation and receive their protection from intellectual property laws.[13] Because many of these new businesses and industries are based on ideas, individual inven-

---

12. See Thomas P. Hughes, *American Genesis: A Century of Invention and Technological Enthusiasm* (New York: Penguin Books, 1989).
13. John Markoff, "Microsoft Quietly Puts Together Computer Research Laboratory." *The New York Times,* December 11, 1995, D-1.

tors, creators and thinkers have seen their importance increase. A sign of this trend is the growing list of popular literature on intellectual property.[14]

Bill Gates understands the new paradigm of innovation. He founded Microsoft based on the belief that the use of computers would become a pervasive part of life and that communications costs would drop as a result of new equipment such as fiber-optic cable and switching hardware. In a recent interview, Gates declared that "Now that we are at critical mass, there's a wild dynamic taking place, which is a gold rush. That is, nobody can be left out. Your companies and businesses have to be there."[15]

Competitiveness begins with an investment of time and money into cutting-edge scientific research and into creative works like movies, music, and literature. Although investment leads to innovation, to take these ideas from a laboratory or a studio to the marketplace requires a critical next step, gaining protection for this new intellectual property. Knowing that they can safely exploit their works in the marketplace is what provides authors, inventors, and companies an incentive to create and invest in the first place.

As the U.S. economy grew beyond markets that were local to markets that were regional, then national and then global, intellectual property protection from patents, trademarks and copyrights provided U.S. enterprises with vital protection. At each step, the new forms of growth and creation built on the existing foundation, not eliminating it, but strengthening it. For example, the automobile industry has been made far more competitive because of computer-aided design and manufacturing. In the industrial age, innovators like Ford and Edison relied on patent law to protect their intellectual property. In the knowledge-based world economy, copyright laws will protect many of these products, particularly multimedia works that provide the content for the national and global information infrastructures.

THE CLINTON ADMINISTRATION: TECHNOLOGY-DRIVEN ECONOMIC GROWTH

The authors of the U.S. Constitution imparted the fundamental precept that government should foster the development of competitive technologies and artistic creations. Congress has historically provided a sound basis for the growth of the U.S. economy by funding the infrastructure for economic growth. Much of today's infrastructure for communications and information resulted from spin-offs of spending on military technology. During World War II, the government paid for the creation of the first computer, the ENAIC, on display at the Smithsonian's

14. Paul Goldstein, *Copyright's Highway: From Gutenberg to the Celestial Jukebox* (New York: Hill and Wang, 1994); and Fred Warshofsky, *The Patent Wars: The Battle to Own the World's Technology* (New York: John Wiley and Sons, 1994).
15. *The Washington Post,* December 3, 1995, A-I and H-6.

Museum of American History. Similar government involvement led to the creation of the Internet by the Defense Advanced Research Projects Agency (now ARPA).

Similarly, the executive branch has always played a vital role in fostering the development of social, technological and other economic infrastructures that will lead to economic growth. As in previous eras of restructuring and change, national leaders have been called on to provide solutions to the pressing problems of their day. In the global knowledge-based economy, entirely new kinds of industries and jobs will need to be created to provide continued economic well-being for our citizens. To foster this type of change requires a comprehensive vision of government policy.[16]

The Clinton administration has responded to this challenge by focusing on creating a leaner, more responsive government, on building a new economy, and on empowering individuals with the tools to succeed and prosper in the modern world. President Clinton has shaped and implemented this vision by advocating policies—intellectual property protection, trade advocacy, reduced export controls and creating incentives for private sector investment in cutting-edge research and development—that will create investment-led, technology-driven, economic growth and that will provide new high-skilled, high-wage jobs for the very people most hurt by the restructuring of the U.S. economy.

THE PATENT AND TRADEMARK OFFICE ACTIVITIES

Shortly after taking office, President Clinton directed Secretary of Commerce Ronald Brown to turn the Commerce Department into an economic powerhouse because commerce is the most effective vehicle to promote investment in technology-driven economic growth and export and job creation. Secretary Brown has aggressively helped lead the government's efforts to usher the United States into the information age. Within the Commerce Department, the PTO is the primary source for creating incentives for technological investment and for protecting the fruits of American creativity. Providing high-quality patents and trademarks allows customers to take their products to the marketplace and compete with the benefit of strong protection for their investment. Because this protection flows from rights granted by nation states, the role of the PTO will become increasingly important to the competitive position of the U.S. economy. The assistant secretary of commerce and commissioner of the U.S. Patent and Trademark Office serves as the administration's primary source for intellectual property policy. In that capacity, the PTO advises the president, the U.S. trade representative, the secretary of commerce and various agencies on improving intellectual property protection both at home and abroad.[17]

---

16. See especially President Clinton's, "Technology for Economic Growth" *President's Progress Report,* November 1993.

The patent office has been working with Congress to implement dozens of important pieces of legislation that would strengthen the country's intellectual property laws. Increasingly, however, because of the globalization of the economy, domestic protection of intellectual property is directly tied to the quality of international intellectual property protection. Several examples illustrate this connection. The report on Intellectual Property and the National Information Infrastructure and efforts to create a Global Information Infrastructure show how copyright law, the standard mode of protection for intellectual property in a digital environment, is both a domestic and an international issue. To protect American intellectual property abroad, the PTO works with foreign governments on a bilateral basis, on a regional basis—as in Latin America under the framework created by the North American Free Trade Agreement (NAFTA)—and on a global basis, as in the General Agreement on Tariffs and Trade (GATT) agreement on the Trade-Related Aspects of Intellectual Property (TRIPs).

The National and Global Information Infrastructures

In the early 1800s the federal government helped foster the growth and development of a national transportation infrastructure. Nothing could illustrate President Clinton's commitment to create new sources of economic growth and new opportunities for employment better than his efforts to harness the full potential of the National Information Infrastructure, a terminology and concept not conceived of in Washington prior to candidate Clinton's campaign. A key element of that commitment is the Information Infrastructure Task Force led by Secretary Brown, bringing together officials from across government to develop a cyberspace marketplace for global commerce. The Working Group on Intellectual Property, chaired by the author, looked at the role of intellectual property laws in protecting the content that flows on the National Information Infrastructure. Without enforceable laws in place, intellectual property holders are unwilling to put their work at risk in the rapidly expanding digital environment. Under such conditions, consumers would be unable to reap the benefits of these new technologies.

On September 5, 1995, the Working Group released a report entitled "Intellectual Property and the National Information Infrastructure."[18] The report explains how intellectual property law applies to the National Information Infrastructure and makes legislative recommendations to Congress to fine-tune copyright law for the digital age. The Working Group found that the Copyright Act is fundamentally adequate and effective in protecting content providers'

---

17. Detailed reviews of PTO activities can be found in our annual reports. The Fiscal Year 1994 Report is available on the PTO World Wide Web home page at http://www.uspto.gov.

18. United States Information Infrastructure Task Force Working Group on Intellectual Property Rights, *Intellectual Property and the National Information Infrastructure: The Report of the Working Group on Intellectual Property Rights,* Bruce A. Lehman. Assistant Secretary of Commerce and Commissioner of Patents and Trademarks, Chair September 1995.

rights on the National Information Infrastructure. In limited areas, the report recommended minor amendments to the Act to adapt existing law to current technology.[19] Bills to implement the report's legislative recommendations are now being considered in the House (H.R. 2441) by Representatives Moorhead, Schroeder and Coble, and in the Senate (S. 1284) by Senators Hatch and Leahy.

A phenomenon common to all of the Information Infrastructure Task Force committees and working groups was the recognition that one could not truly speak in terms of a "national" information infrastructure. The very nature of the technology meant that the emerging information infrastructure was "global." Global access to this technology has required the task force to focus some of its efforts on international issues. Vice President Al Gore and Secretary Brown have provided worldwide leadership at several international summits and other forums where governments from around the world are carefully considering the implications of the Global Information Infrastructure on their national economies and copyright systems.

In February 1995, Vice President Gore and Secretary Brown were in Belgium to lead the ministers of the G7 nations in a discussion of issues relating to the Global Information Infrastructure. The final communiqué of that meeting contains a pledge by G7 governments to provide for protection of content flowing through the Global Information Infrastructure and commits the nations involved to work through the World Intellectual Property Organization, the specialized United Nations agency for intellectual property in Geneva, and in other forums to secure effective global protection for information products marketed in international electronic commerce.

In March 1995, the author hosted a working group in San Francisco of ten industrialized nations and the European Union on behalf of the Clinton Administration to begin determining what new international agreements, if any, are needed to secure effective protection for products sold electronically. Ongoing efforts to draft a protocol to the Berne Convention and a possible new instrument on neighboring rights are being redirected to solve the problems posed by international cyberspace. The San Francisco meeting ended with a general recognition that there will have to be a better understanding of how the differing systems of countries can be made to cooperate whenever a book, periodical or database is uploaded from one country and downloaded, distributed and copied in another. Questions include: when does infringement occur, who will have a cause of action to sue, what national law will apply, and what will be the role of national treatment.

The patent office has taken the lead on questions of intellectual property in the international arena by identifying the essential elements needed to update the Berne Convention for the Protection of Literary and Artistic Works and to provide improved protection for performers and producers of phonograms and by striving

---

19. A copy of the Report and an Executive Summary of the Report can be found on the PTO World Wide Web home page at http://www/uspto.gov.

for international agreement on these issues. The United States urged at a World Intellectual Property Organization meeting last September that the organization continue to focus attention on the digital agenda and more conventional issues, and that it quickly develop a consensus on these issues that would lead to appropriate international agreements.

The PTO: Bilateral Activities

Much of the international work done by the PTO occurs on a bilateral basis in conjunction with the PTO of the U.S. trade representative. The United States works with other countries to harmonize international intellectual property laws, to educate and provide technical assistance to other countries' intellectual property organizations, to work with foreign governments in strengthening their intellectual property laws and to resolve trade disputes that revolve around intellectual property protection.

China's failure to enforce intellectual property rights adequately and effectively resulted in China being investigated under the Special 301 provisions of the 1974 Trade Act. The investigation began on June 30, 1994, and culminated on February 26, 1995, with the United States and China reaching an accord on the protection of intellectual property rights and market access. Officials from the PTO assisted the United States trade representative's office with the investigation and the negotiation of the agreement.

The agreement will safeguard U.S. intellectual property rights and increase U.S. access to the Chinese market. The agreement requires the Chinese government to take immediate steps to address rampant piracy throughout China, to make long-term changes ensuring effective enforcement of intellectual property rights and to provide U.S. intellectual property holders with enhanced access to the Chinese market. In particular, some of the more important obligations China is required to undertake include creation of an effective customs enforcement system modeled after the U.S customs service, creating a title verification system to help prevent the production, distribution, importation, exportation and retail sale of U.S. audio-visual works, and establishing a strong intellectual property enforcement structure composed of working groups and task forces to coordinate and carry out enforcement efforts. The agreement also stipulates that the United States and China hold quarterly consultations on the implementation and effectiveness of the enforcement action plan, as well as quarterly exchanges of statistics and information for verification purposes.

In fiscal year 1995, the United States and China held two quarterly consultations. These consultations covered a broad range of topics, including enforcement, structural changes to China's intellectual property enforcement system and market access. The patent office will continue to participate in the consultations and to work with Chinese officials and assist the Chinese in training judges, lawyers, students, government officials, and business people on intellectual property laws.

NAFTA

The patent office also works on a regional basis to strengthen intellectual property laws that promote increased trade and investment. American relations with Latin America, especially in the commercial arena, were considerably strengthened by the passage of NAFTA in 1993. Exports from the United States to this region grew by 300 percent from 1983 to 1993, and the forces of economic restructuring, integration and trade liberalization will continue to affect this trend in a positive way. Within the NAFTA framework, the United States has been negotiating bilateral investment treaties and intellectual property rights agreements with countries in the region and working with their public and private sectors to remove barriers to trade. In July, the United States, Canada, Mexico and Chile met to discuss the accession of Chile to NAFTA.

On another front, the PTO, in conjunction with the United States trade representative's office and the Departments of State, Treasury and Agriculture and Commerce, took an active role in formulating U.S. proposals to bring NAFTA into conformity with TRIPs and to provide, in certain circumstances, TRIPs-plus levels of protection. Negotiations to effect these changes are ongoing, and progress is being made to ensure that NAFTA continues to provide the highest level of protection for intellectual property.

GATT/TRIPs Implementation: The Uruguay Round Agreements Act

On January 1, 1995, the GATT/TRIPs Agreement, creating the World Trade Organization, entered into force. The TRIPs council, made up of representatives of the members of the World Trade Organization, which includes the United States, has responsibility for overseeing the implementation of the TRIPs obligations by World Trade Organization members. The council met four times in 1995 to discuss a variety of procedural and institutional matters necessary for the smooth functioning of the council, including arrangements for cooperation with the World Intellectual Property Organization.

In order for the United States to fulfill its obligations under the TRIPs agreement, Congress passed the Uruguay Round Agreements Act of 1994 which was signed into law by President Clinton on December 8, 1994. The act amends U.S. patent terms, the treatment of inventive activity, the definition of infringing activity and the establishment of a domestic priority system based on a new provisional patent application.

Patent Term: The TRIPs agreement requires that the term of patent protection be at least twenty years measured from the filing date of the patent application. To satisfy this requirement, the patent law was amended to provide that the patent term end 20 years from the earliest effective filing date of the U.S. patent application. The patent law was also amended to allow the twenty-year term to be extended for up to five years to compensate for delays in the issuance of the patent due to interferences, national security considerations or successful appeals to the Board of Patent Appeals and Interferences or the federal courts.

Prior to the implementation of this act, the practice of a 20-year term measured from the date of filing was common to all industrialized nations except the United States. The 20-year term will in most cases mean longer patent terms. Because it now takes an average of nineteen months for an application to be considered, the length of a patent term from date of grant to expiration will be, on average, twenty years minus nineteen months.

Provisional Applications

The Act establishes a new type of patent application, the provisional patent application. A simple low-cost patent application now lets inventors easily preserve their rights to a patent for up to a year, at which time they must either file a complete application or abandon their provisional application. The provisional application has several important benefits. Most importantly, it places domestic applicants on an even footing with foreign applicants because the filing of a provisional application does not trigger the start of one's patent term. This feature, common in several other countries for years, is now available to inventors in the United States.

Treatment of Inventive Activity

Under previous patent law, no evidence could be introduced by a party seeking to prove a date of invention if that evidence was based on activity that took place outside the United States. The Act removed this restriction so that patents are now available without discrimination as to the place of invention.

Definition of Infringing Activity

Prior to the TRIPs agreement, U.S. patent law did not confer the right to bar others from "offering for sale or importing" a product covered by a patent. Because the TRIPs Agreement requires this protection, the act amended U.S. patent law to enable patent holders to bar such activity. Prior to the TRIPs Agreement, U.S. patent law also did not confer on "process" patent owners the right to "prevent others from offering for sale" products made by a process covered by their patent. This shortcoming was also eliminated by the Act.

INTELLECTUAL PROPERTY PIRACY:
OPPORTUNITY COSTS

As the preceding discussion illustrates, these issues are evidence of the growing importance of intellectual property to our economy. Yet despite efforts to increase protection, the pernicious problem of counterfeiting is growing and attacking some of our nation's most profitable and competitive industries. In industries such as software publishing, biotechnology and pharmaceuticals, and entertainment, research and development expenditures constitute a much larger portion of the cost of production than in many other industries, and the cost for reproducing intellectual property-based goods is a smaller portion of overall cost. Unfortunately, the cost of producing counterfeit products, such as videotapes or records, is also lower.

Counterfeiters, who do not pay for expensive research, development, marketing and other costs, instead act as free riders, usurping the fruits of Americans' creative spirit. It is no wonder that organized crime has become increasingly involved in counterfeiting. Because it is so safe and so profitable, counterfeiting will be a growing area for organized crime in the twenty-first century and a significant problem for the Federal Bureau of Investigation's organized crime and drug operations and the U.S. Customs Service. In a world economy based on ideas, protecting intellectual property from counterfeiters amounts to protecting American economic well-being.

The International Anti-Counterfeiting Coalition has estimated that between five and eight percent of all products and services worldwide are counterfeit and that U.S. trade revenue losses to piracy amount to $200 billion annually (up from $61 billion in 1988). Piracy accounts for $2.5 billion a year in counterfeit recordings alone.[20] Similar losses hurt other industries, including manufacturers of software, pharmaceuticals, videotapes and electronic equipment. From a macroeconomic perspective, these figures are staggering.

The impact of piracy on the software industry is a perfect example. According to the Business Software Alliance, an association of software publishers, software theft annually costs the industry and its distributors over $15.2 billion worldwide. The high cost of software piracy comes not only from illegal reproduction of CD-ROMs, software disks, packaging and manuals, but also from black-market trade in counterfeit products. In addition to hurting software publishers and legitimate software dealers (and their employees), many potential jobs are lost to people who, but for piracy, would have been hired for legitimate positions.

The costs to workers, industries, cities and states, and consumers are equally disturbing. In 1993, the U.S. Customs Service estimated that the United States lost 750,000 jobs to foreign counterfeiting of U.S. products. An auto industry study in 1991 projected that the U.S. auto industry could hire an additional 210,000 workers if the $12 billion per year global manufacture and sale of counterfeit parts were eliminated. These numbers also reduce the tax revenues of U.S. cities and states.

Consumers should be deeply concerned about counterfeit products—their health and safety depend on getting the products they expect. Brand names serve as indicia of origin guaranteeing that the product purchased can do what the

20. "Pirating of Albums Is Put at $2.5 Billion," *The New York Times,* November 25, 1995, 38. This figure was supplied by the International Federation of the Phonographic Industry.

product says it can. Counterfeit pharmaceuticals, cosmetics and health care products can pose grave health risks to people who purchase inferior products. Counterfeit parts for automobiles, airplanes and helicopters can lead to serious or fatal accidents.

Senator Orin Hatch, chairman of the Senate Judiciary Committee, introduced the Anti-Counterfeiting Consumer Protection Act of 1995 to provide stronger and more effective remedies against trademark and copyright counterfeiting. The act would expand the list of officials who may carry out seizure orders, and establish statutory damages in cases involving the use of a counterfeiting mark, in lieu of actual damages and profits. It would also include counterfeiting activity in the definition of prohibited racketeering activity, require Customs to destroy goods rather than return them to the country of origin, and prohibit knowingly trafficking in counterfeit computer programs and computer-program documentation and labeling.

CONCLUSION

Because we are entering an era dominated by the new paradigm of technology and ideas, U.S. competitiveness in the coming decades will increasingly depend on intellectual property protection and an activist federal government. Both corporations and individuals must understand this new reality and act accordingly. Corporations can ensure that their intellectual property counsels are included in strategic planning, especially on an international level, and can more actively promote intellectual property rights by increasing their support for appropriate legislation in the political arena. Further, individuals and consumers, who benefit from a growing economy, should also care about these issues.

The United States has always derived its greatest strength from its inhabitants' creativity. In advertising, marketing, public relations and sales, American brand names, protected by trademark law, have been recognized throughout the world as symbols of quality and value. Our culture, one of our greatest exports, dominates the world, and our artists, composers, musicians, performers, actors or actresses, authors and journalists rely on copyright protection. Individual inventors and corporate laboratories continue to push the boundaries of science at a faster rate than those in any other country and are protected by patent law. Now, more than ever, American businesses are based on activities protected by domestic and international intellectual property laws. Creativity, the key to U.S. success in the past, will continue to ensure that U.S. companies, the U.S. economy, and the country as a whole remain competitive in the twenty-first century.

6

Power Shift: The Age of Non-State Actors

Jessica T. Mathews

THE RISE OF GLOBAL CIVIL SOCIETY

The end of the Cold War has brought no mere adjustment among states but a novel redistribution of power among states, markets, and civil society. National governments are not simply losing autonomy in a globalizing economy. They are sharing power—including political, social, and security roles at the core of sovereignty with businesses, with international organizations, and with a multitude of citizens groups, known as nongovernmental organizations (NGOs). The steady concentration of power in the hands of states that began in 1648 with the Peace of Westphalia is over, at least for a while.[1]

The absolutes of the Westphalian system—territorially fixed states where everything of value lies within some state's borders; a single, secular authority governing each territory and representing it outside its borders; and no authority above states—are all dissolving. Increasingly, resources and threats that matter, including money, information, pollution, and popular culture, circulate and shape lives and economies with little regard for political boundaries. International standards of conduct are gradually beginning to override claims of national or regional singularity. Even the most powerful states find the marketplace and international public opinion compelling them more often to follow a particular course.

The state's central task of assuring security is the least affected, but still not exempt. War will not disappear, but with the shrinkage of U.S. and Russian nuclear arsenals, the transformation of the Nuclear Nonproliferation Treaty into a

1. The author would like to acknowledge the contributions of the authors of the case studies for the Council on Foreign Relations study group, "Sovereignty, Nonstate Actors, and a New World Politics," on which this article is based.

Reprinted by permission of FOREIGN AFFAIRS, Jan/Feb 1997. Copyright © 1997 by the Council on Foreign Relations, Inc.

permanent covenant in 1995, agreement on the long-sought Comprehensive Test Ban treaty in 1996, and the likely entry into force of the Chemical Weapons Convention in 1997, the security threat to states from other states is on a downward course. Nontraditional threats, however, are rising—terrorism, organized crime, drug trafficking, ethnic conflict, and the combination of rapid population growth, environmental decline, and poverty that breeds economic stagnation, political instability, and, sometimes, state collapse. The nearly 100 armed conflicts since the end of the Cold War have virtually all been intrastate affairs. Many began with governments acting against their own citizens, through extreme corruption, violence, incompetence, or complete breakdown, as in Somalia.

These trends have fed a growing sense that individuals' security may not in fact reliably derive from their nation's security. A competing notion of "human security" is creeping around the edges of official thinking, suggesting that security be viewed as emerging from the conditions of daily life—food, shelter, employment, health, public safety—rather than flowing downward from a country's foreign relations and military strength.

The most powerful engine of change in the relative decline of states and the rise of nonstate actors is the computer and telecommunications revolution, whose deep political and social consequences have been almost completely ignored. Widely accessible and affordable technology has broken governments' monopoly on the collection and management of large amounts of information and deprived governments of the deference they enjoyed because of it. In every sphere of activity, instantaneous access to information and the ability to put it to use multiplies the number of players who matter and reduces the number who command great authority. The effect on the loudest voice—which has been governments'—has been the greatest.

By drastically reducing the importance of proximity, the new technologies change people's perceptions of community. Fax machines, satellite hookups, and the Internet connect people across borders with exponentially growing ease while separating them from natural and historical associations within nations. In this sense a powerful globalizing force, they can also have the opposite effect, amplifying political and social fragmentation by enabling more and more identities and interests scattered around the globe to coalesce and thrive.

These technologies have the potential to divide society along new lines, separating ordinary people from elites with the wealth and education to command technology's power. Those elites are not only the rich but also citizens groups with transnational interests and identities that frequently have more in common with counterparts in other countries, whether industrialized or developing, than with countrymen.

Above all, the information technologies disrupt hierarchies, spreading power among more people and groups. In drastically lowering the costs of communication, consultation, and coordination, they favor decentralized networks over other modes of organization. In a network, individuals or groups link for joint action without building a physical or formal institutional presence. Networks have no person at the top and no center. Instead, they have multiple nodes where collections of individuals or groups interact for different purposes. Businesses, citizens organizations, ethnic groups, and crime cartels have all readily adopted the network model. Governments, on the other hand, are quintessential hierarchies, wedded to an organizational form incompatible with all that the new technologies make possible.

Today's powerful nonstate actors are not without precedent. The British East India Company ran a subcontinent, and a few influential NGOs go back more than a century. But these are exceptions. Both in numbers and in impact, nonstate actors have never before approached their current strength. And a still larger role likely lies ahead.

DIAL LOCALLY, ACT GLOBALLY

No one knows how many NGOs there are or how fast the tally is growing. Published figures are badly misleading. One widely cited estimate claims there are 35,000 NGOs in the developing countries; another points to 12,000 irrigation cooperatives in South Asia alone. In fact, it is impossible to measure a swiftly growing universe that includes neighborhood, professional, service, and advocacy groups, both secular and church-based, promoting every conceivable cause and funded by donations, fees, foundations, governments, international organizations, or the sale of products and services. The true number is certainly in the millions, from the tiniest village association to influential but modestly funded international groups like Amnesty International to larger global activist organizations like Greenpeace and giant service providers like CARE, which has an annual budget of nearly $400 million.

Except in China, Japan, the Middle East, and a few other places where culture or authoritarian governments severely limit civil society, NGOs' role and influence have exploded in the last half-decade. Their financial resources and—often more important—their expertise, approximate and sometimes exceed those of smaller governments and of international organizations. "We have less money and fewer resources than Amnesty International, and we are the arm of the U.N. for human rights," noted Ibrahima Fall, head of the U.N. Centre for Human Rights, in 1993. "This is clearly ridiculous." Today NGOs deliver more official development assistance than the entire U.N. system (excluding the World Bank and the International Monetary Fund). In many countries they are delivering the services—in urban and rural community development, education, and health care—that faltering governments can no longer manage.

The range of these groups' work is almost as broad as their interests. They breed new ideas; advocate, protest, and mobilize public support; do legal, scientific, technical, and policy analysis; provide services; shape, implement, monitor, and enforce national and international commitments; and change institutions and norms.

Increasingly, NGOs are able to push around even the largest governments. When the United States and Mexico set out to reach a trade agreement, the two governments planned on the usual narrowly defined negotiations behind closed doors. But NGOs had a very different vision. Groups from Canada, the United States, and Mexico wanted to see provisions in the North American Free Trade Agreement on health and safety, transboundary pollution, consumer protection, immigration, labor mobility, child labor, sustainable agriculture, social charters, and debt relief. Coalitions of NGOs formed in each country and across both borders. The opposition they generated in early 1991 endangered congressional approval of the crucial "fast track" negotiating authority for the U.S. government. After months of resistance, the Bush administration capitulated, opening the agreement to environmental and labor concerns. Although progress in other trade venues will be slow, the tightly closed world of trade negotiations has been changed forever.

Technology is fundamental to NGOs new clout. The nonprofit Association for Progressive Communications provides 50,000 NGOs in 133 countries access to the tens of millions of Internet users for the price of a local call. The dramatically lower costs of international communication have altered NGOs goals and changed international outcomes. Within hours of the first gunshots of the Chiapas rebellion in southern Mexico in January 1994, for example, the Internet swarmed with messages from human rights activists. The worldwide media attention they and their groups focused on Chiapas, along with the influx of rights activists to the area, sharply limited the Mexican government's response. What in other times would have been a bloody insurgency turned out to be a largely nonviolent conflict. "The shots lasted ten days," José Angel Gurria, Mexico's foreign minister, later remarked, "and ever since, the war has been . . . a war on the Internet."

NGOs' easy reach behind other states' borders forces governments to consider domestic public opinion in countries with which they are dealing, even on matters that governments have traditionally handled strictly between themselves. At the same time, cross-border NGO networks offer citizens groups unprecedented channels of influence. Women's and human rights groups in many developing countries have linked up with more experienced, better funded, and more powerful groups in Europe and the United States. The latter work the global media and lobby their own governments to pressure leaders in developing countries, creating a circle of influence that is accelerating change in many parts of the world.

OUT OF THE HALLWAY, AROUND THE TABLE

In international organizations, as with governments at home, NGOs were once largely relegated to the hallways. Even when they were able to shape governments' agendas, as the Helsinki Watch human rights groups did in the Conference on Security and Cooperation in Europe in the 1980s, their influence was largely determined by how receptive their own government's delegation happened to be. Their only option was to work through governments.

All that changed with the negotiation of the global climate treaty, culminating at the Earth Summit in Rio de Janeiro in 1992. With the broader independent base of public support that environmental groups command, NGOs set the original goal of negotiating an agreement to control greenhouse gases long before governments were ready to do so, proposed most of its structure and content, and lobbied and mobilized public pressure to force through a pact that virtually no one else thought possible when the talks began.

More members of NGOs served on government delegations than ever before, and they penetrated deeply into official decision-making. They were allowed to attend the small working group meetings where the real decisions in international negotiations are made. The tiny nation of Vanuatu turned its delegation over to an NGO with expertise in international law (a group based in London and funded by an American foundation), thereby making itself and the other sea-level island states major players in the fight to control global warming. *ECO*, an NGO-published daily newspaper, was the negotiators best source of information on the progress of the official talks and became the forum where governments tested ideas for breaking deadlocks.

Whether from developing or developed countries, NGOs were tightly organized in a global and half a dozen regional Climate Action Networks, which were able to bridge North-South differences among governments that many had expected would prevent an agreement. United in their passionate pursuit of a treaty, NGOs would fight out contentious issues among themselves, then take an agreed position to their respective delegations. When they could not agree, NGOs served as invaluable back channels, letting both sides know where the other's problems lay or where a compromise might be found.

As a result, delegates completed the framework of a global climate accord in the blink of a diplomat's eye—16 months—over the opposition of the three energy superpowers, the United States, Russia, and Saudi Arabia. The treaty entered into force in record time just two years later. Although only a framework accord whose binding requirements are still to be negotiated, the treaty could force sweeping changes in energy use, with potentially enormous implications for every economy.

The influence of NGOs at the climate talks has not yet been matched in any other arena, and indeed has provoked a backlash among some governments. A handful of authoritarian regimes, most notably China, led the charge, but many others share their unease about the role NGOs are assuming. Nevertheless, NGOs have worked their way into the heart of international negotiations and into the day-to-day operations of international organizations, bringing new priorities, demands for procedures that give a voice to groups outside government, and new standards of accountability.

ONE WORLD BUSINESS

The multinational corporations of the 1960s were virtually all American, and prided themselves on their insularity. Foreigners might run subsidiaries, but they were never partners. A foreign posting was a setback for a rising executive.

Today, a global marketplace is developing for retail sales as well as manufacturing. Law, advertising, business consulting, and financial and other services are also marketed internationally. Firms of all nationalities attempt to look and act like locals wherever they operate. Foreign language skills and lengthy experience abroad are an asset, and increasingly a requirement, for top management. Sometimes corporate headquarters are not even in a company's home country.

Amid shifting alliances and joint ventures, made possible by computers and advanced communications, nationalities blur. Offshore banking encourages widespread evasion of national taxes. Whereas the fear in the 1970s was that multinationals would become an arm of government, the concern now is that they are disconnecting from their home countries' national interests, moving jobs, evading taxes, and eroding economic sovereignty in the process.

The even more rapid globalization of financial markets has left governments far behind. Where governments once set foreign exchange rates, private currency traders, accountable only to their bottom line, now trade $1.3 trillion a day, 100 times the volume of world trade. The amount exceeds the total foreign exchange reserves of all governments, and is more than even an alliance of strong states can buck.

Despite the enormous attention given to governments' conflicts over trade rules, private capital flows have been growing twice as fast as trade for years. International portfolio transactions by U.S. investors, nine percent of U.S. GDP in 1980, had grown to 135 percent of GDP by 1993. Growth in Germany, Britain, and elsewhere has been even more rapid. Direct investment has surged as well. All in all, the global financial market will grow to a staggering $83 trillion by 2000, a 1994 McKinsey & Co. study estimated, triple the aggregate GDP of the affluent nations of the Organization for Economic Cooperation and Development.

Again, technology has been a driving force, shifting financial clout from states to the market with its offer of unprecedented speed in transactions—states cannot match market reaction times measured in seconds—and its dissemination of financial information to a broad range of players. States could choose whether they would belong to rule-based economic systems like the gold standard, but, as former Citicorp chairman Walter Wriston has pointed out, they cannot withdraw from the technology-based marketplace, unless they seek autarky and poverty.

More and more frequently today, governments have only the appearance of free choice when they set economic rules. Markets are setting de facto rules enforced by their own power. States can flout them, but the penalties are severe—loss of vital foreign capital, foreign technology, and domestic jobs. Even the most powerful economy must pay heed. The U.S. government could choose to rescue the Mexican peso in 1994, for example, but it had to do so on terms designed to satisfy the bond markets, not the countries doing the rescuing.

The forces shaping the legitimate global economy are also nourishing globally integrated crime—which U.N. officials peg at a staggering $750 billion a year, $400 billion to $500 billion of that in narcotics, according to U.S. Drug Enforcement Agency estimates. Huge increases in the volume of goods and people crossing borders and competitive pressures to speed the flow of trade by easing inspections and reducing paperwork make it easier to hide contraband. Deregulation and privatization of government-owned businesses, modern communications, rapidly shifting commercial alliances, and the emergence of global financial systems have all helped transform local drug operations into global enterprises. The largely unregulated multi-trillion-dollar pool of money in supranational cyberspace, accessible by computer twenty-four hours a day, eases the drug trade's toughest problem: transforming huge sums of hot cash into investments in legitimate business.

Globalized crime is a security threat that neither police nor the military—the state's traditional response—can meet. Controlling it will require states to pool their efforts and to establish unprecedented cooperation with the private sector, thereby compromising two cherished sovereign roles. If states fail, if criminal groups can continue to take advantage of porous borders and transnational financial spaces while governments are limited to acting within their own territory, crime will have the winning edge.

BORN-AGAIN INSTITUTIONS

Until recently, international organizations were institutions of, by, and for nation-states. Now they are building constituencies of their own and, through NGOs, establishing direct connections to the peoples of the world. The shift is infusing them with new life and influence, but it is also creating tensions.

States feel they need more capable international organizations to deal with a lengthening list of transnational challenges, but at the same time fear competitors. Thus they vote for new forms of international intervention while reasserting sovereignty's first principle: no interference in the domestic affairs of states. They hand international organizations sweeping new responsibilities and then rein them in with circumscribed mandates or inadequate funding. With states ambivalent about intervention, a host of new problems demanding attention, and NGOs bursting with energy, ideas, and calls for a larger role, international organizations are lurching toward an unpredictable, but certainly different, future.

International organizations are still coming to terms with unprecedented growth in the volume of international problem-solving. Between 1972 and 1992 the number of environmental treaties rocketed from a few dozen to more than 900. While collaboration in other fields is not growing at quite that rate, treaties, regimes, and intergovernmental institutions dealing with human rights, trade, narcotics, corruption, crime, refugees, antiterrorism measures, arms control, and democracy are multiplying. "Soft law" in the form of guidelines, recommended practices, nonbinding resolutions, and the like is also rapidly expanding. Behind each new agreement are scientists and lawyers who worked on it, diplomats who negotiated it, and NGOs that back it, most of them committed for the long haul. The new constituency also includes a burgeoning, influential class of international civil servants responsible for implementing, monitoring, and enforcing this enormous new body of law.

At the same time, governments, while ambivalent about the international community mixing in states' domestic affairs, have driven some gaping holes in the wall that has separated the two. In the triumphant months after the Berlin Wall came down, international accords, particularly ones agreed on by what is now the Organization for Security and Cooperation in Europe and by the Organization of American States (OAS), drew explicit links between democracy, human rights, and international security, establishing new legal bases for international interventions. In 1991 the U.N. General Assembly declared itself in favor of humanitarian intervention without the request or consent of the state involved. A year later the Security Council took the unprecedented step of authorizing the use of force "on behalf of civilian populations" in Somalia. Suddenly an interest in citizens began to compete with, and occasionally override, the formerly unquestioned primacy of state interests.

Since 1990 the Security Council has declared a formal threat to international peace and security 61 times, after having done so only six times in the preceding 45 years: It is not that security has been abruptly and terribly threatened; rather, the change reflects the broadened scope of what the international community now feels it should poke its nose into. As with Haiti in 1992, many of the so-called Chapter VII resolutions authorizing forceful intervention concerned domestic situations that involved awful human suffering or offended international norms but posed little if any danger to international peace.

Almost as intrusive as a Chapter VII intervention, though always invited, election monitoring has also become a growth industry. The United Nations monitored no election in a member state during the Cold War, only in colonies. But beginning in 1990 it responded to a deluge of requests from governments that felt compelled to prove their legitimacy by the new standards. In Latin America, where countries most jealously guard their sovereignty, the OAS monitored eleven national elections in four years.

And monitoring is no longer the passive observation it was in earlier decades. Carried out by a close-knit mix of international organizations and NGOs, it involves a large foreign presence dispensing advice and recommending standards for voter registration, campaign law, campaign practices, and the training of clerks and judiciaries. Observers even carry out parallel vote counts that can block fraud but at the same time second-guess the integrity of national counts.

International financial institutions, too, have inserted themselves more into states' domestic affairs. During the 1980s the World Bank attached conditions to loans concerning recipient governments' policies on poverty, the environment, and even, occasionally, military spending, a once sacrosanct domain of national prerogative. In 1991 a statement of bank policy holding that "efficient and accountable public sector management" is crucial to economic growth provided the rationale for subjecting to international oversight everything from official corruption to government competence.

Beyond involving them in an array of domestic economic and social decisions, the new policies force the World Bank, the International Monetary Fund, and other international financial institutions to forge alliances with business,

NGOs, and civil society if they are to achieve broad changes in target countries. In the process, they have opened themselves to the same demands they are making of their clients: broader public participation and greater openness in decision-making. As a result, yet another set of doors behind which only officials sat has been thrown open to the private sector and to civil society.

LEAPS OF IMAGINATION

After three and a half centuries, it requires a mental leap to think of world politics in any terms other than occasionally cooperating but generally competing states, each defined by its territory and representing all the people therein. Nor is it easy to imagine political entities that could compete with the emotional attachment of a shared landscape, national history, language, flag, and currency.

Yet history proves that there are alternatives other than tribal anarchy. Empires, both tightly and loosely ruled, achieved success and won allegiance. In the Middle Ages, emperors, kings, dukes, knights, popes, archbishops, guilds, and cities exercised overlapping secular power over the same territory in a system that looks much more like a modern, three-dimensional network than the clean-lined, hierarchical state order that replaced it. The question now is whether there are new geographic or functional entities that might grow up alongside the state, taking over some of its powers and emotional resonance.

The kernels of several such entities already exist. The European Union is the most obvious example. Neither a union of states nor an international organization, the EU leaves experts groping for inadequate descriptions like "post-sovereign system" or "unprecedented hybrid." It respects members' borders for some purposes, particularly in foreign and defense policy, but ignores them for others. The union's judiciary can override national law, and its Council of Ministers can overrule certain domestic executive decisions. In its thousands of councils, committees, and working groups, national ministers increasingly find themselves working with their counterparts from other countries to oppose colleagues in their own government; agriculture ministers, for example, ally against finance ministers. In this sense the union penetrates and to some extent weakens the internal bonds of its member states. Whether Frenchmen, Danes, and Greeks will ever think of themselves first as Europeans remains to be seen, but the EU has already come much further than most Americans realize.

Meanwhile, units below the national level are taking on formal international roles. Nearly all fifty American states have trade offices abroad, up from four in 1970, and all have official standing in the World Trade Organization (WTO). German *Lander* and British local governments have offices at EU headquarters in Brussels. France's Rhône-Alps region, centered in Lyon, maintains what it calls "embassies" abroad on behalf of a regional economy that includes Geneva, Switzerland, and Turin, Italy.

Emerging political identities not linked to territory pose a more direct challenge to the geographically fixed state system. The WTO is struggling to find a method of handling environmental disputes in the global commons, outside all states' boundaries, that the General Agreement on Tariffs and Trade, drafted 50 years ago, simply never envisioned. Proposals have been floated for a Parliamentary Assembly in the United Nations, parallel to the General Assembly; to represent the people rather than the states of the world. Ideas are under discussion that would give ethnic nations political and legal status, so that the Kurds, for example, could be legally represented as a people in addition to being Turkish, Iranian, or Iraqi citizens.

Further in the future is a proposed Global Environmental Authority with independent regulatory powers. This is not as far-fetched as it sounds. The burden of participating in several hundred international environmental bodies is heavy for the richest governments and is becoming prohibitive for others. As the number of international agreements mounts, the pressure to streamline the system—in environmental protection as in other areas—will grow.

The realm of most rapid change is hybrid authorities that include state and nonstate bodies such as the International Telecommunications Union, the International Union for the Conservation of Nature, and hundreds more. In many of these, businesses or NGOs take on formerly public roles. The Geneva-based International Standards Organization, essentially a business NGO, sets widely observed standards on everything from products to internal corporate procedures. The International Securities Markets Association, another private regulator, oversees international trade in private securities markets—the world's second-largest capital market after domestic government bond markets. In another crossover, markets become government enforcers when they adopt treaty standards as the basis for market judgments. States and NGOs are collaborating ad hoc in large-scale humanitarian relief operations that involve both military and civilian forces. Other NGOs have taken on standing operational roles for international organizations in refugee work and development assistance. Almost unnoticed, hybrids like these, in which states are often the junior partners, are becoming a new international norm.

FOR BETTER OR WORSE?

A world that is more adaptable and in which power is more diffused could mean more peace, justice, and capacity to manage the burgeoning list of humankind's interconnected problems. At a time of accelerating change, NGOs are quicker than governments to respond to new demands and opportunities. Internationally, in both the poorest and richest countries, NGOs, when adequately funded, can outperform government in the delivery of many public services. Their growth, along with that of the other elements of civil society, can strengthen the fabric of the many still-fragile democracies. And they are better than governments at dealing with problems that grow slowly and affect society through their cumulative effect on individuals—the "soft" threats of environmental degradation, denial of human rights, population growth, poverty, and lack of development that may already be causing more deaths in conflict than are traditional acts of aggression.

As the computer and telecommunications revolution continues, NGOs will become more capable of large-scale activity across national borders. Their loyalties and orientation, like those of international civil servants and citizens of nonnational entities like the EU, are better matched than those of governments to problems that demand transnational solutions. International NGOs and cross-border networks of local groups have bridged North-South differences that in earlier years paralyzed cooperation among countries.

On the economic front, expanding private markets can avoid economically destructive but politically seductive policies, such as excessive borrowing or overly burdensome taxation, to which governments succumb. Unhindered by ideology, private capital flows to where it is best treated and thus can do the most good.

International organizations, given a longer rein by governments and connected to the grassroots by deepening ties with NGOs, could, with adequate funding, take on larger roles in global housekeeping (transportation, communications, environment, health), security (controlling weapons of mass destruction, preventive diplomacy, peacekeeping), human rights, and emergency relief. As various international panels have suggested, the funds could come from fees on international activities, such as currency transactions and air travel, independent of state appropriations. Finally, that new force on the global scene, international public opinion, informed by worldwide media coverage and mobilized by NGOs, can be extraordinarily potent in getting things done, and done quickly.

There are at least as many reasons, however, to believe that the continuing diffusion of power away from nation-states will mean more conflict and less problem-solving both within states and among them.

For all their strengths, NGOs are special interests, albeit not motivated by personal profit. The best of them, the ablest and most passionate, often suffer most from tunnel vision, judging every public act by how it affects their particular interest. Generally, they have limited capacity for large-scale endeavors, and as they grow, the need to sustain growing budgets can compromise the independence of mind and approach that is their greatest asset.

A society in which the piling up of special interests replaces a single strong voice for the common good is unlikely to fare well. Single-issue voters, as Americans know all too well, polarize and freeze public debate. In the longer run, a stronger civil society could also be more fragmented, producing a weakened sense of common identity and purpose and less willingness to invest in public goods, whether health and education or roads and ports. More and more groups promoting worthy but narrow causes could ultimately threaten democratic government.

Internationally, excessive pluralism could have similar consequences. Two hundred nation-states are a barely manageable number. Add hundreds of influential nonstate forces—businesses, NGOs, international organizations, ethnic and religious groups—and the international system may represent more voices but be unable to advance any of them.

Moreover, there are roles that only the state—at least among today's polities—can perform. States are the only nonvoluntary political unit, the one that can impose order and is invested with the power to tax. Severely weakened states will encourage conflict, as they have in Africa, Central America, and elsewhere. Moreover, it may be that only the nation-state can meet crucial social needs that markets do not value. Providing a modicum of job security, avoiding higher unemployment, preserving a livable environment and a stable climate, and protecting consumer health and safety are but a few of the tasks that could be left dangling in a world of expanding markets and retreating states.

More international decision-making will also exacerbate the so-called democratic deficit, as decisions that elected representatives once made shift to unelected international bodies; this is already a sore point for EU members. It also arises when legislatures are forced to make a single take-it-or-leave-it judgment on huge international agreements, like the several-thousand-page Uruguay Round trade accord. With citizens already feeling that their national governments do not hear individual voices, the trend could well provoke deeper and more dangerous alienation, which in turn could trigger new ethnic and even religious separatism. The end result could be a proliferation of states too weak for either individual economic success or effective international cooperation.

Finally, fearsome dislocations are bound to accompany the weakening of the central institution of modern society. The prophets of an Internetted world in which national identities gradually fade, proclaim its revolutionary nature and yet believe the changes will be wholly benign. They won't be. The shift from national to some other political allegiance, if it comes, will be an emotional, cultural, and political earthquake.

DISSOLVING AND EVOLVING

Might the decline in state power prove transitory? Present disenchantment with national governments could dissipate as quickly as it arose. Continuing globalization may well spark a vigorous reassertion of economic or cultural nationalism. By helping solve problems governments cannot handle, businesses, NGOs, and international organizations may actually be strengthening the nation-state system.

These are all possibilities, but the clash between the fixed geography of states and the nonterritorial nature of today's problems and solutions, which is only likely to escalate, strongly suggests that the relative power of states will continue to decline. Nation-states may simply no longer be the natural problem-solving unit. Local government addresses citizens' growing desire for a role in decision-making, while transnational, regional, and even global entities better fit the dimensions of trends in economics, resources, and security.

The evolution of information and communications technology, which has only just begun, will probably heavily favor nonstate entities, including those not yet envisaged, over states. The new technologies encourage noninstitutional, shifting networks over the fixed bureaucratic hierarchies that are the hallmark of the single-voiced sovereign state. They dissolve issues' and institutions' ties to a fixed place. And by greatly empowering individuals, they weaken the relative attachment to community, of which the preeminent one in modern society is the nation-state.

If current trends continue, the international system 50 years hence will be profoundly different. During the transition, the Westphalian system and an evolving one will exist side by side. States will set the rules by which all other actors operate, but outside forces will increasingly make decisions for them. In using businesses, NGOs, and international organizations to address problems they cannot or do not want to take on, states will, more often than not, inadvertently weaken themselves further. Thus governments' unwillingness to adequately fund international organizations helped NGOs move from a peripheral to a central role in shaping multilateral agreements, since the NGOs provided expertise the international organizations lacked. At least for a time, the transition is likely to weaken rather than bolster the world's capacity to solve its problems. If states, with the overwhelming share of power, wealth, and capacity, can do less, less will get done.

Whether the rise of nonstate actors ultimately turns out to be good news or bad will depend on whether humanity can launch itself on a course of rapid social innovation, as it did after World War II. Needed adaptations include a business sector that can shoulder a broader policy role, NGOs that are less parochial and better able to operate on a large scale, international institutions that can efficiently serve the dual masters of states and citizenry, and, above all, new institutions and political entities that match the transnational scope of today's challenges while meeting citizens' demands for accountable democratic governance.

Part Two

A Tool Kit for Businesses in the Knowledge-Based Economy

Introduction

Jacquelyn Cefola

In Part One, Dr. Neef describes several macro-level forces that are drastically altering the way our economy works. He identifies knowledge, new technology and global strategies as three key impacts that are changing the nature of market competition. These impacts are also changing the nature of business strategy as we know it. For as the knowledge-based economy continues to evolve, businesses will be forced to develop new competitive advantages—and strategies to match. But how exactly should businesses go about creating these new competitive advantages?

To tackle this question we need to explore how businesses can and should respond to the economic forces of knowledge. The following six articles will do just that by providing a more micro-level analysis of how businesses can create competitive advantage in the knowledge-based economy. The articles I have selected present a tool kit of ideas that will help managers understand and plan for the changes that lie ahead.

Specifically, Part Two will address three questions:

- How can businesses more carefully define the value gained from knowledge?
- What new theories in economics will help managers to analyze how knowledge is reshaping the economy?
- What strategies can businesses implement to create competitive advantages in the knowledge-based economy?

CHAPTERS 7 AND 8: DEFINING THE ECONOMIC VALUE GAINED FROM KNOWLEDGE

These two chapters present the reader with a working definition of knowledge and a synopsis of the economic frameworks that have been used to value knowledge.

In their article titled "The Knowledge-based Economy: From the Economics of Knowledge to the Learning Economy," Dominique Foray and Bengt-Åke Lundvall define four different kinds of knowledge that contribute economic value.[1] "Know what" represents special sets of facts such as, how many flats are there in the key of b minor, or what are the positions on a soccer team. "Know why" encompasses the laws of nature, the scientific knowledge that is often employed to facilitate technological innovation. "Know how," includes the core competencies and skills that individuals utilize when accomplishing a task. A material handler uses know how to move pallets with a forklift as does a researcher conducting a literature search or a manager making a product pricing decision. Finally, "Know who" refers to the knowledge that is used to form and sustain social relationships. Know who allows individuals to access the knowledge of others.

Foray and Lundvall refine their definition of knowledge by differentiating between tacit and codified knowledge. Tacit knowledge is contained within its possessor. It is not "easily transferred because it has not been stated in an explicit form."[2] Complementing tacit knowledge, codified knowledge has been processed and systematized by its possessor so that it is easily communicated to and understood by others. Ikujiro Nonaka, author of the following article in Chapter 12, theorizes that the transference between tacit into codified knowledge continuously spirals: tacit knowledge becomes codified when attempts are made to communicate it; the newly codified knowledge is interpreted and processed by the receiver, and becomes part of that individual's tacit knowledge base.[3] This spiral continues to revolve as knowledge is communicated and interpreted to new individuals.

Having established a working definition for the types of knowledge of interest, let us examine how the impact of knowledge has been treated previously in the field of economics. In "The Contribution of Economic Theory to the Understanding of a Knowledge-based Economy," Giovanni Dosi details how economics has contributed to our understanding of the force of knowledge.[4] As Dosi writes, two conflicting conclusions can be made about the treatment of knowledge in economics. The first conclusion is that the field of economics has always created frameworks for valuing knowledge because it has examined market exchanges among individuals that are made according to the knowledge those individuals possess. The second conclusion is that economics "has very little to say" about the value of knowledge because of the assumptions used in the economic analysis of knowledge.[5] The remainder of this article is dedicated to exploring these conclu-

1. Dominique Foray and Bengt-Ake Lundvall. "The Knowledge-Based Economy: From the Economics of Knowledge to the Learning Economy." *Employment and Growth in the Knowledge-based Economy*. OECD Documents, OECD 1996, p. 19.

2. Foray and Lundvall, p. 21.

3. Nonaka, Ikujiro. "The Knowledge-Creating Company," *Harvard Business Review*, November–December, 1991.

4. Giovanni Dosi. "The Contribution of Economic Theory to the Understanding of a Knowledge-Based Economy." *Employment and Growth in the Knowledge-based Economy*. OECD Documents, OECD 1996, pp. 81–85.

5. Dosi, p. 81.

sions through a description of the past and current economic frameworks that model the value of knowledge.

CHAPTERS 9 AND 10: THE NEW ECONOMICS OF KNOWLEDGE

Most of the theories described by Dosi for valuing knowledge reinforce the idea that diminishing returns prevail in competition. Diminishing returns describe a relationship between the quantity of a good and the value that is derived from that good, where the value diminishes as the quantity increases. The theory of diminishing returns is described succinctly in Ormerod's *The Death of Economics*[6]:

"The consumption of yet more of a product will never reduce the total amount of utility derived from its consumption, but the extra satisfaction . . . derived from each additional amount will diminish as the absolute amount consumed rises."

Recently, controversial economic theories put forth by Brian Arthur have challenged the idea that diminishing returns govern market competition for all products in the knowledge-based economy.[7] As described in Arthur, increasing returns happen when a consumer's marginal utility increases as more of the product is consumed. For example, a consumer of a fax machine gains utility when additional consumers purchase compatible fax machines because their faxes can be sent to more locations. Increasing returns change the rules of competition among businesses.

Businesses that compete in markets with increasing returns are either propelled to the top or driven to the bottom—at least temporarily. Firms with products that succeed gain tremendous market share as consumers increase their utility by increasing their consumption. If this rapid market penetration occurs, businesses can be locked-in as market leaders with products that are the market standard. Such market leaders can only be ousted by competing businesses that create new products that incorporate grand scale innovation. "A new product often has to be two or three times better in some dimension—price, speed, convenience—to dislodge a locked-in rival."[8]

In order to develop such innovation, firms are required to invest in large upfront costs for research and development in order to cultivate the knowledge that leads to such product innovation. Yet once such an investment in knowledge has been made and the product has been developed, the costs of reproducing the good can be minimal; the firm's marginal costs of production may be very small. Because of this difference between the costs of production and the costs of reproduction, the true product costs may not be reflected in prices that consumers are

---

6. Paul Ormerod, *The Death of Economics,* London: Faber and Faber, 1994, p. 51.
7. W. Brian Arthur. "Increasing Returns and the New World of Business." *Harvard Business Review.* July–August 1996, pp. 100–109.
8. Arthur, p. 105.

willing to pay. Knowing that they may not be able to recover their initial investments, firms may be tempted to under-invest in knowledge.

Paul Romer analyzes this externality in terms of national-level investment policies for two developing countries, Mauritius and Taiwan.[9] Romer's growth theories are founded on the concept that knowledge is the only sustainable competitive advantage for nations or businesses. How then does a nation sustain investment in knowledge when its private sector may be unwilling to make the investment?

Romer speculates that there is a clear need for government intervention. Comparing the tracks of Mauritius and Taiwan, Paul Romer describes two different strategies, producing ideas and using ideas, which spur rapid development and increase income levels. "The idea of ideas," from Jim Rohwer's book is included as Chapter 9 because it provides a summary of Paul Romer's theories for growth.[10]

In "Knowledge Buyers, Sellers, and Brokers: The Political Economy of Knowledge," Laurence Prusak and Don Cohen bring the discussion of the market for knowledge and its externalities back to the organizational level. Prusak and Cohen propose that a micro-level knowledge market has a similar cast of characters as other markets and can be described in terms of buyers, sellers, and brokers.[11] Knowledge buyers are those who are in search of knowledge. Knowledge sellers are those who are in possession of the knowledge that is being sought. Knowledge brokers link the buyers and sellers, facilitating the knowledge exchange.

Prusak and Cohen continue to describe the "communities of practice" that influence the transactions in the knowledge market. Thomas Stewart elaborates on the point, explaining that such a community "has an enterprise but not an agenda; that is, it forms around a value-adding something-we're-all-doing."[12] These communities develop over time through shared experiences. They are often formed through social interaction and are not usually predetermined by management.

It is important to realize that the roles of participants in the knowledge market are dynamic over time, for example a knowledge buyer during one exchange will become a seller at the next. Similarly, communities of practice change frequently. It is also important to realize that the knowledge market is rife with potential externalities that threaten to impede effective knowledge transfer. Managers and employees must work together to avoid some of the negative consequences of the knowledge market externalities described by Prusak and Cohen.

9. Paul Romer. "Two Strategies for Economic Development: Using Ideas and Producing Ideas," Proceedings of the World Bank Annual Research Conference 1992, supplement to the World Bank Economic Review, March 1993, pp. 63–91.

10 Jim Rohwer. "The idea of ideas." *Asia Rising: Why America Will Prosper as Asia's Economics Boom*. New York: Touchstone, 1996, pp. 73–78.

11. Laurence Prusak and Don Cohen. "Knowledge Buyers, Sellers, and Brokers: The Political Economy of Knowledge." Center for Business Innovation, Working Paper: January 1997, pp. 1–27.

12. Thomas A Stewart. "The Invisible Key to Success." *Fortune* August 5, 1996, p. 2.

CHAPTERS 11 AND 12: STRATEGIES FOR THE KNOWLEDGE-BASED ECONOMY

Let us progress to think about how managers can synthesize the information contained in the previous articles and create new strategies for the knowledge-based economy. New strategies must improve the internal processing of knowledge—the business systems that perpetuate knowledge use. New strategies must also help to expand the organization's knowledge base and spur innovation.

Dr. W. Edwards Deming's "A System of Profound Knowledge," tackles the first strategic need, describing four critical components of a well-functioning knowledge organization.[13] The first two components will be highlighted here. The first component involves the business organization recognizing that it exists as a composite of independent but networked parts, a system—and must be managed as such. Dr. Deming gives the example of an orchestra, but let us consider a jazz band.

During a standard jazz performance, the band will first present the listener with the theme of the piece. All of the performers work together and play their combined, interdependent, interpretation of the music. Later the musicians deviate from the theme and use their improvisational skills: individual players solo using their individual talents. But throughout the process of improvisation, the players remain a unit, a system, unified by their knowledge and commitment to the standard theme that initiated the performance. This example relates directly to a business operating in the knowledge-based economy: managers must conduct their businesses, ensuring that all employees are unified under one goal; one theme for their organization. Managers must also be flexible and adaptive to allow their employees to improvise—to use their individual talents and skills, so long as their solos adhere to the original goal.

The second component of the system of profound knowledge involves gaining knowledge about variation. Dr. Deming has classified two forms of variation: variation from special causes and variation from common causes. Variation from special causes results from events that cause upward or downward spikes in the quality of production or service. Special cause variation indicates that production processes are not in control—that the processes are not predictable and are not in what Dr. Deming terms a stable state. Managers must identify the contributing factors for these variations and create strategies to eliminate them. Once all of the variation from special causes is eliminated, the system is in control or stable. But a system that is in control still has process variation. Common causes of variation are built into the system itself. Managers will not be able to avoid the variation from such common causes without changing the production system entirely. Distinguishing special cause variation from common cause variation is essential for developing appropriate control strategies.

---

13. W. Edwards Deming. "A System of Profound Knowledge." *The New Economics for Industry, Government, Education.* Massachusetts Institute of Technology Center for Advanced Engineering Study, Cambridge: 1993, pp. 94–118.

Once businesses implement strategies that systematize the use and transfer of knowledge, strategies must be created to ensure continued innovation: the knowledge creation processes must be established. Ikujiro Nonaka, the first Distinguished Professor of Knowledge at the Haas School of Business, has written the article, "The Knowledge-Creating Company" to address this need.[14] At the heart of a knowledge-creating company is the philosophy that the company is a living organism—a dynamic system with a collective goal.

In this system, all employees are considered knowledge workers because all are capable of creating new organizational knowledge. It is the management team's responsibility not only to spur the knowledge creating processes but also to keep the knowledge creation in line with broad strategic objectives. Nonaka suggests that metaphors and analogies can be used to accomplish both tasks. Nonaka continues to describe organizational strategies that have been used by Japanese businesses that have proven their abilities to create knowledge and innovation over time.

Nonaka, like Deming, mentions that new performance measures are needed to gauge the success of businesses in the knowledge-based economy. In the following Section, Dr. Siesfeld will discuss the newest and most effective knowledge measurement systems.

14. See note 3.

7

The Knowledge-Based Economy: From the Economics of Knowledge to the Learning Economy

Dominique Foray and Bengt-Åke Lundvall

SOME CONCEPTUAL CLARIFICATION

In order to understand the role of knowledge and learning in economic development, it is useful to make a distinction between different kinds of knowledge. It is especially important to make a distinction between knowledge as more or less complex information, and knowledge as a set of skills and competences. The mode of formation and distribution of knowledge differs and later we shall see how the codification of knowledge has different conditions and implications for the two main categories.

Four Different Kinds of Knowledge

In an earlier paper, Lundvall and Johnson (1994) proposed distinctions between four different kinds of knowledge:

- know-what;
- know-why;
- know-how;
- know-who.

Excerpt from © OECD, 1996, *Employment and Growth in the Knowledge-based Economy.* Reproduced by permission of the OECD.

Know-what refers to knowledge about "facts." How many people live in New York? What are the ingredients used in pancakes? And when was the battle of Waterloo (or of Austerlitz!)? are examples of this kind of knowledge. Here, knowledge is close to what is normally called information—it can be broken down into bits. There are complex areas where experts must hold a great deal of this kind of knowledge in order to fulfill their jobs—practitioners of law and medicine belong to this category. It is interesting to note that many of these experts will, typically, work in independent, specialized, consulting firms.

Know-why refers to scientific knowledge of principles and laws of motion in nature, in the human mind, and in society. This kind of knowledge has been extremely important for technological development in certain areas, for example the chemical and electric/electronics industries. To have access to this kind of knowledge will often speed up advances in technology and reduce the frequency of errors in trial-and-error processes. Again, the production and reproduction of know-why is often organized in specialized organizations, such as universities. To access this kind of knowledge, firms have to interact with these organizations, either through recruiting scientifically trained labor or through direct contacts with university laboratories.

Know-how refers to skills—that is, the capability to do something. It can relate to production, but also to many other activities in the economic sphere. The businessperson judging the market prospects of a new product, or the personnel manager selecting and training staff, have to use their know-how, and the same is true for the skilled worker operating complicated machine-tools. However, it is important to realize that it is not only "practical people" who need skills. One of the most interesting and profound analyses of the role and formation of know-how is actually about the need for skills among scientists (Polanyi, 1958/1978). Know-how is typically the kind of knowledge developed and kept within the borders of the individual firm. But, as the complexity of the knowledge-base increases, a mix of division of labor and co-operation between organizations is also tending to develop in this field.

This is why *know-who* is becoming increasingly important. It refers to a mix of different kinds of skills, including what might be characterized as social skills. Know-who involves information about who knows what, and who knows how to do what. But, especially, it involves the formation of special social relationships with the expertise involved that makes it possible to get access to and use their knowledge efficiently. This kind of knowledge is important in the modern economy where there is a need to access many different kinds of knowledge and skills which are widely dispersed due to the highly developed division of labor among organizations and experts.

Learning Different Kinds of Knowledge

Mastering these four kinds of knowledge takes place through different channels. While know-what and know-why can be obtained through reading books, attending lectures and accessing databases, the other two categories are rooted primarily in practical experience. Written manuals may help but, in order to use them, some basic skills in the field of application may be needed.

Know-how will typically be learned in apprenticeship-relationships where the apprentice follows his master and relies upon him as his trustworthy authority (Polanyi, 1958/1978, p. 53 *et passim*). This is reflected in the education system leading to these professions. Most natural sciences involve field work or work in laboratories to enable students to learn some of the necessary skills. In management-science, the emphasis on case-based training reflects an attempt to simulate learning from practical experience. Know-how will typically develop into a mature form only through years of experience in everyday practice—through learning-by-doing and learning-by-interacting with colleagues. This is true for lawyers, doctors and businesspeople, as well as for connoisseurs and artists.

Know-who is learned through social practice and, sometimes, through specialized education environments. Communities of engineers and experts are kept together through informal connections as well as by reunions of alumnae and through professional societies giving the participant access to information bartering with professional colleagues (Carter, 1989). Know-who also develops in day-to-day dealings with customers, sub-contractors and independent institutes. One important reason why large firms engage in basic research is that it gives them access to the networks of academic experts crucial for their innovative capability (Pavitt, 1991).

UNDERSTANDING CHANGES IN THE KNOWLEDGE BASE

As can be seen from the overview of empirically based studies, it is clear that the overall economic performance of the OECD economies is increasingly and more directly based upon their knowledge stock and their learning capabilities. As suggested above (Section 3), radical changes in the way knowledge is produced, stored and diffused are being accelerated by ICT. A firm understanding of the character of these changes is fundamental for the analysis of the issues related to growth and employment and for policies focusing on institutional design. In this section, we will briefly investigate two aspects of these changes: changes in the relationship between codified and tacit knowledge; and the increased importance of networked knowledge.

Codified vs. Tacit Knowledge: Definition

Codification of knowledge implies that knowledge is transformed into "information" that can be easily transmitted through information infrastructures. It is a process of reduction and conversion which renders especially easy the transmission, verification, storage and reproduction of knowledge. As explained by David (1993), codified knowledge is typically expressed in a format that is compact and standardized in order to facilitate and reduce the cost of such operations.

Codified knowledge can normally be transferred over long distances and across organizational boundaries at low cost.

However, information and codified knowledge are not easily exchanged in the market. The seller normally keeps access to his information, and it is difficult to prevent the buyer from distributing it to other potential customers. Furthermore, it is not a straightforward matter to reach agreement on the price since the buyers do not know in advance what they are buying (if it was fully revealed, they would not be willing to pay for it).

In contrast with codified knowledge, tacit knowledge refers to knowledge that cannot be easily transferred because it has not been stated in an explicit form. One important kind of tacit knowledge is skills. The skilled person follows rules which are not recognized as such by the person following them (Polanyi, 1958 p. 49). Another important kind of tacit knowledge has to do with the implicit but shared beliefs and modes of interpretation which make intelligent communication possible (*op. cit.*, p. 212).

According to Polanyi, the only way to transfer this kind of knowledge is through a specific kind of social interaction similar to apprenticeship relationships. This implies that it cannot be sold and bought in the marketplace, and that its transfer is extremely sensitive to the social context.

These distinctive features of knowledge as an economic resource establish the context in which the dramatic changes in knowledge generation and use are occurring. At the center of these changes is a transformation in the character of society's knowledge stock involving codification and in the techniques for using codified knowledge.

The Relationships Between Codified and Tacit Knowledge

The most important result of the new steps in the codification of knowledge, which are documented below, is that they change the border between tacit and codified knowledge. They make it technically possible and economically attractive to codify kinds of knowledge which so far have remained in tacit form. However it is important to realize that they do not necessarily reduce the relative importance of tacit knowledge in the form of skills, competencies, and other elements of tacit knowledge. Easier and less expensive access to information makes the skills and competencies relating to the selection and efficient use of information ever more crucial.

That codified and tacit knowledge are complementary is therefore indisputable. In other words, codification is never complete, and some forms of tacit knowledge will always continue to play an important role. What is important is that the borders as well as the forms of complementarity between the two kinds of knowledge are in a state of flux.

The construction of new ensembles of codified and tacit knowledge is a complication issue: as suggested by Hatchuel and Weil (1995), codification processes cannot be considered as a simple transfer between the tacit and the codified domains. Codification entails fundamental transformation, and the codified knowledge base does not cover exactly the tacit knowledge base for which it tries to substitute. In this sense, codification is an irreversible process: once knowledge is transformed into information, it is not possible to return to the original tacit state. It is also clear that moving the boundary between the codified and the tacit parts of the knowledge stock is by no means an instantaneous and simple task. It is usually a matter of long-term technological and organizational evolution, involving changes in incentive structures, as well as an increase in the benefits, and a decrease in the costs, of codification.

The most fundamental aspect of learning is perhaps the spiral movement where tacit is transformed into codified knowledge, followed by a movement back to practice where new kinds of tacit knowledge are developed. According to Nonaka (1991), such a spiral movement is at the very core of individual as well as organizational learning.

REFERENCES

Abramovitz, M. and P. David (1994), "Convergence and Deferred Catch-up: Productivity Leadership and the Waning of American Exceptionalism," *Centre for Economic Policy Research Publication No. 401*, Stanford University.

Archibugi, D. and M. Pianta (1996), "Innovation Surveys and Patents as Technology Indicators: The State of the Art," in OECD (1996), Innovation, Patents and Technological Strategies, Paris.

Arrow, K. J. (1994), "Methodological Individualism and Social Knowledge," Richard T. Ely Lecture, in *AEA Papers and Proceedings*, Vol. 84, No. 2, May.

Barabaschi, S. (1992), "Managing the Growth of Technical Information," in Rosenberg, Landau and Mowery (eds.), *Technology and the Wealth of Nations*, Stanford University Press.

Cambridge Journal of Economics (1995), Special Issue on Technology and Innovation, Vol. 19, No.1.

Carter, A. P. (1989), "Know-how Trading as Economic Exchange," *Research Policy*, Vol. 18, No.3.

Carter, A. P. (1994a), "Production Workers, Meta-investment and the Pace of Change," paper prepared for the meeting of the International J.A. Schumpeter Society, Munster, August.

Carter, A. P. (1994b), "Change as Economic Activity," Working paper, No. 333, Department of Economics, Brandeis University.

Cowan, R. and D. Foray (1995), "The Changing Economics of Technological Learning," *IIASA Working Papers*, 95–39.

David, P. (1991), "Computer and Dynamo: The Modem Productivity Paradox in a Not-too-distant Mirror," in OECD, 1991.

David, P. (1993), "Knowledge, Property and the System Dynamics of Technological Change," Proceedings of the World Bank Annual Conference on Development Economics.

David, P. and D. Foray (1995), "Accessing and Expanding the Science and Technology Knowledge Base," *STI Review,* No. 16, OECD, Paris.

Eirma (1993), "Speeding up Innovation," Conference papers for the EIRMA Helsinki Conference, May.

Eliasson, G., S. Folster, T. Lindberg, T. Pousette and E. Taymaz (1990), *The Knowledge-based Information Economy,* Stockholm: Almqvist & Wiksell.

Ergas, H. (1994), "The New Faces of Technological Change and Some of its Consequences," mimeo.

Foray, D. and C. Freeman (1992), *Technology and the Wealth of Nations,* London: Pinter Publishers.

Freeman, C. (1991), "Networks of Innovators: A Synthesis of Research Issues," *Research Policy,* Vol. 20, No. 5.

Freeman, C. (1995), "The National System of Innovation in Historical Perspective," *Cambridge Journal of Economics,* Vol. 19, No. 1.

Freeman, C. and C. Perez (1988), "Structural Crisis of Adjustment: Business Cycles and Investment Behaviour," in G. Dosi et al., *Technical Change and Economic Theory,* London: Pinter Publishers.

Freeman, C. and L. Soete (1993), *Information Technology and Employment,* Universitaire Pers Maastricht.

Hatchuel, A. and B. Weil (1995), *Experts in Organizations: A Knowledge-based Perspective on Organisational Change,* Berlin-New York: Walter de Gruyter.

Howitt, P. (1994), *Towards an Operational Definition of Knowledge-Based Growth,* Conference on Implications of Knowledge-Based Growth for Microeconomic Policies, Ottawa.

Industry Canada (1993), "Knowledge, Technology and Employment Trends," memo by Pat Murray, July.

Industry Canada (1994), "Employment Growth in Canada," memo by N. Stephens.

Katz, L. F. and K. M. Murphy (1992), "Changes in Relative Wages 1963–1987: Supply and Demand Factors," *Quarterly Journal of Economics,* February.

Komatsuzakt, S., T. Tanimitsu, G. Ohira and K. Yamamoto (undated), "An Analysis of the Information Economy in Japan from 1960 to 1980," Research Institute of Telecommunications and Economics, Tokyo.

Krueger, R. B. (1993). "How Computers have Changed the Wage Structure: Evidence from Micro-data, 1984–89," *Quarterly Journal of Economics,* February.

Lundvall, B -A. (ed) (1992), National Systems of Innovation: Towards a Theory of Innovation and Interactive Learning, Pinter Publishers, London.

Lundvall, B.-A and B. Johnson (1994), "The Learning Economy," *Journal of Industry Studies,* Vol. 1, No. 2, December, pp. 23–42.

Lundvall, B.-A. (1995), "The Global Unemployment Problem and National Systems of Innovation," in D. O'Doherty (ed.), *Globalisation, Networking and Small Firm Innovation,* Graham & Trotman, London.

Machlup, F. (1962), *The Production and Distribution of Knowledge in the United States,* Princeton University Press, Princeton.

Nelson, R. (1993), *National Innovation Systems: A Comparative Analysis,* Oxford University Press, Oxford.

Nonaka, K. (1991), "The Knowledge Creating Company," *Harvard Business Review,* November-December.

OECD (1986), *Trends in the Information Economy,* Pans.

OECD (1991), *Technology and Productivity: The Challenge for Economic Policy,* Paris.
OECD (1994a), The OECD Jobs Study—Facts, Analysis, Strategies, Paris.

OECD (1994b), The OECD Jobs Study—Evidence and Explanation Part I, Paris.

OECD (1994c), Manufacturing Performance: A Scoreboard of Indicators, Paris.

Pavitt, K. (1991), "What Makes Basic Research Economically Useful?," *Research Policy,* Vol. 20, No. 2.

Polanyi, M. (1958/1978), *Personal Knowledge,* Routledge & Kegan Paul.

Porat, M. and M. Rubin (1977), *The Information Economy,* US Department of Commerce, Government Printing Office, Washington, DC.

Rubin, M. R. and M. Taylor (1984), *The Knowledge Industry in the United States: v 1960–1980,* Princeton University Press, Princeton.

Steinmueller, E. (1992), "The Economics of Production and Distribution of User-specific Information via Digital Networks," in Antonelli (ed.), *The Economics of Information Networks,* North-Holland.

8

The Contribution of Economic Theory to the Understanding of a Knowledge-Based Economy

Giovanni Dosi

INTRODUCTION

When I was asked to present at this Conference what economic theory has to offer to the understanding of a knowledge-based economy, two opposite answers came to my mind. The first one was that in one sense, which I shall specify shortly, economic theory is intrinsically about knowledge-based economies. The opposite answer, which I consider at least equally true, is that most strands of current theory have very little to say by way of an analysis of the nature of the particular form of economy that one observes nowadays and the transformation in its knowledge bases. Some words on the first point might help to clarify the second point.

One of the central objects of inquiry of economic theory since its origin as a discipline has been precisely the interactions among a multitude of decentralized agents and the ensuing collective outcomes. (Everyone has heard of Adam Smith's "invisible hand" conjecture on the properties of decentralized markets . . .). But in an essential sense, asking how a decentralized economy works is equivalent to asking how socially-distributed knowledge is collectively put to work in ways that are not socially detrimental and, possibly, increase the welfare of everyone. A. Smith's conjecture (subject to several qualifications, many of which have been missed by later theorists) was indeed that markets are able to elicit private knowledge, propelled by the pursuit of self-interest, and yield orderly outcomes, superior—in terms of welfare—to, say, an autarkic system of production and con-

Excerpt from © OECD, 1996, *Employment and Growth in the Knowledge-based Economy.* Reproduced by permission of the OECD.

sumption. The point that an economy is basically a system of distributed, diverse, pieces of knowledge has been emphasized, among others by von Hayek. And, of course, this is also a way of reading the most rigorous formalization of the economy as an interdependent system, namely General Equilibrium Analysis as put forward in the 1950s and 1960s by Arrow, Debreu, Hahn, McKenzie. The existence theorems, there, are a way of saying that, among all the imaginable worlds, one can also coherently conceive of an economy wherein every selfishly motivated agent, by making the best use of his own information, contributes to "share its use" with all other agents in ways that are mutually consistent and also mutually beneficial. (I am provisionally using here "information" and "knowledge" as equivalent concepts, but I shall come back to this later.)

So, yes, in this general and rather abstract sense, economic theory has always been about interdependencies in knowledge-intensive systems. However, it is enough to check the long list of assumptions that one has to make in the canonical General Equilibrium (GE) model in order to fully appreciate the distance between what it says and the interpretative requirements of any one historically observed economy. Incidentally, note that the very pioneers of the theory are well aware of this, unlike many of the following believers: compare the writings of Kenneth Arrow or Frank Hahn with any random sample of articles from the *Journal of Economic Theory* or *Econometrica*. Indeed when I see works on empirically applied GE models, I must confess that I have the same feeling I had when I saw a while ago at UC Berkeley the announcement of a seminar on "Applied Heidegger"!

The long list of restrictive assumptions is also an indicative proxy for the phenomena that economic theory is unable to account for (at least in that analytical format): the progresses (and regresses) that have been recently made; the humility that economists should, but generally do not, put into their policy prescriptions; and, last but not least, the healthy amount of scepticism that non-economists should have when listening to economists' wisdom.

INFORMATION, KNOWLEDGE
AND ECONOMIC THEORY

As mentioned, GE is a very elegant, very parsimonious on the assumptions, representation of how agents use at their best the available information and interact with each other accordingly. But "information" is not an ordinary good which can be treated, say, like a machine tool or a pair of shoes (again, on the economic characteristics of information, Arrow is a pioneering reference). Shoes wear out as one uses them, while information has typically got a high upfront cost in its generation but can be used repeatedly without decay thereafter, or there might even be learning-by-using type phenomena (as from the first to the n-th time one applies Pythagoras' theorem in high school, . . .). Moreover, information might be appropriable, in the sense that other agents might have significant obstacles to access it (ranging from legal protections, such as patents, all the way to the sheer difficulty of fully appreciating what a particular piece of information means: see also below). But information as such typically entails a non-rival use (in the sense that it can be utilized indifferently by one or one million people, which, again, is not the case of ordinary commodities like shoes or machine tools, . . .).

In my view, some of the most important advances of the theory over the last two or three decades have concerned precisely the economic consequences of these features of information. Without entering into any detail, one might telegraphically mention for example the wide literature on the "economics of information" and of "information processing" (see, for example, the works of Herbert Simon, George Akerlof and Joseph Stiglitz); on "principal-agent" models, most often studying the incentive implications of imperfect, asymmetric information, on the grounds of otherwise quite orthodox assumptions; on the organizational implications of information-related transaction costs and collective rents (for example, the works of Oliver Williamson and Masahiko Aoki); and on "new growth models" explicitly incorporating the generation of technological information (see the contributions of Paul Romer and colleagues).

For our purposes here, let me just recall three major implications of even the most rudimentary account of the specificity of information for economic theory.

First, the "invisible hand" properties of the canonical GE model do not generally carry over to economic models where the most restrictive informational assumptions are relaxed (for example on the perfect access to information by all agents and on the fact that information itself drops freely from the sky). So, the theory may easily predict equilibria and growth paths that are socially sub-optimal, systematic divergences between rewards and marginal products, and also the possibility of long-term unemployment.

Second, the social distribution of information, and thus the institutional architecture of the system, matters a lot in terms of microeconomic incentives and aggregate performance.

Third, by adding the highly plausible assumption of locality of learning, one easily obtains path-dependent models of development—at the levels of individual firms, technologies, industries and whole countries—(cf. the contributions of Paul David, Brian Arthur, Richard Nelson, Sidney Winter and, in general, "evolutionary" models of economic change). Impressionistically, "locality" stands for the fact that you most likely learn by building upon what you already know (so that for example it is much easier to learn differential equations after having taken the course of calculus than without it; or, even at an aggregate level, the probability that the next generation of microprocessors will be invented in the United States, conditional on the past innovative performance in the field, is much higher than in Burkina Faso). And locality/path-dependence stands also for the relative incremental coherence in the domains of exploration that individuals, organizations and possibly countries may attain (so that, for example, becoming a great economist does not make it easier for you to become a good football player, being a competitive textile manufacturer is not likely to help in competing in bioengineering, etc.).

Incidentally, note also that path-dependence in learning is likely to entail tricky dilemmas between "exploitation" and "exploration"—in the terminology of James March—that is, between allocations of efforts aimed at improving what one is already good at doing vs. activities of search for uncertain novelties.

Putting it somewhat bluntly, even simple accounts of some essential characteristics of information analytically shake the naive and Paglossian belief that unhindered market mechanisms yield the best of possible worlds. To use a term that I do not like too much, "market failures" are generally associated with the production and use of information. Intuitively, for this to happen it is sufficient to acknowledge the properties mentioned above concerning: *i)* increasing returns; and *ii)* non-rivalry in the use of information. The former obviously tend to conflict with the idea that pure competition is normatively the best form of market organization (and also with the idea that competition can sustain itself as a viable market structure). The latter decouples the costs of generation and the benefits of use of information (after all, one could say that the cost of production of, say, Pythagoras' theorem was entirely born by Pythagoras himself, while all subsequent generations benefited from it for free). In a related way, such a decoupling is likely to induce under-investment in information generation (and attempts to tackle the problem via an increased appropriability of its benefits might even have perverse outcomes).

Moreover, as is well known in the theory, necessary conditions for some close link to hold between (marginal) productivities of inputs, relative prices and distributive shares are decreasing returns with respect to the use of the inputs whose productivity we are measuring (even neglecting the paramount difficulties involved in the measurement itself). Again, the acknowledgement of the role of information as a "factor of production" breaks that link because of the increasing returns and externalities associated with its generation and use. (Has anyone ever tried to measure the "marginal productivity" of Fermi and Openheimer within the Manhattan Project? Link them to their relative price? Account for their inputs into subsequent "atomic bomb production functions"? Well, it follows from the economics of information that similar overwhelming difficulties apply to the GM or Microsoft or Boeing "production functions," and, more so, to their aggregation, such as the "US production function.")

I would like to emphasize that all the argument so far can comfortably rest upon rather conventional assumptions regarding in particular the "rationality" of agents—at least in their ability to make the best use of the information they access (whatever that means)—and on collective "equilibrium" set-ups (which is a very strong assumption on the collective consistency of individual plans). Some economists (notably those with "evolutionary" and "institutionalist" inclinations) depart even further from the canonical assumptions and suggest the following points (admittedly more controversial among practitioners):

- A distinction is drawn between information and knowledge. The former entails well-stated and codified propositions about "states-of the-world" (e.g., "it is raining"), properties of nature (e.g., "A causes B") or explicit algorithms on how to do things. On the other hand, knowledge, in the definition I am proposing here, includes: i) cognitive categories; ii) codes of interpretation of the information itself; iii) tacit skills; and iv) problem-solving and search heuristics irreducible to well-defined algorithms.

So, for example, the few hundred pages of demonstration of the last Fermat theorem would come under the heading of "information." Having access to that, some dozen mathematicians in the world will have the adequate knowledge to understand and evaluate it. Conversely, a chimpanzee facing those same pages of information might just feel like eating them, and the majority of human beings would fall somewhere in-between these two extremes . . . Similarly, a manual on "how to produce microprocessors" is "information," while knowledge concerns the pre-existing abilities of the reader to understand and implement the instructions contained therein. Moreover, in this definition, knowledge includes tacit and rather automatic skills like operating a particular machine or correctly driving a car to overtake another one (without stopping first in order to solve the appropriate system of differential equations involved!). And, finally, it includes, "visions" and ill-defined rules of search, like those involved in most activities of scientific discovery, and in technological and organisational innovation (for example, proving a new theorem, designing a new kind of car, figuring out the behavioral patterns of a new kind of crook that has appeared on the financial market).

In this definition, knowledge is partly tacit, at the very least in the sense that the agent himself, and even a very sophisticated observer, would find it very hard to explicitly state the sequence of procedures by which information is coded, behavioral patterns are formed, problems are solved, etc. This is certainly a major admission of ignorance on the part of the analyst, but there are good—almost "ontological"—reasons for this. After all, as Arrow himself pointed out long ago, if an innovation is truly an innovation it is impossible for a finite observer to precisely forecast it. And, indeed, there are powerful uncomputatibility theorems that confirm this intuition. But "tacitness"—some of us suggest—extends also to domains where little invention is involved (as mentioned above, driving cars, operating machine tools, debugging computer programs and, even more so, efficiently running production flows, interpreting market trends, etc.).

- In modern economies, firms are major, albeit by no means unique, repositories of knowledge. Individual organizations embody specific "ways of solving problems" that are often very difficult to replicate in other organizations or even within the organization itself. In turn, organizational knowledge is stored to a large extent in the operating procedures (the "routines") and the higher level rules (concerning for example "what to do when something goes wrong," or "how to change lower level routines") that firms enact while handling their problem-solving tasks in the domains of production, research, marketing, etc.

Dynamically, technological knowledge is modified and augmented partly within individual firms, and partly through interaction with other firms (competitors, users, suppliers, etc.) and other institutions (universities, technical societies, etc.).

- Over the last two decades, at least, a good deal of effort—within the broad field of the "economics of innovation"—has gone into a better understanding of the variety of processes by which knowledge is augmented and diffused in the economy (major contributions in this area include those by Christopher Freeman, Nathan Rosenberg, Keith Pavitt, Richard Nelson, among others).

  A first broad property—probably not surprising to non-economists, but with important analytical and normative implications—is the diversity of learning modes and sources of knowledge across technologies and across sectors. For example, in some activities, knowledge is accumulated primarily via informal mechanisms of learning-by-doing, learning by interacting with customers and suppliers, etc. In others, it involves much more formalized activities of search (such as those undertaken in R&D laboratories). In some fields, knowledge is mostly generated internally and is specific to particular applications. In others, it draws much more directly upon university research and scientific advances. I am mentioning all this because recent research suggests that this diversity of learning modes might be a major determinant of the diverse patterns of evolution in industrial structures (for example, in terms of distribution of firm sizes, natality and mortality of firms, corporate diversification, etc.). Moreover, the identification of sectoral specificities in the forms of knowledge and in learning patterns bears straightforward normative consequences (for example, R&D policies or policies aimed at speeding up the diffusion of innovations are likely to have quite diverse effects in the textile industry or in bioengineering). In a related way, an important step in the understanding of the "anatomy" of contemporary systems of production and knowledge accumulation has involved taxonomic exercises (Keith Pavitt's taxonomy is probably the most famous one), trying to map "families" of technologies and sectors according to their sources of innovative knowledge and their typical innovative procedures.

  At the same time, one has tried to identify possible invariances, which hold across technologies, in the patterns of learning (notions like "technological paradigms," "regimes" and "technological trajectories" belong to this domain of analysis), and descriptive indicators for these same patterns. So, for example, variables like the levels of "innovative opportunity" associated with each technological paradigm, the degrees of "cumulativeness" displayed by technical advances, etc., have turned out to be quite useful in interpreting the determinants of the particular "trajectories" of innovation that one observes.

- Building upon the considerations made so far on the nature of technological learning and on the ways organizations incorporate knowledge, a few scholars have started to explore an explicitly co-evolutionary view, whereby the accumulation of technological knowledge is shaped and constrained by the nature of the organizations and institutions where this knowledge is embedded, and, conversely, new forms of knowledge demand and possibly trigger changes in corporate organizations and broader institutions.

To sum up, it seems to me that various strands of research within the fields of the economics of information, the economics of innovation and organizational theory, have recently contributed a lot to our understanding of how knowledge-rich economies work (and, equally important, of how they do not work!). However the thrust of most of the works that I have discussed so far is a microeconomic one. This does not mean to say that they are void of macroeconomic content: on the contrary, it turns out to be relatively easy and highly promising to incorporate some of the mentioned findings on the economics of information and learning into macroeconomic models.

So, for example, self-sustained growth can be shown to be a general property of knowledge-based economies, even independently from capital accumulation (of course, in less abstract models, knowledge accumulation and capital accumulation are intertwined, and self-propelled dynamics apply).

The introduction of asymmetric information into simple macro models generally yields "Keynesian" outcomes, such as persistent involuntary unemployment, credit rationing, etc. (*cf.* the "New Keynesian" contributions pioneered by Stiglitz and colleagues).

In addition, an expanding family of evolutionary models, microfounded in a multitude of heterogeneous agents that imperfectly learn and are selected by the market, is proving capable of accounting for a wide set of aggregate regularities, ranging from the patterns of international growth of incomes and productivities all the way to "meso" phenomena such as size distributions of firms and their persistent asymmetries in efficiency (*cf.* the works spurred by Richard Nelson and Sidney Winter's evolutionary theory of economic change).

All this notwithstanding, it seems to me equally true that there is still an enormous gap between the wealth of microeconomic findings, on the one hand, and the understanding that we have of how knowledge is distributed in the economy as a whole and the ways this affects its performance and dynamics, on the other. This holds at analytical level and bears all its consequences at a normative one. For example, the theory is still ill-equipped to tackle questions like the conditions under which "technological unemployment" emerges, the effects of particular patterns of technical change on growth, or the collective impact of specific institutional arrangements. Correspondingly it is particularly weak in answering policy questions like those concerning unemployment in knowledge-based economies. Let me briefly turn to these issues.

9

The Idea of Ideas

Jim Rohwer

Even so, there are reasons for thinking that at least some active government interventions in East Asia have borne fruit. The most convincing of these reasons is an idea of Paul Romer's, an economist at the University of California at Berkeley, about ideas and economic growth.

Ideas are not human capital, the level of which can be thought of as a sign of how well a country is capable of putting ideas into practice. Ideas are the world's pool of existing knowledge—the most efficient sequence, in an example of Mr. Romer's, for sewing twenty pieces of cloth together to make a shirt—and of new knowledge that people tinkering with the processes on an assembly line or with a string of symbols like this sentence come up with.

The main reason the rich world is rich—and why half or more of its economic growth comes from productivity increases—is not because it has physical and human capital in abundance (though that helps) but because it is rich in ideas it knows how to apply. An example from another North American thinker, Jane Jacobs, who writes about cities, suggests why the difference between the stock of capital and the stock of ideas is crucial. After noting that billions in American foreign-aid spending have had little or no effect in raising incomes in many poor countries, Mrs. Jacobs draws a contrast with San Francisco after the earthquake of 1906. San Francisco's physical capital (though little of its human capital) was abolished overnight. The "foreign aid" that then poured into the city from governments, charities, and insurance companies allowed San Francisco to recover quickly and thrive, but "nobody was addled enough to suggest that the Red Cross should therefore go into the business of rushing aid indiscriminately to economically declining or stagnant cities on the ground that this would make them prosper like San Francisco."

It may seem that San Francisco's quick recovery (or that of West Germany or Japan after the Second World War) was simply a matter of its wealth of human capital; but there is much more to it than that. The post-1945 German example

From *Asia Rising: How History's Biggest Middle Class Will Change the World*, pp. 73–78. Published in 1996 by Nicholas Brealey Publishing, London, for the international market. Reprinted by permission of the publisher.

gives an indication of why. At the start of the Cold War, East Germany was no poorer in human capital than West Germany, but as the years wore on, it fell further and further behind despite continued large investments in education and training. The East had less physical investment, but not that much less. What it increasingly lacked, however, was contact with the newest ideas and best practices in the West.

In the world described by Mr. Romer, "ideas are the critical input in the production of more valuable human and nonhuman capital." If so, for a poor country ideas have a spectacular virtue. Once they exist anywhere, anybody can acquire them and use them—and, just as important, use them at the same time as everybody else without doing any harm to anyone else (which is not the case with, for example, an office building). These days you not only do not have to reinvent the wheel, you can find out how to make the car and then improve on the carmaking process yourself. This is why countries starting out very far behind the rich world have the chance—if they get things right—to make up ground so fast.

Getting things right means, above all, making an economy as open as possible to foreign influences. In Mr. Romer's view, by far the most common mistake made by poor-country governments is to practice a sort of "neo-mercantilism" of ideas: the belief that a country must "own" some ideas of its own and reap monopoly profits (and technological advancement) from them even if this means restricting the entry of ideas from the rest of the world via trade and foreign investment. This sort of approach—which is what advocates of industrial policy usually have in mind when they argue for active government intervention to support "strategic industries"—is almost invariably disastrous. It makes an economy poorer than it would otherwise be and retards rather than accelerates the acquisition of ideas and their dispersion through the economy.

The clearest recent case of a failed policy of this sort was Brazil's attempt in the 1980s to build a home-grown computer industry through subsidies and a near-total prohibition on the import of foreign semiconductors and computers. This not only failed miserably to create a computer industry in Brazil but also did grave damage to other industries, notably cars and aerospace, which fell ever further behind the foreign competition because they were starved of modern electronics. The evidence is not yet in, but it is likely that Indonesia's lavish and premature promotion of an aerospace industry this decade will prove another fiasco—not least through its colossal waste of the country's scarce engineering talent.

By Mr. Romer's calculations, the consequences of closing an economy to the ideas embodied in foreign goods and foreign investment can be catastrophic, far worse even than traditional trade theory predicts. His studies show that a vast underestimate of the benefits from either trade or investment occurs when the yardstick being used fails to take account of the difference between new (improved) goods, which carry with them the potent brew of new ideas, and mere extra portions of goods that already exist.

The impact of failing to draw a distinction between old goods and new can be huge. Mr. Romer reckons that, in a world that has only old goods, a country imposing a 25 percent tariff suffers a loss of national income equal to 6.25 percent (though the revenue the government gets from the tariff can be thought to make up for some of that). With new goods also available, the loss from the same tariff zooms to some 50–60 percent of national income.

The story is similar with investment. High accumulation of only old capital goods quickly leads to declining returns on investment. But, by Mr. Romer's calculation, if new capital goods are brought in (and with them the new ideas they embody), the returns to the economy as a whole from capital-goods investment can rise as more investment is made and can exceed by a factor of two to three the private cost of making the investment.

Thus, the surest good policy for a poor country to follow is to do nothing—that is, to open its doors as wide as possible to foreign goods and foreign investment and then sit back to watch nature take its course. But there is a catch. The market for ideas is inevitably what economists call imperfect. The reason is that, once ideas exist, it costs almost nothing to replicate them over and over; so, by normal economic standards, their price should be almost zero. But ideas are usually owned by private firms, which therefore must be paid what is by definition a monopoly profit if they are to be persuaded to part with them.

For society as a whole it is worth paying this monopoly profit because the benefit of introducing new ideas in terms of employment, wages, productivity, and growth—is higher (usually enormously higher) than the monopoly profit paid to the owner of the ideas. The trouble is that sometimes no one firm will benefit enough from the new ideas to pay for them itself. Thus, pure market-pricing mechanisms may not deliver the incentive needed to get the ideas introduced into an economy in the first place, even though, without the idea, nothing at all of a particular kind of item can be produced no matter how much capital and labor is invested in it. This imperfect-market quirk is what makes limited government intervention potentially beneficial.

In Mr. Romer's terminology, ideas can be used or they can be produced. It is possible even for a very backward country to use the advanced ideas of the West if it allows the owners of those ideas to profit from employing them in that country. The simplest way for a poor country to do this is to encourage multinational companies to set up shop there and start producing goods. Mr. Romer gives the example of Mauritius, a small island in the Indian Ocean which had so bleak a future as it neared independence in the 1960s that the government was urging the country's educated young people to emigrate.

In fact, Mauritius prospered. This happened almost entirely because of the arrival of Hong Kong entrepreneurs who set up clothing factories on the island. They were encouraged to come by the elimination of tariffs on imports of capital goods, unrestricted profit repatriation, a ten-year tax holiday, and centralized wage setting by the government, which made sure wages did not rise too fast and that there were no strikes. This was a clear case of exploitation in both the everyday sense of the word and in the technical economic sense: The workers were paid less than the value of their marginal product. Yet this wicked system caused personal incomes to rise three times faster in Mauritius than they were going up in

India and twice as fast as in Sri Lanka and produced full employment on the island by 1988. The reason is that the ideas brought in by the Hong Kongers—about how to run a factory, how to sew the clothes, and how to sell the output—caused a great expansion in investment (both foreign and domestic) and economic growth. The entrepreneurs could be paid the monopoly profits that would induce them to come, and there was still enough left over to raise incomes significantly and generate the domestic expertise for the island's future growth.

As countries move up the income scale, they have to start producing ideas as well as just importing them. And here, too, government intervention of the right sort can play a role. Two of Taiwan's consistent interventions have been to require foreign investors to bring technology with them and to set up research parks where pooled work is done for the myriad small Taiwanese companies that cannot finance it individually. (The research parks, now at world-class high-tech levels, are being created even more frequently these days.) The ideas brought into Taiwan, or generated there, by these methods create more value than is reflected in the pricing of purely private transactions. This is why judicious government intervention can help.

For it to work, though, intervention must satisfy a punishing set of conditions. This is where modern East Asia came into its own. For a complicated mixture of reasons, an unusually high share of the interventions undertaken even by supremely activist governments, such as South Korea's, avoided the mistakes that plague government intervention elsewhere. East Asia's authoritarian governments, single-mindedly dedicated to economic growth as the highest national ambition, rarely succumbed to special pleading from individual beneficiaries of their interventions. When the beneficiaries floundered, they were cut off; when the programs failed (whether in South Korea, Indonesia, or Malaysia), policy was smartly turned around. The aim of intervention was not to protect the beneficiary firms from competition, from foreign influences, or from change itself but to accelerate the impact of all these things as a way of upgrading the firms' abilities. Intervention that provides a spur is very different from the sort that acts as a cushion.

The idea of ideas helps to solve the great puzzle about East Asia: why an apparently wide variety of methods attained similar spectacular results. Hong Kong threw the doors open to foreigners and let domestic producers fend for themselves in every market. Singapore strongly encouraged multinationals to set up shop, though it imposed several restraints on the domestic market. Japan and South Korea were hostile to foreign investment but excellent at listening to market signals from their foreign forays and at buying foreign-technology licenses. China has both exported a lot and welcomed foreign investment. And Taiwan placed technology-transfer conditions on foreign investment, while its thousands of returning entrepreneurs brought with them business practices and technology learned in Silicon Valley.

The common thread running through all this is a willingness, one way or another, to be hooked into the outside world and judged according to its standards. And behind this willingness lies probably the deepest and most important characteristic of modern Asia: its passion for discipline, for change, and for the future. Lee Kuan Yew, Singapore's former prime minister and (since his retirement) something of the philosopher-king of the East Asian way, put it this way in conversations in 1993 and 1994:

> *Europe is too featherbedded. They took the wrong path. The more you mollycoddle and cosset a society, the less capable they are of adjusting to changes of life. After a while they become soft and a burden to themselves. This idea of your entitlement. Where can you cash this entitlement? Is there a counter up in heaven where you can say, "Look, this chap's not honoring it, now you honor it"?*
>
> *The one striking difference I find between Central Europe coming out from communism and East Asia is that Central Europe is resentful and bewildered that the Russians have brought this darkness, this blight upon them. They say, "America, Europe, help us." They want to be helped out of this hole.*
>
> *But in Guangzhou they don't look for a free lift. They say, "These Hong Kongers are doing well, how did they do it? Better find out, catch up with them." Xiamen's the same. They want to catch up with the Taiwanese. There's none of this "Please help me." Instead it's "Please come and do business with me." They do not believe that somebody owes them a living or that they have to be bailed out.*
>
> *Asians know they've got to make it on their own. Their willingness to endure hardship and to learn to do new things, whatever that may require, is the biggest single advantage that's driving East Asia forward.*

The main question now is whether Asia will continue to be driven forward.

10

Knowledge Buyers, Sellers, and Brokers: The Political Economy of Knowledge

Laurence Prusak and Don Cohen

Grace is given of God, but knowledge is bought in the market.

—Arthur Hugh Clough

Rapidly or slowly, usefully or unproductively, knowledge moves through organizations. It is exchanged, bought, bartered, found, generated, and applied to work. Organizational knowledge is dynamic: It is moved by a variety of forces. If we want knowledge to move and be used more effectively, we need to better understand the forces that drive it.

We believe its movement is powered by market forces similar to those that animate markets for more tangible goods. There is a genuine market for knowledge in organizations.[1] Like markets for goods and services, the knowledge market has buyers and sellers who negotiate to reach a mutually satisfactory price for the goods exchanged. It has brokers who bring buyers and sellers together and even some entrepreneurs who use their market knowledge to create internal power bases. Knowledge market transactions occur because all of the participants believe that they will benefit from them in some particular way. In economists' jargon, they expect the transactions to provide "utility." People search for knowledge because they expect it to help them succeed in their work. Knowledge is the most sought-after remedy to uncertainty. We all try to reach knowledgeable peo-

---

1. It is actually what economists call a "quasi market," since its transactions cannot be enforced by formal contracts.

From a Center for Business Innovation[SM] Working Paper, January 1997. Copyright © 1997 Ernst & Young LLP. All Rights Reserved. Reprinted by permission of the publisher.

ple as soon as we are confronted with the need to deliver a solution to a problem. When we supply knowledge, we expect to benefit too. Cash is usually not involved in these transactions, but that should not disguise the fact that a market price system exists and payment is made or assumed. The knowledge market, like any other, can be defined as a system in which a scarce unit is exchanged for present or future value.

Understanding that there are knowledge markets and that they operate similarly to other markets is essential to managing knowledge successfully in organizations. Many knowledge initiatives have been based on the utopian assumption that knowledge moves without friction or motivating force, that people will share knowledge with no concern for what they may gain or lose by doing so. Companies install e-mail or collaborative software and expect knowledge to flow freely through the electronic pipeline. When it doesn't happen, they are more likely to blame the software or inadequate training than they are to face a basic fact of life: that people rarely give away valuable possessions (including knowledge) without expecting some return. This may be especially true in our current business climate. Even if only semi-mindful of doing so, people make choices about how to spend their limited time and energy and those choices are usually based on perceived self-interest. We don't expect a car salesman to sell us a car at cost, sacrificing his commission simply because we want to pay less. Nor does the salesman expect us to hand him money and walk out of the showroom without a vehicle. No one believes that such one-sided transactions happen in the marketplace or in most of life—even social transactions are generally based on some sort of exchange, as many sociological studies in exchange theory have shown. Just because the object of exchange is intangible does not mean that the market forces are less strong. Knowledge initiatives that ignore the dynamics of markets (and, of course, human nature) are doomed to failure.

We wish to describe these markets for knowledge in organizations, developing a preliminary taxonomy, as the only way to have a market that works well is, first of all, to recognize that market forces exist, second, to try to understand how the market functions, and third, to make it more efficient. By talking about knowledge market inefficiencies and pathologies, we can get at some of the problems that inhibit knowledge exchange and the transformation of corporate knowledge into value and can sketch the outlines of a more efficient market.

SOME BASICS

There really are no such things as "pure" markets—markets that can be understood solely in economic terms. As analysts from John Stuart Mill to Karl Marx to Thorstein Veblen to James March have argued, every market system is embedded in and affected by social and political realities. The value of anything exchanged depends strongly on the context of the transaction. Someone who pays $20,000 for a wristwatch no more accurate than a $20 Timex is obviously not buying a mechanism for telling time. Even the beauty of the watch, while it may give pleasure, cannot explain his or her willingness to pay one thousand times the cost of an ordinary timepiece. The value of the $20,000 watch is mainly social; it buys the owner status in a society that looks up to or envies people who can afford to purchase and display such items.

Harrison White has said that sociology, economics, and political science are the three lenses needed to see organizations fully; no one discipline can capture their whole meaning. We strongly agree that social, economic, and political realities must be taken fully into account to understand virtually anything that happens in organizations, and markets for knowledge are no exception. If the political reality of an organization is such that calculating and secretive hoarders of knowledge thrive, then potential knowledge buyers will have no currency valuable enough to tempt them to share their expertise: knowledge exchange will be minimal. If the social norm of a company is that admitting to a problem you can't solve on your own is considered a sign of weakness or incompetence, then the social cost of "buying" knowledge will be too high and, once again, the knowledge market won't operate well. At Mobil Oil, where disapproval of "bragging" is part of the culture, the efficiency of the knowledge market was reduced because knowledge owners were reluctant to "advertise" their knowledge and were distrusted by their colleagues if they did. Similarly, a Hewlett-Packard vice president transferred from America to Australia found it difficult to encourage individuals to advertise their individual expertise in a very democratic culture of "mateship" that discourages calling attention to individual performance. While these cultural norms can also have positive impacts, they did inhibit internal knowledge markets. In any case, we have to take these and other political and social realities into account when trying to understand why some knowledge markets are efficient and others are not.

We will look first at the players in the knowledge market: the buyers, sellers, and brokers who take part in knowledge transactions and drive knowledge markets. An individual can perform all three roles in a single day and sometimes takes more than one role at the same time. It is quite common, for instance, to be a knowledge buyer, seller, and broker during the same conversation. For the purposes of this discussion, though, we will look at the roles separately.

Buyers

Knowledge buyers are usually people trying to resolve an issue whose complexity and uncertainty preclude an easy answer. Clearly, asking about the GNP of France or a list of the twenty largest U.S. banks is not a knowledge search; it is a request for data. Knowledge seekers are looking for insights, judgments, and understanding. As distinguished from seekers of information, they want answers to questions, such as "What is this particular client like?" or "How did we manage to win that sale?", that require complex answers—answers imbued with all the emotional sub-texts so important to our sensemaking. They go in search of knowledge because it has distinct value to them. It will help them make a sale or accomplish a task more efficiently; it will improve their judgments and skills and help them make better decisions. In short, it will make them more successful at their work.[2]

This task of searching for knowledge accounts for a fairly substantial part of what many managers and executives do. A recent study done at Hughes Aerospace by Arian Ward estimated that between fifteen and twenty percent of managerial time is spent specifically searching for knowledge and responding to requests for knowledge.

Sellers

Knowledge sellers are people in an organization with an internal market reputation for having substantial knowledge about a process or subject. Although virtually everyone is a knowledge buyer at one time or another, not everyone is necessarily a seller. Some people are skilled but inarticulate and can't make their tacit knowledge explicit. Others have knowledge that is too specialized, personal, or limited to be of much value on the knowledge market. Some potential knowledge sellers keep themselves out of the market, because they believe they benefit more from hoarding their knowledge than they would from sharing it. In many organizations, of course, this is a rational belief. If knowledge is power, then the owners of knowledge have power that may be dissipated if other people come to know what they know. This is a reality of knowledge politics that needs to be dealt with in designing knowledge initiatives. One of the challenges of knowledge management is to ensure that knowledge-sharing is rewarded more than knowledge-hoarding.[3]

Brokers

Knowledge brokers (also known as "gatekeepers" and "boundary spanners") make connections between buyers and sellers: those who need knowledge and those who have it.[4] According to a study we developed for a client, eight to twelve percent of managers across industries are boundary spanners and potential knowledge brokers. They enjoy exploring their organizations, finding out what people do and who knows what. They like to understand the big picture, which puts them in a position to know where to go for knowledge, especially if it falls outside their official area of responsibility.

2. This concept of search is slightly modified from March and Simon's *Organizations* (Cambridge, MA: Blackwell Publishers, 1993) and many works based on their insights.
3. See "Information Politics," by Thomas Davenport, Robert Eccles, and Laurence Prusak (*Sloan Management Review*, Fall 1992).
4. See, for instance, "Boundary Spanning Individuals: Their Role in Information Transfer and Their Antecedents," by Michael Tushman and Thomas Scanlan (*Academy of Management Journal*, 1981, Vol. 24, No. 2) pp. 289–305.

Librarians frequently act as covert knowledge brokers, suited by temperament and their role as information guides to the task of making people-to-people as well as people-to-text connections. For instance, when someone in a high tech firm asks the corporate librarian to do research on thinking about the next generation of RISC chips, the librarian is likely to say, "Did you know that John Smith has been asking about the same subject? You might want to talk to him." Because corporate libraries often serve the whole organization, librarians are among the few employees who have contact with people from many departments. In the course of their work, they come to understand a great deal about the various knowledge needs and resources of the company. Traditionally, librarians value customer service and have highly developed techniques for finding out what they don't already know. All of these factors make them natural knowledge brokers. One of Larry's consulting experiences, described below, vividly showed the contribution of corporate librarians in this area.

About eight years ago, when NYNEX decided to develop benchmarks for all major technical and managerial functions, they asked me to help identify which library activities should be identified for benchmarking. I worked with the director of the corporate resource center to develop a list of the most valuable services the library provided. Between us, we had twenty-five years of experience in library and information science, so we should have been able to figure out what libraries do. We came up with eight activities and sent the list to a wide group of NYNEX library users, asking them if these were in fact the most valued library activities. To our astonishment, we found that we had omitted the single most valuable function: knowledge brokering. We had left it out because it was informal and tacit, but it was the service people cared about most. Librarians were key players in creating efficient knowledge markets, in helping buyers and sellers find each other.

The importance of librarians' role as knowledge workers is often neglected, and their status and compensation seldom reflect their real value to a firm. In fact, knowledge brokers of all kinds are frequently underrated, though they play an essential role in the knowledge market. Because of their broad, boundary-spanning interests, they may be thought of as unfocussed or undisciplined and characterized as "nosey" or as "gossips." Making knowledge connections mainly by talking to people, they are sometimes criticized for spending their time "chatting" rather than doing "real work." Since they are facilitators of other people's success, their contribution may not be visible to managers who think in terms of traditional productivity. Their activities are never measured or captured by human resource systems based on Hay points. It is much harder to measure the profit they help generate than what they cost the company in salary and benefits. One of the first things firms do when they cut costs (and one of the last things they should do!) is close the corporate library.[5] They see it as pure expense—the cost of staff, space, books, periodicals, and online subscriptions. They have no familiar ways to quantify the benefits of the library as an information source and knowledge market-

5. See Jim Matarazzo, *Closing the Corporate Library* (Washington, D.C.: SLA, 1987).

place. Even though they "know" value exists there, their inability to express it in traditional accounting or financial terms makes them behave as if it didn't.

Some knowledge brokers can be categorized as knowledge entrepreneurs. They intentionally set out to become experts on the subject of who has knowledge and how to exploit it. They then "sell" this expertise, not for money but in exchange for future favors. In effect, they develop an internal knowledge business.

The Price System

All markets are characterized by having a price system, so value exchanges can be efficiently rendered and recorded. What is the price system of the knowledge market? What sort of currency is exchanged?

When knowledge is acquired from outside an organization, it is frequently (though not at all invariably) bought with cash. A lawyer, investment banker, or consultant is paid several thousand dollars a day because the client company perceives that his or her special knowledge is worth that much. Within organizations, the medium of exchange is seldom money, but there are agreed upon currencies (or "entities," in the sociological language of exchange theory) that drive the knowledge market. As we have said, knowledge is exchanged because the sellers as well as the buyers believe they gain from the transaction. Look at this example, a real-life experience of Larry's, and a common kind of event in the lives of knowledge sellers.

> It's six PM on a mid-winter evening and snowing again. If I leave my office now, I can be home by seven. That's when my wife expects me. I'm looking forward to a quiet evening at home: a nice hot dinner, maybe a fire in the fireplace. As I'm putting my coat on, the phone rings. It's a consultant from another area of the company—not someone I know well; I met him once or twice at meetings. He apologizes for calling at the last minute and says he's just been told he has to fly out to see a major company client in the morning. He knows I've worked with this client in the past. Would I tell him about them? Who are the best people to talk to? What is the company culture like? What do they value? What are they looking for from us?

My caller wants knowledge, not data or even information, so I can't just answer him in a few sentences or direct him to an online repository. While these tools might help him, they wouldn't be sufficient. It will take me at least half an hour to give him a useful response. If I choose to stay in my office and talk to him (delaying my return home and possibly ruining a pleasant evening), what do I get in return? How does the silent auctioneer that exists in all our heads operate here, weighing considerable inconvenience against possible help to a fellow consultant? What sort of payment could I receive for sharing my knowledge that would make it worthwhile for me to extend my long day and disrupt my personal life?

This situation raises the question of what kinds of payment exist in the knowledge market. We have come to the conclusion that there are three entities at work. In order of significance from greatest to least, they are reciprocity, repute, and altruism.

Reciprocity

A knowledge seller will spend the time and effort needed to share knowledge effectively, if he expects the buyer or people associated with the buyer to be willing sellers when *he* is in the market for their knowledge. This is what Tom Wolfe calls "the favor bank," in *Bonfire of the Vanities*. Larry may choose to miss his dinner and help his fellow consultant if he believes that the caller has knowledge that *he* may need to call on in the future. If the caller knows nothing that could possibly be of use and is unlikely to have valuable knowledge to offer in the future, Larry may decide to go home instead.

What about "just being nice?" Altruism is real—we discuss it below—but time, energy, and knowledge are finite. They are in fact very scarce resources in most people's workdays. In general, scarce resources won't be spent unless the expenditure results in a meaningful return. As nice a person as Larry may be, as much as he might like to help a colleague who has a problem, he doesn't have the time or strength to respond to every knowledge request that comes his way. The choices he makes will usually depend on his perceived self-interest.

Reciprocity may take less direct, but no less real, forms than expecting to get knowledge back from others as payment for providing it to them. In firms structured as partnerships, knowledge sharing that improves profitability will return a benefit to the sharer, now and in the future. Individuals who have significant stock options in a firm are in a similar position. Whether or not a knowledge seller expects to be paid with equally valuable knowledge from the buyer, he may believe that his being known for sharing knowledge readily will make others in the company more willing to share with him. That is a rational assumption, since his reputation as a seller of valuable knowledge will make others confident of *his* willingness to reciprocate when he is the buyer and they have knowledge to sell: His knowledge credit is good. Larry (standing in his office with his coat on and the phone in his hand) may talk to his colleague to enhance his own reputation as a knowledge seller, because that will make it more likely that people throughout the company will respond in kind when he needs their knowledge. So reciprocity and repute are related.

Repute

A knowledge seller develops the reputation of being a knowledgeable person, of having expertise of value that he is willing to share with others in the company. Repute may seem intangible but in fact it produces tangible results. As we have suggested, a reputation for knowledge sharing makes reciprocity more likely: Being known as a knowledge seller makes one a more effective knowledge buyer. Having a reputation as a valuable knowledge source can also lead to the tangible benefits of job security, promotion, and all the other rewards and trappings of internal guru-hood. Although a seller is not paid cash directly, he may receive a higher salary or bonus as a result of his sharing knowledge with others. In many consulting firms, consultants' bonuses are tied to demonstrated knowledge generation and transfer. In any organization, however, the value of repute in the knowledge market will depend on the political and social structures of the organization. There is no fixed or universal market value attached to knowledge sharing. In fact, the range extends from being penalized (for "wasting time" talking to people instead of "working") to significant advancement based mainly on knowledge contributions. In businesses such as consulting, investment banking, and entertainment, success depends significantly on repute. In most businesses today, the importance of repute is increasing as the old social contract between firm and worker based on length of service and loyalty is eroded. As the promise of continued employment in exchange for long, loyal service fades, workers at all levels feel considerable pressure to heighten their individual repute for their demonstrated knowledge, skills, and competencies.

In Larry's winter evening case, the hope of enhancing his reputation may lead him to stay late at the office and answer his colleague's questions. If this consultant tells others how helpful and knowledgeable Larry is, especially via the firm's informal networks, that may enhance his reputation. (It may also lead to further requests for knowledge sharing, one of the potential problems of being a successful seller.) If Larry's company formally tracks and rewards knowledge sharing, the likelihood of his cooperation leading to some future tangible benefit will increase.

Altruism

It is possible, of course, that Larry may just be a nice guy who wants to help out whether or not he gets anything beyond a "thank you" in return. Or he may be so passionate about his knowledge that he is happy to share it whenever he gets a chance. Such people do exist (whether or not Larry happens to be one of them). Many knowledge sharers are motivated in part by a love of their subject and to some degree by altruism. Altruism, whether "for the good of the firm" or based on a natural impulse to help others, does exist.

We all know individuals who simply like helping. (We also know some who don't.)

Mentoring is a form of knowledge transfer based, in part, on altruism. Erik Erickson, among others, has pointed out that people go through a "generative stage" (usually in later middle age) when it becomes important and valuable to them to pass on what they have learned to others. Firms cannot create this impulse, but they do have the power to encourage or discourage it. Formally recognizing mentoring relationships, giving managers time to pass on their knowledge, and understanding that experienced employees *have* valuable knowledge are ways to foster mentoring. Many firms ignore the contribution that older workers can make to their younger colleagues, because they have no way of evaluating or efficiently capturing exactly what it is that the older worker actually *knows*. An interesting exception is occurring at Chrysler Corporation, where it is well understood that master mechanics and engineers have a stock of productive knowledge that is essential to the firm's viability. With many of these individuals approaching retirement age, Chrysler is constructing a "book of knowledge"—an easily accessible interactive electronic system which will allow younger mechanics and engineers to benefit from at least a representation of what these craftsmen know. The book of knowledge will be a kind of formalized mentoring tool.

Altruism is real and can be encouraged. It is constrained, though, by increasing demands on the time and energy of employees and by cultural factors: C.B. MacPherson argues that our national culture is characterized by "possessive individualism." It clearly doesn't make sense to depend entirely on goodwill to motivate something as important as knowledge sharing.

SOME NECESSARY MARKET CONDITIONS

Markets cannot function without some sort of price system: If potential buyers and sellers have no agreed-upon currency of exchange (whether monetary or not), then market transactions will not take place. Scarcity is also a necessary condition of a functioning market.

Scarcity

We have already seen that the scarcity of time and energy affects the knowledge market. Scarcity of knowledge is also an essential factor. If Larry's caller already knew everything he needs to know about the client, he would not ask for help. If Larry's time and energy were infinite, he would be willing to give his knowledge away for nothing. Doing so would involve no measurable loss to him. Like all other markets, the knowledge market assumes and reflects the scarcity of things exchanged. Without scarcity, markets need not exist. No one will pay for—and therefore no one can sell—an item that is available universally and without restriction. There is no market for air and sunlight at the beach; there is a market for beach umbrellas because shade is in short supply. (In Mexico City, people pay to enter air pavilions because clean air is becoming scarce.) Specialization and the natural limits of any one person's experience and learning create scarcity in the knowledge market. Especially in lean or downsized organizations, this scarcity is a fact of life: The need for knowledge grows as fewer people try to do more things more quickly; time to learn and teach, always in short supply, becomes especially scarce and precious.

Trust

Trust[6] trumps the other factors that affect the efficiency of knowledge markets. Without trust, knowledge initiatives will fail, regardless of how thoroughly they are supported by technology and rhetoric and even if the survival of the organization depends on effective knowledge transfer. For the knowledge market to operate in an organization:

1. Trust must be visible. The members of the organization must see people get credit for knowledge sharing. They must directly experience reciprocity. There must be direct evidence of trust; a declaration of the importance of trust in the corporate mission statement is not sufficient.
2. Trust must be ubiquitous. If part of the internal knowledge market is untrustworthy, the market becomes asymmetric and less efficient.
3. Trustworthiness must exist at the top. Trust tends to flow downwards through organizations. Upper management's example can often define the norms and values of the firm. If top managers are trustworthy, trust will seep through and come to characterize the whole firm; if they are not, distrust will propagate throughout. Their values become known to the firm through signals, signs, and symbols.

Personal contact and trust are intimately related. The U.S. Army recognizes what it calls "face time" as an essential element in building trust within groups. They measure it as one of the determinants of successful teamwork. In addition to being a necessary condition for knowledge exchange, trust can be a product of it as well. British Petroleum's Virtual Teamworking pilot project succeeded because of the atmosphere of mutual trust established by management, the VT project team, and the participants. Face-to-face meetings among participants established rapport. The frequent video conferences during which knowledge was exchanged actually increased the level of trust and led to measurable improvements in honoring commitments to meet the delivery dates of promised work.

Trust is an essential condition of a functioning knowledge market, as it is of any market that does not depend on binding and enforceable contracts. Of course, even transactions bound by written contracts depend to some degree on trust. Buying a new car, we need to trust the dealer enough to believe that he is representing his product reasonably accurately (not foisting off a used car as a new one, for instance), that he will deliver the car as promised, and that he will be available to resolve problems after the sale. If he reneges, we have recourse to the courts to require him to meet the terms of the contract or return our money. When we buy the car on credit, the seller or the bank handling the loan must assure themselves that we are trustworthy enough not to default.

---

6. An interesting analysis of trust as an economic and social value is Francis Fukuyama's *Trust: The Social Virtues and the Creation of Prosperity* (London, U.K.: Penguin Press, 1995).

The knowledge market—with no written contracts and no court to appeal to—is very much based on credit, not cash. The word "credit" means "to believe" or "to trust" and mutual trust is at the heart of knowledge exchange. When we sell knowledge within an organization, our receiving adequate payment now or in the future depends on the trustworthiness of the buyer and of management. In most cases, we will gain repute for a knowledge transaction only if the buyer gives us credit for it. If he pretends the knowledge was his all along, we gain nothing. If someone claims our research results as his own, we are no more likely to make any more of our knowledge available to him than we are to offer our house to someone who stole our car. A buyer who fails to give credit and recognize his debt to us is also unlikely to reciprocate when we need knowledge. Similarly, management that pays lip service to the value it attaches to knowledge sharing, but rewards employees who hoard knowledge will not create the level of trust needed to make the knowledge market effective.

The importance of trust in knowledge transactions—and the fact that reciprocity and repute are often the currency that pays for knowledge—helps explain why knowledge initiatives based solely on the belief that infrastructure creates communication seldom deliver the expected benefits. The impersonality of groupware that allows anyone to post information and invites anonymous access to that information does not, first of all, create the same confidence in the quality of knowledge that personal acquaintance and reputation can supply. The promise of reciprocity is also weak in such a system. The buyer who downloads an item from a server does not feel the same obligation to the provider that he would if he got the same material through a phone call or meeting. The most successful groupware systems are moderated and facilitated to assure that posted material is accurate and timely. Some have mechanisms for metering the use of posted items and crediting or rewarding the suppliers.

Market Signals

By "market signals" we mean information that indicates where knowledge actually *is* in the organization and how to gain access to it. Accessibility is another way of looking at cost, since it is a measure of the time and effort that need to be expended to get knowledge—to connect buyer and seller. There are formal and informal signals in knowledge markets. The informal ones are generally more accurate guides to where knowledge can be "bought."

Position and Education

Title or position is the most common formal signal indicating who has or should have valuable knowledge. If we need to learn about a particular research project, it seems to make sense to go to the project manager; if we need to know what is happening in marketing, why not ask the director of the Marketing Department? This approach sometimes works, but not at all consistently. The organizational chart is generally not a very effective guide to company knowledge. The project director may know a lot, but be unwilling to share his knowledge. He may have had no direct involvement with the aspects of the project we need to understand. It may be that the marketing director once knew a lot about marketing but now mainly knows about the politics of running a marketing department. It is possible he never was a marketing expert and has been successful thanks to managerial or other skills. Clearly, advancement within a firm is not solely based on knowledge, even tacit or social knowledge. There are other key variables such as drive, ambition, energy, intuition, judgment, ego (or lack thereof), and luck. The expert who knows exactly what we need to learn and would be willing to tell us may be sitting in one of the cubicles we pass on the way to the director's office. The trick is to know which one.

Education is a similar formal market signal that may or may not be helpful. If Lorraine has a Ph.D. in a subject we need to find out about, it is logical to go to her: She is a subject matter expert and has the credentials to prove it. ("Credentials," like "credit," comes from a root meaning "to believe.") She may in fact have just the knowledge we want, but it is possible that Lorraine hasn't learned anything new since she defended her thesis a couple of decades ago. Or her knowledge may be too academic to apply usefully to a practical situation. Or, again, she may not be willing to tell us what she knows.

Informal Networks

Probably the best knowledge market signals—though they are still imperfect—flow through the informal networks of practice that develop in organizations. Within these webs, people ask each other who knows what—who has provided knowledge in the past that turned out to be reliable and useful. If the person you ask where to go for specific knowledge doesn't know an appropriate seller, she probably knows someone who does know. Much of the work that goes on in firms gets done because people are continually asking one another, through informal networks, who knows how to do things. The informal networks of buyers, brokers, and sellers move knowledge through the organization. Knowledge markets clump around formal and informal networks, so providing information about these networks is a good way to make knowledge visible.

Informal networks have the benefits and drawbacks of their informality. Because they function through personal contact and word-of-mouth, they engender the trust that is an essential engine of successful knowledge exchange. A recommendation that comes from someone we know and respect or is "known" and respected within the firm is more likely to lead us to a trustworthy seller with appropriate knowledge than a cold call based on the organizational chart or corporate phone directory. Such informal networks are also very dynamic and fast. Because they consist of people more-or-less continually in communication with each other, they tend to update themselves as conditions change: People share information about who has left the company or moved to new projects, who has recently shown themselves to be surprisingly useful sources of knowledge and who has become unexpectedly reticent. Notable changes and events touch off a chain of conversation that quickly spreads the news. If this sounds a lot like gossip, it is. Most corporate gossip is a form of knowledge transfer concerning internal processes. Gossip in the work place—often considered wasted time—is the way the company's knowledge network updates itself. More formal systems, such as printed as well as electronic repositories of employee skills and interests, begin to go out of date as soon as they are established and generally lack the interactivity that makes informal networks work.

The main disadvantage of these networks is that, by being informal and undocumented, they are not reliably available to all the people who need them. Their working depends on chance conversations and connections that work well sometimes but at other times do not happen at all. Imagine that information about new cars (or restaurants) came only through similar informal networks because advertisements, articles, and reviews did not exist. We would have to depend entirely on advice from acquaintances. They would sometimes give us valuable, authentic information, but it would be limited to their own experience or the experience of people they know well, usually a very small sample. The informal network may help us avoid some bad decisions but it would not give us the full spectrum of choices in our area. To get even a reasonably wide range of recommendations we would have to spend a good deal of time following the branches of personal, undocumented connections.

COMMUNITIES OF PRACTICE

Sometimes people who have complementary knowledge and related knowledge needs will form themselves into a group. The group is self-organized in that it is not created by managerial mandate and may not even begin with the intention of becoming a group. It is likely to start as individuals who communicate with each other because they share common work practices, interests, or aims. They are often called a "community of practice."[7] If their communications prove useful over time, the individuals may formalize the arrangement, giving themselves a group name and establishing a regular system of interchange. A number of British Petroleum scientists and engineers with a shared interest in water produced as a by-product of drilling formed themselves into a group that eventually communicated through e-mail, newsletters, and occasional meetings. The Produced-Water Group later became one of the BP Exploration Virtual Teamworking pilot groups and used VT video-conferencing technology to enrich the closeness of their interaction. Similarly, the people involved in CitiCorp Bank's commercial lending ac-

---

7. John Seely Brown of Xerox and researchers at the Institute for Research on Learning have developed and discussed the idea of communities of practice.

tivities in the Southeast Asian region organized themselves into a group so they could pool expertise and solve problems together.

Too literal an application of reengineering principles, with their emphasis on efficiency, has weakened some of these informal knowledge networks and groups by driving out the "slack" necessary for informal networks and groups to function well. A reengineered organization is likely to have eliminated the jobs of some of the knowledge brokers whose role is not recognized as essential to the firm's work, though they hold the knowledge networks together. By focussing on measurable "work" and underestimating the value of talk, reengineering can discourage the conversations and self-forming groups in which so much of the firm's knowledge work gets done.

KNOWLEDGE MARKET INEFFICIENCIES

In efficient markets, buyers and sellers find each other and exchange their goods readily. Because a clear pricing system exists, they agree on the value of the goods being sold with the least possible friction. They have identical or similar ideas of the value of the currency used to buy them. In practice, efficient markets generate the most good at the least cost. Markets for knowledge, however, are notably inefficient in most organizations. The right seller is often hard to locate and hard to get to even if her location is known. It is difficult if not impossible to judge the quality of knowledge before "purchasing" it. Both the knowledge value and likelihood of payment are uncertain.

To get a feel for the inefficiencies of the knowledge market, think of it in comparison to the market for new cars. In the car market, it is easy to get information about the sellers and products. All car dealers are listed in the yellow pages. Newspapers are full of information about what cars are available, where they can be bought, and what they cost. In many cases, a buyer will have a choice of vendors for the same product. *Consumer Reports* and a host of other publications provide detailed independent evaluations of cars and reveal dealer costs. Shoppers have opportunities to examine and test cars before they buy. Both the product and the currency used to purchase it are tangible and have clearly definable value. A written contract defines what is being bought and how much is to be paid for it. Warranties and lemon laws protect the buyer if the product is defective. Sellers have legal remedies available to them if the buyer fails to pay. It is clear exactly what the buyer and seller hope to gain from the transaction.

Knowledge markets are obviously much murkier. The value of the knowledge is rarely as tangible or explicit as the value of a car. There are no *Consumer Reports* articles on knowledge sellers and brokers. As our discussion of the price system makes clear, payment is much less certain and less tangible than in the new car market. Information about where knowledge resides in the organization is highly imperfect. Much of the current interest in knowledge management has derived from the fact that organizations do not have good information about where their knowledge is and therefore have difficulty getting it and making use of it. Also, the written contracts, guarantees, and legal system that protect buyers and sellers in the automotive market are generally not part of the internal market for knowledge.

As our discussion so far suggests, the **incompleteness** of information about the knowledge market is a principal cause of its inefficiency. Remember that much of the interest in knowledge management has been driven by the realization that firms do not know where to find their own existing knowledge. The lack of knowledge maps or knowledge "yellow pages" to guide a knowledge buyer to a seller is a fundamental problem. The absence of explicit information about the pricing structure is also a source of inefficiency, with knowledge transactions inhibited by uncertainty about what the likely return on shared knowledge will be.

The **asymmetry** of knowledge in organizations also contributes to market inefficiency. There often is abundant knowledge on a subject in one department and a shortage somewhere else. Marketing may have extensive knowledge about a particular set of customers that sales needs but lacks. Strategic knowledge that resides at the top may not be available to the middle managers who are expected to embody that knowledge in action. A certain amount of asymmetry must exist in any market. As we have said, markets cannot exist without scarcity. But strong asymmetry means knowledge will not get where it is needed. Buyers and sellers won't meet. There are always knowledge feasts and famines in organizations. As is true of other kinds of famines, the problem usually has more to do with information patterns, purchasing power, and distribution systems than with an absolute scarcity.

The **localness** of knowledge also inhibits knowledge market efficiency, especially in large organizations. People usually get knowledge from their organizational neighbors. The knowledge market depends on trust and individuals generally trust the people they know; face-to-face meetings are often the best way to get knowledge; and, as we have said, reliable information about more distant knowledge sources is usually not available. Also, mechanisms for getting access to distant knowledge tend to be weak or non-existent. People will buy whatever knowledge the person in the next office may have, rather than deal with the effort and uncertainty of trying to discover who in the company may know more. Simon and March use the term "satisficing" to describe the human tendency to settle for the knowledge or information that is "good enough" for their purposes. They balance the quality of what they get against the effort they must expend to get it. Knowledge initiatives will run into problems if they are based on the assumption that individuals will go to considerable lengths to get the best possible knowledge, an assumption that is not borne out in practice.[8] Localness adds to market inefficiency because it causes people to make do with less than optimal knowledge, while a much better "product" is unsold and unused because the unbridged distance between buyer and seller prevents a transaction from taking place. The realities of limited time and energy and uncertainty about how much better that distant knowledge is prevent a transaction from taking place.

---

8. March and Simon, op. cit.

CASE IN POINT: JAVELIN DEVELOPMENT CORPORATION

Javelin Development Corporation,[9] a real but disguised engineering and construction company, developed a plan to make knowledge available across projects in hopes of reducing construction time and costs by applying existing design solutions to new situations. The centerpiece of the initiative was an online knowledge warehouse that engineers could draw from as they developed their designs. A year after implementation began, less than 15 percent of the planned features were in place and support for the initiative seemed to be fading.

The disappointing results can be analyzed in terms of knowledge market inefficiencies. Chief among them was the lack of a clear price paid to individuals who shared their knowledge. Having been through a period of layoffs and fearing that more were coming, employees saw their unique knowledge as a source of job security and felt that sharing it would weaken their position. Although management supported knowledge-sharing in a general way, its actions did not communicate assurance that sharing knowledge was genuinely important and would be rewarded. For instance, employees were expected to learn on their own time (not during office hours), a company norm that implied that acquiring knowledge was less important than "real work." The knowledge initiative had verbal support but was not backed with a sufficient investment of money and personnel. Some designated knowledge facilitators spent only ten percent of their time on the project. No mechanism was put in place for making knowledge sharing a criterion for performance evaluation. As a result of all these signals, trust in the genuineness of corporate commitment to knowledge exchange was low.

Also, the knowledge warehouse proved not to be a very effective marketplace. Potential sellers felt they gained little from adding to the stock of online knowledge. Potential buyers did not like the way warehouse content was organized. Project designers had favored a rather loosely structured organization so that knowledge would not be forced into old categories. But the engineers who were the intended users of the system favored a hierarchical system that would make it easy for them to find just the information they needed to solve a specific problem.

With uncertainty and skepticism about the value of offering or acquiring knowledge, lukewarm management support, and a marketplace poorly matched to the habits of potential buyers, the knowledge market at Javelin could not function efficiently. In fact, the company has not yet begun to see the benefits it hoped to get from its knowledge project.

---

9. For additional detail, see "Implementing Knowledge Management at Javelin Development Corporation," a 1996 case study prepared by David De Long at the Ernst & Young Center for Business Innovation.

KNOWLEDGE MARKET PATHOLOGIES

Some knowledge markets have deep flaws that we call knowledge market pathologies: distortions that drastically inhibit the flow of knowledge. The pathologies described below overlap to some extent, but the distinctions suggested by the analogies to external markets may help identify and explain serious knowledge market problems in organizations.

Monopolies and Cartels

If widely important knowledge is held by only one person or group, a knowledge monopoly exists. The effect is similar to that of monopolies in the market for goods and services: the knowledge will come at a high price because there is no competition to moderate it. Everyone who has worked in an organization knows individuals who have exclusive ownership or control of key corporate knowledge and use that fact to establish a position of power and control. Such a person may "rent" his expertise to accomplish a task or solve a problem rather than sell his knowledge—even at a high price—since his monopoly will cease to exist once his knowledge is genuinely shared. (In this regard, a knowledge monopoly is different from a monopoly on goods or services.) The drawbacks for the organization are obvious. Important knowledge locked in a monopoly will not always be available when and where it is needed to benefit the company. It will also be held back from the interplay of knowledge that can generate new knowledge. According to Nonaka and Takeuchi, authors of *The Knowledge-Creating Company,* one of the conditions that encourage knowledge creation is "redundancy," which they describe as shared information that allows individuals to "invade" each other's boundaries and offer advice and a new perspective.[10] The idea of redundancy is clearly the antithesis of monopolistic thinking.

If the owner of important knowledge leaves the firm, the effect can be devastating. Knowledge monopolists have negotiated very lucrative severance agreements in exchange for knowledge that their employers must have almost literally at all costs.

Artificial Scarcity

A knowledge monopoly can be seen as one form of artificial scarcity. In general, a corporate culture in which knowledge hoarding is the norm creates scarcity. Knowledge becomes very expensive, not because it doesn't exist but because

---

10. Ikujiro Nonaka and Hirotaka Takeuchi, *The Knowledge-Creating Company* (New York, NY: Oxford University Press, 1995), p. 81.

it is hard to get at. Departments and groups may lack the knowledge they need to work effectively because the hoarding culture keeps it scarce.

Downsizing can create real knowledge scarcity by an artificial means by eliminating employees whose absence shows them to be owners of essential knowledge. The cost of scarcity is high, leading to failed processes or the expense of luring back the laid off knowledge workers or buying the equivalent of their knowledge from outside sources. Jonathan Low, Deputy Assistant Secretary of Labor for Work and Technology Policy under Robert Reich, describes the aerospace companies that offered buyout packages as part of their downsizing programs and saw knowledge walk out the door with employees who took the offer. The companies had to rehire the same people they had encouraged to leave.[11]

Trade Barriers

Organizational markets are hampered by a variety of trade barriers. The hoarding that characterizes monopolies and artificial scarcity is a barrier erected by the possessiveness of the hoarding individual or department. The not-invented-here mentality that refuses to accept new knowledge is a mirror image of the barrier created by hoarding, a refusal to buy knowledge rather than a refusal to sell it. A variation on knowledge hoarding and the not-invented-here barrier is what we might call a class barrier: an unwillingness to give knowledge to or accept it from people in the organization who are perceived to have relatively low status. An instructive experiment some years ago involved providing an executive with information on a subject from a variety of sources: the corporate librarian, the IT department, and a senior strategist. Though the librarian's information was objectively the best (and was identified as best by managers who were not told from where it came), the executive judged the strategist's information the most valuable, his judgment influenced by his opinion of the sources.

A barrier—in fact, a trade ban—is sometimes established by an executive who has the power to enforce a corporate orthodoxy by forbidding discussion of subjects that threaten it. Ken Olsen, the founder of Digital Equipment Corporation, insisted that the word "PC" and the concepts behind it could not be mentioned at DEC, closing off the possibility of work in an area that should have been getting attention. Rather than face the challenge of microcomputer open systems, he tried to pretend that it did not exist and, by doing so, damaged the company. Digital employees were powerless to respond to a threat that they were not allowed to discuss.

There is also a set of trade barriers that result from not having a good knowledge-transfer infrastructure or effective market mechanisms. An obvious example is the lack of an effective computer network or communications system. Without the technology needed to codify knowledge and make it or information about it available, knowledge transactions will be limited and local. The lack of

---

11. From a conversation between Jon Low and Don Cohen, August, 1996.

virtual and real places for buyers and sellers to meet is an infrastructure problem, as is the absence of time for knowledge-seeking, knowledge generation, and knowledge exchange. Both downsizing and reengineering, which tend to reduce the time available to look for and share knowledge, are likely to damage the knowledge market infrastructure.

The infrastructure of knowledge exchange is an essential component of the knowledge market, and many techniques for improving knowledge market efficiency have to do with infrastructure improvements.

IMPROVING KNOWLEDGE MARKET EFFICIENCY

Technology

Technological developments and innovations have the potential to change market dynamics dramatically. In 1400, Western Europe was a market backwater compared with the rich, active markets of the Chinese, Islamic, and Indian empires. It was Europe's development and use of the armed ship that forced open markets for them and shifted the balance of power so that, by 1600, market dominance had shifted to the West.[12]

There are many pitfalls and limitations in using electronic technology for knowledge work, especially the drawbacks of trying to force fluid knowledge into rigid data structures and the related danger of focusing too much on the system and not enough on content. But networks and desktop computers, with their ability to connect people and store and retrieve virtually unlimited amounts of content, can dramatically improve knowledge market efficiency, providing an infrastructure for moving knowledge and information about knowledge and building virtual knowledge marketplaces.

Some organizations have developed electronic knowledge "yellow pages" to provide better information about where knowledge resides in the firm and how to get it. BP's Virtual Teamworking project is, in effect, an effort to expand the definition of "local" or reduce the difference between local and distant by linking team members electronically. A co-worker you can reach (and talk to and see) by clicking a button on your computer monitor may seem more "local" than someone three floors up in your own building, although he is physically one thousand miles away.

Building *Marketplaces*

Recognizing knowledge exchange as a market activity leads to common-sense strategies that can make the market more robust. One is to create market-

---

12. See Carlos Cipolla's *Guns, Sails, and Empire* (Manhattan, KS: Sunflower University Press, 1992).

places—physical and virtual spaces dedicated to knowledge exchange. The rationale is the same as for the sale of goods and services: buying and selling are human activities; people need a place to meet so they can carry them out. The ancient Greek Agora and Roman Forum, places of assembly for political discussion and decision, sharing of the day's news, and buying and selling of goods, provide a striking image of the importance of a public space for the human interactions needed to make a society (or an organization) function. Tellingly, NationsBank gave the name "Project Agora" to an internal knowledge project.

Many Japanese firms, including Dai-Ichi Pharmaceuticals (which one of the authors visited), have established "talk rooms" where researchers are expected to have a cup of tea and spend twenty minutes or half an hour discussing each other's work. There is no agenda set for a talk room and no conference table, only an expectation that the talk shared by colleagues will benefit them and the company. Talk rooms are formalized and sanctioned locations for conversation that, in American companies, more often happen at the water cooler, coffee machine, or cafeteria.

Several organizations have held knowledge fairs at which knowledge sellers display their expertise and buyers can search for what they need or serendipitously find knowledge that they did not know they needed but can use. Like a trade show or farmers' market, a knowledge fair is a temporary gathering of sellers that attracts potential buyers. One of the authors visited such a fair held by CSIRO in Australia. The energy created by the meeting—often for the first time—of researchers and managers was tangible. Perhaps the most frequently heard comment was, "I didn't know we had people doing *that!*"

Corporate universities and live and electronic forums that bring people together to consider subjects of mutual interest are another kind of knowledge marketplace. Although they are typically more structured than a knowledge fair, the successful ones leave time and space for participants to talk to each other. As much or more valuable knowledge exchange is likely to happen in the hallway between participants than from the podium.

Electronic knowledge markets such as the Internet, intranet discussion groups, and groupware databases have much the same advantages and drawbacks as commercial electronic shopping. The plusses are convenience and choice, with desktop access to a vast variety of material. The downside is variable quality and a lack of personal contact that tends to reduce trust and commitment. In the electronic home shopping industry, the result is a lot more browsing than buying. In the electronic knowledge market, it is likely to mean a devaluing of online knowledge. Online knowledge is likely to be ignored or treated with suspicion, unless it has been evaluated and edited by a respected online broker.

Implicit in building a marketplace—even an electronic one—is the need to give members of the organization enough time to shop for knowledge, or sell it. A Catch-22 of the corporate world is that employees are too busy working to take time to learn things that will help them work more efficiently. Engineers may spend weeks or months solving a problem because they can't find the time to ask if anyone else in the company has dealt with it before. If a company's most valuable, influential employees are the very ones who are too busy to attend a knowledge fair or forum, then the knowledge market is not working well.

CREATING AND DEFINING KNOWLEDGE MARKET VALUE

Lack of good information is one of the causes of market inefficiency. As in the Javelin case, the absence of reliable information about the value attached to sharing knowledge (or evidence that the value is low) will reduce market activity. The most reliable information is empirical; direct evidence of employees being recognized, promoted, and otherwise rewarded for sharing knowledge is the clearest proof that an attractive price system exists. A firm's investment in knowledge exchange is another kind of empirical evidence that it genuinely values knowledge. Putting highly-regarded people in knowledge-enabling jobs (rather than making those jobs the part-time responsibility of employees who don't have much else to do), holding fairs and forums, and giving people time to learn and exchange knowledge are forms of commitment that show the value attached to knowledge much more effectively than a mission statement. "Put your money where your mouth is" or "walk the talk" is appropriate advice for developing a healthy knowledge market.

A number of consulting companies have made knowledge-sharing one of the basic criteria of the performance evaluation process, which is yet another concrete demonstration that a reasonable market price will be paid for knowledge. It is a response to the fact that recognized and rewarded behaviors will flourish while those that are ignored or penalized will wither.

Unambiguous demonstrations of the value of knowledge sharing is one aspect of developing an organizational culture that creates knowledge consumer and provider confidence. We repeat that an atmosphere of trust is the most important factor. It is essential that employees trust that other participants in the knowledge market will reciprocate and give appropriate credit, that management will not only say it values knowledge sharing but will reward it both now and in the future.

Knowledge evangelists can also help establish a thriving knowledge market. Enthusiastic, talented managers who are committed to knowledge work and can effectively make the case for it to senior management can have an important impact. When knowledge management work gets its power and authority from one person, though, its existence may be precarious, especially at the beginning. If the manager leaves or is assigned to a new, demanding task, the knowledge project may well collapse.

Non-Market Benefits

The direct benefits of an efficient knowledge market accrue to both the firm as a whole and its employees as individuals. When knowledge flows freely, its potential value is made actual. Productivity increases and innovations spring from the timely application of existing knowledge and the generation of new ideas in the knowledge marketplace. Knowledge buyers, sellers, and brokers get the knowledge they need to do their work well and get appropriate "payment" for knowledge they share in the form of recognition and advancement.

A thriving knowledge market also creates benefits that are peripheral to the principal market aim of making knowledge available when and where it is needed. These gains, which we call non-market benefits, also contribute to the success of the firm.

More Satisfied Workforce

A healthy knowledge market means that employees see that their expertise is valued and acted on and know that others in the organization will cooperate with them when they need expert assistance. They may be more satisfied with their work and work harder than those frustrated by lack of communication, wasted effort, and uninformed decisions. Employee cynicism ("This company never does anything right"; "They never ask the people who really know"; "The empty suits get the promotions.") can have a devastating effect on corporate success.

Corporate Coherence[13]

An active exchange of information and ideas in an atmosphere of openness and trust makes it possible for employees at all levels to understand what is happening in the company. Walsh and Ungson in part define an organization as "a network of . . . shared meanings."[14] A shared awareness of corporate goals and strategies gives individuals cues for directing their own work toward a cooperative goal and makes them feel that their work is meaningful as part of a larger aim. Nonaka and Takeuchi touch on this point when they talk about the importance of making individuals aware of an overall "organizational intention."[15] Kao, Japan's largest household and chemical products maker, values corporate coherence so highly that any meeting in the company, including top-management meetings, is open to any employee. The meetings have the potential to be extremely open knowledge marketplaces. As Nonaka and Takeuchi remark, "Through this practice, top management can acquire insights from those most familiar with the issues at hand, while employees can gain a better understanding of the general corporate policy."[16]

13. David Teece has written on this subject.
14. Quoted by Karl Weick, *Sensemaking in Organizations* (Thousand Oaks: Sage Publications, 1995), p. 38
15. Nonaka and Takeuchi, op. cit., p. 75.
16. Ibid. p. 173.

Creation of a Richer Knowledge Stock

Knowledge markets are unlike markets for goods in that every sale increases the total stock of knowledge in the organization. The seller both keeps his knowledge and gives it away; more importantly, the transaction itself often generates new knowledge. Newly acquired knowledge interacts with existing knowledge to spark ideas that neither the buyer nor seller has had before. One of the major sources of new knowledge is *fusion*, the bringing together of people with different ideas to work on the same problem.

A knowledge transaction, especially a face-to-face exchange, tests the validity of knowledge offered. Knowledge is seldom passively received. It is evaluated by the buyer and then tested in action, since the purchase probably was made to meet a specific need. So an active knowledge market continually validates and refines organizational knowledge.

Countering Orthodoxy and Rigid Hierarchies

A genuinely open knowledge market will test official beliefs and expose the flaws of the faulty ones before they can do much damage. If Ken Olsen had not been able to dominate the knowledge market at Digital, the company's response to changes in the computer industry would probably have come sooner and been more effective. At Polaroid, Edwin Land's insistence that Polavision (an instant movie film) would be an important product inhibited discussion almost to the point of crippling that company. Dr. Wang's exertion of control over knowledge concerning the future direction of the computer industry had a similar effect at Wang Labs.

Knowledge markets tend to break down or circumvent hierarchies, much as the emerging middle classes in Europe began eroding the power of the church and aristocracy in the 16th century. They follow networks of knowers, not the architecture of a reporting structure. Knowledgeable people exist at all levels in organizations. The knowledge market has its own shifting hierarchy based on who knows what and how helpful they are. A healthy, undistorted market is a meritocracy of ideas. Talking about Apple Computer during its most creative years, Steve Jobs said, "It doesn't make sense to hire smart people and then tell them what to do; we hired smart people so they could tell us what to do."

THINKING IN MARKET TERMS

Even familiar markets for material goods are complex and difficult to analyze and influence. The knowledge market, less tangible and not seen *as* a market until now, is no easier to understand. But applying what we do know about markets to knowledge exchange in organizations gives us an important grounding in the reality of why exchange does and doesn't happen. In giving us some tools to understand knowledge transfer, in showing what really drives transfer, it gives us the means to improve it. In fact, all knowledge management can be fruitfully analyzed as efforts to increase the efficiency of knowledge markets.

11

A System of Profound Knowledge[1]

W. Edwards Deming

AIM OF THIS CHAPTER

The prevailing style of management must undergo transformation. The transformation requires profound knowledge. The individual components of the system, instead of being competitive, will for optimization reinforce each other for accomplishment of the aim of the system. The same transformation is required in government and in education.

The system of profound knowledge provides a lens. It provides a new map of theory by which to understand and optimize the organizations that we work in, and thus to make a contribution to the whole country.

As a good rule, profound knowledge comes from the outside, and by invitation. A system cannot understand itself. The transformation will require leaders.

A company that seeks the help of profound knowledge is already poised for the transformation.

The aim of this chapter is to present to the reader a system of profound knowledge. A later chapter will describe a leader.

THE FIRST STEP

The first step is transformation of the individual. This transformation is discontinuous. It comes from an understanding of the system of profound knowl-

---

1. The text here on profound knowledge is in large part the work of Dr. Barbara Lawton. Figure 11.1, with the bowling team and the orchestra, is hers. I am deeply indebted also to Dr. Nida Backaitis for much help.

Reprinted from *The New Economics for Industry, Government, Education* by W. Edwards Deming by permission of MIT and The W. Edwards Deming Institute. Published by MIT, Center for Advanced Educational Services, Cambridge, MA 02139. Copyright 1993 by The W. Edwards Deming Institute.

edge. The individual, transformed, will perceive new meaning to his life, to events, to numbers, to interactions between people.

Once the individual understands the system of profound knowledge, he will apply its principles in every kind of relationship with other people. He will have a basis for judgment of his own decisions and for transformation of the organizations that he belongs to. The individual, once transformed, will:

Set an example
Be a good listener, but will not compromise
Continually teach other people
Help people to pull away from their current practice and beliefs and move
    into the new philosophy without a feeling of guilt about the past

The word *metanoia* (me ta' no ia) is more suitable than transformation. Metanoia is a Greek word which means penitence, repentance, reorientation of one's way of life, spiritual conversion. Transformation means change of form, shape, or appearance. (*Oxford English Dictionary*, 2d edition, vol. ix, Clarendon Press, Oxford, 1989.)[2]

A SYSTEM OF PROFOUND KNOWLEDGE

The layout of profound knowledge appears here in four parts, all related to each other:

- Appreciation for a system
- Knowledge about variation
- Theory of knowledge
- Psychology

One need not be eminent in any part of profound knowledge in order to understand it and to apply it. The 14 points for management in industry, education, and government follow naturally as application of the system of profound knowledge, for transformation from the present style of Western management to one of optimization.

PRELIMINARY REMARKS

The various segments of the system of profound knowledge cannot be separated. They interact with each other. Thus, knowledge of psychology is incomplete without knowledge of variation. A manager of people needs to understand that all people are different. This is not ranking people. He needs to understand

2. This suggestion comes from Dr. Eulogio Romero-Simpson.

that the performance of anyone is governed largely by the system that he works in, the responsibility of management. A psychologist that possesses even a crude understanding of variation as will be learned in the experiment with the Red Beads could no longer participate in refinement of a plan for ranking people.

Further illustrations of entwinement of psychology and use of the theory of variation (statistical theory) are boundless. For example, the number of defective items that an inspector finds depends on the size of the work load presented to him (documented by Harold E. Dodge in the Bell Telephone Laboratories around 1926). An inspector, careful not to penalize anybody unjustly, may pass an item that is just outside the borderline. The inspector in the illustration on page 265 of the same book, to save the jobs of 300 people, held the proportion of defective items below 10 percent. She was in fear for their jobs.

A teacher, not wishing to penalize anyone unjustly, will pass a pupil that is barely below the requirement for a passing grade.

Fear invites wrong figures. Bearers of bad news fare badly. To keep his job, anyone may present to his boss only good news.

A committee appointed by the president of a company will report what the president wishes to hear. Would they dare report otherwise?

An individual may inadvertently seek to cast a halo about himself. He may report to an interviewer in a study of readership that he reads in the *New York Times,* when actually this morning he bought and read a tabloid.

Statistical calculations and predictions based on warped figures may lead to confusion, frustration, and wrong decisions.

Accounting-based measures of performance drive employees to achieve targets of sales, revenue, and costs, by manipulation of processes, and by flattery or delusive promises to cajole a customer into purchase of what he does not need (adapted from the book by Thomas H. Johnson, *Relevance Regained,* The Free Press, 1992).

A leader of transformation, and managers involved, need to learn the psychology of individuals, the psychology of a group, the psychology of society, and the psychology of change.

Some understanding of variation, including appreciation of a stable system, and some understanding of special causes and common causes of variation, are essential for management of a system, including management of people.

A SYSTEM

What Is a System?

As we learned in Chapter 3, a system is a network of interdependent components that work together to try to accomplish the aim of the system. A system must have an aim. Without an aim, there is no system.

We learned also in Chapter 3 that a system must be managed. We learned that optimization is a process of orchestrating the efforts of all components toward achievement of the stated aim.

Interdependence

The greater the interdependence between components, the greater will be the need for communication and cooperation between them. Also, the greater will be the need for overall management. Figure 11.1 illustrates degree of interdependence, from low to high.

Failure of management to comprehend interdependence between components is in fact the cause of loss from use of M.B.O. in practice. The efforts of the various divisions in a company, each given a job, are not additive. Their efforts are interdependent. One division, to achieve its goals, may, left to itself, kill off another division. Peter Drucker is clear on this point.[3]

An example of a system, well optimized, is a good orchestra. The players are not there to play solos as prima donnas, each one trying to catch the ear of the listener. They are there to support each other. Individually, they need not be the best players in the country.

Thus, each of the 140 players in the Royal Philharmonic Orchestra of London is there to support the other 139 players. An orchestra is judged by listeners, not so much by illustrious players, but by the way they work together. The conductor, as manager, begets cooperation between the players, as a system, every player to support the others. There are other aims for an orchestra, such as joy in work for the players and for the conductor.

FIGURE 11.1 Interdependence, from low to high.

Obligation of a Component

The obligation of any component is to contribute its best to the system, not to maximize its own production, profit, or sales, nor any other competitive measure. Some components may operate at a loss to themselves in order to optimize the whole system, including the components that take a loss.

Basis for Negotiation

Optimization for everyone concerned should be the basis for negotiation between any two people, between divisions, between union and management, be-

---

3. Peter Drucker, *Management Tasks, Responsibilities, Practices* (Harper & Row, 1973).

tween companies, between competitors, between countries. Everybody would gain.

The possibility of optimization is voided if one party goes into negotiation with the avowed aim to defend his rights, or if he makes a game of it, shifting position, or if he sets out with demands and stands firm on them with a time limit for assent.

The fruits of negotiation will be impaired if not demolished if one party drops out of the agreement to follow a path of selfish reward.

KNOWLEDGE ABOUT VARIATION

Life is Variation

Variation there will always be, between people, in output, in service, in product. What is the variation trying to tell us about a process, and about the people that work in it?

Need a teacher understand something about variation? Mr. Heero Hacquebord sent his six-year-old daughter to school. She came home in a few weeks with a note from the teacher with the horrible news that she had so far been given two tests, and this little girl was below average in both tests. Warning to the parents that trouble lies ahead. Other parents received the same note, and were worried. They wished to believe Mr. Hacquebord's words of comfort that such comparisons meant nothing, but they were afraid to. Other parents received notes. For example, your little boy was above average in both tests. Prepare for a genius coming up. Or, your little girl was above average on the first test, but sank to below average on the second test.

The little girl learned that she was below average in both tests. The news affected her adversely. She was humiliated, inferior. Her parents put her into a school that nourishes confidence. She recovered.

What if she had not recovered? A life lost. How many children were affected and had not the benefit of such supportive help? Nobody knows.

The teacher failed to observe that roughly half of her pupils will be above average on any test, and the other half below. Half of the people in any area will be above average for that area in test of cholesterol. There is not much that anyone can do about it.

When do data indicate that a process is stable, that the distribution of the output is predictable? Once a process has been brought into a state of statistical control, it has a definable capability. A process that is not in statistical control has not a definable capability: Its performance is not predictable.

There are two mistakes frequently made in attempts to improve results, both costly.

> Mistake 1. To react to an outcome as if it came from a special cause, when actually it came from common causes of variation.

Mistake 2. To treat an outcome as if it came from common causes of variation, when actually it came from a special cause.

Shewhart prescribed procedures aimed at minimum economic loss from the two mistakes.

Stable and Unstable States

A process may be in statistical control; it may not be. In the state of statistical control, the variation to expect in the future is predictable. Costs, performance, quality, and quantity are predictable. Shewhart called this the stable state. If the process is not stable, then it is unstable. Its performance is not predictable.

Management of people (leader, supervisor, teacher) is entirely different in the two states, stable and unstable. Confusion between the two states leads to calamity.

Management requires knowledge about interaction of forces. Interaction may reinforce efforts, or it may nullify efforts. Management of people requires knowledge of the effect of the system on the performance of people (Ch. 6). Knowledge of dependence and interdependence between people, groups, divisions, companies, countries, is helpful.

Use of data requires knowledge about the different sources of uncertainty. Measurement is a process. Is the system of measurement stable or unstable?

Use of data also requires understanding of the distinction between enumerative studies and analytic problems. An enumerative study produces information about a frame. The theory of sampling and design of experiments are enumerative studies. Our Census is an enumerative study. Another example is a shipload of iron ore. Buyer and seller need to know how much iron is on board.

The interpretation of results of a test or experiment is something else. It is prediction that a specific change in a process or procedure will be a wise choice, or that no change would be better. Either way the choice is prediction.

This is known as an analytic problem, or a problem of inference, prediction. Tests of significance, t-test, chi-square, are useless as inference—that is, useless for aid in prediction. Test of hypothesis has been for half a century a bristling obstruction to understanding statistical inference.

Question in a seminar. Please elaborate on your statement that profound knowledge comes from outside the system. Aren't the people in the system the only ones that know what is happening, and why?

Answer: The people that work in any organization know what they are doing, but they will not by themselves learn a better way. Their best efforts and hard work only dig deeper the pit that they are working in. Their best efforts and hard work do not provide an outside view of the organization.

Again, a system cannot understand itself. One may learn a lot about ice, yet know very little about water.

THEORY OF KNOWLEDGE[4]

Management Is Prediction

The theory of knowledge helps us to understand that management in any form is prediction. The simplest plan—how may I go home tonight—requires prediction that my automobile will start and run, or that the bus will come, or the train.

Knowledge Is Built on Theory

The theory of knowledge teaches us that a statement, if it conveys knowledge, predicts future outcome, with risk of being wrong, and that it fits without failure observations of the past.

Rational prediction requires theory and builds knowledge through systematic revision and extension of theory based on comparison of prediction with observation.

> *The barnyard rooster Chanticleer had a theory. He crowed every morning, putting forth all his energy, flapped his wings. The sun came up. The connexion was clear: His crowing caused the sun to come up. There was no question about his importance.*
>
> *There came a snag. He forgot one morning to crow. The sun came up anyhow. Crestfallen, he saw his theory in need of revision.*

Without his theory, he would have had nothing to revise, nothing to learn.

> *Plane Euclidean geometry served the world well for a flat earth. Every corollary and every theorem in the book is correct in its own world.*
>
> *Use of the theory for a flat earth fails on this earth when man extends his horizon to bigger buildings, and to roads that go beyond the village.*
>
> *Parallel lines with a north declination are not equidistant. The angles of a triangle do not add up to 1800. Spherical correction is required—a new geometry.*

It is extension of application that discloses inadequacy of a theory, and need for revision, or even new theory. Again, without theory, there is nothing to revise. Without theory, experience has no meaning. Without theory, one has no questions to ask. Hence without theory, there is no learning.

4. Clarence Irving Lewis, *Mind and the World-Order* (Scribner's, 1929). Reprinted by Dover Press, New York. My advice to a reader is start with Chs. 6, 7, or 8, not with page 1.

Theory is a window into the world. Theory leads to prediction. Without prediction, experience and examples teach nothing. To copy an example of success, without understanding it with the aid of theory, may lead to disaster.

Any rational plan, however simple, is prediction concerning conditions, behavior, performance of people, procedures, equipment, or materials.

Use of Data Requires Prediction

Interpretation of data from a test or experiment is prediction—what will happen on application of the conclusions or recommendations that are drawn from a test or experiment? This prediction will depend largely on knowledge of the subject matter. It is only in the state of statistical control that statistical theory provides, with a high degree of belief, prediction of performance in the immediate future.

An example is contained in the following conclusion, based on tests of two methods, A and B. I will continue to use Method A, and not change to Method B, because at this moment evidence that Method B will be dependably better in the future is not convincing.

A statement devoid of rational prediction does not convey knowledge.

No number of examples establishes a theory, yet a single unexplained failure of a theory requires modification or even abandonment of the theory.

No True Value

There is no true value of any characteristic, state, or condition that is defined in terms of measurement or observation. Change of procedure for measurement (change in operational definition) or observation produces a new number.

There is a true value of the number of prime numbers under 100. Just write them down, and count them—2, 3, 5, 7, 11. This is information, not knowledge. It predicts nothing except that anybody else would get the same number. Likewise, it is a fact—information—that the reader is reading these lines.

There is no true value of the number of people in a room. Whom do you count? Do we count someone that was here in this room, but is now outside on the telephone or drinking coffee? Do we count the people that work for the hotel? Do we count the people on the stage? the people managing the audio-visual equipment? If you change the rule for counting people, you come up with a new number.

> *The procedure will depend on the purpose. If our job is to prepare lunch for the people that will stay through lunch, then we need to count the people that will be here for lunch.*
>
> *If the problem is the total weight of the people in this room (are we in violation of fire regulations?), then we should count everybody in the room.*
>
> *There is no true value of the amount of iron in a shipload of iron ore. Why? Change of procedure for taking samples of the ore from the shipload will produce a new number for the proportion of iron in the iron ore. Repetition of any procedure will produce a new number.*
>
> *How would you count the people on boats in San Diego?*

There is no such thing as a fact concerning an empirical observation. Any two people may have different ideas about what is important to know about any event. Get the facts! Is there any meaning to this exhortation?

Communication and negotiation (as between customer and supplier, between management and union, between countries) require for optimization operational definitions. An operational definition is a procedure agreed upon for translation of a concept into measurement of some kind.

Operational Definitions: An Example

Dr. Mary Leitnaker, Professor of Statistics at the University of Tennessee at Knoxville, uses a simple exercise in her teaching of operational definitions. She goes to the grocery store and buys half a dozen packages of animal crackers, dumps them onto a table in her classroom, and asks her pupils to count the cows, horses, and pigs. Straightaway comes this question, "Is this a cow? One leg is missing. Should I count her as a cow?" Neither yes or no is correct, but the pupil needs to know the rules. Change of rule, count her as a cow, or do not, changes the count of cows.

Information Is Not Knowledge

We are today in possession of instant communication with any part of the world. Unfortunately, speed does not help anyone to understand the future and the obligations of management. Many of us deceive ourselves into the supposition that we need constant updating to cope with the rapidly changing future. But you cannot, by watching every moment of television, or by reading every newspaper, acquire a glimpse of what the future holds.

To put it another way, information, no matter how complete and speedy, is not knowledge. Knowledge has temporal spread. Knowledge comes from theory. Without theory, there is no way to use the information that comes to us on the instant.

A dictionary contains information, but not knowledge. A dictionary is useful. I use a dictionary frequently when at my desk, but the dictionary will not prepare a paragraph nor criticize it.

Losses From Successive Application of Random Impulses

Wild results and losses may come from successive application of random forces or random changes that may individually be unimportant. Examples:

1. Worker training worker in succession
2. Management of a company, or a committee in industry or in government, working with best efforts on policy, leading themselves astray without guidance of profound knowledge

Some Important Signposts for Profound Knowledge

Enlargement of a committee does not necessarily improve results. Enlargement of a committee is not a reliable way to acquire profound knowledge.

Corollaries of this theorem are frightening. True, popular vote acts as a ballast over a dictator, but does it provide the right answer?

Does the House of Bishops serve the church better than governance vested in the Archbishop? History leads to grave doubts.

Psychology[5]

Psychology helps us to understand people, interaction between people and circumstances, interaction between customer and supplier, interaction between teacher and pupil, interaction between a manager and his people and any system of management.

People are different from one another. A manager of people must be aware of these differences, and use them for optimization of everybody's abilities and inclinations. This is not ranking people. Management of industry, education, and government operate today under the supposition that all people are alike.

People learn in different ways, and at different speeds. Some learn a skill by reading, some by listening, some by watching pictures, still or moving, some by watching someone do it.

There are intrinsic sources of motivation, extrinsic sources of motivation, and the phenomenon of overjustification.

5. A number of friends have contributed to this section. I am especially indebted to Dr. Wendy Coles and Dr. Linda Doherty.

People are born with a need for relationships with other people, and need for love and esteem by others.

One is born with a natural inclination to learn. Learning is a source of innovation. One inherits a right to enjoy his work. Good management helps us to nurture and preserve these positive innate attributes of people.

Family environment may shatter at an early age dignity and self-esteem, and thereby shatter also intrinsic motivation. Some practices of management (e.g., ranking people) complete the destruction.

Extrinsic motivation may indirectly bring positive results. For example, a man takes a job and receives money. Money is an extrinsic reward. He arrives at work on time, and comes in a clean shirt, and discovers some of his abilities, all of which helps his self-esteem.

Some extrinsic motivation helps to build self-esteem. But total submission to extrinsic motivation leads to destruction of the individual. Joy in learning is submerged in order to capture top grades. On the job, under the present system, joy in work and innovation become secondary to a good rating. Extrinsic motivation in the extreme crushes intrinsic motivation.

A bonus for high rank in the ranking of people, teams, divisions, regions, brings demoralization to all the people concerned, including him that receives the bonus.

I repeat here Norb Keller's famous statement made on 8 November 1987 in a meeting with General Motors: "If General Motors were to double the pay of everybody commencing the first of December, performance would be exactly what it is now."

He was, of course, talking about pay above that needed to maintain quality of life. He also meant to include everybody, not a selected group.

Some of his friends told him afterward that they would be willing to take part in an experiment in double pay, but they acknowledged in the same breath that double pay would make no difference in their performance.

No one, child or grown-up, can enjoy learning if he must constantly be concerned about grading and gold stars for his performance. Our educational system would be improved immeasurably by abolishment of grading. No one can enjoy his work if he will be ranked with others.

The Phenomenon of Overjustification

Systems of reward now in place may actually be overjustification. Monetary reward to somebody, or a prize, for an act or achievement that he did for sheer pleasure and self-satisfaction may be viewed as overjustification. The result of monetary reward under these conditions is at best meaningless and a source of discouragement. He that receives an award from someone that he does not respect will feel further degraded.

To clarify overjustification, I relate here an example told to me by Dr. Joyce Orsini.

A little boy took it into his head for reasons unknown to wash the dishes after supper every evening. His mother was pleased with such a fine boy. One evening, to show her appreciation, she handed to him a quarter. He never washed another dish. Her payment to him changed their relationship. It hurt his dignity. He had washed the dishes for the sheer pleasure of doing something for his mother.

Further Remarks on Rewards[6]

When children are given rewards such as toys and money for doing well in school, music, and sports, they learn to expect rewards for good performance. As they become adults, their desire for tangible reward begins to govern action. They are now extrinsically motivated. They come to rely on the world to provide things to make them feel good. They will often work hard to earn lots of money, only to find in middle age that their work has no meaning. Anyone that derives meaning from extrinsic sources of motivation brings detrimental effects on his self esteem. He feels that he has no control over the world. He is powerless, and may become despondent.

The loving mother, the kind teacher, the patient coach, can through praise, respect, and support for improvement, reinforce a child's dignity and self-esteem. Children feel good about themselves when they learn how to master a new activity. They become more intrinsically motivated. They develop self-esteem and confidence. They develop self-efficacy. Their work is meaningful, and they will make improvements in what they do.

My son Tad was on a swimming team from the time that he was 5 until 17. When the younger children were in a race, all got medals. They were very excited about the medals. The parents liked them. Important people, the coaches, gave them out. The swimmers were extrinsically motivated to swim better. As the children grew older, medals lost their importance. They found enjoyment and meaning in improvement of performance. My son knew how fast he swam. He would not even pick up the medals. He had become intrinsically motivated and developed self-discipline. The four-hour-a-day workouts, at times in the rain and cold, would have been too difficult had he not found reward in the activity. Some parents offered money or presents to their children to swim better. These children did not pursue swimming.

The most important act that a manager can take is to understand what it is that is important to an individual. Everyone is different from everyone else. All people are motivated to a different degree extrinsically and intrinsically. This is

6. This section is contributed by Dr. Linda Doherty.

why it is so vital that managers spend time to listen to an employee to understand whether he is looking for recognition by the company, or by his peers, time at work to publish, flexible working hours, time to take a university course. In this way, a manager can provide positive outcomes for his people, and may even move some people toward replacement of extrinsic motivation with intrinsic motivation.

Examples of Overjustification

A man, not an employee of the hotel, picked up my bag at the registration desk of a hotel in Detroit, and carried it to my room. The bag was heavy. I was exhausted and hungry, hoping to get into the dining room before it would close at 11 p.m. I was ever so grateful to him; fished out two dollar bills for him. He refused them. I had hurt his feelings, trying to offer money to him. He had carried the bag for me, not for pay. My attempt to pay him was, in effect, an attempt to change our relationship. I meant well, but did the wrong thing. I resolved to be careful.

And then I did it again. As I arrived via U.S. Air at National Airport, Washington, a member of the crew picked up my bag (heavy), carried it off the airplane, escorted me with the other hand through the airport, down and out to my driver waiting for me. Grateful, I hurriedly found a five-dollar bill and pushed it toward her. "Oh, no." I had done it again! Stupefied, I asked her name. Debbie. I wrote to the president of the airline to ask for Debbie's full name and address, so that I could apologize to her. He replied that he had several Debbies in Washington, and could not be sure which one assisted me.

I wonder how many times I have made this same mistake.

An award in the form of money for a job done for the sheer pleasure of doing it is demoralizing, overjustification. Merit awards and ranking are demoralizing. They generate conflict and dissatisfaction. Companies with wrong practices pay a penalty. The penalty can not be measured.

Rewards motivate people to work for rewards.[7]

Recognition? Certainly

A show of appreciation to someone may mean far more to him than monetary reward.

A physician, Dr. Dv, immunologist, prescribed a vaccine for me when I was in the hospital with an infected leg. He sent to me, in due time, a bill. Along with the check to him, I enclosed a brief note of thanks and appreciation for his knowledge and for the care that he showed to me. I encountered him by chance one day,

---

7. Alfie Kohn, Cincinnati, 11 August 1992.

weeks later. The check we had both forgotten, but the letter? No. He had it in his pocket. It meant a lot to him, he told me, to know that someone cared.

Two years later, when I went to see Dr. Sh in Washington, he remarked to me in passing, "I ran across Dr. Dv the other day: he asked about you."

What if I had added five dollars to the Dr. Dv check in appreciation? That would have wounded him. That would have been a horrible example of overjustification.

A good plan of appreciation, I submit, would be to donate a sum of money to a hospital to be dispensed under the guidance of Dr. Dv for medical care for patients that cannot pay.

Question in a seminar. If management does not reward employees for a good job, people will move to a company that is willing to reward them. Some people go where they can get more money.

Answer: Everyone that I work with could get higher pay in some other company. Why does he stay here? He stays here because he likes it here. He has a chance to use his knowledge for the benefit of the whole system. He takes joy in his work. Money, above a certain level, is not enticement. Money may entice someone that knows that he is inferior. Certainly a boss should give a pat on the back for a job well done.

Many managers of people understand that the current methods of rating people do not distinguish the contribution of the individual from the rest of the process, yet they hold on to the belief or hope that a method of appraisal could be developed that would do so.

It is easy to miss the point that even if a method were developed to rank people with precision and certainty, distinct from the process that they work in, why would anyone suppose that this would improve people or the process? (This is a further contribution from Mr. Norb Keller of General Motors on 8 November 1987.)

12

The Knowledge-Creating Company

Ikujiro Nonaka

ABSTRACT

Manufacturers around the world have learned much from Japanese manufacturing techniques. However, any company that wants to compete on knowledge must also learn from Japanese techniques of knowledge—creation. Managers at Japan's most successful companies recognize that creating knowledge is not simply a matter of processing objective information. Rather, it depends on tapping the tacit and often highly subjective insights, intuitions, and ideals of employees.

BODY

In an economy where the only certainty is uncertainty, the one sure source of lasting competitive advantage is knowledge. When markets shift, technologies proliferate, competitors multiply, and products become obsolete almost overnight, successful companies are those that consistently create new knowledge, disseminate it widely throughout the organization, and quickly embody it in new technologies and products. These activities define the "knowledge-creating" company, whose sole business is continuous innovation.

And yet, despite all the talk about "brain power" and "intellectual capital," few managers grasp the true nature of the knowledge-creating company—let alone know how to manage it. The reason: they misunderstand what knowledge is and what companies must do to exploit it.

Deeply ingrained in the traditions of Western management, from Frederick Taylor to Herbert Simon, is a view of the organization as a machine for "informa-

Reprinted by permission of *Harvard Business Review.* "The Knowledge Creating Company" by Ikujiro Nonaka, November–December 1991, pp. 96–104. Copyright © 1991 by the President and Fellows of Harvard College; all rights reserved.

tion processing." According to this view, the only useful knowledge is formal and systematic—hard (read: quantifiable) data, codified procedures, universal principles. And the key metrics for measuring the value of new knowledge are similarly hard and quantifiable—increased efficiency, lower costs, improved return on investment.

But there is another way to think about knowledge and its role in business organizations. It is found most commonly at highly successful Japanese competitors like Honda, Canon, Matsushita, NEC, Sharp, and Kao. These companies have become famous for their ability to respond quickly to customers, create new markets, rapidly develop new products, and dominate emergent technologies. The secret of their success is their unique approach to managing the creation of new knowledge.

To Western managers, the Japanese approach often seems odd or even incomprehensible. Consider the following examples: How is the slogan "Theory of Automobile Evolution" a meaningful design concept for a new car? And yet, this phrase led to the creation of the Honda City, Honda's innovative urban car.

Why is a beer can a useful analogy for a personal copier? Just such an analogy caused a fundamental breakthrough in the design of Canon's revolutionary mini-copier, a product that created the personal copier market and has led Canon's successful migration from its stagnating camera business to the more lucrative field of office automation.

What possible concrete sense of direction can a made-up word such as "optoelectronics" provide a company's product-development engineers? Under this rubric, however, Sharp has developed a reputation for creating "first products" that define new technologies and markets, making Sharp a major player in businesses ranging from color televisions to liquid crystal displays to customized integrated circuits.

In each of these cases, cryptic slogans that to a Western manager sound just plain silly—appropriate for an advertising campaign perhaps but certainly not for running a company—are in fact highly effective tools for creating new knowledge. Managers everywhere recognize the serendipitous quality of innovation. Executives at these Japanese companies are managing that serendipity to the benefit of the company, its employees, and its customers.

The centerpiece of the Japanese approach is the recognition that creating new knowledge is not simply a matter of "processing" objective information. Rather, it depends on tapping the tacit and often highly subjective insights, intuitions, and hunches of individual employees and making those insights available for testing and use by the company as a whole. The key to this process is personal commitment, the employees' sense of identity with the enterprise and its mission. Mobilizing that commitment and embodying tacit knowledge in actual technologies and products require managers who are as comfortable with images and symbols—slogans such as Theory of Automobile Evolution, analogies like that between a personal copier and a beer can, metaphors such as "optoelectronics"— as they are with hard numbers measuring market share, productivity, or ROI.

The more holistic approach to knowledge at many Japanese companies is also founded on another fundamental insight. A company is not a machine but a living organism. Much like an individual, it can have a collective sense of identity and fundamental purpose. This is the organizational equivalent of self-knowledge—a shared understanding of what the company stands for, where it is going, what kind of world it wants to live in, and, most important, how to make that world a reality.

In this respect, the knowledge-creating company is as much about ideals as it is about ideas. And that fact fuels innovation. The essence of innovation is to re-create the world according to a particular vision or ideal. To create new knowledge means quite literally to re-create the company and everyone in it in a nonstop process of personal and organizational self-renewal. In the knowledge-creating company, inventing new knowledge is not a specialized activity—the province of the R&D department or marketing or strategic planning. It is a way of behaving, indeed a way of being, in which everyone is a knowledge worker—that is to say, an entrepreneur.

The reasons why Japanese companies seem especially good at this kind of continuous innovation and self-renewal are complicated. But the key lesson for managers is quite simple: much as manufacturers around the world have learned from Japanese manufacturing techniques, any company that wants to compete on knowledge must also learn from Japanese techniques of knowledge creation. The experiences of the Japanese companies discussed below suggest a fresh way to think about managerial roles and responsibilities, organizational design, and business practices in the knowledge-creating company. It is an approach that puts knowledge creation exactly where it belongs: at the very center of a company's human resources strategy.

THE SPIRAL OF KNOWLEDGE

New knowledge always begins with the individual. A brilliant researcher has an insight that leads to a new patent. A middle manager's intuitive sense of market trends becomes the catalyst for an important new product concept. A shop-floor worker draws on years of experience to come up with a new process innovation. In each case, an individual's personal knowledge is transformed into organizational knowledge valuable to the company as a whole.

Making personal knowledge available to others is the central activity of the knowledge-creating company. It takes place continuously and at all levels of the organization. And as the following example suggests, sometimes it can take unexpected forms.

In 1985, product developers at the Osaka-based Matsushita Electric Company were hard at work on a new home bread-making machine. But they were having trouble getting the machine to knead dough correctly. Despite their efforts, the crust of the bread was overcooked while the inside was hardly done at all. Employees exhaustively analyzed the problem. They even compared X-rays of dough kneaded by the machine and dough kneaded by professional bakers. But they were unable to obtain any meaningful data.

Finally, software developer Ikuko Tanaka proposed a creative solution. The Osaka International Hotel had a reputation for making the best bread in Osaka. Why not use it as a model? Tanaka trained with the hotel's head baker to study his kneading technique. She observed that the baker had a distinctive way of stretching the dough. After a year of trial and error, working closely with the project's engineers, Tanaka came up with product specifications—including the addition of special ribs inside the machine—that successfully reproduced the baker's stretching technique and the quality of the bread she had learned to make at the hotel. The result: Matsushita's unique "twist dough" method and a product that in its first year set a record for sales of a new kitchen appliance.

Ikuko Tanaka's innovation illustrates a movement between two very different types of knowledge. The end point of that movement is "explicit" knowledge: the product specifications for the bread-making machine. Explicit knowledge is formal and systematic. For this reason, it can be easily communicated and shared, in product specifications or a scientific formula or a computer program.

But the starting point of Tanaka's innovation is another kind of knowledge that is not so easily expressible: "tacit" knowledge like that possessed by the chief baker at the Osaka International Hotel. Tacit knowledge is highly personal. It is hard to formalize and, therefore, difficult to communicate to others. Or in the words of the philosopher Michael Polanyi, "We can know more than we can tell." Tacit knowledge is also deeply rooted in action and in an individual's commitment to a specific context—a craft or profession, a particular technology or product market, or the activities of a work group or team.

Tacit knowledge consists partly of technical skills—the kind of informal, hard-to-pin-down skills captured in the term "know-how." A master craftsman after years of experience develops a wealth of expertise "at his fingertips." But he is often unable to articulate the scientific or technical principles behind what he knows. At the same time, tacit knowledge has an important cognitive dimension. It consists of mental models, beliefs, and perspectives so ingrained that we take them for granted, and therefore cannot easily articulate them. For this very reason, these implicit models profoundly shape how we perceive the world around us.

The distinction between tacit and explicit knowledge suggests four basic patterns for creating knowledge in any organization:

1. From Tacit to Tacit. Sometimes, one individual shares tacit knowledge directly with another. For example, when Ikuko Tanaka apprentices herself to the head baker at the Osaka International Hotel, she learns his tacit skills through observation, imitation, and practice. They become part of her own tacit knowledge base. Put another way, she is "socialized" into the craft.

   But on its own, socialization is a rather limited form of knowledge creation. True, the apprentice learns the master's skills. But neither the apprentice nor the master gain any systematic insight into their craft knowledge. Because their knowledge never becomes explicit, it cannot easily be leveraged by the organization as a whole.

2. From Explicit to Explicit. An individual can also combine discrete pieces of explicit knowledge into a new whole. For example, when a comptroller of a company collects information from throughout the organization and puts it together in a financial report, that report is new knowledge in the sense that it synthesizes information from many different sources. But this combination does not really extend the company's existing knowledge base either.

   But when tacit and explicit knowledge interact, as in the Matsushita example, something powerful happens. It is precisely this exchange between tacit and explicit knowledge that Japanese companies are especially good at developing.

3. From Tacit to Explicit. When Ikuko Tanaka is able to articulate the foundations of her tacit knowledge of bread making, she converts it into explicit knowledge, thus allowing it to be shared with her project-development team. Another example might be the comptroller who, instead of merely compiling a conventional financial plan for his company, develops an innovative new approach to budgetary control based on his own tacit knowledge developed over years in the job.

4. From Explicit to Tacit. What's more, as new explicit knowledge is shared throughout an organization, other employees begin to internalize it—that is, they use it to broaden, extend, and reframe their own tacit knowledge. The comptroller's proposal causes a revision of the company's financial control system. Other employees use the innovation and eventually come to take it for granted as part of the background of tools and resources necessary to do their jobs.

In the knowledge-creating company, all four of these patterns exist in dynamic interaction, a kind of spiral of knowledge. Think back to Matsushita's Ikuko Tanaka:

1. First, she learns the tacit secrets of the Osaka International Hotel baker (socialization).

2. Next, she translates these secrets into explicit knowledge that she can communicate to her team members and others at Matsushita (articulation).

3. The team then standardizes this knowledge, putting it together into a manual or workbook and embodying it in a product (combination).

4. Finally, through the experience of creating a new product, Tanaka and her team members enrich their own tacit knowledge base (internalization). In particular, they come to understand in an extremely intuitive way that products like the home bread-making machine can provide genuine quality. That is, the machine must make bread that is as good as that of a professional baker.

This starts the spiral of knowledge all over again, but this time at a higher level. The new tacit insight about genuine quality developed in designing the home bread-making machine is informally conveyed to other Matsushita employees. They use it to formulate equivalent quality standards for other new Matsushita products—whether kitchen appliances, audiovisual equipment, or white goods. In this way, the organization's knowledge base grows ever broader.

Articulation (converting tacit knowledge into explicit knowledge) and internalization (using that explicit knowledge to extend one's own tacit knowledge base) are the critical steps in this spiral of knowledge. The reason is that both require the active involvement of the self—that is, personal commitment. Ikuko Tanaka's decision to apprentice herself to a master baker is one example of this commitment. Similarly, when the comptroller articulates his tacit knowledge and embodies it in a new innovation, his personal identity is directly involved in a way it is not when he merely "crunches" the numbers of a conventional financial plan.

Indeed, because tacit knowledge includes mental models and beliefs in addition to know-how, moving from the tacit to the explicit is really a process of articulating one's vision of the world—what it is and what it ought to be. When employees invent new knowledge, they are also reinventing themselves, the company, and even the world.

When managers grasp this, they realize that the appropriate tools for managing the knowledge-creating company look very different from those found at most Western companies.

FROM METAPHOR TO MODEL

To convert tacit knowledge into explicit knowledge means finding a way to express the inexpressible. Unfortunately, one of the most powerful management tools for doing so is also among the most frequently overlooked: the store of figurative language and symbolism that managers can draw from to articulate their intuitions and insights. At Japanese companies, this evocative and sometimes extremely poetic language figures especially prominently in product development.

In 1978, top management at Honda inaugurated the development of a new-concept car with the slogan, "Let's gamble." The phrase expressed senior executives' conviction that Honda's Civic and the Accord models were becoming too familiar. Managers also realized that along with a new postwar generation entering the car market, a new generation of young product designers was coming of age with unconventional ideas about what made a good car.

The business decision that followed from the "Let's gamble" slogan was to form a new-product development team of young engineers and designers (the average age was 27). Top management charged the team with two—and only two—instructions: first, to come up with a product concept fundamentally different from anything the company had ever done before; and second, to make a car that was inexpensive but not cheap.

This mission might sound vague, but in fact it provided the team an extremely clear sense of direction. For instance, in the early days of the project, some team members proposed designing a smaller and cheaper version of the Honda

Civic—a safe and technologically feasible option. But the team quickly decided this approach contradicted the entire rationale of its mission. The only alternative was to invent something totally new.

Project team leader Hiroo Watanabe coined another slogan to express his sense of the team's ambitious challenge: Theory of Automobile Evolution. The phrase described an ideal. In effect, it posed the question: If the automobile were an organism, how should it evolve? As team members argued and discussed what Watanabe's slogan might possibly mean, they came up with an answer in the form of yet another slogan: "man-maximum, machine-minimum." This captured the team's belief that the ideal car should somehow transcend the traditional human-machine relationship. But that required challenging what Watanabe called "the reasoning of Detroit," which had sacrificed comfort for appearance.

The "evolutionary" trend the team articulated eventually came to be embodied in the image of a sphere—a car simultaneously "short" (in length) and "tall" (in height). Such a car, they reasoned, would be lighter and cheaper, but also more comfortable and more solid than traditional cars. A sphere provided the most room for the passenger while taking up the least amount of space on the road. What's more, the shape minimized the space taken up by the engine and other mechanical systems. This gave birth to a product concept the team called "Tall Boy," which eventually led to the Honda City, the company's distinctive urban car.

The Tall Boy concept totally contradicted the conventional wisdom about automobile design at the time, which emphasized long, low sedans. But the City's revolutionary styling and engineering were prophetic. The car inaugurated a whole new approach to design in the Japanese auto industry based on the man-maximum, machine-minimum concept, which has led to the new generation of "tall and short" cars now quite prevalent in Japan.

The story of the Honda City suggests how Japanese companies use figurative language at all levels of the company and in all phases of the product development process. It also begins to suggest the different kinds of figurative language and the distinctive role each plays.

One kind of figurative language that is especially important is metaphor. By "metaphor," I don't just mean a grammatical structure or allegorical expression. Rather, metaphor is a distinctive method of perception. It is a way for individuals grounded in different contexts and with different experiences to understand something intuitively through the use of imagination and symbols without the need for analysis or generalization. Through metaphors, people put together what they know in new ways and begin to express what they know but cannot yet say. As such, metaphor is highly effective in fostering direct commitment to the creative process in the early stages of knowledge creation.

Metaphor accomplishes this by merging two different and distant areas of experience into a single, inclusive image or symbol—what linguistic philosopher Max Black has aptly described as "two ideas in one phrase." By establishing a connection between two things that seem only distantly related, metaphors set up a discrepancy or conflict. Often, metaphoric images have multiple meanings, appear logically contradictory or even irrational. But far from being a weakness, this is in fact an enormous strength. For it is the very conflict that metaphors embody that jump-starts the creative process. As employees try to define more clearly the insight that the metaphor expresses, they work to reconcile the conflicting meanings. That is the first step in making the tacit explicit.

Consider the example of Hiroo Watanabe's slogan, Theory of Automobile Evolution. Like any good metaphor, it combines two ideas one wouldn't normally think of together—the automobile, which is a machine, and the theory of evolution, which refers to living organisms. And yet, this discrepancy is a fruitful platform for speculation about the characteristics of the ideal car.

But while metaphor triggers the knowledge-creation process, it alone is not enough to complete it. The next step is analogy. Whereas metaphor is mostly driven by intuition and links images that at first glance seem remote from each other, analogy is a more structured process of reconciling contradictions and making distinctions. Put another way, by clarifying how the two ideas in one phrase actually are alike and not alike, the contradictions incorporated into metaphors are harmonized by analogy. In this respect, analogy is an intermediate step between pure imagination and logical thinking.

Probably the best example of analogy comes from the development of Canon's revolutionary mini-copier. Canon designers knew that for the first personal copier to be successful, it had to be reliable. To ensure reliability, they proposed to make the product's photosensitive copier drum—which is the source of 90% of all maintenance problems—disposable. To be disposable, however, the drum would have to be easy and cheap to make. How to manufacture a throwaway drum?

The breakthrough came one day when task-force leader Hiroshi Tanaka ordered out for some beer. As the team discussed design problems over their drinks, Tanaka held one of the beer cans and wondered aloud, "How much does it cost to manufacture this can?" The question led the team to speculate whether the same process for making an aluminum beer can could be applied to the manufacture of an aluminum copier drum. By exploring how the drum actually is and is not like a beer can, the mini-copier development team was able to come up with the process technology that could manufacture an aluminum copier drum at the appropriate low cost.

Finally, the last step in the knowledge-creation process is to create an actual model. A model is far more immediately conceivable than a metaphor or an analogy. In the model, contradictions get resolved and concepts become transferable through consistent and systematic logic. The quality standards for the bread at the Osaka International Hotel led Matsushita to develop the right product specifications for its home bread-making machine. The image of a sphere leads Honda to its Tall Boy product concept.

Of course, terms like "metaphor," "analogy," and "model" are ideal types. In reality, they are often hard to distinguish from each other; the same phrase or image can embody more than one of the three functions. Still, the three terms capture the process by which organizations convert tacit knowledge into explicit knowledge: first, by linking contradictory things and ideas through metaphor; then, by resolving these contradictions through analogy; and, finally, by crystallizing the created concepts and embodying them in a model, which makes the knowledge available to the rest of the company.

FROM CHAOS TO CONCEPT: MANAGING THE KNOWLEDGE-CREATING COMPANY

Understanding knowledge creation as a process of making tacit knowledge explicit—a matter of metaphors, analogies, and models—has direct implications for how a company designs its organization and defines managerial roles and responsibilities within it. This is the "how" of the knowledge-creating company, the structures and practices that translate a company's vision into innovative technologies and products.

The fundamental principle of organization design at the Japanese companies I have studied is redundancy—the conscious overlapping of company information, business activities, and managerial responsibilities. To Western managers, the term "redundancy," with its connotations of unnecessary duplication and waste, may sound unappealing. And yet, building a redundant organization is the first step in managing the knowledge-creating company.

Redundancy is important because it encourages frequent dialogue and communication. This helps create a "common cognitive ground" among employees and thus facilitates the transfer of tacit knowledge. Since members of the organization share overlapping information, they can sense what others are struggling to articulate. Redundancy also spreads new explicit knowledge through the organization so it can be internalized by employees.

The organizational logic of redundancy helps explain why Japanese companies manage product development as an overlapping process where different functional divisions work together in a shared division of labor. At Canon, redundant product development goes one step further. The company organizes product-development teams according to "the principle of internal competition." A team is divided into competing groups that develop different approaches to the same project and then argue over the advantages and disadvantages of their proposals. This encourages the team to look at a project from a variety of perspectives. Under the guidance of a team leader, the team eventually develops a common understanding of the "best" approach.

In one sense, such internal competition is wasteful. Why have two or more groups of employees pursuing the same product-development project? But when responsibilities are shared, information proliferates, and the organization's ability to create and implement concepts is accelerated.

At Canon, for example, inventing the mini-copier's low-cost disposable drum resulted in new technologies that facilitated miniaturization, weight reduction, and automated assembly. These technologies were then quickly applied to other office automation products such as microfilm readers, laser printers, word processors, and typewriters. This was an important factor in diversifying Canon from cameras to office automation and in securing a competitive edge in the laser printer industry. By 1987—only five years after the mini-copier was introduced—a full 74% of Canon's revenues came from its business machines division.

Another way to build redundancy is through strategic rotation, especially between different areas of technology and between functions such as R&D and marketing. Rotation helps employees understand the business from a multiplicity of perspectives. This makes organizational knowledge more "fluid" and easier to put into practice. At Kao Corporation, a leading Japanese consumer-products manufacturer, researchers often "retire" from the R&D department by the age of 40 in order to transfer to other departments such as marketing, sales, or production. And all employees are expected to hold at least three different jobs in any given ten-year period.

Free access to company information also helps build redundancy. When information differentials exist, members of an organization can no longer interact on equal terms, which hinders the search for different interpretations of new knowledge. Thus Kao's top management does not allow any discrimination in access to information among employees. All company information (with the exception of personnel data) is stored in a single integrated database, open to any employee regardless of position.

As these examples suggest, no one department or group of experts has the exclusive responsibility for creating new knowledge in the knowledge-creating company. Senior managers, middle managers, and front-line employees all play a part. Indeed, the value of any one person's contribution is determined less by his or her location in the organizational hierarchy than by the importance of the information he or she provides to the entire knowledge-creating system.

But this is not to say that there is no differentiation among roles and responsibilities in the knowledge-creating company. In fact, creating new knowledge is the product of a dynamic interaction among three roles.

Front-line employees are immersed in the day-to-day details of particular technologies, products, or markets. No one is more expert in the realities of a company's business than they are. But while these employees are deluged with highly specific information, they often find it extremely difficult to turn that information into useful knowledge. For one thing, signals from the marketplace can be vague and ambiguous. For another, employees can become so caught up in their own narrow perspective, that they lose sight of the broader context.

What's more, even when employees do develop meaningful ideas and insights, it can still be difficult to communicate the import of that information to others. People don't just passively receive new knowledge, they actively interpret it to fit their own situation and perspective. Thus what makes sense in one context can change or even lose its meaning when communicated to people in a different context. As a result, there is a continual shift in meaning as new knowledge is diffused in an organization.

The confusion created by the inevitable discrepancies in meaning that occur in any organization might seem like a problem. In fact, it can be a rich source of new knowledge—if a company knows how to manage it. The key to doing so is continuously challenging employees to reexamine what they take for granted. Such reflection is always necessary in the knowledge-creating company, but it is especially essential during times of crisis or breakdown, when a company's traditional categories of knowledge no longer work. At such moments, ambiguity can prove extremely useful as a source of alternative meanings, a fresh way to think about things, a new sense of direction. In this respect, new knowledge is born in chaos.

The main job of managers in the knowledge-creating company is to orient this chaos toward purposeful knowledge creation. Managers do this by providing employees with a conceptual framework that helps them make sense of their own experience. This takes place at the senior management level at the top of the company and at the middle management level on company teams.

Senior managers give voice to a company's future by articulating metaphors, symbols, and concepts that orient the knowledge-creating activities of employees. They do this by asking the questions: What are we trying to learn? What do we need to know? Where should we be going? Who are we? If the job of front-line employees is to know "what is," then the job of senior executives is to know "what ought to be." Or in the words of Hiroshi Honma, senior researcher at Honda: "Senior managers are romantics who go in quest of the ideal."

At some of the Japanese companies I have studied, CEOs talk about this role in terms of their responsibility for articulating the company's "conceptual umbrella": the grand concepts that in highly universal and abstract terms identify the common features linking seemingly disparate activities or businesses into a coherent whole. Sharp's dedication to optoelectronics is a good example.

In 1973, Sharp invented the first low-power electronic calculator by combining two key technologies—liquid crystal displays (LCDs) and complementary metal oxide semiconductors (CMOSs). Company technologists coined the term "optoelectronics" to describe this merging of microelectronics with optical technologies. The company's senior managers then took up the word and magnified its impact far beyond the R&D and engineering departments in the company.

Optoelectronics represents an image of the world that Sharp wants to live in. It is one of the key concepts articulating what the company ought to be. As such, it has become an overarching guide for the company's strategic development. Under this rubric, Sharp has moved beyond its original success in calculators to become a market leader in a broad range of products based on LCD and semiconductor technologies, including: the Electronic Organizer pocket notebook and LCD projection systems, as well as customized integrated circuits such as masked ROMs, ASICs, and CCDs (charge-coupled devices, which convert light into electronic signals).

Other Japanese companies have similar umbrella concepts. At NEC, top management has categorized the company's knowledge base in terms of a few key technologies and then developed the metaphor "C&C" (for "computers and communications"). At Kao, the umbrella concept is "surface active science," referring to techniques for coating the surface area of materials. This phrase has guided the company's diversification into products ranging from soap detergents to cosmetics to floppy disks—all natural derivatives of Kao's core knowledge base.

Another way top management provides employees with a sense of direction is by setting the standards for justifying the value of the knowledge that is constantly being developed by the organization's members. Deciding which efforts to support and develop is a highly strategic task.

In most companies, the ultimate test for measuring the value of new knowledge is economic—increased efficiency, lower costs, improved ROI. But in the knowledge-creating company, other more qualitative factors are equally important. Does the idea embody the company's vision? Is it an expression of top management's aspirations and strategic goals? Does it have the potential to build the company's organizational knowledge network?

The decision by Mazda to pursue the development of the rotary engine is a classic example of this more qualitative kind of justification. In 1974, the product-development team working on the engine was facing heavy pressure within the company to abandon the project. The rotary engine was a "gas guzzler," critics complained. It would never succeed in the marketplace.

Kenichi Yamamoto, head of the development team (and currently Mazda's chairperson), argued that to stop the project would mean giving up on the company's dream of revolutionizing the combustion engine. "Let's think this way," Yamamoto proposed. "We are making history, and it is our fate to deal with this challenge." The decision to continue led to Mazda's successful rotary-engine sports car, the Savanna RX-7.

Seen from the perspective of traditional management, Yamamoto's argument about the company's "fate" sounds crazy. But in the context of the knowledge-creating company, it makes perfect sense. Yamamoto appealed to the fundamental aspirations of the company—what he termed "dedication to uncompromised value"—and to the strategy of technological leadership that senior executives had articulated. He showed how the rotary-engine project enacted the organization's commitment to its vision. Similarly, continuing the project reinforced the individual commitment of team members to that vision and to the organization.

Umbrella concepts and qualitative criteria for justification are crucial to giving a company's knowledge-creating activities a sense of direction. And yet, it is important to emphasize that a company's vision needs also to be open-ended, susceptible to a variety of different and even conflicting interpretations. At first glance, this may seem contradictory. After all, shouldn't a company's vision be unambiguous, coherent, and clear? If a vision is too unambiguous, however, it becomes more akin to an order or an instruction. And orders do not foster the high degree of personal commitment on which effective knowledge creation depends.

A more equivocal vision gives employees and work groups the freedom and autonomy to set their own goals. This is important because while the ideals of senior management are important, on their own they are not enough. The best that top management can do is to clear away any obstacles and prepare the ground for self-organizing groups or teams. Then, it is up to the teams to figure out what the ideals of the top mean in reality. Thus at Honda, a slogan as vague as "Let's gamble" and an extremely broad mission gave the Honda City product-development team a strong sense of its own identity, which led to a revolutionary new product.

Teams play a central role in the knowledge-creating company because they provide a shared context where individuals can interact with each other and engage in the constant dialogue on which effective reflection depends. Team members create new points of view through dialogue and discussion. They pool their information and examine it from various angles. Eventually, they integrate their diverse individual perspectives into a new collective perspective.

This dialogue can—indeed, should—involve considerable conflict and disagreement. It is precisely such conflict that pushes employees to question existing premises and make sense of their experience in a new way. "When people's rhythms are out of sync, quarrels occur and it's hard to bring people together," acknowledges a deputy manager for advanced technology development at Canon. "Yet if a group's rhythms are completely in unison from the beginning, it's also difficult to achieve good results."

As team leaders, middle managers are at the intersection of the vertical and horizontal flows of information in the company. They serve as a bridge between the visionary ideals of the top and the often chaotic market reality of those on the front line of the business. By creating middle-level business and product concepts, middle managers mediate between "what is" and "what should be." They remake reality according to the company's vision.

Thus at Honda, top management's decision to try something completely new took concrete form at the level of Hiroo Watanabe's product-development team in the Tall Boy product concept. At Canon, the company aspiration, "Making an excellent company through transcending the camera business," became a reality when Hiroshi Tanaka's task force developed the "Easy Maintenance" product concept, which eventually gave birth to the personal copier. And at Matsushita, the company's grand concept, "Human Electronics," came to life through the efforts of Ikuko Tanaka and others who developed the middle-range concept, "Easy Rich," and embodied it in the automatic bread-making machine.

In each of these cases, middle managers synthesized the tacit knowledge of both front-line employees and senior executives, made it explicit, and incorporated it into new technologies and products. In this respect, they are the true "knowledge engineers" of the knowledge-creating company.

Part Three

The Measurement of Knowledge

Introduction

G. Anthony Siesfeld

If you use the wrong measure, or if it doesn't map to economic performance, not only have you wasted a lot of money . . . but you've [also] potentially made disastrous . . . decisions.
> —Chris Ittner, in the *Wharton Alumni Review* (1997)

[A]lthough an organization's knowledge base may be its single most important asset, its very intangibility makes it difficult to manage systematically.
> —Roger E. Bohn, *Sloan Management Review* (Fall, 1994)

Knowledge. It has transformed every economy from time immemorial. It has become more and more embedded in the feedback cycles and factors of production in each economy. It is the foundation of today's emerging economy. Yet what we know about measuring knowledge is epigrammatic. Knowledge is power (Francis Bacon) yet it is meager if not expressed in numbers (Lord Kelvin). It is lost for information and for data (T.S. Eliot). Most important, it is recognized as a vital, if not the vital, source of competitive advantage and of production [see, for instance, Chapter 10, Knowledge: Its Economics and its Productivity, in Peter Drucker's *Post-capitalist Society* (1993)]. We do not yet know very much about how to measure knowledge, as an economic force. Still, we do know a lot about knowledge, from the study of epistemology to the design and validation of achievement tests used for evaluating the proficiency of students. However, what we know about knowledge from these studies is not ready for application to the needs we have in business.

It is not for want of trying. Many efforts are underway to account for knowledge. The Institute of Management Accounting reports that about 70 percent of all businesses are experimenting with nonfinancial performance measurements,[1] many geared to the productivity of human and intellectual capital.

Scholars and thinkers have turned their attention to the topic. Some of them, who are not present in this volume, but have had pieces in previous volumes, include Pete Howitt and Peter Drucker. Others include Paul Cole and Stan Davis. The SEC and FASB, through the Jenkins Committee report, suggested that expanded disclosure of a firm's nonfinancial performance is essential to shareholders to make good investment decisions. The international accounting organizations are in the midst of drafting new rules for measuring and valuing intangible assets. The activity of so many represents a tacit consensus of the importance, and stubborn resistance to solving the problems, of measuring knowledge.

The seven articles in this section provide a broad exposure to three critical themes being played out in the effort to measure, so as to actively manage, both the knowledge of an economy and the knowledge within a firm. The themes are: the particularities unique to knowledge and the measure of its performance; valuation at the firm level; and experiments with tools for managers to make day-to-day decisions about investment in, and deployment of, the firm's knowledge.

WHAT TO EXPECT

This part of the book is comprised of three sections, mirroring the three themes described above: 1) a disquisition of knowledge measurement issues; 2) two studies establishing general boundaries around the value of knowledge to an organization. One study looks at investors' perception of a firm's nonfinancial performance, including things like the ability to attract and retain talented people and innovativeness. The other study examines the contribution of research and development to the value of firms. 3) The final three pieces deal with measurement frameworks and tools, some of them strategic and some of them tactical.

Read together, these articles outline the main issues and contradict one another on what to do. I think the contradiction is important. Measuring knowledge in the economy and at work in the firm is a whole new area of development. It is clear that the traditional input/output approach to determining whether and to what extent a firm's assets are working do not work with knowledge. Larry Prusak, author of a previous volume in this series and one of the progenitors of the exploration of the knowledge economy, insists that knowledge cannot be measured, only its impact can.[2] Indeed, there seems to be a growing idea that knowledge is not a stock, but a flow, and it is in the flows, the mingling of people's experiences and insights, that knowledge is created and applied to business problems. The contradictions in this work reflect the newness of the field and the field's lack of orthodoxy. These differences provoke us to reexamine the reasons for our measurements and the uses of the observations.

1. Edwards, J. B., 1995, *The Use of Performance Measures*, IMA.
2. Personal correspondence.

Let me take each article in turn, to preview their important points. However, I will take more time with the first articles—those laying out the measurement issues—because they provide the critical backdrop for evaluating all frameworks and methods then proposed for measuring the economic value of knowledge.

KNOWLEDGE MEASUREMENT ISSUES

In the first paper, "Measuring the Performance of a Knowledge Based Economy," Anne Carter identifies six problems in measuring knowledge. She lays out her case as an economist, focusing on measurements in the knowledge economy.

1. **Measuring knowledge itself.** Knowledge has three properties that are different from traditional goods and services, causing irremediable problems with the traditional model of measurement. These three properties are:
   a. *Knowledge is not separable.* It remains with the seller even after the buyer has acquired it. This lack of separability is a fundamental challenge to accountants; the ability to isolate a specific input and tie it uniquely to a specific output is required in double-entry bookkeeping and most process control measures. While it is true that money is fungible, once the proverbial discretionary dollar (or any monetary unit) is committed to an activity, it cannot be used elsewhere. This is definitely not true with knowledge. Once it is committed to a specific good, service, or process, the "owner" of the knowledge can provide the same knowledge to another, and another, and so on.
   b. *Additional "units" of the same knowledge yields no extra value to the person with the knowledge.* More is not better, new is better. It is true that one can embody a certain set of procedures in software, to be executed over and over again. And, that once this set of procedures has been codified in a program, the marginal cost of selling it again is virtually nil. There is value in reproducing knowledge, but there is no value to acquiring the same program again, any more than there is value in inventing the exact means of DNA replication over again.
   c. *The value of knowledge is unknowable until it is acquired and applied.* Furthermore, experience shows that when the knowledge is tacit, the value of the knowledge is unknowable until it is gone. The point here, though, is that the influence or contribution a unit of knowledge has on the production of a good or service cannot be fully anticipated. The stock cannot be evaluated; the value is in the flow.
2. **Qualitative changes in conventional goods and service.** Knowledge embedded in products undergoes significant change, making it difficult to evaluate "their levels of output" over time. This is akin to the observations Stan Davis has made about the increasing ratio of intangible to tangible value in products and services, and of the emergence of a class of

products and service which are knowledge-based.[3] That is, there is now emerging a class of products and services that learn and adapt with use, changing what the very product is each time it is used. There is now no time for making comparisons between output levels of differing products and services.

3. **Changing boundaries of producing units.** As the connections grow in the knowledge economy, as suppliers codevelop with manufacturers, as competitors ally to enter new geographic markets, as deregulation causes the separation of once-unified industries, who did what and how much it added value to the product becomes impossible to reckon. The boundaries of the firm are becoming permeable, the locus of value creation diffuse, and the traditional value-chain relationships changing. For instance, see Robert Wayland and Paul Cole's *Customer Connections*[4] for a wonderful discussion of the changing relationship between customer and company, and the role knowledge and knowledge transfer plays in redefining value exchange.

4. **Changing externalities and the externalities of change.** One of the greatest, and most vexing, aspects of knowledge is its spillover effect. Learning a task can enhance the learning of a new task, or can interfere. Discovery is path-dependent—where you are looking is generally where you find new knowledge, but it is seldom what you expect. There is a serendipity to knowledge and its value to the firm, but an ominous side as well. Because of the low transportation costs, and moderately low coordination costs, it is possible to shift employment from region to region. Certain U.S. firms outsource their computer code writing needs to India and Israel, getting back at the beginning of the next business day software considerably less expensive than had it been written in the United States. Who is in the firm and what value each person contributes is harder to gauge as the very benefits of knowledge flow in all directions.

5. **Distinguishing meta-investments from the current account.** Some investments are platform investments as they enable all employees in the firm to work more efficiently. IT systems are often this type of meta-investment.[5] At other times, a capital allocation is an expenditure specific to a product or service. Accounting does not differentiate well these types of "costs." Knowledge tends to be a meta-investment, enabling the firm to do some things it had not been able to do before.

6. **Creative destruction and the "useful life" of capital.** Knowledge can become obsolete. As it does, the value of the "old" stock drops to zero immediately. Further, the timing of the obsolescence of knowledge is highly

3. For instance, see Davis, S. and Davidson, B. (1992) *2020 Vision,* Fireside.
4. Wayland, R. E., and Cole, P. M. (1997) *Customer Connections,* Harvard Business School Press.
5. Gold, C. (1995) "Realizing Business Benefits from IT Expenditures," Ernst & Young Center for Business Innovation, working paper.

uncertain. Some knowledge is forever, some is destroyed with the very next insight. There are no schedules of depreciation. This fact suggests that much of what is invested in knowledge will be unprofitable—all cost, no revenue.

In summary, Anne Carter's article lays out succinctly the fundamental issues that have made measuring the knowledge economy or knowledge in action within a firm so difficult.

At this point, I want to introduce critical concepts about measurement from an article NOT in this volume. It is Marshall Meyer's "The Performance Paradox."[6] In it, he takes less of an economy-level view and much more of an organization-level view. Also, it is less specifically about knowledge than it is about performance and performance measurement in general. Nevertheless, it is as dire as Anne Carter's paper—to develop an effective system for measuring and managing knowledge performance will require new ways of thinking, and acting, as managers.

Meyer's thesis is straightforward: effective management requires multiple, uncorrelated, and changing measures of performance. In other words, simple and static measures lose information content over time—what's useful today won't be tomorrow, and unless the firm changes the measure, its performance is likely to decay. The thesis is built both on observation of changes in the arena of performance measurement and in the general properties of all measures.

There are five properties of all measures that are important to understand, three of which are explicitly detailed in this paper. These three are:

1. Performance measures require comparability and variability to discriminate good from bad. A single measure conveys little information in and of itself. The information comes when the single measure is compared to some other standard, like a base line (a 101°F temperature is bad if you are a human and it is your temperature, but not if you were to be, say, a bird), another measure from a similar process or person (a 15 may be the best grade in the class when you are on "a curve"), or the objectives laid out before the measurement was taken (an increase in earnings can send your stock price down if the increase was not as big as the analysts believed it would be). It is in comparison that we learn whether a measured value is good or not.

   Just as critical is whether or not there is variability in measures. Reflect for a moment—without variability there is no possibility of developing a cause and effect model. If two phenomena do not vary together, then it is unlikely they relate to one another. More importantly, a lack of variation among measurements makes it impossible to tell whether something is good or bad. Indeed, discrimination—detecting important differ-

6. Meyer, M. (1994) "The Performance Paradox," *Research in Organizational Behavior.*

ences; selectivity—identifying the right phenomenon; a difference that matters; and specificity—not misidentifying wrong phenomena as right all require the measurements of phenomena being observed to have variation.

2. Performance measures tend to run down over time. Specifically, these measures tend to run down due to learning, perverse learning, and selection.

   a. Given human agency and the desire to improve, or at least the desire to be paid more and/or be promoted, people tend to change their performance to maximize the measure. If one is evaluated on sales, one tends to work on raising sales numbers. Likewise, one compensated for time tends to put more hours into her work. As one learns what drives performance, one endeavors to change performance. If the performance measures were not changed, over time everyone would tend to perform at the same level. This leads to an attenuation of variation.

   b. In a., the right lessons learned lead to the diminution of the effectiveness of the performance measures. Perverse learning can also occur, whereby the wrong lessons guide performance, diminishing performance. Scott Adams, the creator of Dilbert, has identified many instances of perverse learning. My favorite is about the software company that paid $10 to a programmer for every software bug caught and fixed. The firm paid out a lot of money, more errors than ever were being caught, yet the error rates in the original codes were increasing.[7] To catch an error required an error to be made.

   c. Selection is another way performance measures tends to some average number with little variation. Those who perform well are kept and those who do not are released. Over time, through selection, only the top performers are retained. As a result, the performance measure no longer conveys any new information about performance as the pool grows in homogeneity.

3. When a measure does run down, it needs to be replaced (the firm needs to commit metricide!) with another. However, if the replacement measure is correlated with the original measure (that is, goes up when the other goes up or down when the other goes down), then the new measure adds no information. If there is little variability around an extant measure, then there will be little variability around a new measure correlated to the other. (One can think of a correlation as a transformation of one measure into another. If one measure does not change, the transformation will be a different number, but will be a constant, too.)

I would like to note two other properties essential to all performance measures: reliability and validity.

7. Davis, S. M., and Meyer, C. A. (1998) *BLUR: The speed of change in the connected economy.* Addison-Wesley Pub. Co.

1. A reliable measure is one that returns the same value for the same performance, regardless of the time of measurement, the form or nature of the observation (or observer), and the conditions under which the observations are made. A reliable measure is one that varies with the phenomenon being observed with very little random variation (or error) associated with it. There are several forms of driver's tests and of SATs. This is to prevent cheating. The forms need to be reliable, one test has to be a near perfect substitute for the others, so that an 85 percent correct or a 650 on one means the same as it does on another. Reliability is a necessary condition for all performance measures.[8]

2. A valid measure is one which measures what the measurer intends it to measure. For a measure to be valid, the one designing the measure needs to be clear on what the objective of the measure is and what the assumptions about the relationship between the phenomenon and measure are. A measure can be reliable without being valid as it can return the same measure over and over again but be unrelated to the intended purpose of the measure. As revealed in many examples from the business press, the intention of a company when instituting a performance measure does not always link to (or influence) the intended performance. For example, deferring costs from this year's budget can—while making the numbers work for now—adversely affect next year's budget.

In addition to the properties of performance measures just described, Meyer points to three observations about performance measurement he feels support his thesis.

1. Performance measures are proliferating—from shareholder valuation to quality measures, new types of feedback are spawned and suggested. One would expect that if a perfect performance metric existed, there would be no need for others. As there is apparent need for other measures, then the contrapositive of the argument leads us inexorably to conclude that no perfect measurement exists. Important, too, is that as our economy moves from an industrial one through information into a knowledge one, the opportunity for feedback is proliferating. New information technologies (both hardware and software) allow us to observe transactions never before possible. Further, electronic commerce will permit us not only to observe transactions, but also to get feedback from the entire marketplace, opening up new insights into performance, and providing for new ways to acquire wealth. Measures proliferate because of inadequacies with current ones and because of burgeoning opportunity.

8. As this treatment of reliability, and of validity in the next paragraph, are cursory at best, references to accessible work is important. For example, see Cronbach, L. J. (1990) *Essentials of Psychological Testing*, HarperCollins College Publishers.

2. There is no consensus on what the right performance measurement is. Further, the correlation among the candidate measures is quite low. This means that the measures advanced are specific to the objective, and that the various objectives of a business may not be related. Returning maximum shareholder value, as measured in stock performance or earnings, may not be at all consistent with the strategy of market dominance or long-term growth. Indeed, the "costs" of short-term profit may be deferred costs, which makes it impossible to make the investments necessary to compete well with others in the market. The lower expenditures help now, but destroy opportunity.

3. The dominant measures are changing. It used to be that functional measures, like output or market share, determined what was good and bad. Then, accounting measures determined success. Measures such as ROA and cash back guided management decisions. This was replaced by the ascendancy of financial measures, such as earnings per share and return on shareholder equity. Today's dominant measures are very much about shareholder value. (Who can avoid hearing about Stern Stewart's EVA^{sm} stuff today?) Not only have the dominant measures changed over time, the vogue shifting with new technologies, but also strategies and markets change, requiring new measures.

Taken together, the lesson of The Performance Paradox is that context for measurement changes over time, and the content to be measured changes as well. Some of this change is endogenous. For instance, as people become savvy about the measurement system, they change their behavior to reflect in the best possible light. But a lot of the change is exogenous, caused as markets, industries, companies, and economies connect and separate, calling for new investments and actions. Because things change, measures must as well. Because measures lose their efficacy after a length of time, they need to be renewed with uncorrelated measures. Because the phenomena we manage are complex, and because the interactions among actions, reactions, and outcomes are so rich, many measures are necessary. Only through constant design, development, evaluation, and paring can a manager hope to create a set of measures useful for management. There is no best measure and there is no single good measure which will persist in being good.

Now, back to articles in this section. Zvi Griliches' "Productivity, R&D and Data Constraints," is an in-depth review of the apparent contradiction between an increase in R&D (i.e., investment in knowledge) and the seeming decrease in productivity. He concludes that, although the contradiction is not strictly resolvable with current information, data constraints—what we do know (now) about R&D and productivity—lead us to see a contradiction where one does not exist. The first issue pertains to growth. Is it slowing down? Our traditional measures indicate that it is, yet the stock markets continue to climb. Further, what we count about firms, their book value, continues to decrease as a portion of their total value. Today's ratio stands at about 2.5. Are we growing or are we not? The knowledge economy is not growing according to industrial or agricultural economy numbers. The second and third issues pertain to the effectiveness of R&D and to the link between R&D and productivity. Ironically, in the computer industry, with some of the best measures of the R&D investments, the link between investment in knowledge and growth in firm value is strongest.

One of his final observations is an important reminder to us, again, about the limits to knowledge measurement. The outcome of inventive activity, such as knowledge creation, is not predictable. One cannot reliably anticipate what the next insight will be, or the next new idea leading to new product and service offerings, or change in doing business. This implies that performance measures can only provide weak support to our formative decisions, such as forward looking investment or strategic investments.

In summary the difficulties we have in measuring knowledge are:

1. Knowledge itself is inherently difficult to measure; it is context dependent and differentially valuable to those who might acquire it. Knowledge's expected value-lifetime is short. It is not separable. Input/output models fail. It has been suggested that only the outcome of knowledge is meaningfully measurable.
2. Even if we restrict ourselves to measuring the outcomes of knowledge-in-motion, we encounter the rapid decay of the performance measures themselves, as knowledge requires agency, and human agents can learn. As a consequence, the act of observation (that is, measurement) changes the actors, compromising the measurements. As this happens, new measurements are needed. Because knowledge, its uses and applications, and the motives of the people who have it all change, the performance measures used to observe the productivity of knowledge also have to change.
3. At best, knowledge performance measures will support adaptive decisions. The measures will support best decisions about channels of diffusion and the speed of transfer, not about what knowledge will be created or how much productive use will derive from it. These aspects of knowledge are not fully knowable until they occur.

Despite this bleak view, there is hope. The general boundaries of the value of knowledge, in various instantiations, can be measured at the firm level. Moreover, people are working to develop robust systems of measurement and observation, to provide managers with ways to at least know how well knowledge is working in their firms.

THE VALUE OF KNOWLEDGE

The two articles that constitute this section are both research studies. The first, by Lev and Sougiannis, treats R&D not as an expense,[9] but as a capital expenditure which can be used to adjust the firm's book value. The result is, that by treating R&D as an asset, a firm can show a link between the amount invested in R&D and stock prices and returns. Although the authors cannot link R&D costs with specific future revenues, they have established that R&D—investment in knowledge—acts like a productive asset which is strongly tied to stock price performance. At the market level, investments in knowledge can be valued by their contribution to stock price performance. The basis for their conclusions was a cross-sectional study of publicly traded firms with available and comparable financial information.

The second article, "Measures that Matter: An Exploratory Investigation of Investors' Information Needs and Value Priorities," approaches the issue of valuation from a different perspective. We conducted an experiment with institutional investors, evaluating the degree to which financial and nonfinancial information influenced their stock purchase decisions. We discovered that 33 percent of the investment decisions were accounted for by the independent contribution of the *perception* of nonfinancial performance. What investors think about the firm's nonfinancial performance strongly influences their valuation of a firm's stock, because nonfinancial performance signals future earnings potential. The types of nonfinancial information most important to investors are the talent of a firm's employees, the firm's level of innovation, and the knowledge of the management team.

Taken together, these studies establish that a significant part of the total value of a company is determined by its collective knowledge. Further, these studies provide a way to determine the exact value of this knowledge, as measured in contribution to stock price. This is encouraging; there are ways, though complicated, to show how much, if at all, investment in knowledge activities contribute to the firm. Unfortunately, these methods do not show which investments pay off the best or which investments should be made. Nonetheless, they show that growth in knowledge does drive growth in firm value. The final four papers reflect frameworks for establishing the link between a specific action or investment and a specific outcome.

TOOLS AND FRAMEWORKS

Each of the final three papers presents a method for evaluating performance which can be applied to knowledge performance. One of the papers deals with knowledge performance explicitly. Although the other two do not, it is not difficult to see how the frameworks implicitly account for knowledge performance.

As the title reveals, "Measuring and Managing Technological Knowledge," is a framework for mapping and evaluating levels of knowledge. The intended use of these maps and evaluations is to provide managers the means to make better

---

9. The government requires, except in some limited cases, R&D expenditures to be a same year expense.

use of the knowledge within their organization and to identify where knowledge is needed. In this article, Roger Bohn proposes an eight-level scale of knowledge, anchored by complete ignorance at one end and complete knowledge at the other. The scale is interesting for a number of reasons. One is that measurement is a necessary condition for ability to control, characterize, comprehend, and have theories about the causal nature of a process. This mantra, one cannot manage what one cannot measure, is familiar to us all and is put in a logical developmental sequence. Another interesting discussion is that the gulf between measurement and the next higher level, control, is one of the largest between levels in the scale. The message: getting measurement right is only the first, and not even the most difficult, step in the active and effective management of knowledge. Bohn also proposes how knowledge, at least technological process knowledge, can be managed at each level of knowledge.

The first article in this section poses an internal view of knowledge, with an emphasis on evaluating the efficiencies of knowledge development and of knowledge performance. This is an extremely important view, and one which dominates the lives of many managers. The final two articles shift focus. The first, "Putting the Balanced Scorecard to Work," by Kaplan and Norton, puts forth the argument that the considerations of current performance and expected future performance need to be balanced and that information about both is necessary for managers to make good decisions. The second, "The Options Approach to Capital Investment," shifts focus even further, outlining how financial options pricing models can be applied to strategic decision-making, to put an "exact" value on future firm projects, helping to determine how much capital a firm needs and how best to allocate its capital.

"Putting the Balanced Scorecard to Work" explicitly includes evaluation of a firm's knowledge performance. One of the four critical perspectives essential to the balanced scorecard is that of innovation and learning. Further, innovation and learning serves to improve customer-related performance, thus is related to revenue growth, and serves to improve operational effectiveness, thus is related to cost improvements. Taken together, innovation and learning are integral to profitability, hence to overall firm performance. Strategic performance management is incomplete without consideration of innovation and learning and their links to revenues and costs. The process of developing a balanced scorecard requires management to explicate how knowledge influences the delivery of goods and services and to articulate how these influences will manifest themselves. The article offers some specific "how to" messages for developing a balanced scorecard and provides a number of case examples. The key insights about knowledge are that knowledge drives change, so that the measures established for performance have to be designed in light of the expected change and not in terms of current performance, and that it is more informative to measure the changes knowledge brings than the knowledge itself.

"The Options Approach to Capital Investment" provides a very different framework for evaluating the potential value of a firm's investments, including its investment in knowledge. Conceptually, the authors propose applying financial options pricing models to strategic, or real, investment decisions. The real options approach has several benefits. One, it allows managers to place a premium on types of uncertainty and on firm flexibility. Current methods of strategy assessment, such as NPV or DCF methods (like EVA), do not allow for this. Two, it recognizes and permits managers to handle the contingent nature of strategic investments. Usually, not all money for an investment needs to be committed at the time the decision to go forward is made. Standard evaluation techniques, however, assume in for a penny, in for a pound. Three, the real options approach allows managers to value the timing of their decisions. When using a real options approach to evaluating strategic investment decisions, higher value is realized for those projects that offer a firm more options. Indeed, the value of a firm can be thought of as the combination of the current income derived from extant projects and the future income from projects which can be done. All else being equal, a firm will be more valuable if there are more projects it could pursue. As Carter noted in the first article in this section of the book, knowledge represents a meta-investment; it keeps the options of a firm open. The real options approach is a specific way to determine the likely value of future activity, in order to determine the level of investment necessary to make the future activities possible. It provides an approach to determine what ought to be spent on knowledge.

What have we learned?

1. Exactly why knowledge is so difficult to measure and why traditional methods of measurement are inadequate for the task. Further, it teaches us that despite the difficulties, knowledge performance needs to be measured. Knowing the challenges makes it possible to shape an effective response.
2. That the knowledge at work in a firm can be measured as an incremental contribution to stock price performance or as the premium (or discount) investors are willing to pay for a stock. Importantly, there now exist methods which can provide a tight range of value that knowledge adds to a firm, even if the exact contribution of each knowledge effort is unknown.
3. There are emerging performance measurement frameworks which will permit managers to evaluate, and influence, knowledge performance.

13

Measuring the Performance of a Knowledge-Based Economy

Anne P. Carter

INTRODUCTION

My colleagues in sociology and history love to tease economists by calling economics "Queen of the Social Sciences." This royal status is based largely on measurement; our ability to quantify our variables. Quantification, in turn, allows us to cast our theories in equations and to draw on a powerful base of mathematics. This essay draws attention to some troublesome discrepancies between our traditional economic measures of input and output and the knowledge-based economy whose performance they represent. Traditional systems of accounts, on which both our micro- and macroeconomic analysis rests, give a distorted picture of the rising knowledge-based economy. Is our crown at risk? Dare we admit that we can't really quantify after all? That the emperor's, or, worse yet, the empress's, clothes don't fit? That she may be naked?

As you know, traditional measures of input and output are designed for a world with a fixed list of goods and services with well defined prices. In that world, durable goods have known and stable life expectancies and growth is essentially duplication. Performance can be quantified by levels of output or input-output proportions. Even in that hypothetical static world, the proportions of different goods and services can change, and so we have to deal with index number problems in measuring outputs at the national or even at the industry or firm level. But this slightly soiled linen aside, we inherit a clear and consistent set of concepts extending from the establishment to the macro level. Some, and I plead guilty here, have even dared to model a system for the entire world over a 30-year span, still with a fixed list of commodities and regions.

© OECD, 1996, *Employment and Growth in the Knowledge-based Economy.* Reproduced by permission of the OECD.

Economists have realized for some time that traditional measures don't always measure what we care about. For example, since household activities are excluded from Gross Domestic Product (GDP), that measure counts the transfer of individuals, particularly of women, from household tasks or subsistence farming to the paid labor force as a net increase in production. "Hidden unemployment" and "discouraged workers" lead many to question the meaning of the unemployment rate. Regional and sectoral differences in price movements limit the significance of a general price index. And we know that a given level of aggregate GDP has very different welfare implications depending on its distribution.

Measurement in the knowledge-based economy poses all these problems and more. These "more," the measurement problems to be addressed here, arise from three characteristic features of the knowledge-based economy: *i)* the growing importance of economic transactions—exchanges and accumulations—focused on knowledge itself; *ii)* rapid qualitative change in traditional goods and services; and *iii)* incorporation of the creation and implementation of change itself into the mission of economic agents.

Strictly speaking, aren't *all* economies knowledge-based? Certainly all economic systems depend on an enormous heritage of skills and understanding of the natural and social environment. Today's highly trained scientist, sent abroad to give "technical assistance," might starve fending for himself in a hunter-gatherer economy because he lacked the requisite knowledge. When technology was static, or changing slowly, most knowledge, like sun and air, was "priceless" but "free." Anyone with the necessary aptitude and training or experience to absorb it could have it. Typically, knowledge was outside the market sphere and therefore economists saw no need to measure it.

In today's economy a vast heritage of ideas underlying production is still implicit and free, but the generation of new ideas, of *changes* in the knowledge base, is tied to market incentives and knowledge has become a central subject and object of economic activity. While, for reasons to be discussed later, market transactions in knowledge itself are limited, enterprising individuals and firms find indirect ways to "appropriate" new ideas and to derive market benefits from them. In this context firms now actively pursue novelty. They invest significant resources in the creation, development and application of new ideas and even more in marketing, management, procurement and sales networks to capture profits of innovation. Later on we shall consider the difficult problem of measuring such investments and of assigning them to a product.

The measurement problems I shall enumerate are not entirely new. Seeds of the knowledge-based economy were planted long ago and sprouts have fouled our static measuring equipment ever since. Pre-capitalist economies often had conservative institutions and traditions that discouraged change: guilds, for example, essentially forbade innovation. Nevertheless, significant changes did sneak in; long-term change has always been hard to quantify. Those who compile economic censuses, input-output tables and national accounts know all too well the many arbitrary decisions required to force evolving economic activities into the Procrustean bed of an industrial classification (Postner, 1994, touches on these and deeper problems). Schmookler (1961) showed that, even in the 19th century, economic incentives regulated the generation of technical change. But, except for the very rough gauge of patent counts, he could not quantify the effort invested in developing new technology. Today knowledge-based flora, well past the germination stage, confront our old economic lawnmowers with spreading jungle.

Special measurement problems of a knowledge-based economy. Serious measurement problems are found in six overlapping areas:

Measuring knowledge itself. Ideally, to study a knowledge-based economy, one would wish to measure the knowledge content of economic activity. I have no idea how to measure knowledge content, and as far as I know, nobody else is even close either. To paraphrase a pet expression of physicists, "We are not even wrong." First, we have not quite decided what we're talking about: are we really interested in "knowledge"? "Information"? "Creativity"? "Ideas"? My own preference is for "ideas"; to me "knowledge" connotes properties like wisdom and science, while some very mundane ideas like bubblegum ice cream and pump sneakers belong on the agenda. (I'll continue to use the word knowledge to connote this general family of concepts, however ill-defined.)

Second, brain science investigating such activities is itself in flux. Natural scientists (and there are many specialties involved, from artificial intelligence through psychology to biochemistry) are generating disparate insights into the mechanism whereby we "create," "transmit," "receive" an idea, if those words are relevant to the process we're talking about at all. Economists contrast goods, which are relatively easy to quantify, and services, which are not. Knowledge seems to be the ultimate service.

Understandably, economists prefer to leave brain science to other specialists and to measure only what is "economically relevant." The prototype for this strategy is the economist's production function, which is supposed to tell us everything we need to know about engineering without our knowing anything about engineering. But we are not there yet. We are still trying to decide what really matters. Schumpeter (1934) stressed diffusion: ideas seem slippery, spreading without major cost or effort. This property would account for the fact that knowledge that has been around for a long time becomes a free good. Von Hippel (1994), by contrast, emphasizes "stickiness": some ideas are extraordinarily hard to transmit beyond their initial context (it is quite safe to tell *me* the latest secrets of genetic engineering). Both of these properties are important. Stickiness affects the locus of innovation and the path of diffusion in the window of time when competitors are racing to appropriate temporary gains. This is the crucial time interval that seems to matter in the knowledge economy. Neither slipperiness nor stickiness is measured, at least not yet. In this terrain, our economic lawnmower is stalled for the time being.

Why do we have to measure knowledge at all? I've already suggested that the vast body of common knowledge that underlies our production system need not be measured. But new knowledge is now the focus of major economic effort. If we fail to measure it, we are overlooking an important part of current economic activity and thus distorting our measures of the whole. Consistent with this argument, national accounts include Research and Development (R&D) in measures of total economic activity. But even R&D is "measured" only in terms of the inputs allocated to it; "unsuccessful" and "successful" R&D are not distinguished. Furthermore, we know that R&D is only the tip of a much larger iceberg. It constitutes only a small fraction of knowledge-related effort in today's industry. More and more, we see it as a crude proxy for, rather than a measure of, knowledge creation.

If we can't measure knowledge directly, why not simply add up the values of knowledge transactions? This is, after all, our strategy for measuring other types of services. While we don't have an output unit for, say, travel agencies, we gauge their activities in terms of dollar volume. Unfortunately, our traditional market institutions are ill adapted to pricing knowledge, and knowledge transactions often circumvent the market altogether. The reasons are deep and, I think, interesting. Briefly, we should note three special properties of knowledge "exchange" (Carter, 1989):

- The seller doesn't "give up" the knowledge that he sells. Knowledge is automatically and permanently "vested" in whoever acquires it.
- The potential buyer has no use for additional units of knowledge identical to what he already has.
- The buyer can't really appraise the knowledge that he might acquire without actually acquiring it.

For these reasons, prices of knowledge are one-shot and idiosyncratic rather than the consistent, market-disciplined indicators we expect for normal goods and services. To the extent that knowledge is priced, charges to different individuals for the same idea can vary enormously. And a large proportion of knowledge is not exchanged for money at all. Often it is simply accumulated within firms or networks without ever being assigned a value. The recent business literature emphasizes firm learning as an essential element in modern competition (Prahalad and Hamel, 1990). Clearly the authors see it as a key asset, perhaps a form of "meta-investment," which we will discuss later, but I know of no attempt to quantify learning itself. In addition, new knowledge-sharing institutions outside the conventional market system have sprung up. Knowledge is shared informally or "bartered," as in know-how trading and benchmarking, or through other collaborations of various sorts: joint ventures, foreign direct investment, collaborative research agreements, etc.

Qualitative change in conventional goods and services. Because many products are undergoing significant qualitative change, it is difficult to compare their "levels" of output over time. With a few notable exceptions like steel, coal or wheat, the basic Census information on production is collected in terms of dollars rather than in physical units. To measure changes in "real" output we try to separate out that part of change in the dollar volume of output due to change in the product's price. But when price and quality change simultaneously, we depend on questionable assumptions to distinguish them. One common assumption is that the price change component (of simultaneous change in quality and price) is equal to price change for "matched models" over a given time interval.

There are serious practical problems with this procedure, not the least of which is that old and new models may not overlap in time. Another imaginative strategy is to construct "hedonic" price indices. This means characterizing each product by a series of attributes: the speed, memory size, disk capacity, etc., of a computer, or the acceleration and safety features of a car. Through regression analysis, we then price the essential attributes of the product. In a sense, the quality of the product, as represented by the designated attributes, is quantified.

Such clever procedures can only attenuate the problem; they do not fully solve it. Most products have many more important attributes than we can, in practice, specify, and qualitative change keeps creating new, as yet unspecified, attributes: portability, color, virtual memory in computers; cruise control, air bags, styling in automobiles. At some point we throw up our hands. The time interval for meaningful comparisons is much shorter than it used to be.

Changing boundaries of producing units. Along with change in the nature of the product, the knowledge economy shifts the boundaries of producing units. Thus problems of quantifying how much is produced are compounded by difficulties in identifying who the producer is. This problem of boundaries manifests itself at all levels of aggregation, from the shifting responsibility groups at the individual plant level (see, for example, Hayes and Jaikumar, 1988), to the changing product and process composition of sectors, to regional integration and other complex international linkages that blur national economic boundaries. What is an OEM? An American car? US productivity? As the division of labor shifts, whose performance do we measure?

Changing externalities and externalities of change. We all know that economic activities have non-market or "external" effects—good and bad—like noise, air pollution and urban agglomeration effects. These affect the natural environment, all sorts of individuals and organizations, and the community at large. New technologies may have the same kinds of external effects as older ones but often their external effects will be qualitatively different and it may take some time to recognize what those external effects are. The switch from horses to automobiles brought a welcome reduction of horse manure in city streets. While an imaginative city planner might have anticipated cleaner streets, it is unlikely that anyone anticipated the burden of air pollution or accidents or adolescent mobility that the automobile system would bring.

In addition, the process of change itself has external effects on communities and individuals as employment opportunities shift from one region to another and human capital is rendered obsolete. In sum, the knowledge economy keeps creating new externalities as it evolves and significant externalities stem from the change process.

Distinguishing meta-investment from the current account. Today's firms purposefully pursue new product and process technologies. In doing so, they devote a significant proportion of inputs to "meta-investment," that is, investment in effecting change itself (Carter, 1994). Meta-investment includes not only conventional R&D but also the much larger costs of building markets and supply networks for procuring new inputs, implementing new processes, learning and managing the whole intricate sequence of effecting change. Meta-investments proliferate throughout the economy, as firms in various sectors adjust to changes sparked by an initial innovation. Traditional accounting systems—I include all levels, from the firm to the national accounts—do not generally distinguish between meta-investment and standard expenditures on current account. Thus, the productivity of current account inputs is understated, as is the true level of investment (Carter, 1994).

Accountants have already expressed serious concern for the disjunction between traditional accounting conventions and the decision and control functions they are supposed to serve at the firm level. I quote from a volume aptly titled *Relevance Lost* (Johnson and Kaplan, 1987).

"Although simplistic product costing methods . . . yield values for inventory and for cost of goods sold that satisfy external reporting and auditing requirements, the methods systematically bias and distort costs of individual products . . . leading to enormous cross subsidies across products. The financial accounting system treats many cash outlays as expenses of the period in which they are made even though these outlays will benefit future periods. Discretionary cash outlays for new products and improved processes, for preventive maintenance, for long-term marketing positioning, for employee training and morale, and for developing new systems can produce substantial cash inflows for the future. . . . Financial managers, relying exclusively on periodic financial statements for their view of the firm, become isolated from the real value-creating operations of the organization and fail to recognize when the accounting numbers are no longer providing relevant or appropriate measures of the organization's operations."

Individual firms' accounts are the basic building blocks of aggregate production statistics; if firms accounts do not accurately reflect real production activities, the significance of the national accounts is compromised. Aggregation at the micro level could eliminate problems of allocating costs among the various outputs of a multiproduct establishment; problems of cost allocation in a firm with multiple establishments might still persist. Most important, aggregation does not eliminate the distortion involved in registering meta-investment as expenditure on current account inputs.

How serious are the distortions we are talking about? Since we have not yet proposed an alternative measurement system, we cannot really quantify the biases of the old one. But rough preliminary evidence suggests that the problem is very substantial. We are all aware of the explosive growth of the service sectors and of business services in particular. In these rapidly expanding fields it often seems impossible to measure output at all and the default convention is to gauge output by the cost of inputs. This convention masks a problem but does not solve it.

Another indicator of the seriousness of the problem lies in the growing proportion of non-production workers in manufacturing. These are the employees classified as managers, professional and technical personnel, sales and clerical workers, as contrasted with production workers who have hands-on contact with the product. Non-production workers perform the kinds of tasks that are most difficult to assign to specific units of output, including the "overhead" functions discussed by critics of current firms' accounting practices. These functions are not merely difficult to allocate among specific products in multiproduct firms. They are also hard to assign over time: a substantial proportion is associated with meta-investment.

In the United States, between 1958–92, the proportion of production workers in manufacturing fell from 72 to 67 percent. While this change may appear modest, analysis of the sectoral detail shows that the industries with a small proportion of production workers are the fast-growing, high-technology sectors, while those where production workers predominate are the slower-growing older sectors.

The range is dramatic. In 1992, at the 3-digit Standard Industrial Classification level, the four sectors at the low end of the range (Miscellaneous Publishing, Office and Accounting Machines, Computer Equipment, and Guided Missiles and Space Vehicles) had less than 25 percent of their employment in production workers. The four with the largest proportion (Apparel, Meat Products, Knitting Mills, and Logging) employed 85 percent or more in the production worker category. Sectors with a low proportion of production workers are, it turns out, the ones that show high productivity growth as well as rapid growth in output. These sectors are the core of the emerging knowledge-based economy (Carter, 1994).

Creative destruction and the "useful life" of capital. My final point concerns rising difficulties in the measurement of the entire capital stock, both meta-investment and real capital goods, due to "creative destruction." Consider conventional producer durables first. Each year the capital stock—the measure of how much equipment and buildings are in place to support production—changes because of additions of new durable goods and retirements of old. We keep track of additions by tracking purchases of new durables. But it is notoriously hard to get reliable information on retirements. Old equipment may be kept as standby capacity, re-sold, stored in the basement or carried to the dump. The economic censuses do not, probably cannot, keep track.

Subtraction of depreciation allowances used to provide a token adjustment but no one believes that depreciation even approximates actual retirements any more. The United States Internal Revenue Service used to publish a very detailed set of life tables for different types of machinery and buildings as guides for assigning depreciation rates. They have retreated to very few categories and general guidelines. Essentially they recognize that durability depends more and more on competition from evolving options. Change makes investment in durable goods a gamble. In 1970 our department invested in a thousand dollar mechanical calculating machine; three years later we replaced it with a faster Texas Instrument calculator for US$75.

Since we do not explicitly measure meta-investment, we are not yet ready to worry about its obsolescence. But we realize that its "useful life" certainly won't be known *a priori*. Meta-investment in the IBM XT paid off for a few years, until the next model came along. Digital Equipment's "Rainbow" personal computer sold very poorly: meta-investment in the Rainbow was essentially worthless from the start. Still, Digital's investment was genuine investment, and losers as well as winners are expected, even essential, in today's knowledge economy. Since we rely on trial-and-error and competition to select superior products and processes, we must count the costs of the errors along with those of successes in economy-wide measures of economic activity.

The notion that a significant proportion of investments will be unprofitable is scary and the current mood seems to be one of denial. Sometimes children's stories are telling metaphors. Anderson's little mermaid made a risky investment and lost out. She traded her voice and her 300-year longevity for legs and a chance to marry the prince. Yes, she saved his life, but a second-mover, a beautiful bystander who happened to be "in the right place at the right time," won his heart and married him. In the revisionist Disney version, which captures the current mood, the Little Mermaid marries the prince. Disney doesn't even mention the beautiful second mover, win or lose, to the children

LOOKING AHEAD

In 1947, when I first joined the Econometric Society, its motto was "Science is measurement." I do not think measurement is all there is to science, but there is no science without it. The old metrics designed to quantify duplicative production and accumulation will not quantify new ideas nor will they measure and sort the inputs and outputs of an economic system geared to change. As Professor Dosi (Dosi, 1988) argues so eloquently, we need a new paradigm: new models, new variables. This will mean new measures. The division of labor between model building theorists and suppliers of off-the-rack data, primarily from government sources, is ending. New approaches, perhaps grounded in other disciplines, must be developed to quantify knowledge variables like firm learning, know-how, adaptation.

Measurement is not just an academic problem; it affects real-world economic decisions and policy. As the knowledge-based economy evolves, businesspeople will rely on traditional measures at their peril—and at ours. Economists claim that "no one listens to them," but reports on GDP growth and other measures of input and output certainly reverberate in the capital markets. Now that "the rising tide" no longer "floats all ships," policy makers will need to focus on the details about winners, losers and costs of change. Perhaps most important, they will be called upon to articulate priorities among diverging interests, where previously there was at least an illusory common good, some semblance of broad-based consensus.

In the short run we economists are likely to shuttle between pseudo-quantitative work with unsatisfactory "proxies" and at least a temporary "retreat" to qualitative insights characteristic of the other social sciences. In today's world, after all, royalty changes too. Leaders embrace metamorphosis to survive: *vide* the

British royal family, or Yasser Arafat. The Queen of the Social Sciences really does need new clothes. I hope we can provide something stunning!

REFERENCES

Carter, A. P. (1989), "Know-how Trading as Economic Exchange," *Research Policy,* Vol. 18, No. 3, pp. 155–163.

Carter, A. P. (1994), "Production Workers, Meta-investment and the Pace of Change," paper prepared for the meetings of the International J. A. Schumpeter Society, Munster, August, forthcoming in a volume edited by Mark Perlman, University of Michigan Press.

Dosi, G. and L. Orsenigo (1988), "Co-ordination and Transformation: Environments," Chapter 2 in Dosi *et al.* (eds.), *Technical Change and Economic Theory,* New York: Pinter Publishers.

Hayes, R. H. and R. Jaimkumar (1988), "Manufacturing's Crisis: New Technologies, Obsolete Organisations," *Harvard Business Review,* September–October, pp. 77–85.

von Hippel, E. (1994), "Sticky Information and the Locus of Problem Solving: Implications for Innovation," *Management Science,* Vol. 40, April, pp. 429–439.

Johnson, H. T. and R. S. Kaplan (1987), *Relevance Lost: The Rise and Fall of Management Accounting,* Boston: Harvard Business School Press, p. 2.

Postner, H. (1994), "The 1993 Revised System of National Accounts: Where Do We Go From Here?", paper prepared for the 23rd General Conference, International Association of Income and Wealth, New Brunswick, August 21–27.

Prahalad, C. K. and G. Hamel (1990), "The Core Competence of the Corporation," *Harvard Business Review,* May–June, pp. 79–91.

Schmookler, J. (1961), "Changes in Industry and in the State of Knowledge as Determinants of Industrial Invention" in Universities-NBER, *The Rate and Direction of Economic Activity,* Princeton: Princeton University Press, pp. 195–228.

Schumpeter, J. A. (1934), *The Theory of Economic Development,* Cambridge, MA: Harvard University Press.

14

Productivity, R&D, and the Data Constraint

Zvi Griliches

Forty years ago economists discovered the "residual." The main message of this literature, that growth in conventional inputs explains little of the observed growth in output, was first articulated by Solomon Fabricant in 1954 and emphasized further by Moses Abramovitz (1956), John Kendrick (1956), and Robert Solow (1957).[1] The pioneers of this subject were quite clear that this finding of large residuals was an embarrassment, at best "a measure of our ignorance" (Abramovitz, 1956 p. 11). But by attributing it to technical change and other sources of improved efficiency they turned it, perhaps inadvertently, from a gap in our understanding into an intellectual asset, a method for measuring "technical change." Still, it was not a comfortable situation, and a subsequent literature developed trying to "explain" this residual, or more precisely, to attribute it to particular sources (Griliches 1960, 1963a, b, 1964; Edward Denison, 1962; Dale Jorgenson and Griliches, 1967). The consensus of that literature was that, while measurement errors may play a significant role in such numbers, they could not really explain them away. The major sources of productivity growth were seen as coming from improvements in the quality of labor and capital and from other, not otherwise measured, sources of efficiency and technical change, the latter being in turn the product of formal and informal R&D investments by individuals, firms, and governments, and the largely unmeasured contributions of science and other spillovers. The prescription of additional investments in education, in science, and in industrial R&D followed from this reading of history as did also the hope and

---

1. The message itself was not exactly new. With hindsight, it is visible in the earlier work of Jan Tinbergen (1942), George Stigler (1947), Glen Barton and Martin Cooper (1948), Jacob Schmookler (1952), and Vernon Ruttan (1954, 1956). See Griliches (1994) for a more detailed account of these developments.

From *The American Economic Review,* March 1994, Vol. 84, No. 1. Reprinted by permission of the American Economic Association and Zvi Griliches.

expectation that the recently observed rates of "technical change" would continue into the future.

This general view of the sources of growth was put into doubt by the events of the 1970s and 1980s. Beginning in 1974 (or perhaps already in 1968) productivity growth slowed down significantly in the United States and abroad, and it has not fully recovered yet, at least as far as national aggregates are concerned. The many explanations that were offered for these events were not very convincing (see e.g., Denison, 1979; Martin Baily and Robert Gordon, 1988; Griliches, 1988). As time went on and the direct effects of the energy-price shocks wore off but the expected recovery did not come or came only weakly, more voices were heard arguing that the slowdown might not be temporary; that the energy-price shocks just revealed what was already there—a decline in the underlying trend of technical change in the world economy; that the growth opportunities that had opened up in the late 1930s and had been interrupted by World War II have been exhausted, reflecting perhaps the completion of an even longer cycle, going back to the beginnings of this century (see e.g., Alfred Kleinknecht, 1987; Gordon, 1993a). Even more ominously, the slowdown was blamed on diminishing returns to science and technology in general and the onset of widespread socioeconomic sclerosis (see e.g., William Nordhaus, 1972, 1989; Mancur Olsen, 1982; F. M. Scherer, 1983, 1986; Robert Evenson, 1984; Baily and A. K. Chakrabarti, 1988).

This is a rather pessimistic view of our current situation, and I would like to argue that the observed facts do not really support it. But that will not be easy, both because some of the "facts" are contradictory and because our measurement and observational tools are becoming increasingly inadequate in the context of our changing economy. Nevertheless, I will review some of the evidence for such views and argue with their interpretation. There are several possibilities here: (i) this view is true and that is sad; (ii) it is not true and recovery is around the corner if not already underway; (iii) it may be true, but whatever is or is not happening has little to do with diminishing returns to science or industrial R&D. Or, (iv) it may be that we just do not know. As is the case with global warming, we may not have an adequate understanding of the mechanisms producing growth or adequate data to adjudicate whether there has or has not been an underlying trend shift. If that is true, as is most likely, the question arises as to why we don't know more after years of research done by so many good people. What is it about our data and data acquisition structure, and possibly also our intellectual framework, that prevents us from making more progress on this topic?

In discussing this range of topics, I will concentrate primarily on the R&D component of this story—not because it can explain much of the productivity slowdown (it cannot), and not just because this is where I have done most of my recent work, but because it illustrates rather well the major point I want to make here tonight: that our understanding of what is happening in our economy (and in the world economy) is constrained by the extent and quality of the available data. I will also allude briefly to similar issues which arise in interpreting the productivity contribution of computers in the economy. Parallel tales about data constraining our understanding could also be told about other potential productivity-slowdown villains: energy-price shocks, insufficient investment in physical capital, and possible declines in human-capital investments. Having reached the verdict of "not proven," largely on account of insufficient evidence, I shall make a number of more general remarks on the state of our data and the possible reasons for it. The major message that I will be trying to convey is that we often misinterpret the available data because of inadequate attention to how they are produced and that the same inattention by us to the sources of our data helps explain why progress is so slow. It is not just the measurement of productivity that is affected. Other fields of empirical economics are also struggling against the limitations imposed by the available data. Great advances have been made in theory and in econometric techniques, but these will be wasted unless they are applied to the right data.

I. THE "FACTS"

There are three sets of "facts" to look at: what has happened to productivity, what has happened to investment in R&D and science, and what has happened to the relationship between them. Sometime in the late 1960s measured productivity growth in the United States started to slow down. After a mild recovery in the early 1970s, the world economy was hit by two successive oil-price shocks which dropped economic growth rates in most of the developed economies to levels significantly below those experienced in the 1960s and early 1970s. While the effects of the oil-price shocks wore off and real energy prices declined to close to their earlier levels, productivity growth rates did not recover much. At this point, and also somewhat earlier, many observers started wondering whether something more fundamental than just an energy-price-shock-induced business cycle was afoot. Standing in the early 1980s and looking back at the recent past, one would have observed a decline in total patents granted in the United States beginning in the early 1970s and a decline in the share of GNP being devoted to industrial R&D starting in the mid-1960s, the timing looking suspiciously appropriate for declining productivity growth rates 5–10 years later.

One could also see a continuous and worrisome decline in the number of patents received per corporate R&D dollar (see below). But there were also many other events clouding this picture, making one wonder whether faltering R&D and scientific efforts are really the culprits behind our current woes.

A number of discordant facts are important for an understanding of what happened. First, the productivity-growth decline in many other countries was larger, absolutely, than in the United States, and there it was not associated with declines in R&D investment.[2] Second, as illustrated in Figure 14.1, the sectors

---

2. For example, the role of growth in total factor productivity declined between the 1960s and the 1970s by 4.5 percent in Japan, 3.3 percent in France, and "only" 2 percent in the United States (see Organization for Economic Cooperation and Development, 1993).

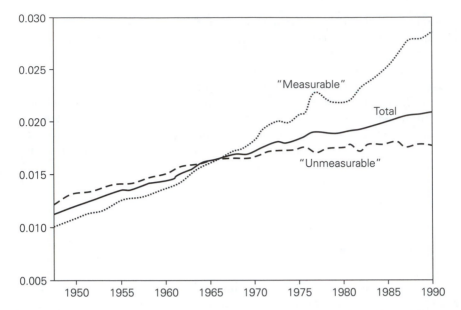

FIGURE 14.1 Gross domestic product per man-hour (thousands of 1982 dollars, United States, 1948–1990).

Notes: Measurable sectors are agriculture, mining, manufacturing, transportation, communications, and public utilities, unmeasurable sectors are construction, trade, finance, other services, and government. Values for 1977–1987 are based on 1987 weights; values for 1941–1976 are based on 1982 weights (the series are linked at 1977).

where the productivity slowdown has persisted in the United States are largely outside of manufacturing, communications, and agriculture (see Gordon, 1987). Besides mining and public utilities, which were affected more specifically by the energy-price shocks, it has lingered particularly in construction, finance, and other services where output measurement is notoriously difficult. Third, the decline in patent grants in the 1970s was just a bureaucratic mirage, an example of fluctuations induced by changes in the data-generating process (a budgetary crisis in the Patent Office) rather than a reflection of the underlying activity itself.[3] The number of patent applications did not decline significantly during this period, but also it did not grow. The latter fact, coupled with a continuous upward growth in the absolute level of company-financed R&D, resulted in a persistent decline in the patents per R&D ratio in the United States (and also in most of the other countries for which we have data). This raised the specter of diminishing returns to R&D and offered the hypothesis of "exhaustion of inventive opportunities" as a potential explanation for the productivity slowdown.

---

3. See Griliches (1990) for more details on this story.

This hypothesis has been examined recently by various authors. There are basically two styles of analysis: one focuses directly on the link, if any, between R&D and productivity growth (see e.g., Griliches, 1986a; Bronwyn Hall, 1993; Scherer, 1993), while the other uses patents as indicators of the output of the R&D effort and looks at what has happened to the "knowledge-production function" (see e.g., Griliches, 1990; Ricardo Caballero and Adam Jaffe, 1993; Robert Evenson, 1993; Samuel Kortum, 1993). The bridge that is missing between these two approaches would examine the units in which patents affect productivity growth and ask whether they have stayed constant over time. Without such constancy, no clear interpretation is possible.

II. PRODUCTIVITY GROWTH AND THE ROLE OF R&D

In parallel to the aggregate "residual" literature, a more micro-oriented approach had developed. It took the study of technical change, diffusion, and the role of formal R&D as its main challenge, with the hope of bringing more of it within the realm of economic analysis, helping thereby also to explain some of this residual away. Using modern language, one can interpret Edwin Mansfield's and my own early work on diffusion and on the role of R&D in agriculture and manufacturing as trying to endogenize as much of technical change as was possible (Griliches, 1957, 1958, 1964; Mansfield, 1961, 1965). Other important contributors to this literature were Richard Nelson, Scherer, Jacob Schmookler, and Nestor Terleckyj. By expanding the notion of capital to include also R&D capital and estimating its effects, this literature documented the contribution of public and private investments in R&D and their spillovers to the growth of productivity.[4] But the magnitude of the estimated effects was modest, not enough to account for the bulk of the observed residual or the fluctuations in it (Griliches, 1988). The experience here was similar to other attempts to account for the residual, such as using "embodiment" theories to magnify the potential effects of capital accumulation (Denison, 1962; Nelson, 1962) or looking for increasing returns to scale (Griliches and Vidar Ringstad, 1972). These various effects are real and nonnegligible, but not large enough.

There is one other way of trying to make something more out of the R&D story: the possibility that the productivity impact of R&D has declined over time—that the coefficients have changed. This hypothesis has been investigated repeatedly by a number of researchers with mixed results. Studies that used data through the 1970s and early 1980s found no decline in the relevant coefficients. More recent studies that analyze data through the late 1980s report more mixed results, varying strongly with how the computer industry and its deflator are handled in the analysis.[5] At the same time, the stock market's valuation of R&D fell

---

4. This literature has been surveyed in Griliches (1979, 1991), Jacques Mairesse and Mohamed Sassenou (1991), Wallace Huffman and Evenson (1993), and M. I. Nadiri (1993).
5. As reported in Griliches (1936a), I found no significant decline in the relevant coefficients

significantly, both in terms of *ex post* returns to R&D in the 1980s (Michael Jensen, 1993) and the market's view of current R&D investments (Bronwyn Hall and Robert Hall, 1993; B. Hall, 1993).

My own recent foray into this type of analysis of industry data at the three-digit SIC level is summarized in Table 14.1.[6] It reports estimates from regressions of growth rates in total factor productivity (TFP) on the rate of investment in R&D (the R&D-sales ratio), where the estimated coefficient can be interpreted as the excess gross rate of return to R&D (Griliches, 1979). The earlier 1958–1973 period yields an estimate on the order of 0.33, while the estimate for the later 1973–1989 period even rises a bit, to 0.36. So far, so good! But when one excludes the outlier computer industry (See Fig. 14.2), the estimated coefficient falls from 0.36 to 0.13 for 1973–1989 and even lower for 1979-1989. Only one observation out of 143 does this![7]

These results raise a major data conundrum: is it right to treat the computer industry as an outlier and exclude it from such calculations just because the pro-

TABLE 14.1   Industry TFP Growth Regressions: Coefficients of the R&D—Sales Ratio by Period, Three-Digit SIC Level (N = 143 or 142)

Row	Period	With computers	Without computers
1	1958–1973	0.332 (0.066)	0.317 (0.066)
2	1973–1989	0.357 (0.072)	0.134 (0.059)
3a	1978–1989	0.300 (0.073)	0.115 (0.062)
3b	1978–1989 "revised"	0.461 (0.070)	0.348 (0.070)

Notes: The equations include also dlog (energy/capital) as an additional utilization variable. Standard errors are shown in parentheses. The ratio of company-financed R&D to total sales in 1974 is from Scherer (1984) for row 1; this ratio is updated for 1984 from National Science Foundation (1992) for rows 2 and 3. Row 3b shows total-factor-productivity growth revised downward for computers and upward for electronic components and drugs (computers = SIC 357).

through the mid-1970s. Frank Lichtenberg and Donald Siegel (1991) replicated and extended this work to the early 1980s and found *increases* in the relevant coefficients through 1985. B. Hall (1993) updated and extended the Griliches and Mairesse (1934) study of publicly traded U.S. manufacturing firms to the end of the 1980s and found that the R&D coefficients came close to disappearing in the 1970s and early 1980s but recovered in the late 1980s to about half or more of their original size. Her result is very sensitive, however, to the particular deflators used in constructing the output measure. When separate industry-level deflators are used, including the newly revised deflator for the output of the computer industry, there is no evidence of a decline in the "potency" of R&D at all; the estimated coefficients rise rather than fall. See also Englander et al. (1988) Pari Patel and Luc Soete (1988), Sveikauskas (1990), and Scherer (1993).

6. The total-factor-productivity numbers come from the National Bureau of Economic Research data base (Wayne Gray, 1992). The R&D numbers come from Scherer (1984), updated to 1984 using 2.5-digit-level information from National Science Foundation (1992).

7. Updating the Griliches and Lichtenberg (1984) results for 28 2.5-digit SIC industries and using a possibly more appropriate R&D-by-product-field measure yields essentially similar results, as does a parallel computation at the more aggregated two-digit SIC level using unpublished Bureau of Labor Statistics data on total (five-factor) productivity.

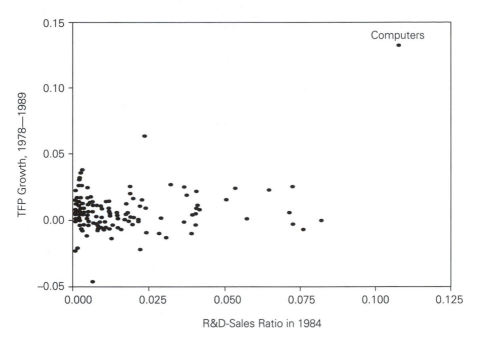

FIGURE 14.2 Total-factor-productivity growth (per annum) and research intensity in U.S. Manufacturing. Three-digit SIC Level, 1978–1989.

ductivity measure may be better there? It is quite possible that if other technologically advanced industries (such as instruments, communications equipment, and pharmaceuticals) had their price indexes adjusted in a similar fashion, Figure 14.2 would look much better, with the computer industry not being as much of an outlier and with the whole period showing much higher (social) returns to R&D. That this is indeed the case can be seen in Figure 14.3, where only three such adjustments are made, but before I discuss it, I need to digress briefly and remind you about the developments in computer price measurement.

Quality change is the bane of price and output measurement. Until 1986, computer prices were treated as unchanged in the national income accounts. It took twenty-five years for the recommendations of the Stigler committee (Griliches, 1961; National Bureau of Economic Research, 1961) to have a noticeable effect on official practice, but when they did, they did it with a bang! In 1986 the Bureau of Economic Analysis (BEA) introduced a new computer price index, based on hedonic regression methods, into the national accounts and revised them back to 1972 (Rosanne Cole et al., 1986).[8] This index was falling by about 15 percent per year or more (as compared to the assumed value of zero before), and that had several major implications, including the fact that it made the apparent recovery in manufacturing productivity in the 1980s much stronger, about one-

8. For historical background on these developments see Jack Triplett (1989) and Ernst Berndt (1991, Ch. 4).

third of the total coming from the introduction of this price index alone (Gordon, 1993b).

There was nothing wrong with the price index itself. It was, indeed, a major advance, and the BEA should be congratulated for making it, but the way it was introduced created some problems. First, it was a unique adjustment. No other high-tech product had received parallel treatment, and thus it stuck out like a sore thumb. This had the unfortunate consequence that the productivity growth in the computer industry itself was seriously overestimated, because some of its major inputs, such as semiconductors, were not similarly deflated. Second, it was introduced into a framework with fixed weights, wreaking havoc on it. Using fixed 1982 weights and a sharply falling price index implied the absence of a "real" computer industry in the early 1970s and a very rapid growth in its importance, leading to a more than doubling of the share of machinery in total manufacturing output by the late 1980s. This last problem has largely been solved recently with the introduction of "benchmark-weighted" estimates of gross domestic product (GDP) and the moving away from fixed-weights national income accounting (Allan Young, 1992). But the first problem, the uniqueness of this adjustment in the face of similar, though perhaps not as extreme, problems elsewhere remains to haunt us.

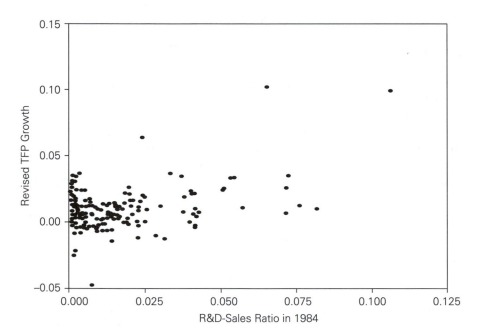

FIGURE 14.3 Revised total-factor-productivity growth (per annum), U.S. Three-digit manufacturing industries, 1978–1989.

Note: Computers adjusted downward; electronic components and drugs adjusted upward.

What I have done in Figure 14.3 (and in row 3b of Table 14.1) is to adjust the estimated TFP growth in the computer industry downward by deflating materials purchases in this industry, which to a significant extent consist of purchases of other computer components and semiconductors, by the same output price index. I have also substituted a similar price index in the semiconductors (electronic components) industry and also adjusted the growth of TFP in the pharmaceuticals industry upward to reflect the exclusion of price declines due to the introduction of generics in the current measurement procedures. (I shall come back to discuss this last adjustment later on.) So adjusted, Figure 14.3 does not look all that bad, and row 3b in Table 14.1 indicates no decline in the R&D coefficient even without the computer industry.

What is one to make of these conflicting stories? It seems that the observed decline in the R&D coefficients did not begin seriously until the latter half of the 1970s, with the second oil-price shock and the rise in the dollar exchange rate. The abruptness of the decline argues against a "supply-side" explanation in terms of exhaustion of inventive opportunities. It is more likely that the peculiar aggregate shocks of that time went against R&D-intensive industries: first, because they hit energy-intensive industries such as chemicals and petroleum refining more severely; and second, because the subsequent rise in value of the dollar and the expansion in imports that followed hit some of the more high-tech R&D-intensive industries even harder, leading to declines in "competitiveness," losses of rents, and the appearance of excess capacity. The subsequent rise in the R&D coefficients (if it did in fact occur), the rise in corporate R&D investments through most of the 1980s, and the rise in patenting in the late 1980s (as we shall see), all argue against interpreting these coefficient movements as reflecting "real" declines in the once and future potency of R&D. What did happen, though, was a sharp widening of the differential between social and private returns to R&D. The internationalization of R&D, the rise in the technical and entrepreneurial skills of our competitors, and the sharp rise in the dollar exchange rate in the mid-1980s, all combined to erode, rather rapidly, the rents accruing to the earlier accumulated R&D capital and to the technical-expertise positions of many of our enterprises. This rise in the rate of private obsolescence and the fall in the "appropriability" of R&D led to sharp declines in both profitability and real product prices. The latter, if they were actually reflected in the appropriate price indexes, would show up as an increase in productivity, rather than a decline.

Before accepting this inconclusive verdict, one still has to face the evidence of declining patent-to-R&D ratios. Figure 14.4 plots domestic patent applications divided by total company-financed R&D expenditures in U.S. industry (in 1972 dollars) and by the total number of scientists and engineers in industry. Looking at the right half of this plot (the last couple of decades) we see a more or less continuous decline with a small, but possibly significant, turnaround in the late 1980s. Similar trends can be seen also in other countries, even in Japan (Evenson, 1991). But before one takes this as an indicator of our recent problems, one should glance also at the left side of this figure, which goes back to the early 1920s. How long has this been going on? This ratio keeps falling, both through good times

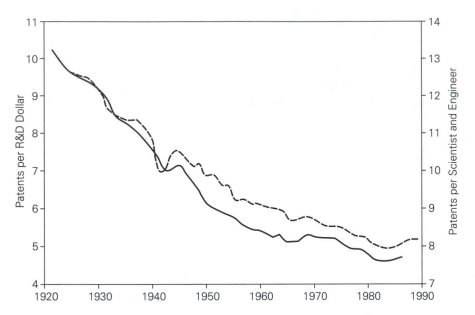

FIGURE 14.4 Domestic patent applications per company-financed R&D in industry (dashed line; in 1972 dollars) and per scientist and engineer (solid line), log scale.

(while productivity growth rates were rising) and bad times. If this was not a cause for worry earlier, why should one worry about it now?[9]

III. PATENTS: A SHRINKING YARDSTICK?

To decide whether we should be worried by what is happening with the patent numbers we need to know what they measure. Since I have discussed this at some length elsewhere (Griliches, 1990), I will make only two points here. First, the interpretation of Figure 14.4 need not be pessimistic. Its message may not be what meets the eye. And, second, the meaning of both the numerator and the denominators of the ratios plotted in Figure 14.4 may have changed significantly over time.

If patents can be taken as indicators of invention, and if the value of an invention is proportional to the size of its market (or economy), then the fact that their total numbers remained roughly constant over long time periods is consistent with nondeclining growth rates of output and overall productivity.[10] If inven-

9. Actually quite a few people worried about it then also: see Griliches (1990) for more detail and W. Fellner (1970), who worried about the rising real cost of R&D as an indicator of diminishing returns.
10. This follows from the nonrival nature of inventions (see Kenneth Arrow, 1962; Paul Romer, 1990).

tions are "produced" by a combination of current R&D and the existing state of knowledge (incorporating the accumulated effects of science and spillovers from the previous research activities of others), and if R&D is invested approximately "optimally," then under reasonable assumptions, a rise (or fall) in the underlying knowledge stock will affect them both in parallel fashion and will leave their ratio unchanged.[11] There will be, therefore, no evidence in this ratio on the underlying state of the "stock of knowledge." Moreover, it will be declining with growth in the size of the market, since a rise in the value of inventions will push R&D up until present costs equal again the present value of future (private) returns.

The rate of growth of domestic patents was close to zero during the last three decades. That by itself should not be worrisome. If their average value had been growing at the same rate as the economy as a whole, there would be no reason for us to worry about it. But there were long periods when the actual numbers were worse than that. During 1965–1985 the number of domestic patent applications declined by –0.6 percent per year while company-financed R&D expenditures were growing by 4.8 percent per year, in constant prices. But a negative growth rate in the number of inventions and a positive one in R&D are inconsistent with an unchanging inventions production function, unless the overall pool of available knowledge is declining, or more likely, unless the relationship between inventions and the number of patents applied for has been changing.

The suspicion that the relationship between the number of patents and the number of inventions (weighted by their relative economic importance) has been changing is not new. Schmookler (1966) stops most of his analysis with pre-World War II data, believing that the meaning of the patent statistics changed at that time. What needs to be reconciled in the data is the sharp contrast between the rapidly growing R&D series during 1953–1968 (and earlier) and the essentially flat patent series. There are a number of not mutually exclusive possibilities here:

(i) The fast-growing R&D expenditures, fueled by the new global opportunities that opened up in the post-World War II period, were being invested in the face of rapidly diminishing returns.

(ii) Some of the observed growth in R&D could be spurious, the result of reclassification of informal technological activities into formal R&D

---

11. Assume an aggregate inventions "production function" of the form $N = R^\gamma Z$, where R is a measure of current R&D inputs and Z represents all other shifters of this function: the accumulation of one's own past R&D successes and also spillovers from the research efforts of others. Then, $\gamma < 1$ implies short-run diminishing returns to current R&D, a "fishing-out" phenomenon given the current "state of the art" Z. To the extent that endogenous (and exogenous) forces "recharge" the pool (in Evenson's [1991] terminology) and change Z as the result of the direct and indirect additions to the overall stock of knowledge, there need not be diminishing returns to R in the long run. If R is chosen so as to equate the value of its marginal product, $V(\gamma N/R)$, to the marginal real cost of R, C, and if V is *the* expected present value of an invention, one can rewrite the first-order condition as $N/R = C/\gamma V$, which yields the major conclusion that the ratio of inventions per unit of R&D is independent of the state of general knowledge Z. Moreover, N/R will be declining in V, the size of the market. For a more detailed elaboration of such models see the "quality ladders" approach of Gene Grossman and Elhanan Helpman (1991), Caballero and Jaffe (1993), and Kortum (1993).

under the pressure of tax accountants, public-relations experts, and R&D tax credits.

(iii) The rise of formal R&D-based invention crowded out smaller, less valuable individual-inventor-based patents, while the rise in the cost of patenting (in terms of the time costs of dealing with the patent system) and the more recent sharp rise in fees may have selected out a large number of potentially low-valued patents. Given the evidence that the value distribution of inventions and patents is extremely skewed, with only a small fraction having a high present value, such a crowding out could raise average values significantly, though the required rate is rather on the high side.[12]

It is also likely that the threshold for what is patentable has risen, given the large influx of foreign patent applications into the U.S. system all impinging on a relatively slow-growing and budget-constrained patent office.[13] On the other hand, the legal status of patents in the United States has improved significantly with the creation of a special patents court, driving up the expected private value of a patent. Given the presence of so many opposing forces, there is no compelling need to reply on the exhaustion-of-inventive-opportunities hypothesis, especially since patents-to-R&D ratios were falling much more drastically during the "good times" of the past than recently.[14] Moreover, if we do take these numbers seriously, then good news is just around the corner: domestic patent applications have risen sharply in the last five years (See Fig. 14.5), implying a potential resurgence in the rate of technological change. This leaves us, however, more or less where we started, with the productivity slowdown largely unexplained.

The impact on productivity is too fast. Rather, it is likely to reflect the impact of the slowdown in the growth of aggregate demand and the recessions of the 1970s. In both cases there is an upturn in the 1980s.

12. There is scattered evidence on the rising "quality" of patents from patent renewal data (see Mark Schankermun and Ariel Pakes, 1986; Pakes and Margaret Simpson, 1989) and from the rising number of claims per patent (see X. Tong and J. D. Frame, 1992). The latter, for example, rose at about 2.5 percent per year between 1970 and 1990. That is about right for this period but far too low for the 6+ percent earlier. On the other hand, Cabellero and Jaffe (1993), using citation data, find that the average size of a patent did not grow during the last 20 years.

13. There is some evidence that such crowding-out may have occurred. Between 1966–1969 and 1981–1985 the "yield ratio" for domestic patent applications in terms of grants received fell by about 15 percent (from 0.68 to 0.58) before recovering somewhat in the late 1980s (to 0.62). See Griliches (1990) for a survey of these issues and citations to the relevant literature.

14. A similar story is also told by other scattered invention "output" indicators. In their study of innovations in the chemical, textile, and machinery-tools industries, Baily and Chukrabarti (1988) found a decline in the number of innovations in the 1970s in two out of these three industries, and some recovery thereafter. Similar patterns were observed in a study of British industrial innovations (see the figure in Gerhard Mensch et al. [1991]). In both cases the timing is not right for an explanation of the slowdown in the 1970s.

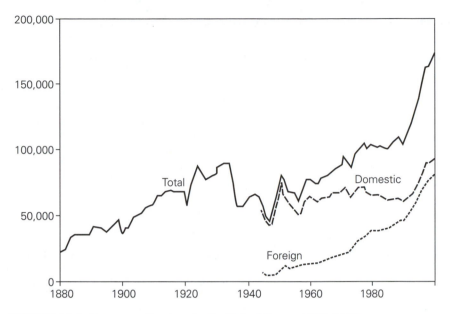

FIGURE 14.5   Patent applications in the United States, 1880–1992.

IV. WHY IS THE GLASS HALF-EMPTY?

Economists have not been very successful in explaining what has happened to the economy during the last two decades, nor have they been able to agree on what should be done about it. I will argue that data and measurement difficulties may in fact be a major source of this failure. This point will be made not to provide us with an alibi, but rather to temper the pretentiousness of some of our pronouncements and to urge us toward the more mundane task of observation and measurement.

Why don't we know more after all these years? Our data have always been less than perfect. What is it about the recent situation that has made matters worse?

The brief answer is that the economy has changed and that our data-collection efforts have not kept pace with it. "Real" national income accounts were designed in an earlier era, when the economy was simpler and had a large agricultural sector and a growing manufacturing sector. Even then, a number of compromises had to be made to get measurement off the ground. In large sectors of the economy, such as construction and most of the services, government, and other public institutions, there were no real output measures or relevant price deflators. Imagine a "degrees of measurability" scale, with wheat production at one end and lawyer services at the other. One can draw a rough dividing line on this scale between what I shall call "reasonably measurable" sectors and the rest, where the situation is not much better today than it was at the beginning of the national income accounts. Table 14.2 shows the distribution of nominal GDP by

TABLE 14.2   The Distribution of GNP by Major Industrial Sector,
in Current Prices (Percentages)

Industry	1947	1959	1969	1977	1990
Agriculture	8.8	4.1	3.0	2.8	2.0
Mining	2.9	2.5	1.8	2.7	1.8
Construction	3.9	4.8	5.1	4.8	4.4
Manufacturing	28.1	28.6	26.9	23.6	18.4
Transportation and utilities	8.9	9.1	8.6	9.1	8.7
Wholesale trade	7.1	6.9	6.7	7.0	6.5
Retail trade	11.7	9.9	9.8	9.6	9.3
Finance, insurance, and real estate	10.1	13.8	14.2	14.4	17.7
Other services	8.6	9.7	11.5	13.0	18.9
Government	8.6	10.2	12.6	12.5	12.2
Measurable sectors[a]	48.7	44.3	40.3	38.2	30.9

Note: Numbers before 1977 are not strictly comparable, since the latest revision was carried back only to 1977.
Source: Tables 6.1 and 6.2 of the National Income and Products Accounts (1928–1982) and Survey of Current Business (May 1993).
[a]Agriculture, mining, manufacturing, and transportation and utilities.

major industrial sector. In the early post-World War II period, the situation was not all that bad: about half of the overall economy was "measurable" in this sense. By 1990, however, the fraction of the economy for which the productivity numbers are half reasonable had fallen to below one-third. Figure 14.6 tells the same story with employment numbers. Measurement problems have indeed become worse. Our ability to interpret changes in aggregate total factor productivity has declined, and major portions of actual technical change have eluded our measurement framework entirely.[15]

An example of the consequences of this shift is what has come to be known as the "computer paradox." We have made major investments in computers and in other information-processing equipment. The share of "information" equipment in total producer investment in durable equipment, in current prices, has more than doubled, from about 17 percent in 1960 to 36 percent in 1992. Computers alone went up from less than 1 percent to 11 percent of the total; and that does not allow for improvements in the quality of this equipment, which has been

---

15. An argument could be made that this story would not be so bleak if we had focused on consumption expenditures instead, since many of the offending industries produce largely intermediate products and services. But personal consumption expenditures account only for about 68 percent of GDP, while services represent 56 percent of personal consumption. Thus, it is unlikely that looking at consumption data in more detail would change the tenor of my remarks much. A cursory look at Personal Consumption Expenditures (Bureau of Economic Analysis, 1990) yields a rough estimate of 47 percent of total consumption expenditures not easily measurable in real terms. The two largest difficult items consist of hard-to-measure services in the medical, insurance, legal, entertainment, and education areas (23 percent) and housing-related services (21 percent).

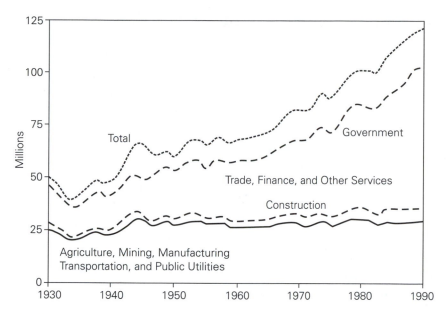

FIGURE 14.6   Persons engaged in production by industry, United States, 1929–1980.

happening at a very fast rate—on the order of 15–30 percent per year (See Jack Triplett, 1989; Berndt and Griliches, 1993). Why has this not translated itself into visible productivity gains? The major answer to this puzzle is very simple: over three quarters of this investment has gone into our "unmeasurable" sectors (see Table 14.3), and thus its productivity effects, which are likely to be quite real, are largely invisible in the data.

That there were gains is not really in doubt. Just observing the changes in the way banks and airlines operate, and in the ways in which information is delivered to firms and consumers, would lead one to conclude that we are in the midst of a major technical revolution. Effective distances are declining rapidly in many parts of the world. The rise of ATM networks in banking has resulted in substantial though largely unmeasured time savings for consumers. It is less clear, however, whether the large expansion of the securities industry has been associated with a similar productivity increase or was primarily a response to a real decline in the cost of rent-seeking induced by the falling price of information-processing (see Timothy Bresnahan et al., 1992).

There is also some scattered evidence for the positive contribution of computers in manufacturing, but given the needle-in-the haystack aspect of this problem, it is not particularly strong (see e.g., Alan Krueger, 1991; Donald Siegel and Griliches, 1992; Erik Brynjolfson and Lorin Hitt, 1993; Igal Hendel, 1993). Some of the gains from computers have been reflected in higher wages of their operators and in the more general rise in the returns to education and "skill" (Chinhui Juhn et al., 1993). More generally, we may be just at the beginning of the computer era,

TABLE 14.3   Investment in Computers (OCAM) in the US Economy
(Percentage of Total)

Industry	1979	1989	1992
Agriculture	0.1	0.1	0.1
Mining	2.4	1.1	0.9
Construction	0.1	0.3	0.2
Manufacturing	29.4	20.3	20.0
Transportation	1.3	2.0	1.0
Communication	1.5	1.4	1.5
Utilities	1.2	2.8	3.7
Trade	19.9	16.3	20.0
Finance, insurance, and real estimate (F.I.R.E.)	32.5	38.7	37.8
Other services	11.6	17.0	13.9
"Unmeasurable" sectors[a]	64.1	72.3	71.9
Plus consumer and government purchases as percentage of all computer (OCAM) purchases	67.7	77.6	77.0

Notes: OCAM = office, computing, and accounting machinery.
Source: Unpublished BEA tabulations.
[a]Construction, trade, F.I.R.E., and other services.

early in its diffusion and learning stages, with most of the productivity contributions still to come, as we learn how to use computers more effectively and integrate them more efficiently into the existing production structures (Paul David, 1991).

Similar arguments can be (and have been) made about the difficulties in measuring the contribution of R&D to productivity growth (see Griliches, 1979). From one-third to over half of all industrial R&D is "sold" to the government, either in the form of research contracts and prototypes or indirectly in the form of weapons and space equipment, and its direct productivity effects do not show up in the data at all. Private R&D investment is also likely to have followed the economy and shifted its targets toward the faster-growing sectors, with more invention and technical change occurring exactly where we have more trouble in measuring them.

Not only has the economy shifted into uncharted waters, but even in the "measurable" sectors, accelerating rates of change have destroyed the basis for some of the older compromises. Currently, new goods are introduced into the various official price indexes rather slowly. While attempts are being made to reduce the revision cycle in the producer price index from five to two years for some of the more high-tech goods, this may still not be fast enough. In the personal-computers market, for example, the life of a model has recently fallen to a year or less (Berndt et al., 1993).

Dealing with the quality-change problem by treating every version of a product sold to a different type of customer as a separate commodity, as is currently the predominant official practice, creates its own problems. By linking out the decline in prices experienced by consumers in their shift to supermarkets, discount stores, and mail-order purchases, it underestimates significantly not only the output of services, but also the output of some of the more "standard" manufacturing industries (Marshall Reinsdorf, 1993). A prime example of that is the treatment of generics in the pharmaceutical price indexes. The stylized facts are as follows:

(i) Generics are introduced at roughly half the price of the original brand.
(ii) The brand price, however, does not decline (it sometimes even goes up), with the ex-monopolist depreciating optimally her original position and with generics gaining between half and three-quarters of the market for the particular drug.
(iii) But because generic versions are treated as separate commodities, in spite of what the FDA says, the price index does not fall, and since the value of shipments declines as the market shifts to generics (and to hospital and HMO formularies), so does measured "output" in this industry and the associated productivity measures (Griliches and Iain Cockburn, 1993).

This might explain the rather strange fact that during the last decade pharmaceuticals, an industry with one of the highest R&D-sales ratios, had a rather dismal productivity-growth performance. This was the period with an increasing penetration of generics, which should have reduced measured prices in this industry but did not.

The measurement environment has also deteriorated in other ways. There is less willingness on the part of firms and consumers to respond to detailed questions, and our government has done little to emphasize the importance of good economic data to its own functioning or the overall understanding of our economy. The consequence of such deterioration can be illustrated by the uncertainty about the level of industrial investment in basic research, an investment which many think is crucial to our long-run economic performance (Griliches, 1986a). Because the question that asks about the allocation of total R&D expenditures by the "character of work" is not mandatory and is also not an easy one to answer, less than half of all the firms surveyed in 1988 answered it. As a result of such nonresponse, the best that can be done is to produce a "reasonable" range of estimates, based on alternative imputation algorithms, from $2.5 to $8.2 billion (and a "central" guess of $3.9 billion), which leaves us really in the dark as to what has happened to such investments recently (Eileen I. Collins, 1990).

V. DATA WOES

Why are the data not better? The facts themselves are not in dispute. Every decade or so a prestigious commission or committee produces a report describing in detail various data difficulties and lacunae: the Stigler committee report on government price statistics (National Bureau of Economic Research, 1961) is still a living document, as are the related Ruggles report (Richard Ruggles, 1977), the Rees productivity report (National Academy of Sciences, 1979), the Bonnen report (J. T. Bonnen, 1981), the Creamer GNP improvement report (D. Creamer, 1977), the recent OTA report (Office of Technology Assessment, 1989), and many others. But life goes on, and change in this area is very slow. Why? I don't really have good answers to this question, and the topic itself is much larger than can be handled in this address, but at least three observations come to mind:

(i)   The measurement problems are really hard.
(ii)   Economists have little clout in Washington, especially as far as data-collection activities are concerned. Moreover, the governmental agencies in these areas are balkanized and underfunded.
(iii) We ourselves do not put enough emphasis on the value of data and data collection in our training of graduate students and in the reward structure of our profession. It is the preparation skill of the econometric chef that catches the professional eye, not the quality of the raw materials in the meal, or the effort that went into procuring them (Griliches, 1986b).

In many cases the desired data are unavailable because their measurement is really difficult. After decades of discussion we are not even close to a professional agreement on how to define and measure the output of banking, insurance, or the stock market (see Griliches, 1992). Similar difficulties arise in conceptualizing the output of health services, lawyers, and other consultants, or the capital stock of R&D. While the tasks are difficult, progress has been made on such topics. The work of Jorgenson and Barbara Fraumeni (1992) on the measurement of educational output is an example both of what can be done and of the difficulties that still remain. But it is not reasonable for us to expect the government to produce statistics in areas where the concepts are mushy and where there is little professional agreement on what is to be measured and how. Much more could be done, however, in an exploratory and research mode.[16] Unfortunately, the various statistical agencies have been both starved for funds and badly led, with the existing bureaucratic structure downplaying the research components of their enterprise when not being outright hostile to them, research being cut first when a budget crunch happens (Triplett, 1991).

Our current statistical structure is badly split, there is no central direction, and the funding is heavily politicized. How else can one explain that the national income accounts and the BEA as a whole receive only one-third, and health and education statistics each less than one-half of the funds allocated to agricultural

---

16. I refrain from offering a detailed list of my own favorite data improvements; but a census of real wealth (i.e., a survey of structure, equipment, and other resources and their utilization—not just what is on the books, but what is actually out there in the field) would be high on my list. I would also like to see a survey of patent owners on the use and potential value of their property rights.

statistics?[17] How does one explain the failure of the most recent attempt at getting more money for economic statistics, the late "Boskin initiative"? Central economic statistics do not have a clear constituency that lobbies on their behalf. Recent governments seem not to care enough, or to have enough energy to fight for something that has a more distant horizon than the next election. One hopes for some improvement in this situation from the current administration. It has people who know better in reasonably important positions. Still, with the main focus on the daily crisis and the continuing budget battles with Congress, I am not all that optimistic. But if we want progress in this area, if we care, we need to make our opinions heard. We need to convince Congress (and ourselves) that the requests for additional funding of the statistical infrastructure are justified as investments in general knowledge and more informed policy formation; that they are not just self-serving, intended to allow us to publish more articles or run thousands more regressions; that it is indeed important to know what is happening and to understand where we might be going or drifting.[18]

We need also to make observation, data collection, and data analysis a more central component of our graduate teaching. How can we expect our community to fight for the budgets of the BEA, BLS, or Census, if the average student doesn't really know how the data that they use are manufactured or what the national accounts are made of?[19] We also need to teach them to go out and collect their own data on interesting aspects of the economy and to rely less on "given" data from distant agencies.[20] There are encouraging signs that some of this is happening, especially in the micro area. One is much more cheered by work such as that of Robert Fogel (1986) on heights and nutrition, Alan Krueger and Orley Ashenfelter (1992) on twins, Richard Levin et al. (1987) on the appropriability of technology, Rebecca Henderson and Cockburn on pharmaceutical R&D, Richard Freeman and Harry Holtzer (1986) on inner-city youths, Schankerman and Pakes (1986) on patent renewal data, Manuel Trajtenberg (1990a) on CT scanners, and Trajtenberg (1990b) and Adam Jaffe et al. (1993) on patent citations, where re-

17. I am not arguing that too much is being currently spent on agricultural statistics. That would require a substantive analysis, which has not been done. I am saying, however, that the other areas of federal statistics could use both more funding and a redirection of existing funding. We are also currently spending far more on monthly employment and average hourly earnings data than we spend to collect all of the other inputs and outputs annually. With Congressional prodding, we spend much more on local-markets data than on national-level data.

18. One should probably worry also about the overall level of support for economic research. As a percentage of total academic research funding, it fell from 1.5 percent in 1979 to 1.2 percent in 1990. While the number of economists doing academic research was rising at 5.5 percent per year, funds per researcher were falling in real terms at -2.3 percent per year, and the federal share in these funds was also dropping from 48 percent to only 27 percent (in 1989). At the same time, real funds per researcher in the academy as a whole were rising at 0.4 percent per year (National Science Board, 1991). What is it that we have been doing wrong?

19. The recent shift toward a "three essays" Ph.D. thesis is also not conducive to a serious involvement with data creation.

20. Unfortunately, the usage is apt. Data already means "given" rather than collected or observed.

searchers go out, collect, and create new data sets, than by the 20,000th regression on the Robert Summers and Alan Heston (1991) data set, illuminating as it may be. But unless we transmit this message to our students, we will not be able to convince others that this is a cause worth supporting.

VI. EXPANDING THE FRAMEWORK

Is there something possibly wrong with the way we ask the productivity question, with the analytical framework into which we force the available data? I think so. I would focus on the treatment of disequilibria and the measurement of knowledge and other externalities. The current measurement framework proceeds as if all investment and employment decisions are made at known and common factor and product prices, throwing all of the heterogeneity and uncertainty—the surprises and the disappointments—into the residual category. An alternative view would see measured productivity growth as a summation of above- (and below-) average returns to various current investment decisions and capital gains (or losses) on existing physical- and human-capital stocks.[21] The appearance of such investment opportunities is the essence of growth and change. They are largely disequilibrium phenomena, resulting in a lurching from one "steady state" to another rather than something smooth and exponential. The presence of locally increasing returns, network externalities, asymmetric information, and heterogeneous expectations, the appearance of new products and technologies, and the changes in the political and regulatory environments are all sources of such "excess" returns, while the ex post fixity of much of the investment in both physical and human capital causes capital gains and losses and unanticipated "obsolescence" in the various stocks. We will have to figure out how to take the residual apart along such lines to make more progress in understanding its proximate sources.

Our theories tend to assume that we are, indeed, at the frontier and that we can only either move along it or try to shift it, the latter being a difficult and chancy business. In fact we may be far from our existing "frontiers." Harvey Leibenstein's (1966) ideas about X-efficiency, or more correctly X-inefficiency, did not get much of a sympathetic ear from us. They were inconsistent with notions of equilibrium, the absence of unexploited profit opportunities, and the possibilities for economic arbitrage. But real economic growth is the consequence of both the appearance of such disequilibria and the devising of ways of closing them. How quickly they are eliminated depends on the strength of incentive systems within enterprises, and on their organizational quality. In spite of the large growth in the literature on organizations, we have not yet developed useful ways of quantifying their strengths and weaknesses. Nor are we close to having measures of such fac-

---

21. This is not a new idea. Versions of it appear in Harry Johnson (1964), Arnold Harberger (1990), and Theodore Schultz (1990) and presumably also elsewhere.

tors as the "work ethic" or aspects of the property-rights system that are likely to contribute much to the observed differences in productivity across nations.

The "new" growth theories have various externalities as their centerpiece (see Solow [1991] for a recent review). It is somewhat ironic that they have come to the fore just when growth started declining and notions of eternal exponential growth began to lose their luster. Knowledge externalities are obviously very important in the growth process, but they do not help us to explain what has happened in the last two decades. There is no reason to believe that they have declined over time. If anything, the communication and transportation advances should have expanded the availability of such externalities.[22] But we have no good models for the measurement of such processes.

Knowledge is not like a stock of ore, sitting there waiting to be mined. It is an extremely heterogenous assortment of information in continuous flux. Only a small part of it is of any use to someone at a particular point of time, and it takes effort and resources to access, retrieve, and adapt it to one's own use. Thus models of externalities must perforce be models of interaction between different actors in the economy. We have, however, very few convincing models of such interactions, and the identification problems are severe (see e.g., Charles Manski, 1993). Our measurement frameworks are not set up to record detailed origin and destination data for commodity flows, much less so for information flows. We do have now a new tool for studying some of this: citations to patents and the scientific literature (see e.g., Jaffe et al., 1993), but anyone currently active in the e-mail revolution and participating in the conferences and workshops circuit knows how small this tip is relative to the informal-communications iceberg itself.

VII. THE GLASS HALF-FULL?

After a long detour I come back to the original question: why don't we know more about the sources of productivity growth and the causes for its recent slowdown? Why does it feel as if the glass is still half-empty? First note that in a trivial sense we are doing better: The residual is smaller. But that is the bad news, not the good. It is smaller not because we have succeeded in providing a substantively fuller explanation of output growth, but rather because measured output growth declined, leaving some of these explanations in the dust. But we are also doing better substantively. We know much more about the components of growth and where our measures are lacking. After decades of work and contributions by Denison, Jorgenson, Kendrick, and many others, the conceptual and measurement underpinnings of the growth accounts are in much better shape today. We now have extensive micro data on firms, their productivity, their R&D expenditures, and other variables. We have more data on individual investments in education

---

22. The story is similar for externalities from human-capital investments, another linchpin of the new growth theories, but I will not pursue it here.

and training, and we also have more asset detail on capital formation. More international data are now available, with the OECD both collecting R&D data and computing TFP numbers for many countries, and with Summers and Heston (1991) providing comparable real GNP numbers for many countries. Finally, we have much more computing power and better econometric techniques and frameworks for attacking many of the problems that arise in the analysis of such data. So what is still missing?

We are caught up in a mixture of unmeasurement, mismeasurement, and unrealistic expectations. The productivity situation is both better than we think and also worse. It is likely that there have been significant unmeasured productivity advances in many of the service sectors (Bresnahan, 1986; Baily and Gordon, 1988). Moreover, rising R&D investment rates in the mid-1980s and the recent rise in the number of patent applications augur well for the future. Also, productivity growth rates are probably underestimated even in the "measurable" sectors because they are based on "book value" estimates of physical- and human-capital stocks and do not reflect the capital losses—the obsolescence that occurred, first as the result of the various energy-price shocks, and later as the result of increased international competition and the melting away of much of the previously existing monopoly rents to both types of capital. That is actually bad news. We are not as wealthy as we thought, but productivity growth, based on the lower remaining levels of input, is probably higher than we have measured it.

A cautionary remark needs to be added here: productivity growth contributes to the potential for welfare, but it is not the same thing. Welfare can move in the opposite direction if the resources released by productivity growth do not find adequate employment in other, economically valuable, activities (including leisure). Also the physical, economic, and political environments can change, both positively and negatively, overwhelming the productivity story.[23] So even though I have been focusing on it here tonight, it is not the be-all of economic welfare. But as George Bernard Shaw used to say when he was accused of money-grubbing: "Yes, I know that money is not happiness, but it is a pretty good substitute."

Nevertheless, the issues I have been discussing here tonight are important. Much depends on whether the "truth" is closer to the upper ("measurable") line in Figure 14.1, or the lower one. The country's mood is affected by bad data and incorrect perceptions. Are we really not much better off than we were in the 1960s? Would we really like to exchange the commodity assortment we have today for that of yesteryear? Our health system, warts and all? The air pollution? The civil-rights situation? The fear of nuclear war? These are not just idle intellectual curiosities. They affect what we feel about ourselves and the future.

Returning to the topic of technical change, our expectations of what economics can deliver here may also be excessive. It is unlikely that we can have a

---

23. Between 1970 and 1989, average hours of work per worker went down by seven percent, air pollution went down significantly, and the crime rate came close to doubling (Baily et al., 1993). Of course, these data are also problematic (see Scott Boggess and John Bound, 1993).

fully "endogenous" theory of technical change. Yes, both the rate and direction of inventive activity are subject to economic influences and analysis. So also is the diffusion of innovations. But the outcome of inventive activity is not really predictable. True "innovation" is an innovation. If it were knowable in advance it would not be one, and the innovators would not be able to collect any rents. In that sense it is futile to expect that we could control it fully or predict it well.[24] Given the fundamental uncertainties entailed in the creative act, in invention, and in innovation, there is no reason to expect the fit of our models to be high or for the true residual to disappear. We should, however, be able to "explain" it better ex post even if we cannot predict it.

The metaphor of the glass half-empty is also misleading. As we fill it, the glass keeps growing. A major aspect of learning is that the unknown keeps expanding as we learn. This should be looked at positively. It is much better this way—especially for those of us who are engaged in research!

REFERENCES

Abramovitz, Moses. "Resource and Output Trends in the U.S. since 1870." *American Economic Review,* May 1956 (Papers and Proceedings), 46(2), pp. 5–23.

Arrow, Kenneth J. "The Economic Implications of Learning by Doing." *Review of Economic Studies,* June 1962, 29(3), pp. 155–73.

———. "Classificatory Notes on the Production and Transmission of Technological Knowledge." *American Economic Review,* May 1969 (Papers and Proceedings), 59(2), pp. 29–35.

Baily, Martin N.; Burtless, G. and Litan, R. E. *Growth with equity: Economic policymaking for the next century.* Washington, DC: Brookings Institution, 1993.

Baily, Martin N. and Chakrbarti, A. K. *Innovation and the productivity crisis.* Washington, DC: Brookings Institution, 1988.

Baily, Martin N. and Gordon, Robert J. "The Productivity Slowdown, Measurement Issues, and the Explosion of Computer Power." *Brookings Papers on Economic Activity,* 1988, (2), pp. 347–420.

Barton, Glen T. and Cooper, M. R. "Relation of Agricultural Production to Inputs." *Review of Economics and Statistics,* May 1948, 30(2), pp. 117–26.

Berndt, Ernst R. *The practice of econometrics: Classic and contemporary.* Reading, MA: Addison-Wesley, 1991.

Berndt, Ernst R. and Griliches, Zvi. "Price Indexes for Microcomputers: An Exploratory Study," in M. E. Manser, M. F. Foss, and A. H. Young, eds., *Price measurements and their uses, NBER Studies in Income and Wealth,* Vol. 57. Chicago: University of Chicago Press, 1993, pp. 63–93.

---

24. The set of opportunities for innovation at any moment are determined by what the physical laws of the world really are and how much has already been learned and is therefore "accidental" from the viewpoint of economics (Arrow, 1969 p. 35).

Berndt, Ernst R.; Griliches, Zvi and Rappaport, Neal. "Econometric Estimates of Price Indexes for Personal Computers in the 1990's." Unpublished paper, Massachusetts Institute of Technology, 1993.

Boggess, Scott and Bound, John. "Did Criminal Activity Increase During the 1980s? Comparison Across Data Sources." *National Bureau of Economic Research* (Cambridge, MA), Working Paper No. 4431, 1993.

Bonnen, J. T. "Improving the Federal Statistical System: Issues and Options." *Statistical Reporter,* February 1981, pp. 133–221.

Bresnahan, Timothy F. "Measuring the Spillovers from Technical Advance." *American Economic Review,* September 1986, 76(4), pp. 741–55.

Bresnahan Timothy F.; Milgrom, P. and Paul, J. "The Real Output of the Stock Exchange," in Z. Griliches, ed., Output measurement in the service sectors, NBER Studies in Income and Wealth, Vol. 56. Chicago: University of Chicago Press, 1992, pp. 195–218.

Brynolfson, Erik and Hitt, Lorin. "Is Information Systems Spending Productive? New Evidence and New Results." Sloan School (Massachusetts Institute of Technology) Working Paper No. 357-93 1993.

Bureau of Economic Analysis, U.S. Department of Commerce. *The National Income and Product Accounts of the United States, 1929–1982.* Washington, DC: U.S. Government Printing Office, 1986.

————. Personal consumption expenditures, Methodology Paper Series MP-6. Washington, DC: U.S. Government Printing Office, 1990.

Caballero, Ricardo J. and Jaffe, Adam B. "How High Are The 'Giants' Shoulders?" in Olivier J. Blanchard and Stanley Fischer, eds., *NBER Macroeconomics Annual,* Cambridge, MA: MIT Press, 1993, pp. 15–74.

Cole, Rosanne; Chen, Y. C.; Barquin-Stolleman, J. A.; Dulberger, E.; Helvecian, N. and Hodge, J. H. "Quality Adjusted Price Indexes for Computer Processors and Selected Peripheral Equipment." *Survey of Current Business,* January 1986, 66(1), pp. 41–50.

Collins, Eileen L. "Estimating Basic and Applied Research and Development in Industry: A Preliminary Review of Survey Procedures," NSF 90-322. Washington, DC: National Science Foundation, 1990.

Creamer, D. *Gross National Product Improvement Project Report.* U.S. Department of Commerce, Office of Federal Statistical Policy and Standards, Washington, DC: U.S. Government Printing Office, 1977.

David, Paul A. "Computer and Dynamo: The Modern Productivity Paradox in a Not-Too-Distant Mirror," in *Technology and Productivity.* Paris: Organization for Economic Cooperation and Development, 1991, pp. 315–48.

Denison, Edward F. "The Sources of Economic Growth in the U.S. and the Alternatives Before Us," *Supplementary Paper No. 13.* New York: Committee for Economic Development, 1962.

————. *Accounting for Slower Economic Growth.* Washington, DC: Brookings Institution, 1979.

Englander, A. S.; Evenson, R. E. and Hanazaki, M. "R&D, Innovation, and the Total Factor Productivity Slowdown." *OECD Economic Studies,* Autumn 1988, (11), pp. 7–42.

Evenson, Robert E. "Technical Change in U.S. Agriculture," in R. R. Nelson, ed., *Government and technical change: A cross industry analysis.* New York: Pergamon, 1984, pp. 233–82.

———. "Patent Data by Industry: Evidence for Invention Potential Exhaustion?" in *Technology and Productivity: The Challenge for Economic Policy.* Paris: Organization for Economic Cooperation and Development, 1991, pp. 233–48.

———. "Patents, R&D, and Invention Potential: International Evidence." *American Economic Review,* May 1993 (Papers and Proceedings), 83(2), pp. 463–68.

Fabricant, Solomon. *Economic Progress and Economic Change.* New York: National Bureau of Economic Research, 1954.

Fellner, W. "Trends in Activities Generating Technological Progress." *American Economic Review,* March 1970, 60(1), pp. 1–29.

Fogel, Robert. "Nutrition and the Decline in Mortality since 1700: Some Preliminary Findings," in Stanley Engerman and Robert Gallman, eds., *Long-term Factors in American Economic Growth, NBER Studies in Income and Wealth,* Vol. 51. Chicago: University of Chicago Press, 1986, pp. 439–555.

Freeman, Richard and Holtzer, Harry. *The Black Youth Employment Crisis.* Chicago: University of Chicago Press, 1986.

Gordon, Robert J. "Productivity, Wages, and Prices Inside and Outside of Manufacturing in the U.S., Japan, and Europe." *European Economic Review,* April 1987, 31(3), pp. 685–739.

———. "Comment on Baily." *Brookings Papers on Economic Activity, Micro-economics* 1993a.

———. "American Economic Growth: One Big Wave." Unpublished manuscript, National Bureau of Economic Research, Cambridge, MA, 1993b.

Gray, Wayne. "Upgrading Productivity Data Through 1989." Mimeo, National Bureau of Economic Research (Cambridge, MA), 1992.

Griliches, Zvi. "Hybrid Corn: An Exploration in the Economics of Technological Change." *Econometrica,* October 1957, *25(4),* pp. 501–22.

———. "Research Cost and Social Returns: Hybrid Corn and Related Innovations." *Journal of Political Economy,* October 1958, 66(5), pp. 419–31.

———. "Measuring Inputs in Agriculture: A Critical Survey." *Journal of Farm Economics,* December 1960, 42(5), pp. 1411–33.

———. "Hedonic Price Indexes for Automobiles: An Econometric Analysis of Quality Change," in The price statistics of the federal government. Washington, DC: National Bureau of Research, 1961, pp, 173–96.

———. "The Sources of Measured Productivity Growth: U.S. Agriculture, 1940–1960." *Journal of Political Economy,* August 1963a, 81(4), pp. 331–46.

———. "Production Functions, Technical Change, and All That." Netherlands School of Economics, Econometric Institute Report No. 6328, 1963b.

———. "Research Expenditures, Education and the Aggregate Agricultural Production Function." *American Economic Review,* December 1964, 54(6), pp. 961–74.

———. "Issues in Assessing the Contribution of R&D to Productivity Growth." *Bell Journal of Economics,* Spring 1979, 10(1), pp. 92–116.

———. "Productivity, R&D and Basic Research at the Firm Level in the 1970s." *American Economic Review,* March 1986a, 76(1), pp. 141–54.

———. "Data Issues in Econometrics," in Z. Griliches and M. Intriligator, eds., *Handbook of econometrics.* Amsterdam: North-Holland, 1986b, pp. 1466–1514.

———. "Productivity Puzzles and R&D: Another Nonexplanation." *Journal of Economic Perspectives*, Fall 1988, 2(4), pp. 9–21.

———. "Patent Statistics as Economic Indicators: A Survey." *Journal of Economic Literature*, December 1990, 18(4), pp. 1661–1707.

———. "The Search for R&D Spillovers." *Scandinavian Journal of Economics*, Supplement 1991, 94, pp. 29–47.

———. "Introduction," in Z. Griliches, ed., Output measurement in the service sectors, NBER Studies in Income and Wealth, Vol. 56. Chicago: University of Chicago Press, 1992, pp. 1–22.

———. "The Residual, Past and Present: A Personal View." Unpublished manuscript, Harvard University, 1994.

Griliches, Zvi and Cockburn, Iain A. "Generics and New Goods in Pharmaceutical Price Indexes." *National Bureau of Economic Research* (Cambridge, MA) Working Paper No. 4272, 1993.

Griliches, ZvI and Lichtenberg, Frank, "Errors of Measurement in Output Deflators." *Journal of Business and Economic Statistics,* January 1989, 7(1), pp. 1–9.

Griliches, Zvi and Mairesse, Jacques. "Productivity and R&D at the Firm level," in Zvi Griliches, ed., *R&D, Patents, and Productivity.* Chicago: University of Chicago Press, 1984, pp. 339–74.

Griliches, Zvi and Ringstad, Vidar. *Economies of Scale and the Form of the Production Function.* Amsterdam: North-Holland, 1971.

Grossman, Gene M. and Helpman, E. *Innovation and Growth in the Global Economy.* Cambridge, MA: MIT Press, 1991.

Hall, Bronwyn H. "New Evidence on the Impacts of R&D." *Brookings Papers on Economic Activity, Microeconomies 1993* (forthcoming).

Hall, Bronwyn H. and Hall, Robert E. "The Value and Performance of U.S. Corporations." *Brookings Papers on Economic Activity,* 1993, (1), pp. 1–50.

Harberger, Arnold C. "Reflections on the Growth Process." Unpublished manuscript, University of California, Los Angeles, 1990.

Hendel, Igal. "The Role of PC's in Manufacturing Industries." Unpublished manuscript, Harvard University, 1993.

Henderson, Rebecca and Cockburn, Iain. "Scale, Scope and Spillovers: The Determinants of Research Productivity in the Pharmaceutical Industry." *National Bureau of Economic Research (Cambridge, MA) Working Paper No. 4466, 1993.*

Huffman, Wallace E. and Evenson, Robert E. *Science for agriculture.* Ames, IA: Iowa State University Press, 1993.

Jaffe, Adam; Trajtenberg, Manuel and Henderson, Rebecca. "Geographic Localization of Knowledge Spillovers as Evidenced by Patent Citations." *Quarterly Journal of Economics,* August 1993, 108(3), pp. 577–98.

Jensen, Michael C. "The Modern Industrial Revolution, Exit, and the Failure of Internal Control Systems." *Journal of Finance,* July 1993, 48(3), pp. 831–80.

Johnson, Harry G. "Comment on Vaizey," in *The Residual Factor and Economic Growth.* Paris: Organization for Economic Cooperation and Development, 1964, pp. 219–27.

Jorgenson, Dale W. and Fraumeni, Barbara M. "The Output of the Education Sector," in Z. Griliches, ed., *Output Measurement in the Service Sectors,* NBER Studies in Income and Wealth, Vol. 56. Chicago: University of Chicago Press, 1992, pp. 303–38.

Jorgenson, Dale W. and Griliches, Zvi. "The Explanation of Productivity Change." *Review of Economic Studies,* March 1967, 34(3), pp. 249–83.

Juhn, Chinhui; Murphy, K. M. and Pierce, B. "Wage Inequality and The Rise in Returns to Skill." *Journal of Political Economy,* June 1993, 101(3), pp. 410–42.

Kendrick, John W. *Productivity Trends: Capital and Labor.* New York: National Bureau of Economic Research, 1956.

Kleinknecht, Alfred. *Innovation Patterns in Crisis and Prosperity.* New York: St. Martin's, 1987.

Kortum, Samuel. "Equilibrium R&D and the Patent-R&D Ratio: U.S. Evidence." *American Economic Review,* May 1993 (Papers and Proceedings), 83(2), pp. 450–57.

Krueger, Man B. "How Computers Have Changed the Wage Structure: Evidence from Microdata, 1984–89." National Bureau of Economic Research (Cambridge, MA) Working Paper No. 3858, 1991.

Krueger, Alan and Ashenfelter, Orley. "Estimates of the Economic Return to Schooling from a New Sample of Twins." National Bureau of Economic Research (Cambridge, MA) Working Paper No. 4143, August 1992.

Leibenstein, Harvey. "Allocative Efficiency vs. 'X-Efficiency'." *American Economic Review,* June 1966, 56(3), pp. 392–415.

Levin, Richard; Klevorick, A.; Nelson, R. and Winter, S. "Appropriating the Returns from Industrial Research and Development." *Brookings Papers on Economic Activity,* Microeconomics 1987, (3), pp.783–820.

Lichtenberg, Frank and Siegel, Donald. "The Impact of R&D Investment on Productivity: New Evidence Using Linked R&D-LRD Data." *Economic Inquiry,* April 1991, 29(2). pp. 203–29.

Mairesse, Jacques and Sassenou, Mohamed. "R&D and Productivity: A Survey of Econometric Studies at the Firm Level." *STI Review* (OECD, Paris), 1991, 8, pp. 9–43.

Mansfield, F. "Technical Change and the Rate of Imitation." *Econometrica,* October 1961, 29(4), pp. 741–66.

———. "Rates of Return from Industrial R&D." *American Economic Review,* May 1965 (Papers and Proceedings), 55(2), pp. 310–22.

Manski, Charles F. "Identification of Endogenous Social Effects: The Reflection Problem." *Review of Economic Studies,* July 1993, 60(3), pp. 531–42.

Mensch, Gerhard; Haag, Gunter and Weidlich, Wolfgang. "The Schumpeter Clock," in '*Technology and Productivity.*' Paris: Organization for Economic Cooperation and Development, 1991, pp. 523–44.

Nadiri, M. I. "Innovations and Technological Spillovers." National Bureau of Economic Research (Cambridge, MA) Working Paper No. 4423, August 1993.

National Academy of Sciences. *Measurement and Interpretation of Productivity.* Washington, DC: National Academy Press. 1979.

National Bureau of Economic Research. *The Price Statistics of the Federal Government, General Series No. 73.* New York: National Bureau of Economic Research, 1961.

National Science Board. Science and engineering indicators—1991. Washington, DC: U.S. Government Printing Office, 1991.

National Science Foundation. *Research and Development in Industry: 1989, NSF 92-307.* Washington, DC: National Science Foundation, 1992.

Nelson, Lehard R. *The Rate and Direction of Inventive Activity.* Princeton, NJ: Princeton University Press, 1962.

Nordhaus, William D. "The Recent Productivity Slowdown." *Brookings Papers on Economic Activity,* 1972, (3), pp. 493–537.

———. "Comment on Griliches." *Brookings Papers on Economic Activity, Micro-economics 1989,* pp. 320–25.

Organization for Economic Cooperation and Development. *OECD Economic outlook, No. 53.* Paris: Organization for Economic Cooperation and Development, June 1993.

Office of Technology Assessment, U.S. Congress. "Statistical needs for a changing U.S. economy," *Background Paper OTA-BP-E-58.* Washington, DC: U.S. Government Printing Office, 1939.

Olsen, Mancur. *The Rise and Decline of Nations.* New Haven, CT: Yale University Press, 1982.

Pakes, Ariel and Simpson, Margaret. "Patent Renewal Data." *Brookings Papers on Economic Activity, Microeconomics 1989,* pp. 331–410.

Patel, Pari and Soete, Luc. "Measuring the Economic Effects of Technology." STI Review (OECD, Paris), 1988, 4, pp. 121–66.

Reinsdorf, Marshall. "The Effect of Outlet Price Differentials on the U.S. Consumer Price Index," in Murray Foss, Marilyn Manser, and Allan Young, eds., *Price Measurements and Their Uses, NBER Studies in Income and Wealth,* Vol. 57. Chicago: University of Chicago Press, 1993, pp. 227–54.

Romer, Paul M. "Endogenous Technological Change." *Journal of Political Economy,* October 1990. 98(5)pp. S71-S102.

Ruggles, Richard. *The Wholesale Price Index.* Washington, DC: Council on Wage and Price Stability, 1977.

Ruttan, Vernon W. "Technological Progress in the Meat Packing Industry, 1910–47," *Marketing Research Report.* Washington, DC: U.S. Department of Agriculture, 1954.

———. "The Contribution of Technological Progress to Farm Output, 1950–1975." *Review of Economics and Statistics,* February 1956, 3S(1), pp 61–69.

Schankerman, Mark and Pakes, Ariel. "Estimates of the Value of Patent Rights in European Countries During the Post-1950 Period." *Economic Journal,* December 1986, 96(384), pp. 1052–76.

Scherer, F. M. "R&D and Declining Productivity Growth." *American Economic Review,* May 1983 (Papers and Proceedings), 73(2), pp. 215–18.

———. "Using Linked Patent and R&D Data to Measure Interindustry Technology Flows," in Z. Griliches, ed., *R&D, Patents, and Productivity.* Chicago: University of Chicago Press, 1984, pp. 417–64.

———. "The World Productivity Growth Slump," in R. Wolff, ed., *Organizing Industrial Development.* Berlin: de Gruyter, 1986, pp. 15–27.

———. "Lagging Productivity Growth: Measurement, Technology and Shock Effects." *Empirica,* 1993, 20(1), pp. 5–24.

Schmookler, Jacob. "The Changing Efficiency of the American Economy 1869–1938." *Review of Economics and Statistics,* August 1952, 34(3), pp. 214–31,369–1938.

———. "Invention and Economic Growth." Cambridge, MA: Harvard University Press, 1966.

Schultz, Theodore W. *Restoring Economic Equilibrium.* Oxford: Blackwell, 1990.

Siegel, Donald and Griliches, Zvi "Purchased Services, Outsourcing, Computers, and Productivity in Manufacturing," in Z. Griliches, ed., *Measuring the Output of Service Sectors, NBER Studies in Income and Wealth,* Vol. 56. Chicago: University of Chicago Press, 1992, pp. 429–60.

Solow, Robert M. "Technical Change and the Aggregate Production Function." *Review of Economics and Statistics,* August 1957, 39(3), pp. 312–20.

———. "Growth Theory," in David Greenaway, Michael Bleaney, and Ian Stewart, eds., *Companion to Contemporary Economic Thought.* London: Routledge, 1991, pp. 393–415.

Stigler, George J. *Trends in Output and Employment.* New York: National Bureau of Economic Research, 1947.

Summers, Robert and Heston, Man. "The Penn World Table (Mark 5): An Expanded Set of International Comparisons, 1950–1988." *Quarterly Journal of Economics,* May 1991, 106(2), pp. 327–68.

Sveikauskas, L. "Productivity Growth and the Depletion of Technological Opportunities." *Journal of Productivity Analysis,* June 1990, 1(4), pp. 301–8.

Tinbergen, J. "Zur Theorie der Langfirstigen Wirtschaftsentwicklung," *Weltwirtschaftliche's Archiv,* January 1942, 55(1), pp. 511–49; reprinted in English translation in J. Tinbergen, Selected papers. Amsterdam: North-Holland, 1959.

Tong, X. and Frame, J, D. "Measuring National Technological Performance with Patent Claims Data." Unpublished manuscript, George Washington University, 1992.

Trajtenberg, Manuel. "Economic analysis of product innovation." *The Case of CT Scanners.* Cambridge, MA: Harvard University Press, 1990a.

———. "A Penny for Your Quotes: Patent Citations and the Value of Innovations." Rand Journal of Economics, Spring 1990b, 21(1) pp. 172–87.

Triplett, Jack E. "Price and Technological Change in a Capital Good: A Survey of Research and Computers," in D. W. Jorgenson and R. Landau, eds., *Technology and Capital Formation.* Cambridge, MA: MIT Press, 1989, pp. 127–213.

———. "The Federal Statistical System's Response to Emerging Data Needs." *Journal of Economic and Social Measurement,* 1991, 17(3-4), pp. 155–201.

Young, Allan H. "Alternative Measures of Change in Real Output and Prices." *Survey of Current Business,* April 1992, 72(4), pp. 32–48.

15

The Capitalization, Amortization, and Value-Relevance of R&D

Baruch Lev and Theodore Sougiannis

1. INTRODUCTION

A direct relationship between research and development costs and specific future revenue generally has not been demonstrated even with the benefit of hindsight. For example, three empirical research studies, which focus on companies in industries intensively involved in research and development activities, generally failed to find a significant correlation between research and development expenditures and increased future benefits as measured by subsequent sales, earnings, or share of industry sales. (Statement of Financial Accounting Standards No 2, p. 14).

The presumed absence of a relation between R&D expenditures and subsequent benefits was a major reason for the FASB's decision in 1974 to require the full expensing of R&D outlays in financial reports of public corporations. The last 20 years have witnessed an unprecedented growth of R&D investment in the U.S. and other developed economies and the emergence of new, science-based industries (e.g., software, biotechnology, and telecommunications). Nevertheless, the requirement for full R&D expensing in the U.S.—based on the assertion that 'a direct relationship between research and development costs and specific future revenue generally has not been demonstrated . . . '—is still in effect.[1] Apparently

---

1. In 1985 the FASB made an exception to the following requirement for some software development cost, see FAS No. 86 (Eccher, 1995). In several other countries R&D capitalization is allowed and even required. For example, in the UK, SSAP 13 requires that expenditures on pure and applied research should be written off as incurred, but development expenditures may, in certain defined cir-

From *Journal of Accounting & Economics*, Vol. 21, pp. 107–138, copyright © 1996. Reprinted with kind permission from Elsevier Science.

U.S. standard-setters are concerned with the reliability and objectivity of the estimates required for R&D capitalization, and with the associated audit risk. The specter of providing managers with additional opportunities for earnings management must also weigh heavily on regulators.

The main objective of this study is to address the issues of reliability, objectivity, and value-relevance of R&D capitalization. We do this by first estimating the relation between R&D expenditures and subsequent earnings for a large cross-section of R&D-intensive firms. This estimation allows us to compute firm-specific R&D capital and its amortization rate, as well as the measurement of the periodic R&D amortization (in contrast with the GAAP expense, which equals the R&D outlay). We then adjust reported earnings and book values of the sample firms for the R&D capitalization and show that the adjusted values are significantly associated with stock prices and returns, indicating the value-relevance to investors of the R&D capitalization process developed here. Finally, we demonstrate in an intertemporal context that R&D capital is reliably associated with *subsequent* stock returns. This intriguing finding may be due to a systematic mispricing of the shares of R&D-intensive firms (market inefficiency), or to the R&D capital proxying for an extra-market risk factor (equilibrium returns). Taken together, the evidence presented here indicates that the association between R&D expenditures and subsequent earnings is, in general, both statistically significant and economically meaningful, in clear contradiction to a major premise of FAS No. 2—the absence of an association between R&D expenditures and subsequent benefits.

R&D research in economics and related areas (e.g., organizational behavior) is extensive and growing (see Cohen and Levine, 1989, for a survey), stimulated primarily by the major role of innovation in the theory of economic growth and social welfare. In contrast, this important subject is only infrequently examined in the accounting literature, as indicated by the following brief research survey. Dukes (1976) examined investors' perceptions of R&D and concluded that they adjust reported earnings for the full expensing of R&D. Similarly, Ben-Zion (1978) showed that firms' market minus book values are cross-sectionally correlated with R&D and advertising expenditures. Hirschey and Weygandt (1985) demonstrated that Tobin's Q values (the ratio of market value to replacement cost of assets) are cross-sectionally correlated with R&D over sales ratios (R&D intensity). A different approach to assess R&D relevance was pursued by Woolridge (1988) and Chan et al. (1990). Using an event methodology they documented a positive investor reaction to firms' R&D announcements. Similar evidence, derived from analysts' forecast errors, was provided by Bublitz and Ettredge (1989). Finally, several studies were aimed at evaluating the economic consequences of FAS No. 2. While some researchers detected a decline in the R&D intensity of small firms subsequent to FAS No. 2 enactment (e.g., Horwitz and Kolodny,

---

cumstances, be deferred to future periods. The Canadian Standard (section 345 of the CICA Handbook) goes further to require the deferment of certain development expenditures. The International Accounting Standard, IAS 9, is generally in line with the Canadian standard with respect to R&D capitalization.

1981; Wasley and Linsmeier, 1992), others failed to observe significant changes in managerial R&D decisions (e.g., Elliott et al., 1984). Overall, while documenting investors' cognizance of the capital aspects of R&D, the accounting research on innovation is sparse indeed. Compared with ours, the above studies generally used *proxies* for R&D investment, such as the R&D to sales ratio, while we estimate firm-specific R&D capital and adjust reported earnings for the full R&D expensing. Furthermore, while we examine whether investors fully adjust for the R&D expensing (market efficiency), previous studies have not investigated this issue.

In the next section we present our methodology for estimating the relation between R&D and earnings, followed by an outline of the R&D capitalization process in Section 3. Section 4 describes the adjustment of reported earnings and book values for R&D capitalization, while Section 5 presents the contemporaneous analysis, relating stock prices and returns to the R&D-adjusted financial variables. Section 6 reports the intertemporal analysis, relating R&D capital to subsequent stock returns, while Section 7 concludes the study.

2. ESTIMATING THE R&D—EARNINGS RELATION

Our estimation of R&D capital and its amortization rate is derived from the fundamental relation between the value of assets and the earnings generated by them. Accordingly, we define the earnings of firm i in period t, E_{it}, as a function of tangible, TA_{it}, and intangible assets, IA_{it}, where the latter includes the R&D capital:[2]

$$E_{it} = g(TA_{it}, IA_{it}).$$ (1)

While the values of earnings and tangible assets (at historical costs) are reported in financial statements, the intangible capital, IA, is not reported and therefore has to be estimated.

Given our focus on R&D, we single it out of intangible assets and define its value, RDC_{it}, as the sum of the *unamortized* past R&D expenditures. Those are the expenditures that are expected to generate current and future earnings:

$$RDC_{it} = \sum_k x_{ik} RD_{i,t-k},$$ (2)

where x_{ik} is the contribution of a dollar R&D expenditure in year $t - k$ ($k = 0$, ..., N) to subsequent earnings (i.e., the proportion of the R&D expenditure in year $t - k$ that is still productive in year t).

---

2. This formulation accords with production function estimations (e.g., Mairesse and Sasenou, 1991; Hall, 1993a) where gross output (e.g., sales) is related to labor and material inputs, as well as to the stocks of physical and intangible capital. Our dependent variable, earnings, proxies for output minus labor and material inputs, leaving the values of tangible and intangible assets as the independent variables.

Substituting expression (2) into (1) yields:

$$E_{it} = g\left(TA_{it}, \sum_k x_{ik}\, RD_{i,t-k}, OIA_{it}\right), \tag{3}$$

where OIA_{it} are other (than R&D) intangible assets. (E_{it} is the R&D-adjusted earnings, namely reported earnings plus current R&D expenditures minus the amortization of R&D capital.)

Note that we derive the value of R&D capital from the firm's earnings. An alternative is to estimate that value from the difference between the firm's market and book (or replacement cost) values (e.g., Cockburn and Griliches, 1988; Hall, 1993a).[3] We prefer to derive R&D capital from its direct benefits—earnings—over its estimation from market values, since the former avoids the notorious circularity in the use of market prices to estimate values of assets or liabilities. This circularity arises from the general presumption that market prices are *determined* by reported financial variables, and therefore such prices cannot be logically used to determine the values of financial variables. Furthermore, the estimation of fundamental variables (e.g., R&D capital or an environmental liability) from market values precludes one from investigating the extent of market emergency with respect to the examined variables. Such an investigation is conducted below.[4]

2.1. Estimation of Expression (3) and Data Sources

The variables in relation (3) are defined thus. Earnings, E_{it}, is measured as operating income before depreciation and the expensing of R&D and advertising. Operating income is used as a measure of R&D benefits, since R&D investment and its consequences seem largely unrelated to nonoperating items, such as administrative expenses and financing charges. Depreciation, R&D, and advertising expenses were excluded from (added back to) operating income since they represent, largely ad hoc, writeoffs of the independent variables in (3)—tangible and intangible assets.[5]

Tangible assets, TA_{it} in (3), consist of three components: plant and equipment, inventories, and investment in unconsolidated subsidiaries and purchased intangibles. Each of these asset items has been separately adjusted for inflation in the data source we use (to be described below). Across our sample firms and years examined (1975–1991), the average shares of tangible assets, inventories, and

---

3. Market values were also used in prior accounting research (e.g., Ben-Zion, 1978; Hirschey and Weygandt, 1985) to estimate R&D amortization rates.
4. It should also be noted that we estimate the value of R&D capital by relating an input measure (R&D expenditures) to an output indicator earnings. There are various attempts in economic literature to estimate the value of R&D capital by other output measures, such as the number of patents granted, the number of inventions resulting from the R&D process, or the frequency of citations in scientific publications and in patent requests (e.g., Pakes, 1985).
5. Replication of our estimates with net income (before extraordinary items) as the dependent variable yielded very similar results to those based on operating income.

other investments are: 0.70, 0.23, and 0.07, respectively. The major intangible asset, R&D capital, is represented here by the lag structure of annual R&D expenditures, expression (2), where these expenditures, $RD_{i,t-k}$, are adjusted for inflation to reflect current-year dollars.

Advertising expenditures on product promotion and brand development may create an additional intangible asset for some sample firms. This may raise an omitted variable problem in expression (3), if R&D capital were the only intangible asset included. Conceptually, advertising capital can be estimated from its lag structure, similarly to the procedure applied to R&D (2). However, inspection of our data source, which focuses on R&D firms, revealed that annual advertising expenditures were occasionally missing for many sample firms, straining the requirement for a reasonable length of lag structure for reliable estimation. We therefore employed a procedure frequently used by economists (e.g., Hall, 1993b), in which the advertising intensity (advertising expenses over sales) is substituted for advertising capital. Empirical evidence (e.g., Bublitz and Ettredge, 1989; Hall, 1993b), indicates that, in contrast to R&D, the effect of advertising expenditures on subsequent earnings is short-lived, typically one to two years only. Accordingly, an advertising proxy based on annual expenditures may account reasonably well for the omitted variable in expression (3).[6]

The estimated expression, sealed by total sales to mitigate heteroscedasticity, is

$$(OI/S)_{it} = x_0 + x_1(TA/S)_{i,t-1} + \sum_k x_{2,k}(RD/S)_{i,t-k} + x_3(AD/S)_{i,t-1} + e_{it}, \qquad (4)$$

OI	=	annual operating income, before depreciation, advertising and R&D expenses, of firm i in year t,
S	=	annual sales,
TA	=	the value of plant and equipment, inventory, and investment in unconsolidated subsidiaries and goodwill, in current dollars, measured at the beginning-of-year values,
RD	=	annual R&D expenditures in current dollars,
AD	=	annual advertising expenses, measured at the beginning-of-year values.

Note that if expression (4) is subject to correlated omitted variables problem, then the estimated values of the x coefficients may be overstated.

Three data bases are used in this study: (1) the 1993 CRSP daily file, (2) the 1993 COMPUSTAT file, and (3) the NBER's R&D Master File (described in detail in Hall et al., 1988).[7] The R&D Master File was constructed from consecutive COMPUSTAT tapes, starting with the 1978 tape. Accordingly, the earliest data on

---

6. Peles (1970), in one of the earliest studies on advertising amortization, also documents the short life (impact on subsequent sales) of advertising capital. His estimated annual amortization rates for advertising were: 100 percent for the car industry, 40–50 percent for beer advertising (i.e., roughly two-year life), and 35–45 percent for cigarettes.
7. The Master File was updated to 1991.

the Master File relate to the year 1959. The COMPUSTAT tapes used as sources for the R&D Master File are: the Industrial (NYSE, AMEX, and large OTC firms), OTC (the remaining OTC firms), Full Coverage (non-NASDAQ firms), and the Research (deleted firms) tapes. The R&D Master File includes about 2,600 manufacturing companies which reported R&D expenditures. It is thus a subset of merged COMPUSTAT tapes, focusing on R&D firms. This file has several attractive features for our study. In particular, asset values and expenses (e.g., R&D) are adjusted to current dollars, and given the frequent use of this data base in time-series analyses, key variables (e.g., plant, sales, R&D expenditures) were scanned to identify large yearly jumps in the data and locate missing values. In such cases, the original annual reports and 10-Ks were examined and the data were completed and corrected when possible (for a detailed discussion of these quality checks, see Hall et al., 1988).[8]

2.2. Simultaneity

Models, such as (4), relating output to capital, generally raise simultaneity issues. Specifically, when a shock to the regression residual affects both the dependent (output) and one or more independent variables (capital), the latter will be correlated with the residual term, leading to inconsistent regressions estimates. For example, an exogenous shock enhancing demand for the firm's products will generally increase both current earnings and the marginal return to capital, the latter leading to increased investment in R&D. In this case, R&D expenditures cannot be considered an exogenous variable, and OLS estimation of (4) will yield inconsistent estimates. This calls for estimating expression (4) in a simultaneous equation context.

To account for simultaneity, we use the instrumental variable method, where an instrument (another variable) is chosen to substitute for the explanatory variable [RD_{it} in expression (4)] which may be correlated with the residual. A successful instrument is one which is correlated with the substituted explanatory variable, yet is uncorrelated with the residual. We chose as the instrument for firm i the average level of R&D expenditures (deflated by sales) of the *other* firms in its four-digit SIC code.[9] The industry R&D instrument is appealing on both theoretical and empirical grounds. Industry R&D level is obviously unaffected by firm idiosyncratic shocks (e.g., a specific managerial strategy or a corporate control change affecting the firm's cost of capital), thereby considerably limiting its correlation with the original regression (4) residual. At the same time, there are strong

---

8. In addition to the checks made in the R&D database we eliminated from the sample firms that had large mergers (those contributing 50% or more to annual sales), since such mergers seriously disrupted the time series examined. The total number of firms eliminated due to mergers was 121.
9. We require at least four other firms in the four-digit SIC group. If less than four firms are available, the industry is defined at the three-digit level in which firm i is classified.

reasons to believe that the correlation between a given firm's R&D expenditures (the original variable) and the industry average (the instrument) is generally high. Corporate activities are often evaluated by investors and financial analysts against industry norms deterring managers from significantly deviating from them.

More fundamentally an association between a firm's R&D expenditures and those of the industry is induced by the well-known "spillover" phenomenon, namely by firms' efforts to learn of and benefit from the innovative activities of other firms. Obviously, in order to benefit from others' knowledge, one has to develop a capacity to exploit that knowledge, achieved by increasing one's own R&D (e.g., hiring scientists who will follow other firms' activities). Indeed, economists have observed that firms that invest more in their own R&D are better able to exploit externally-generated knowledge than firms with lower R&D expenditures (e.g., Evenson and Kislev, 1973; Mowery, 1983). Cohen and Levinthal (1989) found that firms invest in R&D for two purposes: to generate new knowledge and to develop "absorptive capacity"—the ability to recognize, assimilate, and exploit others' knowledge. R&D spillover will thus contribute to a positive association between a firm's R&D expenditures and those of related firms (the industry).

The positive association between firm-specific R&D expenditures and those of the industry (the instrument) is corroborated by the data in Table 15.1. These are mean coefficient estimates, over the years 1975–1991, from regressing cross-sectionally individual firms' R&D expenditures on the corresponding four-digit industry R&D level (both variables scaled by sales). Note that the regressions are estimated by pooling over firms in two-digit industries (e.g., SIC codes 28, 35 . . .), where each of those two-digit industries includes multiple four-digit industry means.[10] For example, the two-digit industry no. 28 (Chemicals and Pharmaceutics) includes 12 four-digit industry groups. Moreover, for each observation of the dependent variable, $(RD/S)_{it}$, we exclude the firm's R&D expenditure from the corresponding four-digit industry average (independent variable). Accordingly, in each cross-section of two-digit industry, the independent variable takes a different value for each observation. It is evident from Table 15.1 that for all industries, the industry R&D level coefficient, b is positive, highly statistically significant, and quite stable (around 0.65 for four of the six industries). There thus exists the desired association between our instrumental variable—the industry R&D—and the substituted explanatory variable, RD_{it}, in expression (4).[11]

10. The industry classification in Table 15.1 (two-digit codes 28, 35, 36, 37, 38 and "Other R&D Industries") is also used in the rest of the study. The individual two-digit industries resulted from their requirement that each one will have at least 20 firms in each year examined (1975–1991). All industries with less than 20 firms in at least one year were grouped into "Other R&D Industries." We also required that each sample firm has at least ten annual lags of R&D data and its R&D Sales ratio is at least 2 percent.

11. The industry R&D was also found by Berger (1993) to be the most significant variable in explaining firm-specific R&D expenditures (the other variables were: cash flow, GNP, Tobin's Q ratio, last year's R&D expenditures, and the R&D tax credit).

TABLE 15.1   The Association Between the Instrumental Variable (Industry R&D) and the Substituted Variable (Firm R&D)

Mean coefficient estimates of yearly cross-sectional regressions (1975–1991) of individual firms' annual R&D expenditures scaled by sales (*RD/S*) on their four-digit industry average R&D (*IRD S*). T-values are presented in parentheses.

$(RD/S)_{it} = a + b(IRD/S)_{it} + u_{it}$

Industry	N**	$\hat{a}$	$\hat{b}$	Adj R^2
Chemicals and Pharmaceutics (28)*	74	0.029	0.458	0.20
		(2.00)	(11.81)	
Machinery and Computer Hardware (35)	118	0.009	0.677	0.34
		(9.00)	(26.54)	
Electrical and Electronics (36)	98	0.012	0.616	0.16
		(9.60)	(13.84)	
Transportation Vehicles (37)	54	0.008	0.613	0.30
		(6.40)	(13.11)	
Scientific Instruments (38)	69	0.015	0.680	0.16
		(7.50)	(24.50)	
Other R&D Industries	412	0.030	0.328	0.14
		(5.64)	(7.28)	

RD/S_{it} = ratio of R&D expenditures to sales of firm *i* in year *t* and $(IRD\ S)_{it}$ = industry R&D) expenditures to sales ratio (four- or three-digit SIC codes), excluding firm *i*.
*Two-digit SIC code.
**Average number of firms in the yearly regressions, 1975–1991.

We apply the instrumental variable method by running a two-stage least squares regression. In the first stage, for every year and two-digit industry, firms scaled R&D expenditures, $(R/S)_{it}$ are cross-sectionally regressed on the four-digit industry R&D level, $(IRD/S)_{it}$:

$$(RD/S)_{it} = a + b(IRD/S)_{it} + u_{it}. \tag{4a}$$

In the second stage, expression (4) is estimated with the fitted value of RD/S_{it} from (4a), substituting for the actual value of $(RD/S)_{it}$.

2.3. Other Estimation Issues

The system of Eqs. (4a) and (4), relating operating earnings to tangible capital, advertising intensity, and the R&D lag structure, is cross-sectionally estimated for each two-digit industry and sample year. The reason for the cross-sectional estimation of (4) is that data limitations preclude an efficient estimation from individual firms' time series. Our estimates of R&D amortization rates [derived from the α_{2k} coefficients in expression (4)] are thus industry-wide estimates which are then applied to individual firms.

A multicolinearity problem is encountered in the estimation of the R&D lag structure, $\sum_k x_{2,k}(RD/S)_{i,t-k}$, in expression (4), since annual R&D expenditures for most companies are relatively stable over time. A frequently used approach to address this problem, which is particularly serious in relatively short time series, is "reduced parameterization," namely the estimation of fewer parameters than the number of lags, k, in the time series. This is achieved by assuming a priori that the lag coefficients, $x_{2,k}$, reflecting the R&D benefits, behave according to some general structure, such as a polynomial. The increased efficiency results from the need to estimate a small number of parameters, relative to the number of lags in the series. The efficiency comes, of course, at the expense of assuming an a priori structure of coefficients. The specific estimation technique we used is the Almon lag procedure (for details see, e.g., Johnston, 1984, pp. 352–358; Maddala, 1992, pp. 424–429). The Almon procedure has a flexibility advantage over several competitors (e.g., the Koyck lag or the binomial lag), since it allows experimentation with polynomials of various degrees and the consequent fitting of a suitable polynomial to the data. In contrast, the Koyck lag imposes a strictly declining pattern on the coefficients, while the binomial and Pascal lag procedures impose quadratic patterns.

3. THE R&D CAPITALIZATION

The system of Eqs. (4a) and (4), relating earnings to assets, was run cross-sectionally, with the instrumental variable (industry R&D level) and the Almon lag procedure, for each two-digit sample industry and year. Table 15.2 provides an example of the estimation procedure for industry 36—Electrical and Electronics Manufacturers—covering the early part of the sample period: 1975–1981. These estimates are used to adjust reported earnings and book values of the sample companies in the *subsequent* year, 1982. Similarly, the 1983 reported earnings and book values were adjusted from R&D capitalization estimates based on data of the preceding years 1975–1982. This is an important feature of our analysis: the adjustment of reported earnings and book values in any sample year is based on estimates derived from expression (4) run over the preceding years, starting with 1975 (the year FAS No. 2 came into effect).[12] Thus, all information used in the R&D adjustment process was ex ante known.

---

12. 1975 was the first year for the estimation of expression (4). Note, however, that the R&D lagged data for the 1975 regression (as well as those for succeeding years) extend back to 1959, the first year on the R&D Master File.

In the industry-wide estimates from expression (4) we ignore the statistically insignificant R&D lag coefficient estimates, $\hat{a}_{2,k}$. For example, in the first row of Table 15.2 (year 1975), the coefficients of lags 6 to 10, $\hat{a}_{2,6}$ to $\hat{a}_{2,10}$ were insignificant and therefore not reported in the table, while in 1980 and 1981, the lags 6 and 7 coefficients were significant (perhaps due to the larger sample size in those years or to a shift in R&D benefits). The horizontal sum of the significant R&D coefficients, $\sum \hat{a}_{2,k}$ (second column from the right), reflects the total (undiscounted) effect of $1 invested in R&D on current and future operating income. For example, based on the 1975 estimation (first row in Table 15.2), the average contribution to operating income of $1 invested in R&D by Electrical and Electronics manufacturers was $2.328. While total benefits of $2.328 from $1.00 R&D expenditure may appear to be large, it should be recalled that these benefits refer to operating income before R&D amortization, and before major expense items, such as selling, general and administrative expenses, as well as financing expenses and income taxes. Furthermore, these benefits accrue over five years but are not discounted.

The estimated regression coefficients for each of the years 1975–1981 are averaged and reported in the second to bottom row in Table 15.2. These averages are used to compute a key R&D capitalization parameter—the annual amortization rates of the R&D capital, δ_k (reported in the bottom line of Table 15.2),

$$\hat{\delta}_k = \hat{x}_{2,k} \Big/ \sum_k \hat{x}_{2,k} .$$ (5)

The R&D amortization in year k is thus the ratio of that year's benefits *expired*, $\hat{x}_{2,k}$ to total benefits, $\sum_k \hat{x}_{2,k}$. For example, the amortization rate of current (year 0) R&D expenditures, δ_0, is 0.268/2.348 = 0.114. Thus, on average, in the Electrical and Electronics industry (over the period 1975–1981), the amortization rate of current R&D expenditures was 11.4 percent. The amortization rate of the preceding year's (year 1) R&D expenditures was 17.7 percent. Accordingly, the amortization of the R&D capital in 1982 (the proper R&D expense, rather than the GAAP expense) consists of 11.4 percent of the 1982 R&D expenditure, plus 17.7 percent. Of the 1981 R&D expenditure, plus 19.7 percent of the 1980 R&D expenditure, and so on back in time over all R&D vintages that are still contributing to year t earnings. The annual amortization rates, bottom line of Table 15.2, are used to compute both the R&D capital and its amortization for 1982, as will be demonstrated in Section 4. Note that prior to 1975 (the year FAS No. 2 came into effect) some firms capitalized part of their R&D expenditures. This introduces noise into our data and increases measurement error, particularly in the early sample years (the 1970s) which rely heavily on pre-FAS No. 2 data. This may explain the apparent shift (nonstationarity) of the R&D coefficients ($\hat{x}_{2,0}$; $\hat{x}_{2,1}$; ...) in Table 15.2, occurring in 1980.

TABLE 15.2 Example: Derivation of Annual Amortization Rates of R&D for 1982, Industry 36 (Electrical and Electronics)

Coefficient estimates of regression (4), run cross-sectionally for each of the years 1975–1981, using instrumental variables and the Almon lag procedure (t-values in parentheses):

$$(OI/S)_{it} = x_0 + x_1(TA/S)_{i,t-1} + \sum_k x_{2,k}(RD/S)_{i,t-k} + x_3(AD/S)_{i,t-1} + e_{it}$$

Year	No. of firms	$\hat{x}_0$	$\hat{x}_1$	$\hat{x}_3$	$\hat{x}_{2,0}$	$\hat{x}_{2,1}$	$\hat{x}_{2,2}$	$\hat{x}_{2,3}$	$\hat{x}_{2,4}$	$\hat{x}_{2,5}$	$\hat{x}_{2,6}$	$\hat{x}_{2,7}$	$\sum_{k=0}^{7}\hat{x}_{2,k}$	Adj. R^2
1975	44	0.266 (0.73)	0.136 (6.01)	1.833 (1.61)	0.361 (4.19)	0.536 (3.74)	0.561 (3.73)	0.471 (3.21)	0.304 (2.41)	0.095 (2.04)	—	—	2.328	0.91
1976	49	−0.346 (−0.84)	0.181 (7.40)	0.856 (0.69)	0.342 (5.18)	0.514 (5.24)	0.547 (5.26)	0.476 (5.28)	0.331 (4.94)	0.146 (2.86)	—	—	2.356	0.91
1977	52	−1.143 (−4.50)	0.191 (7.51)	1.543 (2.06)	0.356 (5.08)	0.543 (5.22)	0.593 (5.54)	0.535 (6.08)	0.402 (7.30)	0.226 (5.14)	0.037 (2.13)	—	2.692	0.89
1978	66	−0.943 (−3.14)	0.236 (7.92)	0.048 (0.08)	0.293 (3.66)	0.451 (3.75)	0.498 (3.89)	0.458 (4.08)	0.356 (4.23)	0.218 (3.63)	0.067 (2.36)	—	2.341	0.86
1979	69	−1.074 (−3.41)	0.249 (7.88)	0.527 (0.87)	0.318 (3.74)	0.490 (3.82)	0.542 (3.98)	0.501 (4.17)	0.393 (4.41)	0.244 (4.06)	0.082 (2.94)	—	2.570	0.88
1980	68	−1.069 (−2.52)	0.189 (6.53)	1.303 (1.57)	0.099 (4.95)	0.180 (5.00)	0.243 (5.06)	0.289 (5.07)	0.316 (5.01)	0.325 (5.07)	0.302 (4.79)	0.269 (4.71)	2.023	0.82
1981	70	−0.387 (−0.89)	0.217 (7.40)	0.906 (1.78)	0.104 (4.00)	0.188 (4.08)	0.254 (4.03)	0.301 (4.06)	0.330 (4.07)	0.339 (4.03)	0.316 (3.90)	0.287 (3.87)	2.119	0.85
Mean		−0.671	0.200	1.002	0.268	0.415	0.463	0.433	0.347	0.228	0.115	0.079	2.348	0.87
R&D amortization δ_k*					0.114	0.177	0.197	0.184	0.148	0.097	0.049	0.034		

*The R&D annual amortization rates are calculated from the mean R&D coefficients $x_{2,k}$ ($k = 0, \ldots, 7$) follows: $\delta_k = \hat{a}_{2,k} / \sum_{k=0}^{7} \hat{a}_{2,k}$.

$(OI/S)_{it}$ = operating income (before depreciation, R&D amortization, and advertising expenses) over sales, of firm i in year t, $(TA/S)_{i,t-1}$ = tangible assets (plant and equipment, investment in unconsolidaries subsidiaries, and inventory), over sales, in current dollars, of firm i for k lag years. $(AD/S)_{i,t-1}$ = advertising expenses over sales, of firm i. The instrumental variable for the $(RD/S)_{i,t}$ term is the four-digit industry-average R&D over sales, expression (4a).

Table 15.2 demonstrates the estimation of the R&D amortization rates for firms in the Electrical and Electronics industry in 1982. Similar estimations were made for all sample years and industries, allowing the adjustment of reported earnings and book values of all sample firms and years (1975–1991). An overview of these estimates is provided in Table 15.3 which reports for each sample industry the mean coefficients of the yearly regressions. The amortization rates, δ_k, in Table 15.3, were computed from the 16 yearly regressions, 1975–1990, and were used in the earnings and book value adjustments made for the last sample year, 1991. Note that in Table 15.3, the coefficients of tangible capital, x_1, indicating the contribution of the beginning-of-year tangible assets to operating income, range from 0.084 (Other Industries) to 0.155 (Electrical and Electronics). These values indicate the industry-average annual return on tangible assets, and they are in line with the estimates of Griliches and Mairesee (1990), ranging from 0.11 to 0.15. The coefficients of advertising intensity, x_3 (a flow variable), range between 0.906 (Transportation Vehicles) to 1.639 (Scientific Instruments). Thus, a \$1 advertising expenditure is associated with an operating income (before advertising) increase of roughly \$1.00–1.60.

The length of the statistically significant lagged R&D coefficients, $x_{2,k}$, in Table 15.3 indicates the average *duration* of R&D benefits (useful life of R&D capital). Thus, in Chemicals and Pharmaceutics, the average useful life of R&D is the longest—nine years ($x_{2,8}$ is the last significant coefficient), while in Scientific Instruments the average R&D life is the shortest—five years. These results are generally consistent with Nadiri and Prucha (1992), whose estimates of the useful life of R&D range between seven and nine years. The different durations of R&D capital are mainly related to the ability of innovators to *appropriate* the benefits of innovations, namely to prevent others from copying or imitating them. Benefit appropriation is primarily achieved by patents, but industries differ widely in the effectiveness of patent protection. Both Mansfield (1986) and Levin et al. (1987) argue that patents are highly effective in appropriating returns in the chemicals and drug industries, moderately effective for mechanical equipment and machinery manufacturers, and least effective (i.e., it is relatively easy for competitors to "invent around" the patents) in instruments and motor vehicles.[13] This ranking generally accords with Table 15.3 estimates regarding the cross-industry differences in the useful life of the R&D investment.

13. Levin et al. (1987) suggest that patents are particularly effective in the chemical and drug industries because of the clear standards that can be applied to assess a patent's validity, e.g., a specific molecular structure. In contrast, it is more difficult to demonstrate and defend the novelty of a new component of a mechanical system. Patents are the major, but not the only means of appropriating R&D benefits. Investment in complementary sales and service efforts and secrecy of the innovative process are other appropriability means (Cohen and Levin, 1989. Sec. 4.3).

TABLE 15.3 R&D Amortization Rates of All Sample Industries for 1991

Mean coefficient estimates of regression (4), over the years 1975–1990, using instrumental variables and the Almon lag procedure.

Industry	Chemicals & Pharmaceutics (28)		Machinery & Computer Hardware (35)		Electrical & Electronics (36)		Transportation Vehicles (37)		Scientific Instruments (38)		All Other R&D Industries	
No. of firm-years	1106		1751		1375		757		990		5653	
Coefficient	$\hat{x}$	δ_k*	$\hat{x}$	δ_k	$\hat{x}$	δ_k	$\hat{x}$	δ_k	$\hat{x}$	δ_k	$\hat{x}$	δ_k
$\hat{x}_0$	0.812		-0.658		-0.517		1.487		0.278		-0.517	
$\hat{x}_1$	0.137		0.135		0.155		0.109		0.132		0.084	
$\hat{x}_3$	1.234		1.493		1.055		0.906		1.639		1.015	
$\hat{x}_{2,0}$	0.215	0.082	0.177	0.106	0.224	0.114	0.146	0.072	0.232	0.135	0.201	0.110
$\hat{x}_{2,1}$	0.350	0.133	0.279	0.168	0.347	0.176	0.249	0.123	0.355	0.207	0.322	0.176
$\hat{x}_{2,2}$	0.415	0.158	0.319	0.192	0.386	0.196	0.313	0.155	0.413	0.240	0.376	0.205
$\hat{x}_{2,3}$	0.424	0.161	0.309	0.186	0.360	0.183	0.344	0.170	0.419	0.244	0.376	0.205
$\hat{x}_{2,4}$	0.387	0.147	0.262	0.157	0.288	0.146	0.347	0.171	0.299	0.174	0.324	0.177
$\hat{x}_{2,5}$	0.317	0.121	0.192	0.115	0.186	0.095	0.327	0.162			0.233	0.127
$\hat{x}_{2,6}$	0.226	0.086	0.125	0.076	0.098	0.050	0.298	0.147				
$\hat{x}_{2,7}$	0.158	0.060			0.079	0.040						
$\hat{x}_{2,8}$	0.136	0.052										
$\displaystyle\sum_{k=0}^{s} \hat{a}_{2,k}$	2.628		1.663		0.968		2.024		1.718		1.832	
Adj. R^2	0.89		0.68		0.73		0.73		0.80		0.59	

*Annual R&D amortization rate $= \delta_k = \hat{a}_{2,k} \Big/ \sum_k \hat{a}_{2,k}$.

All the x coefficients, except for the intercept, are statistically significant at the 0.05 level or better (two-tail t-test).

The estimated total benefits of $1 investment in R&D, $\sum_k \hat{a}_{2,k}$, are reported on the next to bottom line of Table 15-3. These benefits range from $2.628 for chemicals and Pharmaceutics to 1.663 in Machinery and Computer Hardware.[14] Note that these undiscounted benefits accrue over a relatively long period of time—five to nine years. Based on the estimated flow of benefits (the $x_{2,k}$ in Table 15.3), assumed to accrue at year-end, the annual internal rate of return of a $1 R&D investment in chemicals and pharmaceutics is 28 percent. Similarly computed, the estimated annual rates of return on a $1 investment in R&D in the remaining industries are: Machinery and Computer Hardware—15 percent, Electrical and Electronics—22 percent, Transportation Vehicles—19 percent, Scientific Instruments—20 percent, and Other Industries—20 percent. Recall that these are benefits in terms of operating income, namely before depreciation and amortization, general expenses, and taxes. In terms of after tax net income, our return estimates accord well with the Grabowski and Mueller (1978) return estimates of 16.7 percent for chemicals and pharmaceutics and 11.7 percent over all R&D industries, as well as with the Lichtenberg and Siegel (1989) more recent estimates of 13 percent return on R&D investment across all industries (for the period 1972–1985).

4. ADJUSTING REPORTED EARNINGS AND BOOK VALUES

The industry-wide amortization rates, δ_k, are used to compute for each sample firm the annual *R&D amortization*, RA_{it}

$$RA_{it} = \sum_k \delta_k RD_{i,t-k}. \tag{6}$$

The periodic R&D amortization (different, of course, from the GAAP expense, which is the current R&D outlay—RD_{it}) is thus the sum of current and past R&D outlays, $RD_{i,t-k}$, each multiplied by the appropriate amortization rate, δ_k.

Earnings adjusted for the R&D capitalization, X_{it}^C, are equal to reported (GAAP) earnings, X_{it}^E, plus the expensed R&D outlay, RD_{it}, minus the R&D amortization (6):

$$X_{it}^C = X_{it}^E + RD_{it} - RA_{it} \tag{7}$$

---

14. When expression (4) was run without the instrumental variable (industry level R&D), the estimated lagged R&D coefficients were, in general, smaller and somewhat less significant. For example, for the Chemicals and Pharmaceutics industry (SIC code 28), the total R&D benefits of $1.00 investment estimated without the instrumental variable was $2.383, while the estimate with the instrumental variable was $2.628 (Table 15.3).

To avoid complicating the analysis, we do not adjust earnings under R&D capi-talization, X_{it}^C, for deferred taxes.[15] The association documented below between returns and the R&D-adjusted data would have been strengthened by adding de-ferred taxes.

The R&D *capital* at year-end, RDC_{it}, of each sample firm is obtained by cu-mulating for each year, starting with 1975 (the year FAS No. 2 became effective), the unamortized portion of the annual R&D expenditures:

$$RDC_{it} = \sum_{k=0}^{N-1} RD_{i,t-k} \left(1 - \sum_{j=0}^{k} \delta_j \right), \tag{8}$$

where N is useful life or duration of R&D (e.g., nine years in the chemicals and pharmaceutics industry). The R&D capital is thus the sum of the un-amortized portion of the current year R&D outlay, $RD_{i,t} \times (1 - \delta_0)$, plus the un-amortized portion of last year's R&D outlay which is amortized twice, $RD_{i,t-1} \times (1 - \delta_0 - \delta_1)$, and so on back to the end of the useful R&D life. A de-tailed example of the computation of earnings under R&D capitalization (X_{it}^C), the R&D amortization (RA_{it}), and the R&D capital (RDC_{it}), for Merck & Co. is provided in the Appendix.

The impact of the above adjustments on the sample firms' reported data is substantial. The average (over firms and years) understatement of reported earn-ings due to R&D expensing (i.e., the percentage difference between adjusted, X_{it}^C, and reported, X_{it}^E, earnings) ranges from 26.8 percent in Electrical and Electronics to 9.7 percent for "Other Industries." The average earnings understatement for all sample firms and years is 20.55 percent. The understatement of reported equity, resulting from the absence of the R&D capital, ranges from 24.6 percent for both Scientific Instruments and Machinery and Computer Hardware to 12.3 percent in "Other Industries." The mean book value understatement for all sample firms and years is 22.2 percent.

The relation between adjusted and reported return on equity (*ROE*) is more complicated, being a function of the growth rate in R&D expenditures, the amor-tization rate of the R&D capital, and its duration. Holding other things equal, *ROE* based on R&D capitalization will be higher than reported *ROE* for firms with a sufficiently high growth rate of R&D expenditures. This is corroborated by a regression run across all sample firms and years, of the difference between capi-talized and reported ROE on the five-year geometric growth rate of R&D expen-ditures, which yielded a coefficient of 0.115 (*t*-value = 6.49) for the R&D growth rate.

---

15. Note, however, Daley's (1995) finding that the deferred tax component of the reported tax ex-pense is considered an expense by investors.

5. CONTEMPORANEOUS ANALYSIS: STOCK PRICES, RETURNS, AND R&D CAPITALIZATION

We wish to examine the value-relevance of the variables derived from the R&D capitalization process described above. This can be done by examining, in a *contemporaneous* setting, the association between stock prices (or returns) and the R&D capitalization estimates, as well as evaluating the *intertemporal* association between R&D-adjusted variables and subsequent stock returns. The former, contemporaneous analysis, indicates the extent of current recognition of R&D relevance by investors, while the intertemporal analysis may suggest market inefficiency (i.e., investors failing to fully recognize the value-relevance of R&D).

Kothari and Zimmerman (1995) evaluate the adequacy of price and return models for accounting research and conclude that the "use of both return and price models has the potential to yield more convincing evidence." We adopt this recommendation and examine the following return and price models:

5.1. Definition of Variables and Models

P_{it} = share price of firm i three months after fiscal year-end,

R_{it} = annual stock return from nine months before fiscal t year-end through three months after it,

X_{it}^E, X_{it}^C = reported (GAAP) and adjusted (7) earnings-per-share (before extraordinary items), respectively,

$X_{it}^C - X_{it}^E$ = "error" or misstatement in reported earnings due to the R&D expensing; this misstatement is equal to $RD_{it} - RA_{it}$, namely the annual R&D outlay minus the R&D amortization, which in turn is equal to the net (amortized) investment in R&D during t,

X_{it}^B = $X_{it}^E + RD_{it}$ is reported earnings before the R&D expensing.

Return Models

$$R_{it} = x_1 + \beta_1 X_{it}^E + \gamma_1 (X_{it}^C - X_{it}^E) + u_{it}, \tag{11}$$

$$R_{it} = x_2 + \beta_2 X_{it}^E + \gamma_2 \Delta X_{it}^E + \delta_2 (X_{it}^C - X_{it}^E) + \Omega_2 \Delta (X_{it}^C - X_{it}^E) + u_{it}, \tag{12}$$

$$R_{it} = x_3 + \beta_3 X_{it}^B + \gamma_3 \Delta X_{it}^B + \delta_3 (X_{it}^C - X_{it}^E) + \Omega_3 \Delta (X_{it}^C - X_{it}^E) + u_{it}. \tag{13}$$

All right-hand variables in (11)–(13) are deflated by beginning of fiscal year share price, $P_{i,t-1}$. Annual differencing is indicated by A.

Model (11) is the basic returns-earnings relation: stock returns regressed on the price-deflated level of earnings. We single out for examination of value-relevance the estimated "error" or misstatement in reported earnings, $X_{it}^C - X_{it}^E$. Model (12) incorporates the first differences in reported earnings, ΔX_{it}^E, and in the earnings misstatements, $\Delta (X_{it}^C - X_{it}^E)$, because differencing often yields a stationary series (Christie, 1987). Model (13) substitutes X_{it}^B, reported earnings *before* R&D expensing, for the after R&D earnings, X_{it}^E. The reason: when X_{it}^E, is the explanatory variable [model (12)], the R&D expenditure (RD_{it}) is a component of all four independent variables, and thus may be associated with different estimated coefficients. In model (13), on the other hand, the R&D expenditure is only present in the two right-most independent variables.

Price Models

$$P_{it} = x_4 + \beta_4 X_{it}^E + \gamma_4 (X_{it}^C - X_{it}^E) + u_{it}, \tag{14}$$

$$P_{it} = x_5 + \beta_5 X_{it}^E + \gamma_5 (X_{it}^C - X_{it}^E) + \Omega_5 (BV_{it}^C - BV_{it}^E) + u_{it}. \tag{15}$$

Expression (14) is the parsimonious price model, with the "error" in reported earnings singled out. Model (15) accounts for both the misstatements in reported earnings and in book value. The latter, $BV_{it}^C - BV_{it}^E$, equals the total capitalized value of R&D, RDC_{it}, (8). Since the price regressions are not deflated, we applied White's correction for heteroscedasticity. We expect positive values for all the coefficients (except the intercepts) in both the returns and price regressions. The reason: earnings are expected to be positively correlated with stock prices and returns, while the misstatements in reported earnings and book value, which equal the net annual investment in R&D and the total R&D capital, respectively, should on average be associated with market value increases (assuming managers follow the net present value rule in their R&D decisions).

5.2. Findings

Table 15.4 presents estimates of the contemporaneous price and return regressions outlined above. Specifically, for each sample firm and year we adjusted earnings, book values, and R&D capital (expressions 6–8), from data publicly available prior to the year of adjustment. For example, the 1982 adjusted earnings, book values and R&D capital of the sample firms are based on R&D amortization rates computed from 1975–1981 data, as demonstrated in Table 15.2 for the Electric and Electronics industry. The values reported in Table 15.4 are mean regression coefficients and corresponding *t*-values derived from the 16 individual-year regressions, 1976–1991.[16]

It is evident from Table 15.4 that in all the return and price configurations (except for rows 5 and 9), our adjustment to reported earnings, $X_{it}^C - X_{it}^E$ (the difference between earnings under R&D capitalization and GAAP earnings), is as

---

16. We estimate R&D amortization rates for every industry and year. 1975–1990. These estimates enable us to adjust reported data from 1976 (1975 is "lost" in the differencing of earnings) to 1991, the year subsequent to the end of amortization rate estimation.

TABLE 15.4 Contemporaneous Analysis: Prices (Returns)—Financial Variables, 1976–1991

Mean coefficient estimates from stock price and return regressions run on reported earnings (X_{it}^E), the misstatement in reported earnings ($X_{it}^C - X_{it}^E$), and the misstatement in equity ($BV_{it}^C - BV_{it}^E$) T-values in parentheses.

Dependent variable	Intercept	X_{it}^E	ΔX_{it}^E	$(X_{it}^C - X_{it}^E)$	$\Delta(X_{it}^C - X_{it}^E)$	X_{it}^B	ΔX_{it}^B	$(BV_{it}^C - BV_{it}^E)$	Adj. R^2
1. Return (R_{it})—All firms	0.969 (17.38)	1.114 (11.11)	—	2.030 (4.14)	—	—	—	—	0.09
2. Return—Upper quartile*	0.425 (4.21)	1.197 (8.79)	—	2.207 (5.68)	—	—	—	—	0.09
3. Return (R_{it})	-0.004 (-0.07)	0.805 (6.17)	0.854 (7.41)	2.286 (4.48)	0.091 (0.16)	—	—	—	0.12
4. Return—Upper quartile*	-0.031 (-0.53)	0.586 (4.29)	0.767 (5.23)	2.576 (4.70)	-0.928 (-1.13)	—	—	—	0.11
5. Return (R_{it})	-0.036 (-0.59)	—	—	0.746 (1.30)	-0.100 (-0.18)	0.884 (7.13)	0.690 (6.11)	—	0.13
6. Return—Upper quartile*	-0.087 (-1.35)	—	—	2.622 (4.21)	-0.777 (-0.75)	0.718 (7.54)	0.757 (5.86)	—	0.13
7. Price (P_{it})—All firms	9.425 (22.25)	6.240 (11.28)	—	10.612 (14.37)	—	—	—	—	0.44
8. Price—Upper quartile	7.882 (12.93)	6.335 (16.21)	—	8.760 (8.31)	—	—	—	—	0.46
9. Price (P_{it})	9.025 (10.73)	5.193 (8.25)	—	0.963 (0.92)	—	—	—	2.368 (16.11)	0.46
10. Price—Upper quartile*	5.453 (6.50)	4.701 (16.94)	—	2.460 (2.55)	—	—	—	2.070 (11.68)	0.55

Independent variables

X_{it}^C and BV_{it}^C are earnings and book values adjusted for R&D capitalization. X_{it}^B is reported earnings before R&D expensing. X_{it}^E and BV_{it}^E are reported earnings and equity, respectively.

*These regressions were run for firms in the upper quartile of the R&D capital to reported book value ratio (RDC/BV)$_{it}$, namely firms with a relatively large estimated R&D capital.

expected positive and highly statistically significant.[17] Furthermore, the coefficients of the earnings misstatement, $X_{it}^C - X_{it}^E$, are substantially larger than those of reported earnings. For example, in row 1, the mean coefficient of $X_{it}^C - X_{it}^E$ is 2.030, almost twice as large as the earnings level coefficient, 1.114. In the price regressions (rows 7 and 8), the coefficients of $X_{it}^C - X_{it}^E$ are roughly 50 percent larger than the earnings coefficients. Since $X_{it}^C - X_{it}^E$ is equal to the net (of amortization) annual investment in R&D, the large regression coefficients attest to the high value placed on this investment by investors. Such a high value accords with a major theme of this study, namely that R&D investment contributes, on average, to future earnings and cash flows. When the estimated R&D capital $(RDC_{it} = BV_{it}^C - BV_{it}^E)$ is included in the price regressions (rows 9–10), it too is highly statistically significant. Thus, both the annual net investment in R&D and the cumulated R&D capital are value-relevant to investors.[18]

Our sample is large (about 1,300 companies in Table 15.4) and therefore contains a fair number of firms with relatively small R&D expenditures, potentially distorting the above findings. Accordingly, we add a focus on firms with relatively large R&D investment by ranking all sample firms in every year by their R&D capital-to-equity values (i.e., RDC_{it}/BV_{it}^E), and running the price and return regressions over firms in the upper quartile of this ranking. Estimates of these regressions are reported in rows 2, 4, 6, 8, and 10 in Table 15.4. It is evident that, in the returns regressions (rows 2, 4, 6), the coefficients of the earnings misstatement, $X_{it}^C - X_{it}^E$, for intensive R&D capital firms are larger and more significant than the corresponding total sample coefficients. Furthermore, in the two cases where the coefficient of $X_{it}^C - X_{it}^E$ for the total sample are statistically insignificant (regressions 5 and 9), the coefficients of the same variable for firms with large R&D capital (rows 6 and 10) are highly significant.

5.3. A Survivorship Bias?

Can the positive and statistically significant association between the R&D capitalization values and both stock prices and returns (Table 15.4) be driven by a sample selection bias? Could these results be due to our sample consisting of firms which were ex post successful in their R&D activities? We think not.

---

17. The change in this variable, $\Delta(X_{it}^C - X_{it}^E)$, is not significant, probably due to the relative stability for most firms of the R&D expenditures in successive years. Indeed, the standard deviation of $X_{it}^C - X_{it}^E$, is about 50 percent larger than that of $\Delta(X_{it}^C - X_{it}^E)$.

18. To examine whether the earnings and book value adjustments for R&D capitalization, just proxy for expected growth, we reran the regressions in Table 15.4, adding to the independent variables the beginning-of-year market-to-book ratio, which reflects investors' expected growth (used by Collins and Kothari, 1989). The addition of this ratio decreases to some extent the coefficient of the earnings misstatement, $X_{it}^C - X_{it}^E$, but the latter remains statistically significant (at the 0.01 level). For example, in regression 1 (Table 4), the earnings misstatement coefficient is 2.030 ($t = 4.14$). When the market-to-book ratio is added to that regression, the earnings misstatement coefficient is 1.294 ($t = 3.07$).

First, our main source of data, the R&D Master File (Section 2) was compiled from successive COMPUSTAT tapes, starting with 1978. Accordingly, firms which were included in earlier tapes, yet were subsequently dropped because of bankruptcies or mergers, are included in the R&D Master File and in our sample. Moreover, the R&D Master File includes the COMPUSTAT Research File which contains, among others, failed firms. This inclusion in our sample of failed and merged companies mitigates a possible survivorship bias.

We nevertheless wished to examine directly the existence of a survivorship bias, and therefore computed "Jensen's (1968) alphas" for the sample firms (see also Ball and Kothari, 1991, for use of Jensen's alphas). This parameter, reflecting abnormal returns, is derived from the following monthly time-series regression:

$$R_{RD,t} - R_{Ft} = x + \beta(R_{Mt} - R_{Ft}) + e_t, \tag{16}$$

where

$R_{RD,t}$ = value-weighted return on the sample firms in month t (192 months during 1976–1991),

R_{Ft} = risk-free return, measured as the average 90-day rate on Treasury bills, in month t,

R_{MT} = CRSP value-weighted market return in month t.

Regression (16) was run over the 192 months in 1976 through 1991. The estimated x coefficient reflects the average abnormal return of the sample firms relative to the market. Accordingly, if our sample is characterized by unusually good performers (a survivorship bias), then the estimated x should be positive and statistically significant.

The estimated coefficients of expression (16), with t-values in parentheses, are

$$x = -0.0003, \quad \beta = 0.842, \quad \text{Adj. } R^2 = 0.86.$$
$$(-0.25) \qquad (33.81)$$

The estimated Jensen's alpha is thus insignificantly different from zero.[19] Accordingly, the value-relevance of the R&D adjustment to earnings as well as that of the estimated R&D capital, apparent from Table 15.4, do not appear to be driven by a survivorship bias in our sample.

19. When we ran regression (16) on annual rather than monthly returns, the estimated x efficient was 0.0248 ($t = 0.85$), namely statistically insignificant. The annual β coefficient was 1.152 ($t = 6.569$), which appears more reasonable than the monthly β of 0.842 (above).

6. INTERTEMPORAL ANALYSIS: R&D CAPITAL AND SUBSEQUENT STOCK RETURNS

The contemporaneous analysis (Section 5), indicating the value-relevance of the R&D capitalization estimates, leaves open a most intriguing and important question: Do investors fully recognize the value-relevance of R&D information when reported or do they only adjust partially for the R&D expensing under GAAP? Such partial adjustment is analogous to the "post earnings announcement drift" (e.g., Bernard and Thomas, 1990), indicating that while investors generally react to unexpected earnings at the announcement date, such reaction is incomplete (an underreaction), as evidenced by the systematic return drifts subsequent to the earnings announcements. The extent (completeness) of investor reaction to new information bears on the efficiency of capital markets and may also have important regulatory implications. For example, if investors are found to over- or underreact to current R&D information, a case can be made for changing the disclosure environment to improve investors' comprehension of the information.

The extent of investors' reaction to R&D information can be examined in an *intertemporal* setting, where R&D capitalization estimates based on currently available information are associated with subsequent stock returns. A significant association may suggest an incomplete contemporaneous adjustment to R&D information. We examine this association within a model recently used by Fama and French (1992), where stock returns were regressed on *lagged* values of the following fundamentals: systematic risk (β), firm size (market capitalization), the book-to-market ratio, financial leverage, and the earnings-to-price ratio. We add to these fundamentals the firm's estimated R&D capital scaled by its market value. Evaluating the relation between returns and lagged R&D capital within this model assures that the R&D variable does not proxy for other risk or mispricing variables (e.g., the book-to-market or the price-to-earnings ratios) present in the analysis. Accordingly, we estimate the following cross-sectional regression:

$$R_{i,t+j} = c_{0,j} + c_{1,j}\beta_{i,t} + c_{2,j}\ln(M)_{i,t} + c_{3,j}\ln(B/M)_{i,t} + c_{4,j}\ln(A/B)_{i,t}$$

$$+ c_{5,j}(E(+)/M)_{i,t} + c_{6,j}(E/M \ dummy)_{i,t}$$

$$+ c_{7,j}\ln(RDC/M)_{i,t} + e_{i,t+j} \qquad (17)$$

where

$R_{i,t+j}$ = *returns:* monthly stock returns of firm i, starting with the 7th month after fiscal t year-end, $j = 1, \ldots, 12$,

$\beta_{i,t}$ = *risk:* CAPM-based beta of firm i, estimated from 60 monthly stock returns up to month t (one month preceding the return calculation); a minimum of 24 months is required,

$M_{i,t}$ = *size:* market value of firm i, calculated as price times number of shares outstanding at t,

$(B/M)_{i,t}$ = *book-to-market:* ratio of book value of common equity plus deferred taxes to market value of equity of firm *i* at fiscal year-end,

$(A/B)_{i,t}$ = *leverage:* ratio of book value of total assets to book value of common equity of firm *i* at fiscal year-end,

$[E(+)/M]_{i,t}$ = *earnings/price ratio:* ratio of positive earnings before extraordinary items (plus income-statement deferred taxes, minus preferred dividends), to the market value of equity of firm *i* at fiscal year-end; this variable is set equal to 0 when earnings are negative,

$(E/Mdummy)_{i,t}$ = 1 if earnings of firm *i* for fiscal *t* are negative, and 0 otherwise,

$(RDC/M)_{i,t}$ = *R&D capital:* estimated R&D capital [expression (8)] over market value of equity at year-end.

The following time-line clarifies the intertemporal regressions:

		Disclosure of financials		Subsequent returns	
	Fiscal year *t*				
1	12		18		30

Months

The accounting fundamentals—book value, earnings, total assets, and R&D capital (RDC)—pertain to fiscal year *t* (months 1–12). Six months (13–18) are then allowed for the public disclosure of fiscal *t* annual financial statements by all sample firms, followed by 12 monthly stock returns, $R_{i,t+j}$ (months 19–30). For each of the 15 fiscal years examined in this analysis (1975–1989), we run regression (17) cross-sectionally for each of the subsequent 12 return months.[20] In total, 180 cross-sectional regressions were computed (15 years × 12 regressions per year).[21]

     Table 15.5 reports mean coefficient estimates of expression (17) over the 180 months, for the total sample (top panel) and for the firms in the upper quartile of the R&D capital-to-total assets ranking (i.e., firms with a relatively large R&D investment). The first row of coefficients in each panel is generated by a replication of the Fama-French (1992) analysis, namely regression (17) *without* the R&D variable. This was aimed at examining the conformity of our sample of R&D firms with the COMPUSTAT population (Fama-French sample), with respect to the returns-fundamentals' relation. It is evident from Table 15.5 that a close conformity indeed exists: as in Fama-French, the only two variables that are

---

20. In the preceding analyses we examined the years 1975–1991. Here we stop in 1989, since we need stock returns for 1-1/2 years subsequent to each fiscal year.

21. Note that these regressions are not run on overlapping months. For example, for the fiscal year ending in December 1980, the returns range from July 1981 through June 1982. The following fiscal year, ending December 1981, is associated with the nonoverlapping returns starting in July 1982 and ending in June 1983. The numbers of sample firms in each cross-sectional regression range between roughly 900 in the earlier sample years (the 1970s) to 1,500 in the latter period.

TABLE 15.5 Intertemporal Analysis: R&D Capital and Subsequent Stock Returns

Mean coefficient estimates of cross-sectional regressions (17) of monthly stock returns on lagged values of fundamental variables. The returns are for the 12 months after fiscal year-end (plus six months). The means are computed over 180 regressions run for each month in 1975–1989. T-statistics are reported in parentheses.

Regressions	Intercept	Beta	Size	B/M	A/B	E(+)/M	E(−)/M dummy	RDC/M	Adj. R^2
Total sample									
Without R&D[a]	0.0251	−0.0012	−0.0014	0.0033	−0.0007	0.0002	−0.0030	—	
	(5.95)	(−0.66)	(−2.74)	(2.90)	(−0.52)	(0.02)	(−1.46)	—	0.036
With R&D[a]	0.0286	−0.0014	−0.0013	0.0022	−0.0013	0.0022	−0.0031	0.0015[c]	
	(6.32)	(−0.79)	(−2.61)	(1.91)	(−1.00)	(0.27)	(−1.58)	(3.10)	0.042
Upper quartile[b]									
Without R&D	0.0303	−0.0009	−0.0019	0.0043	0.0021	−0.0181	−0.0072	—	
	(5.12)	(−0.30)	(−2.76)	(2.44)	(0.70)	(−0.87)	(−1.60)	—	0.053
With R&D	0.0474	−0.0011	−0.0014	−0.0051	−0.0082	−0.0231	−0.0102	0.0114[d]	
	(5.91)	(−0.41)	(−1.99)	(−1.52)	(−2.12)	(−1.09)	(−2.25)	(3.88)	0.056

[a] "Without R&D" and "With R&D" refers to regression (17) run *without* the R&D capital i.e., the construct used by Fama and French (1992) and *with* the R&D capital, respectively.

[b] These regressions were run on firms in the upper quartile of the R&D capital-to-total assets ratio, namely firms with a large R&D capital.

[c] When R&D capital is scaled by financial variables rather than market value, the coefficient estimates and t-values (in parentheses) of R&D capital are: R&D capital over total assets = 0.0015 (3.10), and R&D capital over book value of equity = 0.0014 (2.95).

[d] The coefficient estimates and t-values (parentheses) of R&D capital over total assets are: 0.0114 (3.88), and R&D capital over book value of equity = 0.0075 (3.41).

Regression: $R_{i,t+j} = c_0 + c_1\beta_{it} + c_2\ln(M)_{it} + c_3\ln(B/M)_{it} + c_4\ln(A/B)_{it} + c_5(E(+)/M)_{it} + c_6(E/M \text{ dummy})_{it} + c_7\ln(RDC/M)_{it} + e_{i,t+j}$, with $R_{i,t+j} = 12$ monthly stock returns of firm i from the 7th month after fiscal year-end, estimated from 60 monthly stock returns (minimum of 24) up to month t, $(M)_{it} = $ market value of equity of firm i at t, $(B/M)_{it} = $ book-to-market ratio of firm i at fiscal year-end, $(A/B)_{it} = $ ratio of book value of total assets of firm i to book value of equity, at fiscal year-end, $(E(+)/M)_{it} = $ ratio of positive earnings to the market value of equity at fiscal year-end and equal to 0 when earnings are negative, $(E/M \text{ dummy})_{it} = 1$ if earnings are negative and 0 otherwise, $(RDC/M)_{it} = $ R&D capital-to-market value of firm i at fiscal year-end.

statistically significant are size and the book-to-market ratio. The systematic risk, β, is in each regression statistically insignificant, as are the remaining fundamentals. Our results are close to Fama-French's in terms of coefficient sizes. For example, Fama and French report that the average risk premium for the book-to-market factor (the premium per unit of the regression slope of book-to-market), is 0.40 percent per month, while our estimated book-to-market (B/M) coefficient (upper panel of Table 15.5) is 0.33 percent. Thus, in terms of the returns-fundamentals relation, our sample of science-based companies does not differ much from the total COMPUSTAT sample.

When the R&D capital-to-market (RDC/M) ratio is included in the regression (second row of each panel), its coefficient is positive and statistically significant (0.0015, t = 3.10) at better than the 0.01 level. This finding is even more pronounced for firms in the upper quartile of the R&D capital-to-total assets ratio, namely those with relatively large R&D capital. The coefficient of R&D capital, 0.0114 (Table 15.5 bottom row), is about eight times larger than the R&D coefficient for the total sample (0.0015). Given the mean value of RDC/M, 0.327, the regression coefficient of 0.0114 (monthly) translates to an annual return of 4.57%, This is our estimate of the average market mispricing of R&D capital in R&D-intensive companies.

Note that for the upper-quartile firms, the statistical significance of the book-to-market ratio vanishes with the introduction of the R&D capital, while leverage (A/B) and the negative earnings dummy, $E(-)/M$, become significant. It should also be noted that the association between R&D capital and subsequent returns does not depend on the scaling of the R&D variable by *market* value. As footnotes c and d to Table 15.5 indicate, when we scale R&D capital by *book* value of total assets (A), or by the *book* value of equity (B), the regression coefficients of R&D capital and their significance level are remarkably close to those in the table.[22]

Summarizing, firms' R&D capital was found to be associated with subsequent stock returns. Given the analysis and discussion of Section 5.3, this association does not appear to be due to a survivorship bias. Similar to other findings of this type (e.g., the book-to-market association with returns in Fama and

---

22. The R&D capital in expression (17) is based on our estimation procedures described in Sections 2–4. As a comparison, we replaced in (17) that estimate with the *sum* of R&D outlays in the current and the preceding two years (i.e., $RD_{it} + RD_{i,t-1} + RD_{i,t-2}$). Over our entire sample and time period, this substitution made little difference with respect to the estimated R&D capital (RDC/M) coefficient and its statistical significance. However, when we focus on firms with relatively large R&D capital we obtain substantial differences.

For example, for the firms in the upper quartile of the R&D capital-to-total assets ratio, the estimated RDC/M coefficient based on the sum of the recent three years R&D is 0.0078 (t = 3.01), while the RDC/M coefficient based on the capitalization procedure (Table 15.5) is 0.114 (t = 3.88). When we focus on the firms in the top decile of the R&D capital-to-total assets ratio, the difference is even more striking. The RDC/M coefficient based on the three-year R&D is statistically insignificant (0.0105, t = 1.20), while that based on the capitalization procedure is large and significant (0.0165, t = 1.85). It appears, therefore, that our R&D estimation procedure yields different and improved results, compared with a mechanistic capitalization, such as the sum of R&D expenditures in the last three years.

French, 1992), this association may result from a mispricing of securities, namely investors' underreaction to R&D information, or it may reflect an extra-market risk factor associated with R&D capital (i.e., equilibrium returns). Disentangling these alternative explanations is a major endeavor, obviously beyond the boundaries of this study. Whether the R&D association with subsequent returns indicates mispricing or the existence of an extra-market risk factor, it enhances our conclusion concerning the value-relevance of R&D capitalization.

7. SUMMARY

The following major conclusions can be drawn from the evidence presented above:

1. The R&D capitalization process developed here yields statistically reliable estimates of the amortization rate of the R&D capital. These amortization rates are used to compute firm-specific R&D capital and adjust reported earnings and equity (book) values to reflect the capitalization of · R&D.
2. The major outcomes of these adjustments—the corrections to reported earnings and book values for R&D capitalization—were found to be strongly associated with stock prices and returns, indicating that the R&D capitalization process yields value-relevant information to investors.
3. The estimated R&D capital does not appear to be fully reflected contemporaneously in stock prices, since R&D capital is associated with subsequent stock returns. This suggests either a systematic mispricing of the shares of R&D-intensive firms (underreaction to R&D information), estimated at an annual rate of 4.57 percent, or that the subsequent excess returns are compensating for an extra-market risk factor associated with R&D.

    Taken together, these findings suggest that R&D capitalization yields statistically reliable and economically relevant information, contradicting a major tenet of FASB Statement No. 2: "A direct relationship between research and development costs and specific future revenue generally has not been demonstrated."

APPENDIX

Merck & Co.: Example of the adjustment of earnings and book values for R&D capitalization

Table 15.6 presents Merck's reported (GAAP) and R&D-adjusted values for the years 1975–1991. The four left-hand columns are derived from Merck's annual financial reports, while the five columns on the right are the adjusted values reflecting R&D capitalization. These adjustments are based on the procedures described in Sections 2–4 above, and are detailed in the footnotes to Table 15.6. The detailed computation of Merck's 1991 R&D amortization and its R&D capital,

TABLE 15.6 Merck & Co.: The Adjustment of Reported Earnings and Book Values for R&D Capitalization (in $ Millions)

Year	Reported data				Adjusted data				
	Earnings*	R&D expenditures*	Equity*	ROE	R&D amortization[a]	R&D capital[b]	Earnings[c]	Equity[d]	ROE
1975	228.78	124.51	947.00	0.28	80.54	334.11	272.76	1281.11	0.25
1976	255.48	136.35	1099.22	0.27	91.06	379.40	300.77	1478.62	0.23
1977	277.52	144.90	1275.03	0.25	102.38	421.92	320.04	1696.95	0.22
1978	307.33	161.35	1452.82	0.24	114.72	468.55	354.17	1921.38	0.21
1979	381.78	188.07	1663.45	0.26	128.63	527.99	441.22	2191.44	0.23
1980	415.40	233.90	1863.32	0.25	146.49	615.40	502.80	2478.72	0.23
1981	398.26	274.17	2001.46	0.21	168.61	720.95	503.82	2722.41	0.20
1982	415.14	320.16	2203.99	0.21	193.78	845.33	539.51	3049.31	0.20
1983	450.85	356.04	2434.61	0.20	227.04	974.33	579.86	3408.95	0.19
1984	492.97	393.12	2544.16	0.20	261.12	1106.34	624.97	3650.50	0.18
1985	539.90	426.26	2634.00	0.21	297.03	1235.56	669.12	3869.56	0.18
1986	675.70	479.80	2569.10	0.26	335.50	1379.86	820.00	3948.96	0.21
1987	906.40	565.70	2116.70	0.35	379.31	1566.25	1092.79	3682.95	0.28
1988	1206.80	668.80	2855.80	0.57	431.53	1803.52	1444.07	4659.32	0.39
1989	1495.40	750.50	3520.60	0.52	491.43	2062.59	1754.47	5583.19	0.38
1990	1781.20	854.00	3834.40	0.51	560.52	2356.07	2074.68	6190.47	0.37
1991	2121.70	987.80	4916.20	0.55	640.81	2703.06	2468.69	7619.26	0.40

*Earnings = Compustat item #18, R&D expenditures = Compustat item #46, Book value of equity = Compustat item #60.

[a] The R&D amortization, RA_{it}, for 1991 ($640.81 million), is calculated as follows:

$$RA_{it} = \sum_k \delta_k RD_{t-k}$$

$= 0.082 \times 987.8 + 0.133 \times 854 + 0.158 \times 750.5 + 0.161 \times 668.8 + 0.147 \times 565.7 + 0.121 \times 479.8 + 0.086 \times 426.3 + 0.06 \times 393.1 + 0.052 \times 356$

$= 640.81$ million

[b] R&D capital, RDC_{it}, for 1991 ($2,703.06 million), is calculated as follows:

$$RDC_{it} = \sum_{k=0}^{N-1} RD_{i,t-k}\left(1 - \sum_{j=0}^{k}\delta_j\right)$$

$= (1 - 0.082) \times 987.8 + (1 - 0.082 - 0.133) \times 854 + (1 - 0.082 - 0.133 - 0.158) \times 750.5 + (1 - 0.082 - 0.133 - 0.158 - 0.161) \times 668.8$

$+ (1 - 0.082 - 0.133 - 0.158 - 0.161 - 0.147) \times 565.7 + (1 - 0.082 - 0.133 - 0.158 - 0.161 - 0.147 - 0.121) \times 479.8$

$+ (1 - 0.082 - 0.133 - 0.158 - 0.161 - 0.147 - 0.121 - 0.086) \times 426.3 + (1 - 0.082 - 0.133 - 0.158 - 0.161 - 0.147 - 0.121$

$- 0.086 - 0.06) \times 393.1 + (1 - 0.082 - 0.133 - 0.158 - 0.161 - 0.147 - 0.121 - 0.086 - 0.06 - 0.052) \times 356$

$= \$2,703$ million

The coefficients 0.082, 0.133 . . . in footnotes a and b are the amortization rates, δ_λ, for the Chemical and Pharmaceuticals industry presented in Table 3.

[c] Income under capitalization (X_{it}^C) = reported net income (X_{it}^E) + reported R&D expenditures (RD_{it}) − R&D amortization (RA_{it}).

[d] Equity under capitalization (BV_{it}^C) = reported equity (BV_{it}^E) + R&D capital (RDC_{it}).

using the Chemicals and Pharmaceutics amortization rates (δ_k in Table 15.3) is presented on the bottom part of Table 15.6.

As expected, Merck's reported earnings and equity values are in every year lower than the corresponding R&D-adjusted values. However, Merck's return on equity (ROE) based on the capitalized numbers (right column) is substantially lower than its reported ROE (e.g., 0.40 vs. 0.55 in 1991). This is mainly due to Merck's relatively low growth rate of R&D expenditures—less than 20 percent a year during 1987–1991—compared with about 35 percent average annual growth rate in earnings over that period. In general, R&D-adjusted ROE will be higher than reported (GAAP) ROE when the growth rate of R&D expenditures is sufficiently large.

REFERENCES

Ball, R. and S. P. Kothari, 1991, "Security returns around earnings announcements." *The Accounting Review* 66, 718–738.

Ben Zion, U., 1978, "The investment aspect of nonproduction expenditures: An empirical test," *Journal of Economics and Business* 30, 224–229.

Berger. P., 1993, "Explicit and implicit tax effects of the R&D tax credit," *Journal of Accounting Research* 31, 131–171.

Bernard. V. and J. Thomas, 1990, "Evidence that stock prices do not fully reflect the implications of current earnings for future earnings." *Journal of Accounting and Economics* 13, 303–340.

Bublitz, B. and M. Ettredge, 1989, "The information in discretion outlays: Advertising, research and development," *The Accounting Review* 64, 108–124.

Chan, S., J. Martin, and J. Kensinger, 1990, "Corporate research and development expenditures and share value," *Journal of Financial Economies* 26, 255–276.

Christie, A., 1987, "On cross-sectional analysis in accounting research," *Journal of Accounting and Economics* 9, 231–238.

Cockburn, I. and Z. Griliches, 1988, "Industry effects and appropriability measures in the stock market's valuation of R&D and patents," *American Economic Review* 78, 419–423.

Cohen, W. and R. Levin, 1989, "Empirical studies of innovation and market structure," in R. Schmalensee and R. Willig, eds., *Handbook of Industrial Organization*, Vol. II (Elsevier Science BV. Amsterdam).

Cohen, W. and D. Levinthal, 1989, "Innovation and learning: The two faces of R&D—Implications for the analysis of R&D investment," *Economic Journal* 99, 569–596.

Collins. D. W. and S. P. Kothari, 1989, "An analysis of intertemporal and cross-sectional determinants of earnings response coefficients," *Journal of Accounting and Economies* 12, 143–181.

Daley, M., 1993, "The impact of deferred tax allocation on earnings as a measure of firm performance," Ph.D. dissertation (University of Rochester, Rochester, NY).

Dukes, R., 1976, "An investigation of the effects of expensing research and development costs on security prices," in *Proceedings of the conference on topical research in accounting* (New York University, New York, NY).

Eccher, E., 1995, "The value relevance of capitalized software development costs," (Northwestern University, Kellogg School of Management. Evanston, IL).

Elliott, J., G. Richardson, T. Dyckman, and R. Dukes, 1984, "The impact of SFAS No. 2 on firm expenditures on research and development: Replications and extensions," *Journal of Accounting Research* 22, 85–102

Evenson, R. and Y. Kislev, 1976, "A stochastic model of applied research." *Journal of Political Economy* 84, 265–281.

Fama, E. and K. French, 1992, "The cross-section of expected stock returns." *Journal of Finance* 47, 427–465.

FASB (Financial Accounting Standards Board), 1974, "Accounting for research and development costs," *Statement of Financial Accounting Standards No. 2.*

FASB, 1985, "Accounting for the costs of computer software to be sold, leased, or otherwise marketed," *Statement of Financial Accounting Standard No. 86.*

Grabowski, H. and D. Mueller, 1978, "Industrial research and development, intangible capital stocks, and firm profit rates," *Bell Journal of Economies* 9, 328–343

Griliches, Z. and J. Mairesse, 1990, "R&D and productivity growth: comparing Japanese and U.S. manufacturing firms," in: C. Hulten, ed., *Productivity growth in Japan and the United States* (University of Chicago Press, Chicago, IL) 317–348.

Hall, B., 1993a, *New evidence on the impacts of research and development* (University of California, Berkeley, CA).

Hall, B., 1993b, "The stock market value of R&D investment during the 1980s," *American Economic Review* 83, 239–264.

Hall, B. C. Cummins, E. Laderman, and J. Mundy, 1988, "The R&D master file documentation," NBER technical working paper no. 72, updated to 1990 in NBER working paper no. 3366, May 1990.

Hirschey, M. and J. Weygandt, 1985, "Amortization policy for advertising and research and development expenditures." *Journal of Accounting Research* 23, 326–333.

Horwitz, B. and R. Kolodny, 1981, "The FASB, the SEC and R&D," *Bell Journal of Economics* 12, 249–262.

Johnston, J. 1984, *Econometric methods*, 3rd ed. (McGraw-Hill, New York. NY).

Kothari, S. and J. Zimmerman, 1995, "Price and return models," *Journal of Accounting and Economics* 20, forthcoming.

Lev, B. and R. Thiagarajan, 1993, "Fundamental information analysis." *Journal of Accounting Research* 31, 190–215.

Levin, R., K. Klevorick, R. Nelson, and S. Winter, (1987). "Appropriating the returns from industrial R&D." *Brookings Papers on Economic Activity,* 783–820.

Lichtenberg, F. and D. Siegel, 1989, "The impact of R&D investment on productivity: New evidence using linked R&D-LED data," NBER working paper no. 2901.

Maddala, G., 1992, *Introduction to econometrics.* 2nd ed. (Macmillan, New York. NY).

Mairesse, J. and M. Sassenou, 1991, "R&D and productivity: A survey of econometric studies at the firm level," NBER working paper no. 3666.

Mansfield, E., 1986, "Patents and innovation: An empirical study." *Management Science* 32, 173–181.

Mowery, D., 1983, "The relationship between intrafirm and contractual form of industrial research in American manufacturing, 1900–1940," *Explorations in Economic History* 20, 351–374.

Nadiri, I. and I. Prucha, 1992, *Estimation of the depreciation rate of physical and R&D capital in the U.S. total manufacturing sector* (New York University, New York, NY).

Pakes, A., 1985, "On patents, R&D, and the stock market rate of return," *Journal of Political Economy 93,* 390–409.

Peles, Y., 1970, "Amortization of advertising expenditures in the financial statements," *Journal of Accounting Research* 8, 128–137.

Wasley, C. and T. Linsmeier, 1992, "A further examination of the economic consequences of SFAS No. 2," *Journal of Accounting Research* 30, 156–164.

Woolridge, R., 1988, "Competitive decline and corporate restructuring: Is a myopic stock market to blame?," *Journal of Applied Corporate Finance 1,* 26–36.

16

Measures that Matter: An Exploratory Investigation of Investors' Information Needs and Value Priorities

Sarah Mavrinac and G. Anthony Siesfeld

Policymaking groups are calling for improved performance evaluation techniques. This study evaluates the validity of those calls by examining investors' use of non-financial performance measures. Empirical results collected using revealed-preference analysis suggest that non-financial measures of quality and strategic achievement have a profound effect on investment and valuation.

An increasing number of private and public organizations are now issuing calls for the reform of traditional financial reporting and disclosure requirements. Among this growing set of critics are executive groups like the Capital Allocation Subcouncil of the Competitiveness Policy Council. In its recently published report, the group presents an extensive criticism of our conventional reporting framework which highlights, for example, the inability of current financial statements to capture or communicate the value of strategy, processes, and such intangible assets as knowledge, innovation, and customer loyalty. The report asserts that accounting's traditional focus on what is historic and tangible has had a profound and depressing impact not only on companies' valuations but also on the nation's growth, productivity, employment levels, and wage rates.

Similar criticisms of traditional performance measurement systems can be found in the academic accounting and performance measurement literature. In this literature, these "rule-bound" systems are referred to as outdated, inaccurate, and increasingly irrelevant in today's service-oriented and knowledge-based economy. Empirical evidence buttressing these criticisms can be found in papers like Baruch Lev's 1996 working paper which presents evidence of a dramatic shift in

From: OECD and Ernst & Young joint publication (1997), *Enterprise Value in the Knowledge Economy: Measuring Performance in the Age of Intangibles.*

the market valuation of publicly traded firms over the past twenty years. Using data compiled for some 300 firms for the period 1973–1992, Lev charts a change in the ratio of market equity to book equity values from a level of approximately 0.811 in 1973 to a level of approximately 1.692 in 1992. According to Lev, this trend represents not only a revolutionary change in the process of economic value creation but, more seriously, a decline in the value relevance of traditional financial measures. Summarizing, Lev writes: "The gap in 1992 indicates that roughly 40 percent of the market valuation of the median corporation was missing from its balance sheet. For high-tech firms, whose median market-to-book ratio in 1992 was 2.09, the proportion of value missing from the balance sheet is over 50 percent." (Lev, 1996, p. 9)

Lev's study is just one among a number of recent academic studies which collectively identify the limitations of traditional performance measurement techniques and simultaneously call for changed perspectives and innovation in valuation. Of particular note in these papers is the increasing importance now ascribed to non-financial measurement and measures of strategic achievement, product and process quality, customer satisfaction, and organizational learning, for examples. The academic accounting literature is particularly devoted to identifying those non-financial measures which can be used to explain or predict share price and share price movements. Amir and Lev (1996), for example, suggest that the single strongest predictor of the share value of cellular phone service providers is not revenues or net income or even earnings expectations but current catchment area population levels or "pops." Ittner & Larcker (1995) similarly find strong association between customer satisfaction and share price levels. Outside the accounting domain, Jarrell & Easton (1996) find that firms recognized for their "above average implementation" of a TQM (total quality management) program accrued excess share returns of some 15 percent over the five-year period following the program launch. Still other studies provide evidence of strong association between firms' equity market values and a) new product announcements (Chaney, Devinney, & Winter, 1991), b) product quality levels (Heller, 1994), and c) employee development programs (Gordon, Pound, & Porter, 1994), for examples.

The central message of these studies is not that financial indicators are unimportant or that investors' concern for the bottom line has abated in any way. The papers imply simply that in a world of increasing technological change and shortened product life-cycles, and in a world where "knowledge-work" and intangible assets have become of profound importance, future financial performance is often better predicted by non-financial indicators than by financial indicators.[1]

---

1. Consider, for example, the development and production processes of a biotechnology firm. Financial analysts following the biotech industry commonly assert that the value of these processes and the value of the company as a whole is based less on the company's investment in property, plant, and equipment—i.e., the assets on the balance sheet—than on the company's investment in intellectual capital or research and development capability. The CFO of one California biotech company described the situation, saying: "Biotechnology is a unique sector in that valuation for emerging

The intent of this study is to pursue this hypothesis and to evaluate critically the influence of non-financial data in the performance evaluation and investment context. When and under what conditions do investors find value in non-financial data? Which types of non-financial data do they value most? To what extent do changes in non-financial performance influence the investment decision? The specific objectives of the study are threefold: 1) to extend prior investigations of investors' information requirements, 2) to investigate the use of non-financial data by investors and their advisors; and 3) to evaluate the influence of non-financial data on the share purchase decision. What distinguishes this study from earlier analyses is its methodology and its direct assessment not only of investors' information requirements but also their decision-making routines and value priorities. This study is also among the first to offer an explicit assessment of the valuation impact of non-financial performance improvement.

Using data collected from over 250 institutional portfolio managers, project investigators have compiled an array of evidence which strongly supports the study's basic hypothesis that non-financial performance data are relevant to shareholder evaluations and investment decisions. According to the results, we conclude that the "typical" institutional investor does devote substantial attention to non-financial performance issues. In brief, it appears that approximately 35 percent of the investment decision is driven by the investor's evaluation of non-financial data.

Not all non-financial data are considered equally useful by the study participants, however. According to the study's respondents, measures of strategy implementation, management credibility, innovativeness, market share, and the firm's ability to "attract and retain talented people" are identified as being substantially more useful than measures of customer complaints, quality award programs, employee training programs, or environmental and social policies, on average. Interestingly, the data suggests little variation across types of investors in the perceived importance of particular types of non-financial data. We interpret this result as an indication of the general applicability of non-financial data. That is, the value of non-financial data appears not to be specific to any particular investment strategy or investor type. Note, however, that these results are derived from our analysis of investors' evaluation of firms with significant capitalization levels. Consequently, the results may not be generalizable to the small-firm population or to investors devoted to small-cap investment strategies.

In the last phase of analysis, we, the project investigators, used experimental data collected through investment simulations to draw association between financial and non-financial data—i.e., to "value" the non-financial data. As will be described in greater detail below, we estimate the relationship between non-financial performance and the propensity of the investor to acquire firm shares. This proce-

companies is largely based on projections of future timing, utility, and performance of research/ development projects which aren't commercializable until years from now. Short-term financial performance is correspondingly of little use in determining corporate value."

dure effectively allows certain elements of non-financial performance improve-ment to be "priced." Results of the analysis conducted specifically for firms in the pharmaceuticals industry show strong variation in the estimated "value" of cer-tain types of non-financial performance improvement. Improvements in the "quality of products and services" appear to be evaluated more highly than im-provements in "investor communications," for example. Nonetheless, the data suggest strong returns to improvements in investor communications. According to our estimates, a "one unit"[2] improvement in the quality of investor communica-tions by a large firm operating in the pharmaceuticals industry would be equiva-lent in the minds of shareholders to a 0.5 percent increase in share price. For a firm like Merck, this measure could translate into a market valuation gain of $140 million.[3]

This paper is organized into a total of six sections, including this introduc-tory section. Section 2 reviews previous studies of investors' information needs and decision styles and attempts to position the issue of investors' use of non-fi-nancial data in its larger economic and managerial context. Section 3 provides in-formation on the research methodology, survey design, and sample selection techniques. Section 4 provides data on investors' stated use of non-financial data and the source of that data, while Section 5, as noted above, provides discussion of the results of the revealed preference study. Section 6 concludes with a brief summary of the results and offers suggestions for continuing policy and research analyses.

INVESTORS' INFORMATION NEEDS AND THE VALUE RELEVANCE OF NON-FINANCIAL DATA

Over the past five years, the management community has witnessed an ex-plosion of interest in non-financial performance measurement. According to a survey conducted recently by the Institute of Management Accountants, fully 64 percent of U.S. controllers surveyed report that their companies are actively ex-perimenting with new ways of measuring, collecting, and reporting non-financial data. This flurry of corporate action has been encouraged by the publication of an expanding number of books and articles which suggest that new "strategic" per-formance measurement systems (Vitale, Mavrinac & Hauser, 1994; Atkinson & Waterhouse, 1996), "balanced scorecard" systems (Kaplan & Norton, 1993, 1995), or "expanded" measurement systems (Kron, 1994) can enhance both managerial understanding and control of the firm's value-creation process. In ef-

2. In this study, a one-unit change in non-financial ranking, e.g., a movement from a rank of 6 to 7, represents a relative change of less than half a standard deviation.
3. To calculate this hypothetical return, the authors need share price and earnings numbers collected for the period. At the end of month, year, Merck's share price was approximately $70 while its earn-ings were $3.50/share.

fect, these papers all suggest that non-financial performance indicators can be used productively as leading indicators of future financial performance.

The financial regulatory community appears to have adopted much the same conclusion. Over the past two years, an increasing number of professional and regulatory bodies have published policy statements calling for expanded disclosure of non-financial data. In 1991, the American Institute of Certified Public Accountants (AICPA) created a Special Committee on Financial Reporting to address increasing public concern over the relevance of current-day financial and disclosure policies. In its final report, the committee concluded that while the current measurement and reporting framework had recognized strengths, it also offered substantial opportunities for improvement. Among the many suggestions the committee made was one encouraging corporations to provide more "forward looking" information and "enhanced discussion of the non-financial performance factors that create longer-term value." The Association for Investment Management & Research (AIMR), a professional body representing U.S. chartered financial analysts, presented similar statements in its 1993 position paper on the future of financial reporting. In its recommendations section, Peter Knutsen, the paper's author, writes:

> *For financial analysts to make sound judgments and draw rational conclusions, they must judge the performance of individual business enterprises . . . To do so, they need information of two types. First, management should explicitly describe its strategies, plans, and expectations. Much of this must come in the form of narrative descriptive material. (1993, p. 85)*

Still more recently, the Securities & Exchange Commission (SEC), acting on the initiative of Commissioner Steven Wallman, sponsored a two-day symposium at which both academic and corporate presentations focused closely on the value of expanding firms' disclosures of intangible assets, strategic aims, and non-financial performance. While the issue of expanded disclosure was hotly debated, there was general consensus among symposium participants on the utility of non-financial metrics as indicators of internal operating performance and strategic achievement.

Despite the increasing interest and support of policymakers and professional bodies in the disclosure of non-financial data to the investor community, there is still only limited evidence of their value relevance. To what extent are non-financial performance data impounded in share prices? Can differences in non-financial performance be used to explain differences in share price and valuation levels? To what extent are non-financial disclosures valued by the market as "new" data? As noted above, there are relatively few studies which address these questions specifically. However, there are a number which touch upon the relationship between financial and non-financial performance more broadly.

Among the handful which address the value relevance of non-financial data *per se* are the studies by Lev (1996), Amir & Lev (1996), and Heller (1994) mentioned above and a study by Larcker & Ittner (1996) which examines the information content of announcements of corporate customer satisfaction rankings. This study offers not only preliminary confirmation of the value relevance of customer satisfaction data but also suggests that the disclosure of such non-financial data offers new information to the market, i.e., data which has not been previously communicated through more traditional accounting media.

In addition to these studies, there are various other research studies which analyze the relationship between non-financial performance and either net income levels or aggregate expense. Descriptions of some of these studies can be found in a series of white papers sponsored by the U.S. Department of Labor. The most recent of these reviewed several hundred research reports examining the financial and non-financial returns to innovative workplace practices.[4] In its conclusion, the report notes that: "In most of the papers reviewed, firm financial performance and intermediate workplace outcomes, like product quality and customer satisfaction, did increase with strategic investments in innovative employee management and compensation programs, process management, and total quality management programs." The explicit conclusion of the report is that non-financial performance indicators, and more specifically, indicators of internal workplace achievement, can serve as leading indicators of future financial performance.

Despite these studies and despite their illustration of the statistical association between non-financial and financial performance, the research community still has little data on the extent of investor demand for non-financial data. Still less is understood about how investors might use non-financial data in the course of their decision-making. What little data do exist are derived from survey studies that solicit from investors either their stated rankings of the "value" of non-financial data or an open-ended list of the most valued types of non-financial data. One such study was conducted in 1987 by the Financial Executives Research Foundation (FERF). This survey suggests that, on average, investors, analysts, and other users of financial reports would find value in more extensive disclosure of the company's market and competitive position, management goals and objectives, and business segment data (SRI, 1987). Another more recent survey study conducted by Eccles and Mavrinac (1995) for the Ernst & Young Center for Business Innovation also found modest interest on the part of investors and analysts for increased non-financial disclosure. Approximately one-third of the analysts and investors responding to the survey agreed with the statement that increased disclosure of non-financial data should be mandated. Interestingly, the proportion is significantly higher for analysts following growth industries than for those following consolidating or mature industries. As noted in Table 16.1 on the following page, approximately 35 percent of the investors and over 40 percent of the

---

4. See "Competitive Renewal through Workplace Innovation: The Financial and Non-financial Returns to Innovative Workplace Practices," authored by Sarah C. Mavrinac and Neil R. Jones with Marshall W. Meyer, and published jointly by the U.S. Department of Labor and Ernst & Young LLP.

TABLE 16.1   Corporate Managers', Analysts', and Investors' Attitudes towards Increased Non-financial Disclosure Requirements

Respondent Group	Percent Approving	Percent Disapproving	Percent Unsure
Corporate Managers			
Consolidating Industries	0	60	40
Mature Industries	7	87	6
Service Growth Industries	10	87	6
High Tech Growth Industries	14	82	4
Financial Analysts			
Consolidating Industries	0	100	0
Mature Industries	26	72	2
Service Growth Industries	44	56	0
High-Tech Growth Industries	41	45	14
Portfolio Managers & Investors	35	56	9

Source: Eccles and Mavrinac (1995).

analysts following growth industries encouraged the institution of new non-financial disclosure requirements.

In another series of questions, the survey asked respondents to evaluate the usefulness of some 26 different financial and non-financial measures. While few non-financial measures were ranked as "extremely useful" by either investors or analysts, some were considered sufficiently useful to be included in the list of these users' top ten most valued measures. As noted in Table 16.2, investors appear to value not only earnings and cash flow measures but also measures of market growth, new-product development, market share, and R&D productivity as among the most valuable measures they receive.

TABLE 16.2   Investment Analysts' and Portfolio Managers' Most Useful Investment Measures by Rank

Rank	Sell-Side Investment Analysts	Portfolio Managers
1	Earnings	Market Growth
2	Cash Flow	Earnings
3	Market Growth	Cash Flow
4	Segment Performance	New Product Development
5	Market Share	Costs
6	Capital Expenditure	Market Share
7	Costs	Capital Expenditure
8	R&D Investment	Segment Performance
9	Strategic Achievement	R&D Investment
10	New Product Development	R&D Productivity

Source: Eccles and Mavrinac (1995).

Not all non-financial measures were evaluated highly, however. Despite the empirical evidence attesting to the return on investments in employee training and development,[5] it appears that neither investors nor analysts place a great deal of value on measures of employee satisfaction, training, or turnover. Like measures of environmental compliance and ethical conduct, employee measures were, on average, ranked as being "of little use."

While survey studies like the Ernst & Young study described above provide valuable description of the perceived needs and interests of capital markets participants, their interpretation is constrained by the fact that their results are based solely upon stated preferences and subjective attitudes which at the time of testing are subject to any number of both overt and subtle influences.[6] Another more recent study attempts to overcome this limitation. The results of the study, presented in a working paper by Mavrinac and Boyle (1996), highlight the relationship between financial analysts' use of non-financial data and those analysts' forecast accuracy. In contrast with survey studies which rely on respondent statements, this study was designed to critique actual behavior as revealed through assessment of the analysts' own published research reports. The study builds upon the content analysis of some 300 investment reports and on an analysis of the frequency with which the authors/analysts considered non-financial performance issues.[7] The results of the study suggest that a wide range of non-financial factors are considered by analysts, although the types of issues considered vary strongly across industry. The results of the study also provide modest support for the hypothesis that analysts who consider non-financial data more frequently are able to generate more accurate earnings predictions. Specifically, the investigators find that forecast error decreases with the frequency of non-financial performance review. In short, the results of the study suggest that analysts do treat non-financial performance data as leading indicators of future financial performance.

This study is one of the first to document analysts' interests in non-financial data. It is also one of the first to identify the consequences of non-financial disclosure; however, its observations and results are limited to the extent that they consider only the routines and information usage patterns of analysts rather than investors *per se*. Do investors also find non-financial data useful? To what extent is the investment decision itself influenced by non-financial data? To what extent do investment patterns change as a result of changes in non-financial performance?

The tests described below in Sections 4 and 5 were designed to extend the findings of this preliminary analysis of analysts' information needs, and, importantly, to shift the focus of attention from the analyst to the investor. Specifically,

---

5. See Mavrinac, Jones & Meyer, 1995.

6. Note also that the stated "importance" of an item need not reflect the utility or actual influence of the item in decision-making. The actual influence of any one particular type of item may be strongly affected by the availability of information substitutes or proxies, for example.

7. A stratified sampling plan was used to select the company reports. The procedure was designed to accommodate variation in the density of the information environment which might result from or be associated with variation in firm size or market value, exchange listing, and industry.

the study was intended: 1) to offer more concrete behavioral evidence of investors' use of non-financial data, 2) to examine the value relevance of non-financial data, and 3) to estimate the relative influence of non-financial data on the investment decision. The study also attempts to extend previous studies documenting investors' stated information needs by soliciting more detailed survey descriptions of preferred non-financial measures.

The primary research tool used to collect the study data was a mailed survey instrument designed using experimental methodologies which allowed the investigators to capture and record behavioral patterns and implicit preferences. By generating this rich, behavioral understanding of investors' information needs and valuation styles, this study should contribute significantly both to policy debates and to managerial development of improved performance measurement and communications strategies. By illustrating the value and potential of a new methodology, the study should also make a contribution to the academic community interested in performance measurement. As will be discussed below, the research methodology used for this study builds upon a set of experimental survey and statistical modeling procedures which are now extensively employed by the marketing research community (see, e.g., Ben-Akiva, Morikawa & Shiroishi, 1990, and Ben-Akiva & Morikawa, 1990). However, this particular methodology has not to date been applied in any investigation of the investor community or performance measurement preferences, despite the opportunity it offers to obtain behavioral insight using controlled procedures. To the extent that it also allows examination of respondents' valuation of data which are not easily quantifiable, this methodology opens up a new avenue of exploration and facilitates examination of information types which to date have not been readily amenable to research.[8]

RESEARCH METHODS

In this section, we provide a brief description of the research method, our sample selection procedures, and our techniques for designing the survey instrument. The subsection below focuses explicitly on the sample selection process and provides a description of the type and variety of respondents participating in the study. Next, we provide information on the structure of the survey instrument and the procedures used to ensure the validity of the instrument. Finally, we provide a description of the analytic tools used to organize and understand the survey results.

Sample Selection Techniques

All research results were generated using information and data provided by 275 portfolio managers representing virtually all major types and classes of active

---

8. See Ben-Akiva, Morikawa, & Shiroishi, 1990, for additional discussion of the benefits of discrete choice experiments incorporating revealed and stated preference data.

institutional investors.[9] The final sample was drawn from a database detailing the population of US portfolio managers which is researched and updated annually by the Georgeson Group, a UK-based investor relations and proxy solicitation firm. At the close of 1995, this database included a total of just over 1,900 individuals representing both private and public funds and institutions. Table 16.3 provides some descriptive information allowing comparison between the study sample and this larger population. Specifically, Table 16.3 presents data on the type of investment account, the portfolio's composition, and the manager's investment style.

Comparison of the population versus the sample suggests that the characteristics of the sample closely approximate those of the population at large, with only slight differences in the proportion of mutual fund and bank representatives.

TABLE 16.3   Population versus Respondent Characteristics: Portfolio Size, Fund Type, and Investment Style

Panel A: Portfolio Size		
	Survey Sample	*Study Population*
Median Assets ($Million)	173	183
Average No. Stocks Held	132	149
% S&P 500 Stocks	64%	58%

Panel B: Fund Type		
	Survey Sample %	*Study Population %*
Mutual Fund	13	19
Bank	22	14
Money Market Fund	51	53
Insurance Company	9	9
Private Pension	4	3
Public Pension	1	2

Panel C: Investment Style		
	Survey Sample %	*Study Population %*
Aggressive Growth	8	14
Growth	35	34
GARP	15	14
Balanced	8	10
Classic Value	11	13
Value Income	22	15

9. Note that the only investors systematically excluded from the sample were those investing exclusively in small to mid-sized firms. The study's focus on "active" investment also necessarily precluded analysis of the decision-making styles of managers controlling indexed funds.

Note also that the sample of 275 represents approximately 14 percent of the total population, a level which minimizes the standard errors of the estimates.

A four-step, mail/telephone procedure was used to collect the study data. In Step 1, investigators posted an introductory letter to all potential respondents informing them of the purpose of the survey and inviting their attention and participation. This initial contact was quickly followed in Step 2 by a telephone call during which paid interviewers confirmed the respondent's appropriateness for the study and solicited their commitment. Those agreeing to participate were mailed the survey in Step 3 and invited to return their responses either by mail or over the phone. Repeated phone calls were used in Step 4 as necessary to encourage response. The return rate from qualified, participating respondents was 42 percent.

Survey Design

As noted above, the primary research tool used to reach this survey sample was a mailed survey instrument which was constructed to allow collection of both "stated" and "revealed" preference data. "Stated" preference data represent respondents' own statements of the influence a particular information item has on their decision-making routines. Stated preference questions are a popular form of survey question and have been the only type of question used to solicit investors' rankings of information usefulness to date. When revealed preference data is collected, the importance of particular information items is identified indirectly by evaluating the subjects' behavioral response to certain choice tasks. For the purposes of this study, respondents were asked to select or reveal their preference for certain equities over others after evaluating various performance data sets. Analysis of the covariation between the subjects' investment choices and changes in the equities' performance attributes reveals the relative importance and/or contribution of each attribute to the subjects' decision-making process.

The instrument itself was divided into four parts. The first and final parts of the survey (Parts 1 and 4) were used to collect essential demographic and investment profile data. The second section (Part 2) was used to collect "stated" preference data, i.e., participants' statements about their use of, or preferences for, particular types of investment data. Specifically, the survey instrument prompted participants: a) to state what percentage of their investment decisions are based on non-financial data; b) to rate the usefulness of 40 different types of non-financial data, and c) to rate the value of different data sources.

The third section (Part 3) was designed to collect the study's experimental or behavioral data, i.e., the respondents' "revealed" preferences. This section presented the respondents with a series of hypothetical share purchase scenarios. In each scenario, the respondent was asked to allocate some portion of an investment fund across four companies operating in either the computer, oil & gas, food processing, or pharmaceutical industry.[10] Specifically, each respondent was asked to allocate 100 percent of their "fund" to one or more of four companies within the industry. To ensure sufficient experimental observations, each industry-specific allocation scenario was run four times for a total of sixteen allocation scenarios. In each scenario, the respondent was provided with a set of financial performance data including, for example, price/earnings ratios, sales growth rates, earnings per share data, etc. As noted above, by varying the characteristics and the performance of these firms and by monitoring how the investment allocations changed along with the firms' changing performance, the investigators were able to deduce or "reveal" through a multinomial regression technique investors' preference for particular performance indicators.[11] With additional modeling and by combining the non-financial data with the financial data in the regression analysis, the investigators were ultimately able to "value" the usefulness of each different type of non-financial data in share price terms.

The process of survey design was constructed to comply with the normative protocol specified in Rossi, Wright & Anderson (1953), Payne (1951/79), and Dillman (1978). Initial drafts of the survey were prepared and reviewed by representatives of all major research constituencies: other researchers, subject experts, typical participants, and potential users of the data. The final draft was tested on a focus panel of six "typical" respondents, each of whom was selected to represent one of the population's significant demographic constituencies. The comments and suggestions received from this group were fully incorporated into the final version mailed to survey respondents.

Data Analysis & Modeling Techniques

Data analysis and modeling procedures used to identify investors' "revealed" preferences for non-financial information were designed following the procedures established by Ben Akiva and Morikawa (1990). The principal statistical test involved estimation of a multinomial logit regression explaining allocation levels as a function of: a) the financial characteristics presented in the experimental scenarios,[12] and b) a set of eight non-financial characteristics whose company-specific values were evaluated by the respondent using an eleven-point Likert scale extending from 0 to 10. Specifically, each respondent was asked to

---

10. Studies by Eccles & Mavrinac (1995) and Lev (1996), for examples, suggest that the usefulness of non-financial data might vary across industries and firm growth categories. To accommodate these findings, the investigators selected industries which varied strongly along the aggregate growth dimension. Using data on average company sales growth rates collected from Standard & Poor's publications, the investigators specifically identified the pharmaceutical and computer industries as "high growth" industries, the food processing industry as a "moderate growth" industry, and the oil & gas industry as a "slow growth" or declining industry.

11. This particular technique has a long history of use in such fields as marketing. The response variable can be either discrete or continuous. With a continuous response, the proportions assigned to each category or choice must sum to one. As a consequence, the responses across choices are negatively correlated and the variance of the response becomes a function of response proportion, making OLS or WLS techniques inappropriate.

12. Repeated measures ensured within-subject variability as well as between-subject variability.

evaluate the performance of all sixteen companies along the following dimensions:

1. Quality of Management,
2. Quality of Products & Services,
3. Customer Satisfaction,
4. Strength of Corporate Culture,
5. Quality of Investor Relations,
6. Executive Compensation,
7. Quality of New Product Development, and
8. Strength of Market Position.[13]

A score of 5 was indicative of "average" performance relative to industry levels; a score of 10 was used to indicate above average performance; and a score of 1, below average performance. Note that virtually all company ratings were highly correlated, raising concerns about the collinearity of the data used for the regression. To reduce the significance of this threat to statistical validity, the investigators decomposed the sources of variability using structural equations modeling techniques. These techniques allowed the investigators to isolate the "brand halo" effects, i.e., the bias or weight introduced to the performance rankings as a result of unique company "reputation." The final regression included only the residual of the model, or the "pure" ranking dissociated from the company halo.[14]

In the process of generating the final statistical model, the investigators evaluated a number of other potential influences on the allocation decision, including the investment style of the portfolio manager, the size of the portfolio, the type of fund managed, and the demographic background of the manager, for examples. None of these factors was found to play a statistically important role in the regression. We consequently interpret the model as being reasonably robust and generalizable across investor groups.

THE STATED VALUE OF NON-FINANCIAL DATA

In many studies of investors' information needs, survey respondents are asked to rank the usefulness of particular types of non-financial data. While certain types of data, like quality of management or measures of market growth, for example, are consistently evaluated as "extremely useful," most discrete elements are evaluated as only modestly useful on average. In contrast with these earlier

13. Note that these ratings were introduced as covariates with only between-subject variability.
14. An often appealing alternative to structural equations modeling is factor analysis. Note, however, that a fundamental assumption of factor analysis is that the variance to be parsed is strictly between-items. In this survey, individuals were asked to evaluate non-financial performance dimensions for each of sixteen companies, raising the possibility of an additional source—i.e., an individual source—of variation. To the extent that structural equations modeling can accommodate multiple sources of variation, it appears preferable to factor analysis for the purposes of this study.

studies, this study attempted to measure the contribution not only of discrete items but also of the non-financial dataset, more generally. That is, while this study assessed the usefulness of discrete data types, it also queried respondents about the value of non-financial data as a whole. For example, we asked respondents to indicate what percent of the investment decision was influenced by non-financial data. The response to this question was, on average, 35 percent. That is, about one-third of the information used to justify the investment decision is non-financial—a significantly larger fraction than anticipated.

Figure 16.1 provides an illustration of how widely responses varied around this average. The data presented here indicate clearly that this average response is not driven by a small fraction of investors who rely entirely on non-financial data. On the contrary, well over 60 percent of the survey population estimated that non-financial data drove between 20 percent and 50 percent of the investment decision. Just slightly less than 20 percent estimated that non-financial data influenced 50–59 percent of the decision.

In addition to this aggregate valuation, the survey asked respondents for their evaluation of certain discrete data elements. To express their evaluation, respondents used a seven-point Likert scale where a score of 1 represented "not at all important" and a score of 7, "very important." Only six of the forty data elements received mean scores of less than 4, signifying that they were considered "somewhat important." Of the remaining 34 items, 31 received scores between 4

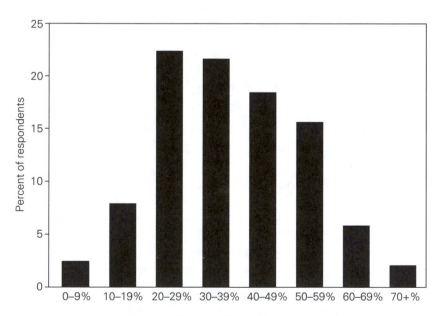

FIGURE 16.1   The stated usefulness of non-financial data. Percent influence of non-financial measures versus percent respondents.

and 5, suggesting that almost all types of non-financial data, from that indicating "innovativeness" (score: 5.77) or quality of the workforce (score: 5.12), to that measuring global capability (score: 4.94), are considered to be valuable to the average shareholder.

Interestingly, in comparison with the results compiled by Eccles & Mavrinac (1995), these data suggest that employee information is reasonably valued by investors. Note, for example, that measures indicating "the company's ability to attract and retain talented people" received an importance score of 5.61, an exceptionally high score in comparison with that associated with other information types. Indeed, the only employee-related data element not receiving a score of at least 4 was the one measuring "use of employee teams." In summary, it appears that investors' most-valued non-financial measures are measures that reveal the productivity and creativity of the organization's people and people-oriented systems. Although the quality of the business plan or strategy is also considered crucial by investors, it appears that investors ultimately place more weight on the ability of the management team to deliver. The focus is on action.

The scores reported provide insight into the "average" valuation, i.e., the ranking provided by the "average" investor. However, exploration of the variation in rankings across respondents reveals the heterogeneity of investor attitudes towards non-financial performance data. To explore the nature and extent of variation in the data scores, the investigators looked specifically at the ten data types which were ranked most important or least important, on average. Table 16.4 provides lists of those data elements along with additional information on the dispersion of the rankings and the percent of respondents who classified the data type as "very important" or "not at all important." Examination of the information displayed in the tables suggests that the ten data types receiving the highest

TABLE 16.4 Investigating Variation in Response Rankings of Least- and Most-Valued Non-Financial Data Types

Panel A		Panel B	
Most-Valued Measures		*Least-Valued Measures*	
Measurement Type	Mean Score	Measurement Type	Mean Score
Execution of Corporate Strategy	6.26	Quality of Guidance	4.48
Management Credibility	6.16	Employee Turnover Rates	4.42
Quality of Corporate Strategy	5.92	Experience of IR Personnel	4.36
Innovativeness	5.77	Number of Cust. Complaints	4.32
Ability to Attract Employees	5.61	Quality of Cust. Service Dept.	4.29
Market Share	5.60	Quality of Published Materials	3.91
Management Experience	5.54	Product Quality Awards	3.53
Quality of Compensation Policies	5.48	Process Quality Awards	3.39
Research Leadership	5.40	Environmental & Social Policies	3.36
Quality of Processes	5.34	Use of Employee Teams	3.26
Customer Satisfaction	5.33	Compensation Ratios	3.22

TABLE 16.5   Collecting Non-financial Information:
Evaluating Alternative Media

Source	Mean Score
Management Presentations	5.54
Company Filings	5.34
Sell-Side Analysts	4.82
Competitors	4.77
Business Press	4.56
Company Investor Relations Personnel	4.56
Customers	4.55
Buy-side Analysts	4.53
Trade Press	4.51
Informal Networks	4.27
Independent Ranking Agencies	3.99
Industry Trade Associations	3.93
On-Line Services	3.77

mean scores were considered "very important" not only by the "average" respondent but by the majority of respondents. For example, almost 90 percent of respondents ranked "execution of corporate strategy" (average score: 6.26) as very important, with scores of either 6 or 7. There appears to be slightly less consensus surrounding the data elements with the lowest scores. For example, far less than 50 percent of the respondents evaluated "use of employee teams" as being "not at all important."

Given that most investors do value and actively use non-financial data, the issue of how investors receive such data becomes critical. To learn more about which media are preferred, we presented our survey respondents with an extensive list of data sources and asked them to rank their value using the traditional seven-point Likert scale. Again, a score of 7 was used to represent a "very important" medium while a score of 1 was used to suggest that the medium was "not at all important." Table 16.5 provides a list of the media considered and the mean scores received. Not unexpectedly, management presentations are ranked as the most important source of non-financial data, on average, suggesting the importance of unstructured discussion and question-and-answer sessions. Interestingly, "on-line services" are considered relatively unimportant, at least in comparison with management presentations or company reports, for example. Apparently, competitors are also a major source of corporate performance data.

THE RELATIVE VALUE OF PERFORMANCE IMPROVEMENT

The first phase of analysis described above offers an extension of previous studies of investors' information requirements and provides important new information on the extent to which non-financial data influence the investment decision in aggregate. Most importantly, however, this phase of analysis offers justification for the more detailed modeling required in the second phase of the study.

As described above, this second phase of work relies upon the data compiled from the experimental investment simulations. As described above, those simulations prompted our survey respondents to allocate a hypothetical portfolio across four firms operating in either the computer, oil and gas, pharmaceuticals, or food processing industry. In every case, these companies were large firms whose non-financial attributes were well recognized by respondents. (See Table 16.6 for a list of the companies included in the study by industry.) By varying the characteristics and performance of these companies in the simulation and by registering the consequent changes in the amount of investment funds allocated to the firm, the investigators were able to estimate the amount of influence each financial and each non-financial characteristic had on the investment decision.

The quantitative results were generated through estimation of a multinomial logit regression. In general, the results of the full study estimation correspond well with the results of the stated preference study described above. According to our statistical estimates, approximately 33 percent of the investment decision can be explained with reference to non-financial data.[15] Recall that the response to our request for an estimate of "how much importance you place on non-financial vs. financial considerations" was 35 percent, on average.

TABLE 16.6   Subject Companies by Industry

Computer Systems Industry	Hewlett-Packard
	Sun Microsystems
	Compaq
	Dell
Food Products Industry	General Mills
	H. J. Heinz
	CPC International
	Ralston-Purina
Pharmaceuticals Industry	Merck
	Pfizer
	Bristol-Meyers
	Warner-Lambert
Oil & Gas Industry	Exxon
	Chevron
	Atlantic Richfield
	Phillips Petroleum

15. Estimates were derived from comparison of relative size of log-likelihood ratios of the models including versus excluding non-financial information.

Table 16.7 provides a description of model output for tests run using data compiled for all four subject industries: the oil & gas, pharmaceuticals, computer systems, and food processing industries. The data presented in this table should be interpreted as the implicit value "scores" received by each of the non-financial factors—i.e., as the revealed values of the non-financial data in the investment allocation context. Note that these are relative scores—i.e., scores determined in relation to the value assigned to the firm's price/earnings ratio. Specifically, each score represents the change in the price/earnings ratio which would have the same utility or value for the investor as a one-unit change in non-financial performance. For example, for a large firm operating in the biotechnology/drug development industry, a one-unit change in the quality of products and services would be equivalent in value, and would have the same impact on investor demand levels, as a 0.9 percent increase in the firm's price/earnings ratio. Similarly, for a firm operating in the food processing industry, a one-unit increase in the quality of products and services would be equivalent in utility or value terms to a 1.4 percent change in the firm's price/earnings ratio.

The implications of these findings can be made more obvious with some simple calculations. Note first that reported earnings do not change frequently. On the contrary, they are reported quarterly at best. Given this fact, we can restate the relationship, defining a one-unit improvement in the quality of products and services in the pharmaceuticals industry as equivalent to a 0.9 percent increase in share price, *ceteris paribus*. For a firm like Merck whose share price was approximately $44.00 in the spring of 1996 and which had over 1,145 million shares outstanding, this 0.9 percent increase in share price would be manifest as a $447 million increase in market value. That is, for the average shareholder, a one-unit increase in the quality of Merck's products and services would be equivalent to, or worth to the shareholder, approximately $447 million.

TABLE 16.7   Model Output: Investor Valuation of Non-financial Performance Improvement

Scores indicate equivalent percentage increase in a company's P/E ratio for a 1-point improvement in investor perceptions of non-financial performance.

	Industry			
	Computer	Drugs	Food	Oil & Gas
Quality of Management	7.6	2.6	1.4	4.2
Quality of Products & Service	2.4	0.9	1.4	5.8
Customer Satisfaction	0.0	0.0	0.0	0.0
Strength of Corporate Culture	0.0	0.0	0.0	0.0
Quality of Investor Relations	0.8	0.5	0.3	0.9
Executive Compensation	0.9	0.6	0.4	1.1
Quality of New Product Dev.	0.0	5.3	0.9	1.6
Strength of Market Position	3.1	0.3	0.0	7.3

Further inspection of the results in Table 16.7 suggest that the largest value gain for a firm operating in the pharmaceutical industry would flow from improvements in the quality of new product development. For a firm like Merck, a one-point improvement in the quality of new product development would be "valued" by investors at a sum topping $2.6 billion.

According to our calculations, improvements in the quality of management would also be valued highly by shareholders. For a firm like Hewlett-Packard, for example, which operates in the computer systems industry, a one-unit improvement in the quality of management would be equivalent in shareholder value terms to a $1.3 billion gain in market value, given the performance of the firm in the spring of 1996.

Interestingly, neither increases in customer satisfaction nor improvements in the strength of corporate culture are valued highly by shareholders. To generate a more complete interpretation of these results, project investigators augmented the statistical analysis with in-depth, unstructured interviews with prototypical respondents. One subject simply dismissed the relatively low customer satisfaction and corporate culture weights, saying:

> *Culture, customers . . . I don't have time to interview employees and customers and no good independent source of information about them exists, so I largely ignore them.*

Another noted that:

> *For these types of companies, if they have high-quality management and are offering a high quality product through well-developed distribution channels, then they must have satisfied customers.*

The data collected to date are insufficient to answer all the questions raised by these findings. Nor is there any point in undertaking such a task. The intent of this study was simply to gain some perspective on investors' perceptions of and need for non-financial data. We also hoped to test and to illustrate the usefulness of an experimental methodology which has not to date been applied in any given study of investor decision-making. Extensions of this study are clearly warranted, however, to realize greater insight into results like those discussed above.

SUMMARY AND CONCLUSIONS

At a recent symposium sponsored by Commissioner Wallman of the Securities and Exchange Commission, it was agreed that if solutions to the problems engendered by traditional reporting systems were to be realized, a more constructive dialogue between users and preparers, regulators, auditors, and policymakers must ensue. A first step in shaping that dialogue will be to make more evident the information needs and interests of shareholders.

The intent of this report is to offer data which might be used not only in this reform dialogue but also and more immediately by corporate managers who have interest in advancing their performance measurement programs, shaping their own communications with shareholders, or, most importantly, assessing the returns to their strategic endeavors. In brief, the results of the study offer new and compelling evidence of shareholders' strong reliance on a broad range of non-financial factors and indication of investors' real appreciation of investments in employee development, process quality, and the corporate innovations which will provide the foundation for tomorrow's financial performance. The study also offers specific information on the types of non-financial metrics which are most valued by the investor community. Most significantly, the study is one of the first to provide quantitative evidence of the value impact of non-financial performance improvements. As illustrated in Table 16.7 above, improvements in investor communications, product quality, and the perceived quality of management can drive hundreds of millions of dollars of shareholder value if these improvements are communicated clearly to the market.

While this paper should offer insight and perspective to the manager attempting to shape his or her strategic agenda, the paper is first intended to provide empirical illustration of the value relevance of non-financial data and to encourage continued academic exploration of the role of expanded performance measurement in the implementation of corporate strategy. It is hoped that the study can also offer an illustration of the usefulness of behavioral and revealed preference experiments in this type of research. Certainly, the topic is deserving of additional exploration.

REFERENCES

AICPA, 1993, Special Committee on Financial Reporting, "The Information Needs of Investors and Creditors," New York, NY: American Institute of Certified Public Accountants.

Atkinson, A. A. and J. Waterhouse, 1996, "Strategic Performance Measurement: Scope and Implementation Issues," Working Paper, University of Waterloo.

Ben-Akiva, M., T. Morikawa, and F. Shiroishi, 1990, "Analysis of the Reliability of Stated Preference Data in Estimating Mode Choice Models," forthcoming in Proceedings of the 5th World Conference on Transport Research.

Ben-Akiva, M., and T. Morikawa, 1990, "Estimation of Travel Demand Models from Multiple Data Sources," submitted to The 11th International Symposium on Transportation and Traffic Theory, Yokohama, Japan.

Capital Allocation Subcouncil, 1995, "Lifting All Boats: Increasing the Payoff from Private Investment in the US Economy," Washington, DC: Competitiveness Policy Council.

Chaney, P., T. Devinney, and R. Winter, 1991, "The Impact of New Product Introductions on the Market Value of Firms," Journal of Business Finance.

Chang, L., and K. Most, 1985, The Perceived Usefulness of Financial Statements, Miami, FL: International University Press.

Dillman, D., 1978, *Mail and Telephone Surveys: The Total Design Method,* New York: Wiley.

Eccles, R., 1991, "The Performance Measurement Manifesto," *Harvard Business Review,* January/February, pp. 131–137.

Eccles, R. and S. Mavrinac, 1995, "Improving the Corporate Disclosure Process," *Sloan Management Review,* Summer, Vol. 36, No. 4, pp. 11–25 .

Gordon, L. A., J. Pound, and T. Porter, 1994, "High-Performance Workplaces: Implications for Investment Research and Active Investing Strategies," Waban, MA: The Gordon Group.

Hawkins, D. and B. Hawkins, 1986, "The Effectiveness of the Annual Report as a Communication Vehicle," Morristown, NJ: Financial Executives Research Foundation.

Heller, T., 1994, "The Superior Stock Market Performance of a TQM Portfolio," *The Center for Quality Management Journal,* 3:1, Winter, pp. 23–32.

Hill and Knowlton, 1984, "The Annual Report: A Question of Credibility," New York, NY: Hill and Knowlton.

Ittner, C. D. and D. Larcker, 1996, "Measuring the Impact of Quality Initiatives on Firm Financial Performance," in *Advances in the Management of Organizational Quality,* Donald B. Fedor and Souman Gosh, eds., Vol. 1, pp. 1–37 .

Ittner, C. D. and J. P. MacDuffie, 1994, "Exploring the Sources of International Differences in Manufacturing Overhead," Working Paper, The Wharton School, University of Pennsylvania.

Jarrell, S. L., and G. S. Easton, 1996, "An Exploratory Empirical Investigation of the Effects of Total Quality Management on Corporate Performance," in *The Practice of Quality Management,* P. Lederer, ed., Boston, MA: Harvard University Press.

Kaplan, R. S., and D. P. Norton, 1992, "The Balanced Scorecard: Measures that Drive Performance," *Harvard Business Review,* pp. 71–79.

Knutson, P., 1992, "Financial Reporting in the 1990s and Beyond: A Position Paper of the Association for Investment Management and Research," Charlottesville, VA: Association for Investment Management and Research.

Kron, N., 1994, "The Crisis in Performance Measurement: An Investigation into Corporate Performance Measurement Practices in Ireland," Masters Thesis, Trinity College.

Lee, T. and D. Tweedie, 1977, "The Private Shareholder and the Corporate Report," London: The Institute of Chartered Accountants in England and Wales.

Mavrinac, S. C., and T. Boyle, 1996, "Sell-Side Analysis, Non-financial Performance Evaluation, and The Accuracy of Short-Term Earnings Forecasts," Ernst & Young Center for Business Innovation Working Paper.

Mavrinac, S., N. Jones, with M. Meyer, 1995, "Competitive Renewal through Workplace Innovation: The Financial and Non-financial Returns to Innovative Workplace Practices," Unpublished Monograph, U.S. Department of Labor and Ernst & Young LLP.

Payne, S., 1951, *The Art of Asking Questions,* Princeton: Princeton University Press.

SRI International, 1987, "Investor Information Needs and the Annual Report," Morristown, NJ: Financial Executives Research Foundation.

Vitale, M., S. C. Mavrinac, and M. Hauser, 1994, "New Process/Financial Scorecard: A Strategic Performance Measurement System," *Planning Review,* Vol. 22, No. 4, pp. 21–26.

17

Measuring and Managing Technological Knowledge

Roger E. Bohn

"Knowledge is power."

—Francis Bacon

As we move from the industrial age into the information age, knowledge is becoming an ever more central force behind the competitive success of firms and even nations. Nonaka has commented, "In an economy where the only certainty is uncertainty, the one sure source of lasting competitive advantage is knowledge."[1] Philosophers have analyzed the nature of knowledge for millennia; in the past half-century, cognitive and computer scientists have pursued it with increased vigor. But it has turned out that *information* is much easier to store, describe, and manipulate than is *knowledge.* One consequence is that, although an organization's knowledge base may be its single most important asset, its very intangibility makes it difficult to manage systematically.[2]

The goal of this paper is to present a framework for measuring and understanding one particular type of knowledge: technological knowledge, that is, knowledge about how to produce goods and services. We can use this framework to more precisely map, evaluate, and compare levels of knowledge. The level of knowledge that a process has reached determines how a process should be controlled, whether and how it can be automated, the key tasks of the workforce, and

1. I. Nonaka, "The Knowledge-Creating Company," *Harvard Business Review,* November-December 1991, pp. 96–104.
2. Peter Drucker has commented, "In fact, knowledge is the only meaningful resource today. The traditional 'factors of production' have not disappeared, but they have become secondary." See P. F. Drucker, *Post-Capitalist Society* (New York: Harper Business, 1993), p. 42.

Reprinted from "Measuring and Managing Technological Knowledge" by Roger E. Bohn. *Sloan Management Review,* Fall 1994, pp. 61–73, by permission of publisher. Copyright © 1994 by Sloan Management Review Association. All rights reserved.

other major aspects of its management. Better knowledge of key variables leads to better performance without incremental physical investment.

Two examples illustrate the importance of technological knowledge in the form of detailed process understanding. Chaparral Steel, a minimill, was able to double output from its original electric furnace and caster. Semiconductor companies routinely increase yields on their chip fabrication lines from below 40 percent to above 80 percent during a period of several years. In these cases, the incremental capital investments are minimal. The improvements are instead due to multiple changes in the manufacturing process, including different procedures, adjustments of controls, changes in raw material recipes, etc. Why weren't these changes implemented at startup? The reason is that the knowledge about the process and how to run it is incomplete and develops gradually through various kinds of learning.

Many authors have noted that there is a difference between data and information. A few have also noted that there is a difference between information and knowledge.[3] Although not always clear-cut, the distinction among the three in production processes is very important. *Data* are what come directly from sensors, reporting on the measured level of some variable. *Information* is "data that have been organized or given structure—that is, placed in context—and thus endowed with meaning."[4] Information tells the current or past status of some part of the production system. *Knowledge* goes further; it allows the making of predictions, causal associations, or prescriptive decisions about what to do.

For example, consider a stream of measurements of the critical dimension of a series of supposedly identical manufactured parts—raw *data*. If the data are plotted on a control chart, they provide *information* about the status of the production process for those parts. The measurements may have a trend, may be beyond the process control limit, may be out of the allowed tolerance, or may even show no discernible pattern. All of these are *information,* but not knowledge. *Knowledge* about the process might include, "When the control chart looks like that, it usually means machine A needs to be recalibrated" (causal association and prescriptive decision), or "When the control chart is in control for the first hour of a new batch, it usually remains that way for the rest of the shift" (prediction). This paper is about technological knowledge, not data or information.

To explain why some types of knowledge are more complete and useful than others, a colleague and I developed an ordinal scale for describing how much is known about a process. Originally we studied ramp-up of new production in high-tech industries (VLSI fabrication, hard disk drives). Subsequently, we found

3. Harlan Cleveland distinguishes data, information, knowledge, and wisdom. However, he then intermixes the four concepts. See: H. Cleveland, "The Knowledge Dynamic," *The Knowledge Executive* (New York: Human Valley Books, 1985).
4. R. Glazer, "Marketing in an Information-Intensive Environment: Strategic Implications of Knowledge as an Asset," *Journal of Marketing* 55 (1991): 1–19.

that the same concepts worked well in traditional industries such as firearms, pulp and paper, and steel cord.[5]

In the next section, I give a detailed scheme for measuring the extent of technological knowledge and several brief examples, ranging from semiconductors to consulting. The third section examines the implications of the level of knowledge for how to manage production processes. The fourth section looks at learning, that is, the evolution of knowledge over time. In the penultimate section, I use a familiar technology, baking, as an extended illustration. In conclusion, I look at some of the implications for managing technological knowledge itself.

A SCALE FOR MEASURING KNOWLEDGE ABOUT A PROCESS

A company's knowledge about its processes may range from total ignorance about how they work to very formal and accurate mathematical models.[6] For our purposes, a process is defined as *any repetitive system for producing a product or service, including the people, machines, procedures, and software, in that system.* A process has inputs, outputs, and state variables that characterize what is happening inside it. The inputs are often further broken down into raw materials, control variables, and environmental variables (See Figure 17.1). For example, environmental variables include temperature, humidity, air pressure, dust, seismic vibration, electrical power, etc.

Here I define technological knowledge as *understanding the effects of the input variables on the output.* Mathematically, the process output, Y, is an unknown function f of the inputs, x: $Y = f(x)$; x is always a vector (of indeterminate dimension). Then technological knowledge is knowledge about the arguments and behavior of the function $f(x)$.[7] The manager's or process engineer's goal is to manipulate the raw materials, controls, and environment to get output that is as good as possible. It is customary to treat the environmental variables as exogenous and uncontrollable. However, with enough knowledge, the environmental variables can be turned into control variables and, therefore, are not exogenous.

I start by looking at well-defined manufacturing processes such as building a car door or cooking in a fastfood restaurant. Later I will show how knowledge

5. R. Jaikumar, "From Filing and Fitting to Flexible Manufacturing: A Study in the Evolution of Process Control" (Boston: Harvard Business School, working paper, 1988); and A. S. Mukherjee, "The Effective Management of Organizational Learning and Process Control" (Boston: Harvard Business School, doctoral dissertation, 1992).
6. R. E. Bohn and R. Jaikumar, "The Structure of Technological Knowledge in Manufacturing" (Boston: Harvard Business School, working paper 93-035, 1992); and R. E. Bohn and Jaikumar, "The Development of Intelligent Systems for Industrial Use: An Empirical Investigation," in *Research on Technological Innovation, Management and Policy,* ed. R. S. Rosenbloom (London and Greenwich, Connecticut: JAI Press, 1986), pp. 213–262.
7. This formalism is pursued in Bohn and Jaikumar (1992).

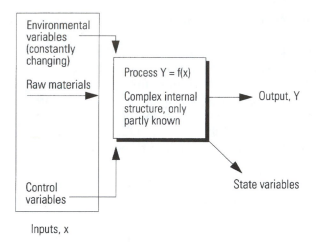

Inputs, x

FIGURE 17.1   Diagram of a process.

about less tangible processes, such as marketing and legal services, can be described by the same scale. Whatever the process, better technological knowledge
gives the operators better ability to manage the process effectively.

I have identified eight stages of technological knowledge, ranging from complete ignorance to complete understanding. Each stage describes the knowledge
about a particular input variable x's effect on the process output, Y. Why so many
stages? We are used to the idea of a spectrum of knowledge "from art to science,"
but intuition suggests that only three or four stages should be sufficient to describe
the spectrum. Most analyses of production processes, however, look only at things
that are already reasonably well understood. Variables in the first three stages are
already reasonably well understood. Variables in the first three stages are usually
considered exogenous, in that it is impossible to control them. Nonetheless, it is
important to recognize their existence since important variables may be at one of
those stages, and management of the process needs to take that into account. The
stages are summarized in Table 17.1.

In contrast to most approaches for measuring knowledge, the nature of the
knowledge changes qualitatively with each stage in this framework. The process
of learning from one stage to the next also changes. Each stage is described as
follows:

Stage One—Complete ignorance.   You do not know that a phenomenon
exists, or if you are aware of its existence, you have no inkling that it may be relevant to your process. The history of technology is full of phenomena that were initially not recognized, yet had potentially major effects on a production process
(e.g., quantum mechanics, germs in the treatment of wounds, contamination in a
number of processes). At stage one, there is nothing you can do with the variable,
and its effects on the process appear as random disturbances.

TABLE 17.1   Stages of Knowledge

Stage	Name	Comment	Typical Form of Knowledge
1	Complete ignorance		Nowhere
2	Awareness	Pure art	Tacit
3	Measure	Pretechnological	Written
4	Control of the mean	Scientific method feasible	Written and embodied in hardware
5	Process capability	Local recipe	Hardware and operating manual
6	Process characterization	Tradeoffs to reduce costs	Empirical equations (numerical)
7	Know why	Science	Scientific formulas and algorithms
8	Complete knowledge	Nirvana	

Stage Two—Awareness.   You know that the phenomenon exists and that it might be relevant to your process. There is still no way to use the variable in your process, but you can begin to investigate it in order to get to the next stage. Learning from stage one to stage two often occurs by serendipity, by making analogies to seemingly unrelated processes, or by bringing knowledge from outside the organization.

Stage Three—Measure.   You can measure the variables accurately, perhaps with some effort. This requires development and installation of specific instrumentation. Stage three variables cannot be controlled. However, if the variable is important enough, you can alter the process in response to the variable in order to exploit or ameliorate its effects. An example of a stage three variable is weather; many outdoor processes are halted or done differently during bad weather.

There are two kinds of learning at stage three. One kind consists of passive, natural experiments to determine the relationship between this variable and the output. A second learning process studies ways of controlling the variable to reach stage four, control. Knowledge about how to control the variable is, in effect, a subprocess with its own inputs and output (the level of the input variable for the main process). For certain variables, knowing how to measure it (stage three) leads almost automatically to knowing how to control it (stage four). These are primarily variables where feedback-based control is feasible, such as furnace temperatures.

Stage Four—Control of the mean.   You know how to control the variables accurately across a range of levels, although the control is not necessarily precise.

That is, you can control the mean level, but there is some variance around that level. Stage four provides a quantum leap in process control, since, at a minimum, you can now stabilize the process with respect to the mean of that variable. Variables that were previously viewed as exogenous disturbances to the process can now be treated as control variables. Reaching stage four also makes further learning easier, because you can now perform controlled experiments on the variable to quantify its impact on the process.

Stage Five—Process capability (**control of the variance**).   You can control the variables with precision across a range of values. When all of the important variables reach stage five, your process can manufacture products by following a "cookbook," that is, a consistent recipe. The product still may not meet quality standards, however, so final inspection will be needed.

Learning from stage four to stage five is a matter of learning to control the various disturbances that affect the input variable. This is a nested subproblem that passes through the stages of knowledge on the way to good control of the input variable. That is, producing the correct level of an input, x, is a process in its own right and must be learned. Fortunately, accumulated technological knowledge gives cookbook methods for controlling many variables. The process engineer can look it up in a catalog or handbook. This means that you do not have to "reinvent the wheel" each time; you just have to learn enough to control the variable using known "wheels."

Stage Six—Process characterization (know how).   You know how the variable affects the result, when small changes are made in the variable.[8] Now you can begin to fine-tune the process to reduce costs and to change product characteristics. You can also institute some feedback control on the output using any stage six variable that is both easy to change and has a major impact. This increases the quality of the output by reducing its variability. To reach stage six, you run controlled experiments with different levels of the variable to determine its effects.

Stage Seven—Know why.   You have a scientific model of the process and how it operates over a broad region, including nonlinear and interaction effects of this variable with other variables. At this stage, you can actually optimize the process with respect to the stage seven variables. Feedback and some feed-forward control are broadly effective. Control can be turned over to microprocessors, which will be able to handle most contingencies. You can even use your knowledge to simulate the process to study settings you have never tried empirically, such as ways of making new products using the same process. Learning from stage six to stage seven involves tapping scientific models, running broad experiments across multiple variables to estimate the models, and finding interactions among input variables.

---

8. $\delta f/\delta x_i$ in a local region.

Stage Eight—Complete knowledge. You know the complete functional form and parameter values that determine the result, Y, as a function of all the inputs. Process and environment are so well understood that you can head off any problems in advance by feed-forward control. Stage eight is never reached in practice because it requires knowing all the interactions among variables. However, it can be approached asymptotically by studying the process in more and more detail.

The stages of knowledge can be applied to diverse tasks and industries:

- High-tech manufacturing requires rapid learning about multiple variables in new products and processes. We can frame a definition in terms of the stage of knowledge: *high-tech processes are those in which many of the important variables are at stage four or below.* This makes the process difficult to control and work with, so a lot of effort goes into raising the knowledge level as quickly as possible. Because of customer and competitive pressures, no sooner is knowledge raised for one product than higher performance products are demanded, which brings in new low-stage variables. Thus managing in high-tech industries requires both rapid learning and the ability to manufacture with "immature" (low stage of knowledge) technologies.

- VLSI semiconductor design and fabrication processes are driven by the ability to reproduce very small features with high reliability at high volume. The process is very complex, with multiple layers and hundreds of variables potentially affecting each layer. As feature sizes get smaller with each new generation, new equipment is needed and new variables become important. These new variables start at low stages of knowledge. For example, as feature sizes go below one micron, heat dissipation problems begin to push designers to engineer chips for three volts instead of five volts. This has a number of advantages but requires many changes in both chip design and fabrication. As these changes are made, the variables that were at stage six or seven for the old process "regress" to stage five; engineers know how to control them, but don't know their effects on the new process.

- Consumer marketing has made many strides toward higher stages of knowledge in the past thirty years. Many of the breakthroughs have been based on developing effective ways to measure variables (stage three). For example, bar-code scanners at supermarket checkouts have provided masses of disaggregated data about who is buying what, whether they use coupons, etc. Some stores are now using customer ID cards to match this data with information about individual households, their demographics, what TV commercials they received, and other environmental variables to allow development of stage six and seven models of the marketing mix's effects on consumer behavior.[9]

9. Glazer (1991); and N. R. Kleinfield, "Targeting the Grocery Shopper," *New York Times*, 26 May

- Professional services such as legal services run the range of knowledge stages. For example, preparing a will has reached stage six or even seven for many people, so that it can be done by a $30 software program. At the other extreme, high-profile criminal trials used to be at stage three or below. Recently, a number of law firms have attempted to move jury selection to stage six, using methods such as customized polling of population groups from which a particular jury will be drawn. Other aspects of trial strategy, presumably, remain at stage three or four; they can be measured but not controlled well. For example, an important type of "input" to litigation is judicial rulings on motions. Lawyers can use the judge's ruling to measure whether the judge agrees with them on a motion, but they have only limited control over chat decision (stage four). Pretrial aspects of litigation, on the other hand, are generally better understood.
- In strategic consulting, the Boston Consulting Group's four-quadrant matrix (cash cows, dogs, stars, and question marks) was an attempt to reduce acquisition and divestiture decisions to two quantitative variables—market share and growth rate.[10] It is possible to write equations that describe the effects of market share and growth rate on business unit profit, so these two variables are at stage six. But there are many other important variables that also influence the outcome and that are at much lower stages of knowledge. Many consulting firms claim knowledge about these other variables, but they perform strategic analysis using a heavy mix of expertise, implying an awareness that some of their knowledge is at a low stage.

DYNAMIC EVOLUTION OF KNOWLEDGE AND PERFORMANCE

Important variables are those that, in fact, have great economic implications for the process. Ideally, a company would like to have a high stage of knowledge about all the important variables and a low stage about all the variables that have negligible effects. But, instead, the organization is likely to know very little about some important variables, especially for immature processes. Conversely, it may have stage six knowledge about unimportant variables, such as the color of paint on the machine and the type of clothing workers wear. Of course, in certain processes, these variables may be important, but there may be little way to know this until you learn enough to bring them to a high stage. For example, paint inside a machine may affect process chemistry, paint outside a machine may affect worker morale, and worker clothing can affect contamination-sensitive processes.

1991.
10. J. A. Seeger, "Reversing the Images of BCG's Growth/Share Matrix," *Strategic Management Journal 5* (1984): 93–97.

One way to visualize overall technological knowledge is as a tree (See Figure 17.2). The trunk of the tree is Y, the process output that we want to control. The branches from the trunk are variables that directly affect Y, (x_1, x_2, ...). Branching off from each of these are subvariables (x_{11}, x_{12}, ...) that collectively determine x_1, and so on, to any level of detail. The shading of each branch represents the organization's stage of knowledge, with white (invisible) representing stage one, while black is stage seven. The thickness of the branch represents its importance. Every knowledge tree trails off into a haze of dimly seen but potentially important variables and eventually becomes invisible, because there are always some variables at a still finer level of detail whose existence is unrecognized.

As the tree illustrates, a single process has many variables that are inevitably at different stages of knowledge. As more is learned about part of the process, old variables are brought to higher stages, but new variables also emerge from the mists of ignorance. The process as a whole can do no better than the knowledge about its most important drivers. If even a few key variables are at low stages of knowledge, the process can be considered at a low stage of knowledge overall.

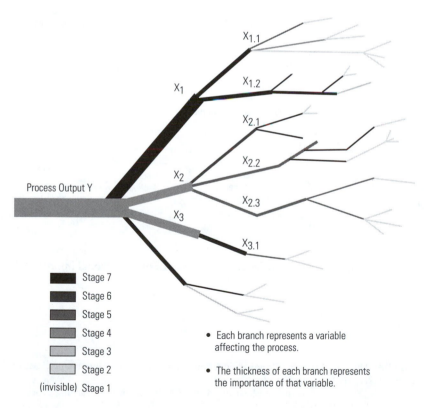

FIGURE 17.2 A knowledge tree.

RELATIONSHIP TO THEORIES OF ORGANIZATIONAL LEARNING

Experience in conducting a task generally leads to improvement, a concept formalized in the literature on learning curves.[11] Most learning curve models skip the intermediate stages of causality and statistically link cumulative production directly to costs (See Figure 17.3, part A). But it is clear that how the production and learning processes are managed has a big impact on whether and how fast learning occurs.[12] Indeed, the large amount of literature on quality improvement concerns systematic learning methods to achieve more improvement in a shorter period of time. Thus learning can be a directed activity, not just a by-product of normal production. Part B in Figure 17.3 shows a more complete model of technological learning, with explicit recognition of knowledge.[13]

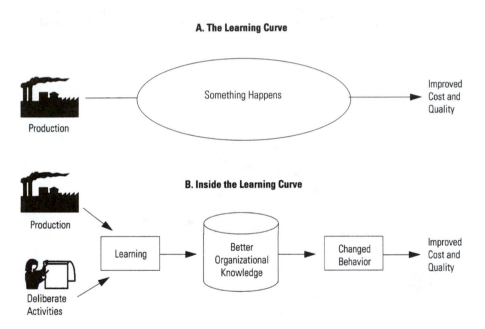

FIGURE 17.3 Learning curve and knowledge-based views of organizational improvement.

11. J. Dutton and A. Thomas, "Treating Progress Functions as a Managerial Opportunity," *Academy of Management Review* 9 (1984): 235–247.
12. P. S. Adler and K. B. Clark, "Behind the Learning Curve: A Sketch of the Learning Process," *Management Science* 37 (1991): 267–281.
13. R. Jaikumar and R. E. Bohn, "A Dynamic Approach to Operations Management: An Alternative to Static Optimization," *International Journal of Production Economics* 27 (1992): 265–282.

It is no coincidence that the knowledge tree of Figure 17.2 resembles causal trees like those used in quality improvement efforts.[14] These trees, also called fishbone or Ishikawa diagrams, are often used as a way of listing potential causes of problems. A process engineer may have fifty variables (or corresponding problems) at stages two through four that are potentially important. Various methods can be used to guess which ones will turn out to be the most important.[15] The stages of knowledge provide a way of mapping current knowledge and estimating how hard it will be to go further on particular variables. That is, they provide a detailed scorecard for process improvement efforts.

HOW TO MANAGE AT EACH STAGE OF KNOWLEDGE

The knowledge stage of different process variables is important because it determines how to manage both the knowledge and the production process. The higher the stage of knowledge, the closer the process is to "science," and the more formally it can be managed. Conversely, low-stage processes, such as creative endeavors, do not do well under formal management methods, and should be treated more as "art."

One of the most basic system-design decisions is the degree of procedure. There are different ways of performing a given task, requiring different kinds of people, training, and tools. At one extreme is pure procedure, i.e., a completely specified set of rules about what to do under every possible set of circumstances. At the other extreme is something we can call pure expertise or pure art—a style of action in which every situation is dealt with as if it were new and unique. This requires experienced and skilled people who use their own judgment at each moment. These people have tacit knowledge, meaning that although they can carry on a task, they are not able to explain it.

Managers can attempt to operate a process anywhere along the spectrum from pure expertise to pure procedure. The microprocessor has made it possible to execute very complex procedures at very low cost.[16] But this does not mean that procedural approaches are always best. There is a natural relationship between degree of procedure and stage of knowledge (See Figure 17.4). For example, in order to automate a process, all key variables should be understood at least to stage six, and preferably to stage seven. If they are not, unanticipated problems will crop up frequently, and the system will not be able to deal with them effectively. Those portions of processes that are at low stages of knowledge should be done using a high degree of expertise and little automation. Locations above the diago-

14. J. M. Juran and F. M. Gryna, eds., *Juran's Quality Control Handbook* (New York: McGraw-Hill, 1988), Chapter 22.

15. These methods include Pareto charts, use of analogies to similar but better understood processes, screening experiments, and other methods discussed in the quality control literature. Notice that screening experiments are possible only if the variable is already at stage four or higher.

16. G. V. Shirley and R. Jaikumar, "Turing Machines and Gutenberg Technologies: The Post-Industrial Marriage," *ASME Manufacturing Review* 1 (1988): 36–43.

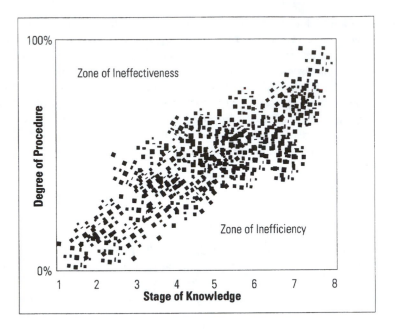

Source: R.E. Bohn and R. Jaikumar, "The Development of Intelligent Systems for Industrial Use: An Empirical Investigation," in *Research on Technological Innovation, Management and Policy,* ed. R. Rosenbloom (London and Greenwich, Connecticut: JAI Press, 1986), pp. 213-262.

FIGURE 17.4   Ideal operating method and the stage of knowledge.

nal in Figure 17.4 correspond to inexpensive but ineffective processes, which do not produce consistently good output.

Conversely, if a process or portion of a process is at a high stage of knowledge, it is inefficient to use lots of expertise to carry it out. An expertise-based process may still work (although people lose attentiveness in purely repetitive situations), but you will pay extra for experts who are not really needed. This is the area below the diagonal in Figure 17.4.

Why do companies find themselves off the diagonal of Figure 17.4? A common reason during the early 1980s was hubris: overoptimism about the firm's knowledge of production processes and its associated ability to build, debug, and operate new factories. This led to numerous attempts to solve manufacturing competitiveness problems by automation, as exemplified by the slogan, "automate, emigrate, or evaporate." When automation was undertaken without a solid base of process knowledge, the results were counterproductive: "The automation of a large, complex, poorly understood, conventional manufacturing process leads to a large, complex, poorly understood, unreliable, expensive, and automated manufacturing process."[17] Perhaps one of the most conspicuous and ex-

17. J. Flanagan, "GM Saga a Lesson four America," *Los Angeles Times,* 27 October 1992, p. A1.

pensive examples of this syndrome was General Motors, which, in the early 1980s, invested approximately $40 billion to build a number of automated auto assembly plants, many of which never worked properly.

At the other, perhaps less common extreme are companies that use expensive labor to perform repetitive tasks, leading to inefficiency. Examples include information-based services such as manual letter sorting (e.g., the U.S. Postal Service) and routine telephone services (directory assistance). Although human judgment is very useful in these processes for handling exceptions, the bulk of the work is routine, well understood, and uses mainly the pattern recognition abilities of the human brain. Industries have taken several approaches to dealing with the resulting inefficiency, including high proceduralizing of workers, which risks dehumanizing the work and suppressing their expertise (e.g., United Parcel Service industrial engineering and automated monitoring of telephone operators), and finding ways of getting data into machine readable form so that human operators do not have to keypunch it (optical character recognition and bar coding).

The degree of procedure is not the only managerial decision affected by the stage of knowledge. Methods of organizing, methods of problem solving, learning, and training, and many other aspects of the process should also be adjusted (See Table 17.2).

Yet, as shown in Figure 17.2, most processes have important variables at widely differing stages of knowledge. The ideal management style for the process as a whole is an uncomfortable hybrid. The traditional approach to this issue was to segregate work into different functional departments, which are then managed according to their own needs. A common example of this in traditional manufacturing companies is R&D (low stages) versus manufacturing functions (high stages, or so it was believed). This Taylorist approach has broken down in modern manufacturing, especially for technologies that are evolving rapidly, because the less mature portions of the process are inevitably at low stages of knowledge.[18]

There are at least two other approaches to this paradox. One is to use microprocessors (or other automation) to execute procedures, but with human oversight to select the appropriate program and to recognize unprogrammed contingencies and take control. Examples include accounting, continuous manufacturing processes such as paper mills, and commercial aviation. A final approach is to use low-skilled workers to execute the better understood tasks, with experts monitoring and directing them. The low-skilled workers may be apprentices to the experts or on a separate career track. For example, law offices use both junior associates (apprentices) and paralegals.

All three approaches have weaknesses. For example, it is difficult for pilots to monitor autopilots reliably during long flights without taking an active role themselves, yet respond quickly and appropriately in emergencies.[19] If lower skilled workers perform the better understood and therefore more procedural

18. Bohn and Jaikumar (1992).
19. K. E. Weick, "Organizational Culture as a Source of High Reliability," *California Management Review,* Winter 1987, pp. 112–127.

TABLE 17.2 Some Effects of Knowledge Stages

Knowledge at Stage . . .	1	2	3	4	5	6	7	8
Nature of production	Expertise based		<————>			Procedure based		
Role of workers	Everything		Problem solving			Learning and improving		
Location of knowledge	Workers' heads		Written and oral			In databases or in software		
Nature of learning	Artistic		Natural experiments			Controlled experiments, simulations		
Nature of problem solving	Trial and error		Scientific method			Table look-up		
Method of training new workers	Apprenticeship, coaching		<————>			Classroom		
Natural type of organization	Organic		Mechanistic			Learning oriented		
Suitability for automation	None		<————>			High		
Ease of transfer to another site	Low		<————>			High		
Feasible product variety	High		Low			High*		
Quality control approach	Sorting		Statistical process control			Feed forward		

*R. Jaikumar,, "From Filing and Fitting to Flexible Manufacturing: A Study in the Evolution of Process Control" (Boston: Harvard Business School, working paper, 1988).

tasks, this can lead to excessive division of labor, poor coordination, and lost opportunities for learning. In addition, cultural conflict is a common result when an organization is split into sections operating at different stages of knowledge. Thus there is no ideal solution to the problem of working at multiple stages of knowledge, or if there is one, we don't yet know it. Nonetheless, this situation is increasingly common.

A SIMPLE EXAMPLE OF KNOWLEDGE PROGRESSION OVER TIME

Knowledge increases through learning. Much learning is simply increasing the precision and accuracy of parameter estimates within a single stage, but sometimes learning shifts the knowledge to the next stage. To illustrate, using familiar technology, suppose you are baking cookies for the first time. You hope to make chocolate chip cookies, but have only a vague idea of a good recipe (raw materials) and procedure (control variables). You have a standard oven, which you were told to set at 350 degrees.[20]

The first step is to define your output measure, Y. It consists of a combination of taste, texture (hard or soft), and appearance.

Stage One—Complete ignorance. You don't even know what influences cookie characteristics, so when the results change, you consider it "random."

Stage Two—Awareness. You rack your memory, observe others in the kitchen, and begin to build a list of possibly relevant input variables, including the list of ingredients, baking time, outdoor weather (rainy, cloudy, clear), time of day, amount and brand name of each ingredient, and a vaguely defined "mixing procedure."

Stage Three—Learning to measure key variables. You use your watch to measure cooking time, measuring cups to measure raw materials, an outdoor thermometer and hygrometer for the weather, and a clock for the time of day. You have no detailed metric for mixing procedure, so you throw everything into one bowl and count strokes of the mixing spoon.

Stage Four—Control of the mean. You get a count-down timer and develop a procedure to take the cookies out of the oven after a set amount of time. You can control outdoor weather only crudely, by baking on days when the weather is of a particular type. You decide not to bother controlling for time of day since it does not seem to make any difference. Control of the ingredients is straightforward, using a standard measuring cup; that is, for the raw materials, stage three leads immediately to stage four.

Stage Five—Process capability and a recipe. You practice measuring ingredients until you can do it with 95 percent repeatability. You write down a set of instructions (recipe) that seems to produce "adequate" cookies. Your cookies now have a reasonably consistent taste, but texture and appearance are still variable and some cookies are burned.

Stage Six—Process characterization. You run a series of experiments on many variables, including baking time, baking temperature, mixing time, and the exact amounts of flour, sugar, and liquid ingredients. You discover the effects of a 10 percent change in each of these variables on the cookie characteristics. If a friend asks for a better baked cookie, you can now achieve it by varying either the time or the temperature. You discover that some variables, including weather and time of day, have no detectable effect on the output.

---

20. Experienced bakers will realize that the following account is highly simplified. A case simulation of some of the following issues is provided in: R. E. Bohn, "Kristen's Cookie Company (B)" (Boston: Harvard Business School, Case 9-686-015, 1986).

Stage Seven—Know why, including interactions among input variables. You go to the local university library and take out textbooks on baking, which give mathematical formulas for outcome variables such as sweetness and surface texture. You calibrate those models using data from your own baking process. You can now produce a "near perfect" chocolate chip cookie. If someone asks for a healthier cookie (less sugar), you can produce it, and you know how much to adjust the baking temperature. Similarly, if you are in a hurry, you know how to increase the temperature and decrease the baking time without burning the cookies.

Repeat for secondary variables. Although you now have stage five control (a recipe) for about ten variables and a stage seven understanding (know why) of five of them, there will always be a host of secondary variables in your knowledge tree that have smaller effects. And there is no guarantee that you will learn about the most important variables first. For example, you may not realize that cookie size is important (stage two) until you are well into stage five for other variables. You can subject these additional variables to the same progression through the stages of knowledge. Variables include the brand and characteristics of raw materials (butter versus margarine versus inexpensive margarine, types of flour), the importance of sifting dry ingredients together before mixing, type of baking tray (aluminum versus glass versus iron), and use of a scale instead of measuring cups for more accurate measurement of raw materials. For casual baking, you would never bother to learn about some of these variables, but if you wanted to reduce costs or improve consistency, you would have to delve much deeper into these secondary variables.

Stage Eight—Complete knowledge. Since there is an infinitude of potential secondary variables, you can never have complete knowledge of the cookie-making process.[21] But for practical purposes, you can say that you have reached stage eight when you have a model that will predict output (cookie) characteristics to an accuracy of one-tenth of the tolerance band, for changes in inputs across a 2:1 range, and including all interactions.

Amateurs may stop when they have stage five knowledge about the primary variables that affect taste. They can then bake decent cookies and throw away batches ruined by low knowledge about secondary variables. But professional bakeries must track down additional secondary variables, especially those that influence costs. Here is a description of the situation at one famous baking company:

> *Since early this decade, Nabisco has been worried about its bakery technology, which, according to a 1981 study, had fallen far behind that of even some tiny rivals. . . . The biscuit company, to this day, uses a lot of equipment made decades ago at Nabisco's former Evanston, Illinois, machine shop.*

---

21. For example, eggs, flour, and chocolate are relatively complex agricultural products, of imperfect consistency over time.

> *And to this day, baking at Nabisco remains something of an art. Oreos have uneven swaths of cream filling. The exact number of Ritz crackers in a box is anybody's guess. Some 5 percent to 7 percent of Nabisco's cookies and crackers emerge from its ovens broken.*
>
> *Similarly, the company still has poor inspection methods for the tons of commodities it purchases, such as flour and cocoa, according to a former executive of the baking unit. The bakers must repeatedly test-bake batches of cookies and crackers to adjust ovens and other gear to slight variations in commodity composition.* [In our terms, they had stage four knowledge of raw materials and were attempting to compensate for it by using stage six knowledge about how to adjust the ovens.] *Such trial-and-error methods make quality control, among other things, difficult.*
>
> *So, sixteen months ago, . . . the company planned to spend some $1.6 billion on complete retrofitting of four existing bakeries and close five other plants.*
>
> *The plan called for a microchip revolution in Nabisco's bakeries. At least one-third of the project's cost was to be for the purchase of computerized weighing, mixing, packaging, and process-control equipment, says a senior Nabisco manufacturing engineer who recently resigned.*
>
> *Such high-tech gear would eventually halve the company's 8 percent "give-away" rate—the overweight amount in an average package of Nabisco biscuits—and sharply reduce its 5 percent to 7 percent breakage.*[22]

Nabisco's automation will be most effective with stage seven knowledge (know why) about all of the key variables. It is possible that Nabisco's equipment vendors sell machines that already embody that knowledge, but it is likely that some of it (including the specific variables uniquely affecting Nabisco's cookies) would have to be developed as part of the automation program.

APPLYING THE STAGES OF KNOWLEDGE

Now that we have a framework for measuring and understanding technological knowledge, we can look at some principles for managing knowledge to improve production processes.

Understand How Much You Know and Don't Know

In order to understand how much you already know about a process, you need to ask a number of questions:

22. P. Waldman, "Change of Pace: New RJR Chief Faces a Daunting Challenge at Debt-Heavy Firm," *Wall Street Journal*, 14 March 1989.

- What are the important variables for the process?
- At what stages are these variables? Which variables in the process would give the most leverage if you could get them to a higher stage?
- How can you manage the process well at these stages of knowledge? What limits and opportunities does the process impose? Are your management methods consistent with knowledge levels (Figure 17.4 and Table 17.2)? How should you handle the inevitable variables that you know less about yet are still important?
- How can you learn to reach higher stages of knowledge?

You also need to beware of what you think you know about a process that you really don't. One of the most painful forms of ignorance is false knowledge. If your company believes that it has stage six or higher knowledge about a variable, but in fact that knowledge is based on past experience and is incorrect for the present process, you will operate the process in an inferior way. A common version of this is the belief that "variable x does not matter." It may not have mattered ten years ago because of a small contribution to process variance. But what was considered small ten years ago may be quite important today. A newer competitor, unburdened with this false knowledge, can control or change the level of x to get superior quality or lower cost.

The countermeasure for this problem is to realize that as your company's process changes, its effective knowledge regresses to earlier stages. In particular, stage six knowledge, which is generally derived by empirical observation, often regresses to stage five for a new process. You still know how to measure and control the variable, but you no longer know its true impact.

Understand and Manage the Locations of Knowledge

Knowing where knowledge resides for the process you are managing is important for effectively managing and using that knowledge. It has implications for accessibility, transmission to new locations, and ability to extend the knowledge, among other things. Technological knowledge may be located in people's heads, word of mouth, or other informal mechanisms; informal procedure sheets for operators, handbooks, other written documentation; or embodied in machinery, firmware, and software. How well is it documented? How easy is it to change? How much do users know about how to use its features?

As I have discussed, the feasible and desirable locations of knowledge depend on its stage. There are also broader issues surrounding more general forms of organizational memory.[23]

---

23. J. P. Walsh and G. R. Ungson, "Organizational Memory," *Academy of Management Review* 16 (1991): 57–91.

Be Wary of Deskilling the Workforce and Freezing Processes

The Taylorist model of manufacturing, as it is commonly applied, moves technological knowledge about the process away from line workers and puts it in the heads of staff engineers. These engineers will be less available when problems come up, or they may leave the company. If workers do not understand the process, they cannot handle unanticipated situations, nor can they do much to improve the process, even if they are motivated. Therefore, one of the revolutionary effects of the total quality management movement has been to return knowledge to the workers and make them capable of doing process improvement in small groups, without relying on the traditional staff experts.

Even if you fully understand a process today, the world will change in a few years. Some of your current knowledge will be obsolete, and it will be important to reevaluate it. Once a firm assumes, for whatever reason, that it has nothing more to learn about a production process, it tends to "lock in" the present production methods by specifying rigid procedures that can deskill the workforce and cut back on product and process engineering. A firm may use time and motion studies to find the "one best way" to produce and lose interest in root cause analysis.[24] While this may work well in the short run, five years from now the company may find competitors making superior products at two-thirds its cost.

For example, Jaikumar compared the development and use of flexible manufacturing systems (FMS) in the United States and in Japan.[25] He found that the U.S. systems had been developed with overly ambitious goals for flexibility, up-time, labor use, etc. These goals were not achieved by the initial designs; the knowledge base was not adequate to make them possible. Yet the projects were often declared complete, and workers with much lower skills were brought in to run the FMS. The result was that the users were afraid to experiment and learn about the systems, and the systems were in fact used in a very inflexible way. In contrast, in the successful Japanese systems, the original developers stayed with the system for the first year or more of operation, and continued to improve it during that time. The results were systems that were very flexible and robust enough to run unattended.

Learn Carefully and Systematically

As we have seen, different stages of knowledge require very different methods of learning. For example, Chew and others recommend sequential use of four different methods of learning about problems that occur during the installation of new technology:

- Vicarious learning—learning from other organizations with similar situations.

---

24. Bohn and Jaikumar (1992).
25. R. Jaikumar, "Postindustrial Manufacturing," *Harvard Business Review*, November-December 1986, pp. 69–76.

- Simulation—building a model of your process and experimenting with the model.
- Prototyping—taking a subset of your process and using it for testing and refining.
- On-line learning—experimenting systematically on the full process.[26]

Many organizations become proficient at only one or a few methods of learning, which makes it difficult for them to deal with variables that are at different stages of knowledge.[27] For example, many plants avoid the use of pilot lines and simulators to pretest process changes.

CONCLUSION

Lord Kelvin, in the 1890s, commented on the value of knowledge:

When you can measure what you are speaking about, and express it in numbers, you know something about it; but when you cannot measure it, when you cannot express it in numbers, your knowledge is of a meager and unsatisfactory kind: it may be the beginning of knowledge, but you have scarcely, in your thoughts, advanced to the stage of science.

In terms of my framework, Kelvin was advocating the value of stage three knowledge (measure) over stage two knowledge (awareness). As I have shown, being able to measure is only the beginning; the stages of knowledge beyond stage three (control, capability, characterization, and know why) give additional power and economic value to a company's processes. The stages-of-knowledge framework provides powerful leverage to efforts to improve processes and conveys information about how to manage. A company can make explicit decisions about which portions of the knowledge tree to pursue most vigorously.

For example, a high-volume, forty-year-old, continuous process was controlled using incremental extensions of the original sensors. These operated on a time scale from seconds to hours. A consultant recognized that the company did not have knowledge of the variables at time scales below a second. Once it learned how to measure events in the millisecond range, a large new subtree of variables became visible. By learning about these variables and their implications for the process, the process engineers were able to reduce quality problems by a factor of three within a few months. Development and exploitation of the new variables continue today.

26. W. B. Chew, D. Leonard-Barton, and R. E. Bohn, "Beating Murphy's Law," *Sloan Management Review*, Spring 1991, pp. 5–16.
27. Learning is obviously of central importance in knowledge-based competition, but detailed analysis is beyond the scope of this paper. A very interesting study of how machine developers become aware of new variables (stage two) through field use is provided by: E. von Hippel and M. Tyre, "How Learning by Doing Is Done: Problem Identification in Novel Process Equipment," *Research Policy*. forthcoming.

18

Putting the Balanced Scorecard to Work

Robert S. Kaplan and David P. Norton

Today's managers recognize the impact that measures have on performance. But they rarely think of measurement as an essential part of their strategy. For example, executives may introduce new strategies and innovative operating processes intended to achieve breakthrough performance, then continue to use the same short-term financial indicators they have used for decades, measures like return-on-investment, sales growth, and operating income. These managers fail not only to introduce new measures to monitor new goals and processes but also to question whether or not their old measures are relevant to the new initiatives.

Effective measurement, however, must be an integral part of the management process. The balanced scorecard, first proposed in the January-February 1992 issue of HBR "The Balanced Scorecard—Measures that Drive Performance", provides executives with a comprehensive framework that translates a company's strategic objectives into a coherent set of performance measures. Much more than a measurement exercise, the balanced scorecard is a management system that can motivate breakthrough improvements in such critical areas as product, process, customer, and market development.

The scorecard presents managers with four different perspectives from which to choose measures. It complements traditional financial indicators with measures of performance for customers, internal processes, and innovation and improvement activities. These measures differ from those traditionally used by companies in a few important ways:

Clearly, many companies already have myriad operational and physical measures for local activities. But these local measures are bottom-up and derived from ad hoc processes. The scorecard's measures, on the other hand, are grounded in an organization's strategic objectives and competitive demands. And, by requir-

Reprinted by permission of *Harvard Business Review.* "Putting the Balanced Scorecard to Work" by Robert S. Kaplan and David P. Norton, September-October 1993, pp. 134–142. Copyright © 1993 by the President and Fellows of Harvard College; all rights reserved.

ing managers to select a limited number of critical indicators within each of the four perspectives, the scorecard helps focus this strategic vision.

In addition, while traditional financial measures report on what happened last period without indicating how managers can improve performance in the next, the scorecard functions as the cornerstone of a company's current *and* future success.

Moreover, unlike conventional metrics, the information from the four perspectives provides balance between external measures like operating income and internal measures like new product development. This balanced set of measures both reveals the trade-offs that managers have already made among performance measures and encourages them to achieve their goals in the future without making trade-offs among key success factors.

Finally, many companies that are now attempting to implement local improvement programs such as process reengineering, total quality, and employee empowerment lack a sense of integration. The balanced scorecard can serve as the focal point for the organization's efforts, defining and communicating priorities to managers, employees, investors, even customers. As a senior executive at one major company said, "Previously, the one-year budget was our primary management planning device. The balanced scorecard is now used as the language, the benchmark against which all new projects and businesses are evaluated."

The balanced scorecard is not a template that can be applied to businesses in general or even industry-wide. Different market situations, product strategies, and competitive environments require different scorecards. Business units devise customized scorecards to fit their mission, strategy, technology, and culture. In fact, a critical test of a scorecard's success is its transparency: From the 15 to 20 scorecard measures, an observer should be able to see through to the business unit's competitive strategy. A few examples will illustrate how the scorecard uniquely combines management and measurement in different companies.

ROCKWATER: RESPONDING TO A CHANGING INDUSTRY

Rockwater, a wholly owned subsidiary of Brown & Root/Halliburton, a global engineering and construction company, is a worldwide leader in underwater engineering and construction. Norman Chambers, hired as CEO in late 1989, knew that the industry's competitive world had changed dramatically. "In the 1970s, we were a bunch of guys in wet suits diving off barges into the North Sea with burning torches," Chambers said. But competition in the subsea contracting business had become keener in the 1980s, and many smaller companies left the industry. In addition, the focus of competition had shifted. Several leading oil companies wanted to develop long-term partnerships with their suppliers rather than choose suppliers based on low-price competition.

With his senior management team, Chambers developed a vision: "As our customers' preferred provider, we shall be the industry leader in providing the highest standards of safety and quality to our clients." He also developed a strategy to implement the vision. The five elements of that strategy were: services that surpass customers' expectations and needs; high levels of customer satisfaction; continuous improvement of safety, equipment reliability, responsiveness, and cost effectiveness; high-quality employees; and realization of shareholder expectations. Those elements were in turn developed into strategic objectives (see the chart "Rockwater's Strategic Objectives"). If, however the strategic objectives were to create value for the company, they had to be translated into tangible goals and actions.

Rockwater's senior management team transformed its vision and strategy into the balanced scorecard's four sets of performance measures (see the chart "Rockwater's Balanced Scorecard"):

Financial Measures: The financial perspective included three measures of importance to the shareholder. Return-on-capital-employed and cash flow reflected preferences for short-term results, while forecast reliability signaled the corporate parent's desire to reduce the historical uncertainty caused by unexpected variations in performance. Rockwater management added two financial measures. Project profitability provided focus on the project as the basic unit for planning and control, and sales backlog helped reduce uncertainty of performance.

Customer Satisfaction: Rockwater wanted to recognize the distinction between its two types of customers: Tier I customers, oil companies that wanted a high value-added relationship, and Tier II customers, those that chose suppliers solely on the basis of price. A price index, incorporating the best available intelligence on competitive position, was included to ensure that Rockwater could still retain Tier II customers' business when required by competitive conditions.

The company's strategy, however, was to emphasize value-based business. An independent organization conducted an annual survey to rank customers' perceptions of Rockwater's services compared to those of its competitors. In addition, Tier I customers were asked to supply monthly satisfaction and performance ratings. Rockwater executives felt that implementing these ratings gave them a direct tie to their customers and a level of market feedback unsurpassed in most industries. Finally, market share by key accounts provided objective evidence that improvements in customer satisfaction were being translated into tangible benefits.

Internal Processes: To develop measures of internal processes, Rockwater executives defined the life cycle of a project from launch (when a customer need was recognized) to completion (when the customer need had been satisfied). Measures were formulated for each of the five business-process phases in this project cycle (see the chart "How Rockwater Fulfills Customer Needs"):

- *Identify:* number of hours spent with prospects discussing new work;
- *Win:* tender success rate;
- *Prepare and Deliver:* project performance effectiveness index, safety/loss control, rework;
- *Closeout:* length of project closeout cycle.

The internal business measures emphasized a major shift in Rockwater's thinking. Formerly, the company stressed performance for each functional department. The new focus emphasized measures that integrated key business processes. The development of a comprehensive and timely index of project performance effectiveness was viewed as a key core competency for the company. Rockwater felt that safety was also a major competitive factor. Internal studies had revealed the indirect costs from an accident could be 5 to 50 times the direct costs. The scorecard included a safety index, derived from a comprehensive safety measurement system, that could identify and classify all undesired events with the potential for harm to people, property, or process.

The Rockwater team deliberated about the choice of metric for the identification stage. It recognized that hours spent with key prospects discussing new work was an input or process measure rather than an output measure. The management team wanted a metric that would clearly communicate to all members of the organization the importance of building relationships with and satisfying customers. The team believed that spending quality time with key customers was a prerequisite for influencing results. This input measure was deliberately chosen to educate employees about the importance of working closely to identify and satisfy customer needs.

Building a Balanced Scorecard

Each organization is unique and so follows its own path for building a balanced scorecard. At Apple and AMD, for instance, a senior finance or business development executive, intimately familiar with the strategic thinking of the top management group, constructed the initial scorecard without extensive deliberations. At Rockwater, however, senior management had yet to define sharply the organization's strategy, much less the key performance levers that drive and measure the strategy's success.

Companies like Rockwater can follow a systematic development plan to create the balanced scorecard and encourage commitment to the scorecard among senior and mid-level managers. What follows is a typical project profile:

1. Preparation

The organization must first define the business unit for which a top-level scorecard is appropriate. In general, a scorecard is appropriate for a business unit that has its own customers, distribution channels, production facilities, and financial performance measures.

2. Interviews: First Round

Each senior manager in the business unit—typically between 6 and 12 executives—receives background material on the balanced scorecard as well as internal documents that describe the company's mission and strategy.

The balanced scorecard facilitator (either an outside consultant or the company executive who organizes the effort) conducts interviews of approximately 90 minutes each with the senior managers to obtain their input on the company's strategic objectives and tentative proposals for balanced scorecard measures. The facilitator may also interview some principal shareholders to learn about their expectations for the business unit's financial performance, as well as some key customers to learn about their performance expectations for top-ranked suppliers.

3. Executive Workshop: First Round

The top management team is brought together with the facilitator to undergo the process of developing the scorecard (see chart "Begin by Linking Measurements to Strategy"). During the workshop, the group debates the proposed mission and strategy statements until a consensus is reached. The group then moves from the mission and strategy statement to answer the question, "If I succeed with my vision and strategy; how will my performance differ for shareholders; for customers; for internal business processes; for my ability to innovate, grow, and improve?"

Videotapes of interviews with shareholder and customer representatives can be shown to provide an external perspective to the deliberations. After defining the key success factors, the group formulates a preliminary balanced scorecard containing operational measures for the strategic objectives. Frequently, the group proposes far more than four or five measures for each perspective. At this time, narrowing the choices is not critical, though straw votes can be taken to see whether or not some of the proposed measures are viewed as low priority by the group.

4. Interviews: Second Round

The facilitator reviews, consolidates, and documents the output from the executive workshop and interviews each senior executive about the tentative balanced scorecard. The facilitator also seeks opinions about issues involved in implementing the scorecard.

5. Executive Workshop: Second Round

A second workshop, involving the senior management team, their direct subordinates, and a larger number of middle managers, debates the organization's vision, strategy statements, and the tentative scorecard. The participants, working in groups, comment on the proposed measures, link the various change programs under way to the measures, and start to develop an implementations plan. At the end of the workshop, participants are asked to formulate stretch objectives for each of the proposed measures, including targeted rates of improvement.

6. Executive Workshop: Third Round

The senior executive team meets to come to a final consensus on the vision, objectives, and measurements developed in the first two workshops; to develop stretch targets for each measure on the scorecard; and to identify preliminary action programs to achieve the targets. The team must agree on an implementation program, including communicating the scorecard to employees, integrating the scorecard into a management philosophy, and developing an information system to support the scorecard.

7. Implementation

A newly formed team develops an implementation plan for the scorecard, including linking the measures to databases and information systems, communicating the balanced scorecard throughout the organization, and encouraging and facilitating the development of second-level metrics for decentralized units. As a result of this process, for instance, an entirely new executive information system that links top-level business unit metrics down through shop floor and site-specific operational measures could be developed.

8. Periodic Reviews

Each quarter or month, a blue book of information on the balanced scorecard measures is prepared for both top management review and discussion with managers of decentralized divisions and departments. The balanced scorecard metrics are revisited annually as part of the strategic planning, goal setting, and resource allocation processes.

Innovation and Improvement: The innovation and learning objectives are intended to drive improvement in financial, customer, and internal process performance. At Rockwater, such improvements came from product and service innovation that would create new sources of revenue and market expansion, as well as from continuous improvement in internal work processes. The first objective was measured by percent revenue from new services and the second objective by a continuous improvement index that represented the rate of improvement of several key operational measures, such as safety and rework. But in order to drive both product/service innovation and operational improvements, a supportive climate of empowered, motivated employees was believed necessary. A staff attitude survey and a metric for the number of employee suggestions measured whether or not such a climate was being created. Finally, revenue per employee measured the outcomes of employee commitment and training programs.

The balanced scorecard has helped Rockwater's management emphasize a process view of operations, motivate its employees, and incorporate client feedback into its operations. It developed a consensus on the necessity of creating partnerships with key customers, the importance of order-of-magnitude reductions in safety-related incidents, and the need for improved management at every phase of multiyear projects. Chambers sees the scorecard as an invaluable tool to help his company ultimately achieve its mission: to be number one in the industry.

APPLE COMPUTER: ADJUSTING
LONG-TERM PERFORMANCE

Apple Computer developed a balanced scorecard to focus senior management on a strategy that would expand discussions beyond gross margin, return on equity, and market share. A small steering committee, intimately familiar with the deliberations and strategic thinking of Apple's Executive Management Team, chose to concentrate on measurement categories within each of the four perspectives and to select multiple measurements within each category. For the financial perspective, Apple emphasized shareholder value; for the customer perspective, market share and customer satisfaction; for the internal process perspective, core competencies; and, finally, for the innovation and improvement perspective, employee attitudes. Apple's management stressed these categories in the following order:

Customer Satisfaction: Historically, Apple had been a technology- and product-focused company that competed by designing better computers. Customer satisfaction metrics are just being introduced to orient employees toward becoming a customer-driven company. J. D. Power & Associates, a customer-survey company, now works for the computer industry. However, because it recognized that its customer base was not homogeneous, Apple felt that it had to go beyond J. D. Power & Associates and develop its own independent surveys in order to track its key market segments around the world.

Core Competencies: Company executives wanted employees to be highly focused on a few key competencies: for example, user-friendly interfaces, powerful software architectures, and effective distribution systems. However, senior executives recognized that measuring performance along these competency dimensions could be difficult. As a result, the company is currently experimenting with obtaining quantitative measures of these hard-to-measure competencies.

Employee Commitment and Alignment: Apple conducts a comprehensive employee survey in each of its organizations every two years; surveys of randomly selected employees are performed more frequently. The survey questions are concerned with how well employees understand the company's strategy as well as whether or not they are asked to deliver results that are consistent with that strategy. The results of the survey are displayed in terms of both the actual level of employee responses and the overall trend of responses.

Market Share: Achieving a critical threshold of market share was important to senior management not only for the obvious sales growth benefits but also to attract and retain software developers to Apple platforms.

Shareholder Value: Shareholder value is included as a performance indicator, even though this measure is a result—not a driver—of performance The measure is included to offset the previous emphasis on gross margin and sales growth, measures that ignored the investments required today to generate growth for tomorrow. In contrast, the shareholder value metric quantifies the impact of proposed investments for business creation and development. The majority of Apple's business is organized on a functional basis—sales, product design, and worldwide manufacturing and operations—so shareholder value can be calculated only for the entire company instead of at a decentralized level. The measure, however, helps senior managers in each major organizational unit assess the impact of their activities on the entire company's valuation and evaluate new business ventures.

While these five performance indicators have only recently been developed, they have helped Apple's senior managers focus their strategy in a number of ways. First of all, the balanced scorecard at Apple serves primarily as a planning device, instead of as a control device. To put it another way, Apple uses the measures to adjust the "long wave" of corporate performance, not to drive operating changes. Moreover, the metrics at Apple, with the exception of shareholder value, can be driven both horizontally and vertically into each functional organization. Considered vertically, each individual measure can be broken down into its component parts in order to evaluate how each part contributes to the functioning of the whole. Thought of horizontally, the measures can identify how, for example, design and manufacturing contribute to an area such as customer satisfaction. In addition, Apple has found that its balanced scorecard has helped develop a language of measurable outputs for how to launch and leverage programs.

The five performance indicators at Apple are benchmarked against best-in-class organizations. Today they are used to build business plans and are incorporated into senior executives' compensation plans.

The Scorecard's Impact on External Reporting

Several managers have asked whether or not the balanced scorecard is applicable to external reporting. If the scorecard is indeed a driver of long-term performance, shouldn't this information be relevant to the investment community?

In fact, the scorecard does not translate easily to the investment community. A scorecard makes sense primarily for business units and divisions with a well-defined strategy. Most companies have several divisions, each with its own mission and strategy, whose scorecards cannot be aggregated into an overall corporate scorecard. And if the scorecard does indeed provide a transparent vision into a unit's strategy, then the information, even the measures being used, might be highly sensitive data that could reveal much of value to competitors. But most important, as a relatively recent innovation, the scorecard would benefit from several years of experimentation within companies before it becomes a systematic part of reporting to external constituencies.

Even if the scorecard itself were better suited to external reporting, at present the financial community itself shows little interest in making the change from financial to strategic reporting. One company president has found the outside financial community leery of the principles that ground the scorecard: "We use the scorecard more with our customers than with our investors. The financial community is skeptical about long-term indicators and occasionally tells us about some empirical evidence of a negative correlation between stock prices and attention to total quality and internal processes."

However, the investment community has begun to focus on some key metrics of new product performance. Could this be an early sign of a shift to strategic thinking?

ADVANCED MICRO DEVICES: CONSOLIDATING STRATEGIC INFORMATION

Advanced Micro Devices (AMD), a semiconductor company, executed a quick and easy transition to a balanced scorecard. It already had a clearly defined mission, strategy statement, and shared understanding among senior executives about its competitive niche. It also had many performance measures from many different sources and information systems. The balanced scorecard consolidated and focused these diverse measures into a quarterly briefing book that contained seven sections: financial measures; customer-based measures, such as on-time delivery, lead time, and performance-to-schedule; measures of critical business processes in wafer fabrication; assembly and test; new product development; process technology development (e.g., submicron etching precision); and, finally, measures for corporate quality. In addition, organizational learning was measured by imposing targeted rates of improvements for key operating parameters, such as cycle time and yields by process.

At present, AMD sees its scorecard as a systematic repository for strategic information that facilitates long-term trend analysis for planning and performance evaluation.

DRIVING THE PROCESS OF CHANGE

The experiences of these companies and others reveal that the balanced scorecard is most successful when it is used to give the process of change. Rockwater, for instance, came into existence after the merger of two different organizations. Employees came from different cultures, spoke different languages, and had different operating experiences and backgrounds. The balanced scorecard helped the company focus on what it had to do well in order to become the industry leader.

Similarly, Joseph De Feo, chief executive of Service Businesses, one of the three operating divisions of Barclays Bank, had to transform what had been a captive, internal supplier of services into a global competitor. The scorecard highlighted areas where, despite apparent consensus on strategy, there still was considerable disagreement about how to make the strategy operational. With the help of the scorecard, the division eventually achieved consensus concerning the highest priority areas for achievement and improvement and identified additional areas that needed attention, such as quality and productivity. De Feo assessed the impact of the scorecard, saying, "It helped us to drive major change to become more market oriented, throughout our organization. It provided a shared understanding of our goals and what it took to achieve them."

Analog Devices, a semiconductor company, served as the prototype for the balanced scorecard and now uses it each year to update the targets and goals for division managers. Jerry Fishman, president of Analog, said, "At the beginning, the scorecard drove significant and considerable change. It still does when we focus attention on particular areas, such as the gross margins on new products. But its main impact today is to help sustain programs that our people have been working on for years." Recently, the company has been attempting to integrate the scorecard metrics with *hoshin* planning, a procedure that concentrates an entire company on achieving one or two key objectives each year. Analog's hoshin objectives have included customer service and new product development, for which measures already exist on the company's scorecard.

But the scorecard isn't always the impetus for such dramatic change. For example, AMD's scorecard has yet to have a significant impact because company management didn't use it to drive the change process. Before turning to the scorecard, senior managers had already formulated and gained consensus for the company's mission, strategy, and key performance measures. AMD competes in a single industry segment. The top 12 managers are intimately familiar with the markets, engineering, technology, and other key levers in this segment. The summary and aggregate information in the scorecard were neither new nor surprising to them. And managers of decentralized production units also already had a significant amount of information about their own operations. The scorecard did enable them to see the breadth and totality of company operations, enhancing their ability to become better managers for the entire company. But, on balance, the scorecard could only encapsulate knowledge that managers in general had already learned.

AMD's limited success with the balanced scorecard demonstrates that the scorecard has its greatest impact when used to drive a change process. Some companies link compensation of senior executives to achieving stretch targets for the scorecard measures. Most are attempting to translate the scorecard into operational measures that become the focus for improvement activities in local units. The scorecard is not just a measurement system; it is a management system to motivate breakthrough competitive performance.

19

The Options Approach to Capital Investment

Avinash K. Dixit and Robert S. Pindyck

Companies make capital investments in order to create and exploit profit opportunities. Investments in research and development, for example, can lead to patents and new technologies that open up those opportunities. The commercialization of patents and technologies through construction of new plants and expenditures for marketing can allow companies to take advantage of profit opportunities. Somewhat less obviously, companies that shut down money-losing operations are also investing: The payments they make to extract themselves from contractual agreements, such as severance pay for employees, are the initial expenditure. The payoff is the reduction of future losses.

Opportunities are options—rights but not obligations to take some action in the future. Capital investments, then, are essentially about options. Over the past several years, economists including ourselves have explored that basic insight and found that thinking of investments as options substantially changes the theory and practice of decision making about capital investment. Traditionally, business schools have taught managers to operate on the premise that investment decisions can be reversed if conditions change or if they cannot be reversed, that they are now-or-never propositions. But as soon as you begin thinking of investment opportunities as options, the premise changes. Irreversibility, uncertainty, and the choice of timing alter the investment decision in critical ways.

The purpose of our article is to examine the shortcomings of the conventional approaches to decision-making about investment and to present a better framework for thinking about capital investment decisions. Any theory of investment needs to address the following question: How should a corporate manager facing uncertainty over future market conditions decide whether to invest in a new project? Most business schools teach future managers a simple rule to apply to such problems. First, calculate the present value of the expected stream of cash

Reprinted by permission of *Harvard Business Review*. "The Options Approach to Capital Investment" by Avinash K. Divit and Robert S. Pindyck, May-June 1995, pp. 105–115. Copyright © 1995 by the President and Fellows of Harvard College; all rights reserved.

that the investment will generate. Then, calculate the present value of tbe stream of expenditures required to undertake the project. And, finally, determine the difference between the two—the net present value (NPV) of the investment. If it's greater than zero, the rule tells the manager to go ahead and invest.

Of course, putting NPV into practice requires managers to resolve some key issues early on. How should you estimate the expected stream of operating profits from the investment? How do you factor in taxes and inflation? And, perhaps most critical, what discount rate or rates should you use? In working out those issues, managers sometimes run into complications. But the basic approach is fairly straightforward: calculating the net present value of an investment project and determining whether it is positive or negative.

Unfortunately, this basic principle is often wrong. Although the NPV rule is relatively easy to apply, it is built on faulty assumptions. It assumes one of two things: either that the investment is reversible (in other words, that it can somehow be undone and the expenditures recovered should market conditions turn out to be worse than anticipated); or that, if the investment is irreversible, it is a now-or-never proposition (if the company does not make the investment now, it will lose the opportunity forever).

Although it is true that some investment decisions fall into those categories, most don't. In most cases, investments are irreversible and, in reality, capable of being delayed. A growing body of research shows that the ability to delay an irreversible investment expenditure can profoundly affect the decision to invest. Ability to delay also undermines the validity of the net present value rule. Thus, for analyzing investment decisions, we need to establish a richer framework, one that enables managers to address the issues of irreversibility, uncertainty, and timing more directly.

Instead of assuming that investments are either reversible or that they cannot be delayed, the recent research on investment stresses the fact that companies have *opportunities* to invest and that they must decide how to exploit those opportunities most effectively. The research is based on an important analogy with financial options. A company with an opportunity to invest is holding something much like a financial call option: It has the right but not the obligation to buy an asset (namely, the entitlement to the stream of profits from the project) at a future time of its choosing. When a company makes an irreversible investment expenditure, it "exercises," in effect, its call option. So the problem of how to exploit an investment opportunity boils down to this: How does the company exercise that option optimally? Academics and financial professionals have been studying the valuation and optimal exercising of financial options for the past two decades.[1] Thus we can draw from a large body of knowledge about financial options.

---

1. For an overview of financial options and their valuation, see John C. Cox and Mark Rubinstein, *Options Markets* (Englewood Cliffs, N.J.: Prentice-Hall, 1985); John C. Hull, *Options, Futures, and Other Derivative Securities* (Englewood, Cliffs, N.J.: Prentice-Hall, 1989), or Hans R. Stoll and Robert E. Whaley, *Futures and Options: Theory and Applications* (Cincinnati, Ohio: South-Western Publishing Co., 1993).

The recent research on investment offers a number of valuable insights into how managers can evaluate opportunities, and it highlights a basic weakness of the NPV rule. When a company exercises its option by making an irreversible investment, it effectively "kills" the option. In other words, by deciding to go ahead with an expenditure, the company gives up the possibility of waiting for new information that might affect the desirability or timing of the investment; it cannot disinvest should market conditions change adversely. The lost option value is an opportunity cost that must be included as part of the cost of the investment. Thus the simple NPV rule needs to be modified: Instead of just being positive, the present value of the expected stream of cash from a project must exceed the cost of the project by an amount equal to the value of keeping the investment option alive.[2]

Numerous studies have shown that the cost of investing in an opportunity can be large and that investment rules that ignore the expense can lead the investor astray. The opportunity cost is highly sensitive to uncertainty over the future value of the project; as a result, new economic conditions that may affect the perceived riskiness of future cash flows can have a large impact on investment spending—much larger than, say, a change in interest rates. Viewing investment as an option puts greater emphasis on the role of risk and less emphasis on interest rates and other financial variables.

Another problem with the conventional NPV rule is that it ignores the value of creating options. Sometimes an investment that appears uneconomical when viewed in isolation may, in fact, create options that enable the company to undertake other investments in the future should market conditions turn favorable. An example is research and development. By not accounting properly for the options that R&D investments may yield, naive NPV analyses lead companies to invest too little.

Option value has important implications for managers as they think about their investment decisions. For example, it is often highly desirable to delay an investment decision and wait for more information about market conditions, even though a standard analysis indicates that the investment is economical right now. On the other hand, there may be situations in which uncertainty over future market conditions should prompt a company to speed up certain investments. Such is the case when the investments create additional options that give a company the ability (although not the obligation) to do additional future investing. R&D could lead to patents, for example; land purchases could lead to development of mineral reserves. A company might also choose to speed up investments that would yield information and thereby reduce uncertainty.

As a practical matter, many managers seem to understand already that there is something wrong with the simple NPV rule as it is taught—that there is a value to waiting for more information and that this value is not reflected in the standard calculation. In fact, managers often require that an NPV be more than merely

---

2. Of course, one can always redefine NPV by subtracting from the conventional calculation the opportunity cost of exercising the option to invest and then saying that the rule "invest if NPV is positive" holds. But to do so is to accept our criticism. To highlight the importance of valuing the option, we prefer to keep it separate from the conventional NPV. But if others prefer to continue to use positive NPV terminology, they should be careful to include all relevant option values in their definition of NPV.

positive. In many cases, they insist that it be positive even when it is calculated using a discount rate that is much higher than their company's cost of capital. Some people have argued that when managers insist on extremely high rates of return they are being myopic. But we think there is another explanation. It may be that managers understand a company's options are valuable and that it is often desirable to keep those options open.

In order to understand the thought processes such managers may be using, it is useful to step back and examine the NPV rule and how it is used. For anyone analyzing an investment decision using NPV, two basic issues need to be addressed: first, how to determine the expected stream of profits that the proposed project will generate and the expected stream of costs required to implement the project; and, second, how to choose the discount rate for the purpose of calculating net present value. Textbooks don't have a lot to say about the best way to calculate the profit and cost streams. In practice, managers often seek a consensus projection or use an average of high, medium, and low estimates. But however they determine the expected streams of profits and costs, managers are often unaware of making an implicit faulty assumption. The assumption is that the construction or development will begin at a fixed point in time, usually the present. In effect, the NPV rule assumes a fixed scenario in which a company starts and completes a project, which then generates a cash flow during some expected lifetime—without any contingencies. Most important, the rule anticipates no contingency for delaying the project or abandoning it if market conditions turn sour. Instead, the NPV rule compares investing today with never investing. A more useful comparison, however, would examine a range of possibilities: investing today, or waiting and perhaps investing next year, or waiting longer and perhaps investing in two years, and so on.

As for selecting the discount rate, a low discount rate gives more weight to cash flows that a project is expected to earn in the distant future. On the other hand, a high discount rate gives distant cash flows much less weight and hence makes the company appear more myopic in its evaluation of potential investment projects.

Introductory corporate-finance courses give the subject of selecting discount rates considerable attention. Students are generally taught that the correct discount rate is simply the opportunity cost of capital for the particular project—that is, the expected rate of return that could be earned from an investment of similar risk. In principle, the opportunity cost would reflect the nondiversifiable, or *systematic,* risk that is associated with the particular project. That risk might have characteristics that differ from those of the company's other individual projects or from its average investment activity. In practice, however, the opportunity cost of a specific project may be hard to measure. As a result, students learn that a company's weighted average cost of capital (WACC) is a reasonable substitute. The WACC offers a good approximation as long as the company's projects do not differ greatly from one another in their nondiversifiable risk.[3]

---

3. For a more comprehensive discussion of the standard techniques of capital budgeting, see a corporate finance textbook such as Richard A. Brealey and Stewart C. Myers, *Principles of Corporate Finance* (New York: McGraw-Hill, 1991).

Irreversibility and Uncertainty in Everyday Life

The decisions that individuals face in their personal lives do not typically involve billions of dollars. In many cases, the highest costs and the biggest benefits are emotional. However, we have found that the option view of investment can be applied fruitfully to all sorts of personal choices and that presenting examples that are "closer to home" can help individuals get a firmer grasp of the central ideas.

For example, one's career choice is a major and largely irreversible decision, which is made in the face of considerable uncertainty about the future prospects of one's chosen sector, one's skill in it, one's future enjoyment of it, and so on. Examples of large-scale mistakes are legendary. In the 1950s, many bright students chose physics as an exciting and rewarding career, only to find that a surplus of physicists developed in the 1970s. There are signs that the same may happen to today's medical students during the next two decades.

The option view suggests appropriate caution. First, it suggests proceeding in steps. For example, instead of committing oneself in the freshman year of college to a specialized program that leads only to medical school, one should follow a more general program to acquire a more flexible set of skills and find out more about one's own tastes. As one acquires that information and gathers more data about the likely career prospects in medicine versus, say, chemical engineering, one can gradually fine-tune decisions about the appropriate direction. Second, one should not take the final and irreversible plunge into a very specialized line unless the rate of return to the investment is sufficiently greater than the cost, with high enough rewards to justify killing the option of flexibility.

Marriage is another decision that can be analyzed in the same manner. It is costly to reverse, and there is significant uncertainty about future happiness or misery. Therefore, one should enter into it with due caution and only when the expected return is sufficiently high. The criteria should become stiffer as the social costs of separation increase: for example, in some religions or cultures. Courtship is the equivalent of exploratory or R&D investment. Even if the expected return is not very high, one should be willing to undertake courtship because it creates a valuable option—namely the opportunity but not the obligation to follow up or not to, according to the information revealed by the initial steps.

Most students leave business school with what appears to be a simple and powerful tool for making investment decisions: Estimate the expected cash flows for a project, use the company's weighted average cost of capital (perhaps adjusted up or down to reflect the risk characteristics of the particular project) to calculate the project's NPV; and then, if the result is positive, proceed with the investment.

But both academic research and anecdotal evidence bear out time and again the hesitancy of managers to apply NPV in the manner they have been taught. For example, in a 1987 study, Harvard economist Lawrence Summers found that companies were using hurdle rates ranging from 8 percent to 30 percent, with a median of 15 percent and a mean of 17 percent. Allowing for the deductibility of interest expenses, the nominal interest rate during the period in question was only

4 percent, and the real rate was close to zero. Although the hurdle rate appropriate for investment with a nondiversifiable risk usually exceeds the riskless rate, it
is not enough to justify the large discrepancies found. More recent studies have
confirmed that managers regularly and consciously set hurdle rates that are often
three or four times their weighted average cost of capital.[4]

Evidence from corporate disinvestment decisions is also consistent with that
analysis. In many industries, companies stay in business and absorb large operating losses for long periods, even though a conventional NPV analysis would indicate that it makes sense to close down a factory or go out of business. Prices can
fall far below average variable cost without inducing significant disinvestment or
exit from the business. In the mid-1980s, for example, many U.S. farmers saw
prices drop drastically, as did producers of copper, aluminum, and other metals.
Most did not disinvest, and their behavior can be explained easily once irreversibility and option value are taken into account. Closing a plant or going out
of business would have meant an irreversible loss of tangible and intangible capital: The specialized skills that workers had developed would have disappeared as
they dispersed to different industries and localities, brand name recognition
would have faded, and so on. If market conditions had improved soon after and
operations could have resumed profitably, the cost of reassembling the capital
would have been high. Continuing to operate keeps the capital intact and preserves the option to resume profitable production later. The option is valuable,
and, therefore, companies may quite rationally choose to retain it, even at the cost
of losing money in the meantime.

The slow response of U.S. imports to changes in the exchange rate during
the early 1980s is another example of how managers deviate from the NPV rule.
From mid-1980 to the end of 1984, the real value of the U.S. dollar increased by
about 50 percent. As a result, the ability of foreign companies to compete in the
U.S. market soared. But the volume of imports did not begin to rise substantially
until the beginning of 1983, when the stronger dollar was already well established. In the first quarter of 1985, the dollar began to weaken; by the end of
1987, it had almost declined to its 1978 level. However, import volume did not
decline for another two years; in fact, it rose a little. Once established in the U.S.
market, foreign companies were slow to scale back or close their export operations when the exchange rate moved unfavorably. That behavior might seem inconsistent with traditional investment theory, but it is easy to understand in the
light of irreversibility and option value: The companies were willing to suffer tem-

4. See Lawrence H. Summers, "Investment Incentives and the Discounting of Depreciation Allowances," in *The Effects of Taxation on Capital Accumulation*, ed. Martin Feldstein (University of Chicago Press, 1987) p. 300; James M. Poterba and Lawrence H. Summers, "Time Horizons of
American Firms: New Evidence from a Survey of CEOs" (MIT Working Paper, October 1991), Michael L. Dertouzos, Richard K. Lester, Robert M. Solow, and the MIT Commission on Industrial
Productivity, *Made in America* (Harper Paperback, 1990) p. 61; and Robert H. Hayes and David A.
Garvin, "Managing As If Tomorrow Mattered," HBR May-June 1982, pp. 70–9.

porary losses to retain their foothold in the U.S. market and keep alive their option to operate profitably in the future if the value of the dollar rose.

So far, we have focused on managers who seem shortsighted when they make investment decisions, and we have offered an explanation based on the value of the option for waiting and investing later. But some managers appear to override the NPV rule in the opposite direction. For example, entrepreneurs sometimes invest in seemingly risky projects that would be difficult to justify by a conventional NPV calculation using an appropriately risk-adjusted cost of capital. Such projects generally involve R&D or some other type of exploratory investment. Again, we suggest that option theory provides a helpful explanation because the goal of the investments is to reveal information about technological possibilities, production costs, or market potential. Armed with this new information, entrepreneurs can decide whether to proceed with production. In other words, the exploratory investment creates a valuable option. Once the value of the option is reflected in the returns from the initial investment, it may turn out to have been justified, even though a conventional NPV calculation would not have found it attractive.

Before proceeding, we should elaborate on what we mean by the notions of irreversibility, ability to delay an investment, and option to invest. What makes an investment expenditure irreversible? And how do companies obtain their options to invest?

Investment expenditures are irreversible when they are specific to a company or to an industry. For example, most investments in marketing and advertising are company specific and cannot be recovered. They are sunk costs. A steel plant, on the other hand, is industry specific in that it cannot be used to produce anything but steel. One might think that, because in principle the plant could be sold to another steel producer, investment in a plant is recoverable and is not a sunk cost. But that is not necessarily true. If the industry is reasonably competitive, then the value of the plant will be approximately the same for all steel companies, so there is little to be gained from selling it. The potential purchaser of the steel plant will realize that the seller has been unable to make money at current prices and considers the plant a bad investment. If the potential buyer agrees that it's a bad investment, the owner's ability to sell the plant will not be worth much. Therefore, an investment in a steel plant (or any other industry-specific capital project) should be viewed largely as a sunk cost: that is, irreversible.

Even investments that are not company or industry specific are often partly irreversible because buyers of used equipment, unable to evaluate the quality of an item, will generally offer to pay a price that corresponds to the average quality in the market. Sellers who know the quality of the item they are selling will resist unloading above-average merchandise at a reduced price. The average quality of used equipment available in the market will go down and, therefore, so will the market price. Thus cars, trucks, office equipment, and computers (items that are not industry specific and can be sold to buyers in other industries) are apt to have resale values that are well below their original purchase costs, even if they are almost new.

Irreversibility can also arise because of government regulations, institutional arrangements, or differences in corporate culture. For example, capital controls may make it impossible for foreign (or domestic) investors to sell their assets and reallocate their funds. By the same token, investments in new workers may be partly irreversible because of the high costs of hiring, training, and firing. Hence, most major investments are to a large extent irreversible.

The recognition that capital investment decisions can be irreversible gives the ability to delay investments added significance. In reality, companies do not always have the opportunity to delay their investments. For example, strategic considerations can make it imperative for a business to invest quickly in order to preempt investment by existing or potential competitors. In most cases, though, it is at least feasible to delay. There may be a cost—the risk of entry by other companies or the loss of cash flows—but the cost can be weighed against the benefits of waiting for new information. And those benefits are often substantial.

We have argued that an irreversible investment opportunity is like a financial call option. The holder of the call option has the right, for a specified period, to pay an exercise price and to receive in return an asset—for example, a share of stock—that has some value. Exercising the option is irreversible; although the asset can be sold to another investor, one cannot retrieve the option or the money that was paid to exercise it. Similarly, a company with an investment opportunity has the option to spend money now or in the future (the exercise price) in return for an asset of some value (the project). Again, the asset can be sold to another company, but the investment itself is irreversible. As with the financial call option, the option to make a capital investment is valuable in part because it is impossible to know the future value of the asset obtained by investing. If the asset rises in value, the net payoff from investing increases. If the value declines, the company can decide not to invest and will lose only what it has spent to obtain the investment opportunity. As long as there are *some* contingencies under which the company would prefer not to invest, that is, when there is some probability that the investment would result in a loss, the opportunity to delay the decision—and thus to keep the option alive—has value. The question, then, is when to exercise the option. The choice of the most appropriate time is the essence of the optimal investment decision.

Recognizing that an investment opportunity is like a financial call option can help managers understand the crucial role uncertainty plays in the timing of capital investment decisions. With a financial call option, the more volatile the price of the stock on which the option is written, the more valuable the option and the greater the incentive to wait and keep the option alive rather than exercise it. This is true because of the asymmetry in the option's net payoffs: The higher the stock price rises, the greater the net payoff from exercising the option; however, if the stock price falls, one can lose only what one paid for the option.

The same goes for capital investment opportunities. The greater the uncertainty over the potential profitability of the investment, the greater the value of the opportunity and the greater the incentive to wait and to keep the opportunity alive rather than exercise it by investing at once. Of course, uncertainty also plays a role in the conventional NPV rule—the fact that a risk is nondiversifiable creates an uncertainty that is added on to the discount rate used to compute present values. But in the option view of investment, uncertainty is far more important and fundamental. A small increase in uncertainty (nondiversifiable or otherwise) can lead managers to delay some investments (those that involve the exercising of options, such as the construction of a factory). At the same time, uncertainty can prompt managers to accelerate other investments (those that generate options or reveal information, such as R&D programs).

In addition to understanding the role of irreversibility and uncertainty, it is also important to understand how companies obtain their investment opportunities (their options to invest) in the first place. Sometimes investment opportunities result from patents or from ownership of land or natural resources. In such cases, the opportunities are probably the result of earlier investments. Generally, however, investment opportunities flow from a company's managerial resources, technological knowledge, reputation, market position, and possible scale, each of which may have been built up gradually. Such resources enable the company to undertake in a productive way investments that individuals or other companies cannot undertake.

Regardless of where a company gets its options to invest, the options are valuable. Indeed, a substantial part of the market value of most companies can be attributed to their options to invest and grow in the future, as opposed to the capital they already have in place. That is particularly true for companies in very volatile and unpredictable industries, such as electronics, telecommunications, and biotechnology. Most of the economic and financial theory of investment has focused on how companies should (and do) exercise their options to invest. But managers also need to understand how their companies can obtain investment opportunities in the first place. The knowledge will help them devise better long-term competitive strategies to determine how to focus and direct their R&D, how much to bid for mineral rights, how early to stake out competitive positions, and so on.

To illustrate the implications of the option theory of investment and the problems inherent in the traditional net present value rule, let us work through the process of making a capital investment decision at a hypothetical pharmaceutical company.

Suppose that you are the CEO of a company considering the development and production of a new drug. Both the costs and the revenues from the venture are highly uncertain. The costs will depend on, among other things, the purity of the output of the chemical process and the compound's overall effectiveness. The revenues will depend on the company's ability to find a principal market for the compound (and for whatever secondary uses might be discovered) and the time frame within which rival companies are able to introduce similar products.

Suppose that you must decide whether to make an initial investment of $15 million in R&D. You realize that later, if you decide to continue the project, additional money will have to be invested in a production facility. There are three possible scenarios for the cost of production: low ($40 million), middle ($80 million), and high ($120 million). To keep matters simple, we will assume that each of the scenarios is equally likely (in other words, that each has a $\frac{1}{3}$ probability of occurring). Let us also assume that there are two equally likely cases for the revenue (probability $\frac{1}{2}$ each): low ($50 million) and high ($130 million). To focus on the question of how uncertainty and option values modify the usual NPV analysis and to keep the example simple, we will also assume that the time frame is short enough that the usual discounting to reflect the time value of money can be ignored.

Should you make the $15 million investment in R&D? First, let us analyze the problem by using a simple NPV approach. The expected value (i.e., the probability-weighted average) of the cost of the production facility is ($\frac{1}{3}$ × $40 million) + ($\frac{1}{3}$ × $80 million) + ($\frac{1}{3}$ × $120 million) = $80 million. Likewise, the expected value of the revenue is ($\frac{1}{2}$ × $50 million) + ($\frac{1}{2}$ × $130 million) = $90 million. Therefore, the expected value of the operating profit is $10 million, which does not justify the expenditure of $15 million on R&D. So the conventional thinking would kill the project at the outset.

However, suppose that by doing the R&D, you are able to narrow the uncertainty by finding out which of the three possibilities for the cost of the production facility is closest to reality. After learning about the cost, you would be able to make a decision to go ahead and continue the project or to drop it. Thus the $15 million you invest in R&D creates an option—a right with no obligation to proceed with the actual production and marketing.

For a moment, we will put aside the market uncertainty and suppose that the revenue will always be $90 million. If the high-cost ($120 million) scenario is the one that materializes, you will decide not to proceed with the production, and your operating profit will be zero. In the other two cases, however, you will proceed. The operating profit is $90 million – $80 million = $10 million in the middle-cost case and $90 million – $40 million = $50 million in the low-cost case. The probability-weighted average of your operating profit across all three possible outcomes is ($\frac{1}{3}$ × 0) + ($\frac{1}{3}$ × $10 million) + ($\frac{1}{3}$ × $50 million) = $20 million. That exceeds your research and development cost of $15 million, and, therefore, the investment in R&D would be justified.

The logic shows that an action to *create* an option should be valued more highly than a naive NPV approach would suggest. The gap between the naive calculation and the correct one arises because the option itself is valuable. You can exercise it selectively when doing so is to your advantage, and you can let it lapse when exercising it would be unprofitable. The amount that an option should be valued over and above the $10 million expected profit (calculated on the assumption of immediate go-ahead) depends on the sizes and the probabilities of the losses that you are able to avoid.

Now let us reintroduce the notion of uncertainty with regard to the expected revenue. Suppose that you have found out that the middle-cost scenario ($80 million) is the reality. If you need to make a go or no-go decision about production at this point, you will choose to proceed because the expected revenue of ($\frac{1}{2}$ × $130 million) + ($\frac{1}{2}$ × $50 million) = $90 million exceeds the production cost of $80 million, resulting in an operating profit of $10 million. But suppose you can postpone the production decision until you have found out the true market potential. By waiting, you can choose to go ahead only if the revenue is high, and you can avoid the loss-making case where the revenue turns out to be low. If revenue is high (which occurs with probability $\frac{1}{2}$), you will earn an operating profit of $130 million – $80 million = $50 million, and if revenue is low (also probability $\frac{1}{2}$), you will earn zero, for an average or expected value of $25 million, which is more than the $10 million you would get if you went ahead at once.

Here the opportunity to proceed with production is like a call option. Making a go or no-go decision amounts to exercising that option. If you can identify some eventualities that would cause you to rethink a go-ahead decision (such as a drop in market demand for your product), then the ability to wait and avoid those eventualities is valuable: The option has a time value or a holding premium. The fact that the option is "in the money" (going ahead would yield a positive NPV) does not necessarily mean that you should exercise the option (in this case, proceeding with production). Instead, you should wait until the option is deeper in the money—that is, until the net present value of going ahead is large enough to offset the loss of the value of the option.

In this example, we have intentionally left out any explicit cost of waiting. But you can easily include potential waiting costs in the calculation. Suppose that while you wait to gauge the market potential, a rival will grab $20 million worth of your anticipated revenues. The revenues under your most favorable scenario will be only $110 million and under the unfavorable one only $30 million. Now, if you wait, you can expect an outcome of $110 million – $80 million = $30 million with probability and an outcome of zero with probability $\frac{1}{2}$, for an expected value of $15 million. That is still better than the $10 million you get if you go ahead at once.

There's an important lesson here: Just as an action that creates an option needs to be valued more than the NPV analysis would indicate, an action that exercises or uses up an option should be valued less than a simple NPV approach would suggest. The reason is that the option itself is valuable. You can exercise an option selectively when the action is to your advantage, or you can let it lapse when such a course would be unprofitable. Again, the extra value gain depends on the sizes and the probabilities of the losses you are able to avoid.

It is even possible to put the revenue uncertainty and the cost uncertainty together. Thus if the R&D investment reveals that costs will be at the high end, you should again wait for the resolution of the revenue uncertainty before you proceed, earning $\frac{1}{2} \times$ ($130 million – $120 million) = $5 million. If the costs fall in the middle, it is best to wait, as we saw above; the expected operating profit will be $25 million. If the cost is at the low end ($40 million), however, the operating profit is positive at both revenue levels. In that case, it is best to proceed with production at once because the expected profit is ($\frac{1}{2} \times$ $130 million) + ($\frac{1}{2} \times$ $50 million) – $40 million = $50 million. The proper calculation for NPV that results from the $15 million R&D investment is ($\frac{1}{3} \times$ $5 million) + ($\frac{1}{3} \times$ $25 million) + ($\frac{1}{3} \times$ $50 million) = $26.7 million, which is even bigger than the $20 million we calculated when we left out the revenue uncertainty. We are now valuing the production options correctly, whereas earlier we assumed, in effect, that those options would be exercised immediately; in the high-cost and middle-cost scenarios, exercising the options wouldn't have been optimal.

All of the numbers in this pharmaceutical example were chosen to facilitate simple calculations. But the basic ideas represented in the case can be applied in a variety of real-life situations. As long as there are contingencies under which the company would not wish to proceed to production, the R&D that conveys information about which contingency will materialize creates an option. And insofar as there is a positive probability that production would be unprofitable, building the plant (rather than waiting) exercises an option.

The option theory of investing also has clear implications for companies attempting to raise capital. If financial market participants understand the nature of the options correctly, they will place greater value on the investments that *create* options, and they will be more hesitant to finance those that *exercise* options. Therefore, as the pharmaceutical company proceeds from exploratory R&D (which creates options) to production and marketing (which exercises them), it will find the hurdle rate rising and sources of eager venture capital drying up. It is interesting to note that this is exactly what has been going on recently in the biotechnology industry as it has progressed from searching for several new products to trying to exploit the few it has found.[5] The increased difficulty of finding venture capital for biotechnology can be explained in other ways—disappointments over earlier biotechnology products, problems securing and enforcing patents, the risk of a health care cost crunch, to name a few. But we believe that, to a large extent, the market is making an astute differentiation between the creation of options and the exercising of options.

As companies in a broad range of industries are learning, opportunities to apply option theory to investments are numerous. Below are a few examples to illustrate the kinds of insight that the options theory of investment can provide.

INVESTMENTS IN OIL RESERVES

Nowhere is the idea of investments as options better illustrated than in the context of decisions to acquire and exploit deposits of natural resources. A company that buys deposits is buying an asset that it can develop immediately or later, depending on market conditions. The asset, then, is an option—an opportunity to choose the future development timetable of the deposit. A company can speed up production when the price is high, and it can slow it down or suspend it altogether when the price is low. Ignoring the option and valuing the entire reserve at today's price (or at future prices following a preset rate of output) can lead to a significant underestimation of the value of the asset.

The U.S. government regularly auctions off leases for offshore tracts of land, and oil companies perform valuations as part of their bidding process. The sums involved are huge—an individual oil company can easily bid hundreds of millions

---

5. See "Panic in the petri dish," *The Economist,* July 23, 1994, pp 61–2.

of dollars. It should not be surprising, then, that unless a company understands how to value an undeveloped oil reserve as an option, it may overpay, or it may lose some very valuable tracts to rival bidders.[6]

Consider what would happen if an oil company manager tried to value an undeveloped oil reserve using the standard NPV approach. Depending on the current price of oil, the expected rate of change of the price, and the cost of developing the reserve, he might construct a scenario for the timing of development and hence the timing (and size) of the future cash flows from production. He would then value the reserve by discounting these numbers and adding them together. Because oil price uncertainty is not completely diversifiable, the greater the perceived volatility of oil prices, the higher the discount rate that he would use; the higher the discount rate, the lower the estimated value of the undeveloped reserve.

But that would grossly underestimate the value of the reserve. It completely ignores the flexibility that the company has regarding when to develop the reserve—that is, when to exercise the reserve's option value. And note that, just as options are more valuable when there is more uncertainty about future contingencies, the oil reserve is more valuable when the price of oil is more volatile. The result would be just the opposite of what a standard NPV calculation would tell us: In contrast to the standard calculation, which says that greater uncertainty over oil prices should lead to *less* investment in undeveloped oil reserves, option theory tells us it should lead to *more*.

By treating an undeveloped oil reserve as an option, we can value it correctly, and we can also determine when is the best time to invest in the development of the reserve. Developing the reserve is like exercising a call option, and the exercise price is the cost of development. The greater the uncertainty over oil prices, the longer an oil company should hold undeveloped reserves and keep alive its option to develop them.

SCALE VERSUS FLEXIBILITY IN UTILITY PLANNING

The option view of investment can also help companies value flexibility in their capacity expansion plans. Should a company commit itself to a large amount of production capacity, or should it retain flexibility by investing slowly and keeping its options for growth open? Although many businesses confront the problem, it is particularly important for electric utilities, whose expansion plans must balance the advantages of building large-scale plants with the advantages of investing slowly and maintaining flexibility.

Economies of scale can be an important source of cost savings for companies. By building one large plant instead of two or three smaller ones, companies might be able to reduce their average unit cost while increasing profitability. Perhaps companies should respond to growth opportunities by bunching their invest-

---

6. The application of option theory to offshore petroleum reserves was pioneered by James L. Paddock, Daniel R. Siegel, and James L. Smith, "Option Valuation of Claims on Real Assets: The Case of Offshore Petroleum Leases," *Quarterly Journal of Economics* 103, August 1988, pp. 479–508.

ments—that is, investing in new capacity only infrequently but adding large and efficient plants each time. But what should managers do when demand growth is uncertain, as it often is? If the company makes an irreversible investment in a large addition to capacity and then demand grows slowly or even shrinks, it will find itself burdened with capital it doesn't need. When the growth of demand is uncertain, there is a trade-off between scale economies and the flexibility that is gained by investing more frequently in small additions to capacity as they are needed.

Electric utilities typically find that it is much cheaper per unit of capacity to build large coal-fired power plants than it is to add capacity in small amounts. But at the same time, utilities face considerable uncertainty about how fast demand will grow and what the fuel to generate the electricity will cost. Adding capacity in small amounts gives the utility flexibility, but it is also more costly. As a result, knowing how to value the flexibility becomes very important. The options approach is well suited to the purpose.

For example, suppose a utility is choosing between a large coal-fired plant that will provide enough capacity for demand growth over the next 10 to 15 years or adding small oil-fired generators, each of which will provide for about a year's worth of demand growth as needed. The utility faces uncertainty over demand growth and over the relative prices of coal and oil in the future. Even if a straightforward NPV calculation favors the large coal-fired plant, that does not mean that it is the more economical alternative. The reason is that if it were to invest in the coal-fired plant, the utility would commit itself to a large amount of capacity and to a particular fuel. In so doing, it would give up its options to grow more slowly (should demand grow more slowly than expected) or to grow with at least some of the added capacity fueled by oil (should oil prices, at some future date, fall relative to coal prices). By valuing the options using option-pricing techniques, the utility can assess the importance of the flexibility that small oil-fired generators would provide.

Utilities are finding that the value of flexibility can be large and that standard NPV methods that ignore flexibility can be extremely misleading. A number of utilities have begun to use option-pricing techniques for long-term capacity planning. The New England Electric System (NEES), for example, has been especially innovative in applying the approach to investment planning. Among other things, the company has used option-pricing techniques to show that an investment in the repowering of a hydroelectric plant should be delayed, even though the conventional NPV calculation for the project is positive. It has also used the approach to value contract provisions for the purchase of electric capacity and to determine when to retire a generating unit.[7]

---

7. For a more detailed discussion of utility industry applications and NEES's experience in this area, see Thomas Kaslow and Robert S. Pindyck, "Valuing Flexibility in Utility Planning," *The Electricity Journal* 7. March 1994, pp. 60–5.

PRICE VOLATILITY IN COMMODITIES

Commodity prices are notorious for their volatility. Copper prices, for example, have been known to double or drop by half in the space of several months. Why are copper prices so volatile, and how should producers decide whether to open new mines and refineries or to close old ones in response to price changes? The options approach to investment helps provide answers to such questions.

Investment and disinvestment in the copper industry involve large sunk costs. Building a new copper mine, smelter, or refinery involves a large-scale commitment of financial resources. Given the volatility of copper prices, managers understand that there is value to waiting for more information before committing resources, even if the current price of copper is relatively high. As we showed in the earlier pharmaceutical example, a positive NPV is not sufficient to justify investment. The price of copper and, correspondingly, the NPV of a new copper mine, must be high enough to cover the opportunity cost of giving up the option to wait. The same is true with disinvestment. Once a mine, smelter, or refinery is closed, it cannot be reopened easily.

As a result, managers will keep these facilities open even if they are losing money at current prices. They recognize that by closing a facility, they incur an opportunity cost of giving up the option to wait for higher future prices. Thus many copper mines built during the 1970s, when copper prices were high, were kept open during the mid-1980s, when copper prices fell to their lowest levels in real terms since the Great Depression.

Given the large sunk costs involved in building or closing copper-producing facilities and given the volatility of copper prices, it is essential to account for option value when making investment decisions. In reality, copper prices must rise far above the point of positive NPV to justify building new facilities and fall far below average variable cost to justify closing down existing facilities. Outside observers might see that approach as a form of myopia. We believe, however, that it reflects a rational response to option value.

Understanding option value and its implications for irreversible investment in the copper industry can also help us understand why copper prices are so volatile in the first place. Corporate inertia in building and closing down facilities feeds back into prices. Suppose that the demand for copper rises in response to higher-than-average GNP growth, causing the price of copper to rise. Knowing that the price might fall later, producers typically wait rather than respond immediately with new additions to capacity. Since greater supply is not readily forthcoming, the pressure of demand translates into rapid increases in price. Similarly, during downturns in demand, as mines remain open to preserve their options, the price collapses. Recent history has illustrated this phenomenon: The reluctance of producers to close mines during the mid-1980s, when demand was weak, allowed the price to fall even more than it would have otherwise. Thus the reaction of producers to price volatility in turn sustains the magnitude of price volatility, and any underlying fluctuations of demands or costs will appear in an exaggerated way as price fluctuations.

The economic environment in which most companies must now operate is far more volatile and unpredictable than it was 20 years ago—in part because of growing globalization of markets coupled with increases in exchange-rate fluctuations, in part because of more rapid technology-induced changes in the marketplace. Whatever its cause, however, uncertainty requires that managers become much more sophisticated in the ways they assess and account for risk. It's important for managers to have a better understanding of the options that their companies have or that they are able to create. Ultimately, options create flexibility, and in an uncertain world, the ability to value and use flexibility is critical.

Decisions that enhance a company's flexibility by creating and preserving options (decisions, for example, about R&D and test marketing) have value that transcends a naive calculation of NPV. More readily than conventional calculations suggest, managers should make decisions that increase flexibility. Choices that reduce flexibility by exercising options and committing resources to irreversible uses (construction of specific plants and equipment, advertising of particular products) will be valued less than their conventional NPV. Such choices should be made more hesitantly—and subjected to stiffer hurdle rates than the cost of capital—or delayed until circumstances are exceptionally favorable.

The bottom line for managers is that learning how to apply the net present value rule is not sufficient. To make intelligent investment choices, managers need to consider the value of keeping their options open. In this case, we don't think there is any option.

Index